BUSINESS AND DEMOCRACY IN SPAIN

BUSINESS AND DEMOCRACY IN SPAIN

Robert E. Martínez

Foreword by Juan J. Linz

PRAEGER

Westport, Connecticut
London

338.7
M38b

Library of Congress Cataloging-in-Publication Data ℡

Martínez, Robert Esteban.
    Business and democracy in Spain / Robert E. Martínez; foreword by
Juan J. Linz
        p. cm.
    Includes bibliographical references and index.
    ISBN 0-275-94391-7 (alk. paper)
    1. Business enterprises−Spain. 2. Employers' associations−
Spain. 3. Industrial relations−Spain. 4. Business and politics−
Spain. 5. Spain−Politics and government−1975- I. Title.
HD2887.M365 1993
338.7'0946−dc20   92-31845

British Library Cataloguing in Publication Data is available.

Library of Congress Catalog Card Number: 92-31845
ISBN: 0-275-94391-7

First published in 1993

Praeger Publishers, 88 Post Road West, Westport, CT 06881
An imprint of Greenwood Publishing Group, Inc.

Printed in the United States of America

The paper used in this book complies with the
Permanent Paper Standard issued by the National
Information Standards Organization (Z39.48-1984).

10 9 8 7 6 5 4 3 2 1

To my wife, Cristina

Contents

Illustrations

Foreword

The transition from non-democratic to democratic government in the past few decades--first in Southern Europe,
then in South America, and later in Eastern Europe--
has generated important scholarly literature and debate.
In that "third wave" of democratization, to use the expression of Samuel Huntington, the Spanish transition
from the authoritarian Franco regime to democracy occupies a special place. I would almost say that in the
thinking about democratization it occupies a place comparable to the breakdown of the Weimar Republic in
Germany in the study of the crisis of democracies. The
change of regime in Spain that has been described with
the terms reforma-pactada and ruptura-pactada, having
been one of the earliest successful regime changes, has
both attracted scholarly attention and served as a model
in a number of other transitions. One is tempted to
think that the successful outcome was over-determined
by the changes that had taken place in Spanish society,
economy, and culture before the death of Franco. We tend
to forget that many people, particularly foreigners
remembering the civil war of 1936-1939, felt that it
would prove a difficult process to dismantle the regime
created by Franco in over thirty-five years of rule.

This work is an important monographic contribution
to our understanding of that process of transition to,
and consolidation of, the new democracy. There is a vast
literature arguing that business and business elites are
fearful of democracy, particularly when it also represents the mobilization of labor and its demands that an
authoritarian regime presumably is able not only to re-
press but also to limit. In the case of Spain, there is
little doubt that during the later years of the Franco

regime Spanish capitalism succeeded in transforming the economy and society and that business enjoyed a relatively privileged position, particularly since some of its antagonists were prevented from organizing freely. Many would have thought that business would be hostile to a process of democratization and that, under the impact of the presence of anti-business movements, parties and free trade unions mobilizing the demands of the working class would turn against that change. Roberto Martínez, using solid empirical research shows that this was not the case. The pragmatic response of businessmen and their leaders made an important contribution to the success of the transition. This book contributed to an explanation of why this was so and how business responded to the transition and contributed to the consolidation of the new democracy. Only monographs like that of Roberto Martínez on business and that of Robert Fishman on working-class organization and the return of democracy can deepen our understanding of the processes involved in successful democratization. Unfortunately, there are few such monographic studies in spite of the large number of transitions that have taken place in recent decades; therefore, their work can serve as a model for other scholars. This work is not like some of the writings on business and democracy that are based on a speculative analysis of either the incompatibility between capitalism and democracy, or the hypothetical interest of some sectors of business in democratization, or the inevitable affinity between a market economy and democracy; instead, it is a solid study based on a survey of 115 leaders of national business organizations and regional organizations located in the most industrialized areas of Spain and on a survey of chief executives of businesses with over fifty workers in Madrid, Barcelona, Vizcaya, Valencia, and Sevilla. These surveys allow a better understanding of the diversity of responses or business people toward regime change; their expectations about their own business organizations; and their political preferences, voting behavior, and attitudes toward the socialists and Felipe González before he came to power in 1982. There is no comparable study in any other country.

This work also contributed to the rich literature on business organizations and representation and on the debates about corporatism and pluralism in the representation of business interests that has occupied the attention of distinguished social scientists in recent decades, since the seminal contribution of Philippe Schmitter. It is an important contribution to the history of interest representation in Spain without falling into the trap of Howard Wiarda's cultural explanation

of corporatism in Iberic societies. For students of
interest-group politics, it also provides some insights
into both the continuity and discontinuity in leadership
of such organizations. The institutional analysis of the
CEOE, Confederación Española de Organizaciones Empresariales (the peak organization for Spanish business),
places this work among classics like the Henry Ehrmann
book on organized business in France, Stephen Blank on
business in the United Kingdom, and Gerhard Braunthal
on organized business in Germany. Martínez successfully
highlights the complexity of an organization representing business people in a multinational society and
quasi-federal polity and in an organization that
encompasses very diverse interests from the few large
corporations in some fields to the myriad of small and
medium businesses in others. It is an outstanding study
of an organization, the functions that the leaders
assign to it, and the response of constituents (the
businessmen interviewed) to both the CEOE and its member
organizations.

For those interested in the politics of multinational, multilingual, and federal societies, this
study provides invaluable insights into the way in which
Catalan and Basque businesses relate to the Spanish
polity and to a statewide interest representation within
a Spanish market economy and the new polity. It should
provide some food for thought to those who believe that
only a unitary state, and the denial of autonomy to nationalities within it, can assure both democracy and an
integrated market. For the students of European integration, the chapter on attitudes toward the Common
Market will be of special interest. Ultimately, the
success of larger political-economic units like the
Common Market depends on the attitudes of business
elites toward them.

Finally, there is another audience for this work:
all those who are interested in the relations between
employers and workers; employers organizations and trade
unions; and the assumptions under which successful collective bargaining, restructuring of an economy, and
economic policy limiting inflation can develop. The
Spanish experience has often been invoked in Latin
America in dealing with these problems, but very often
the instruments and attitudes necessary to follow the
Spanish example have not been available there. The
reader of this book can learn much about these problems
in the process of transition from authoritarianism to
democracy.

The author is modest and careful not to draw too
many implications from the Spanish experience for other
cases, noting the uniqueness of the Spanish and to some

extent other Southern European experiences when compared
to Eastern Europe in particular. However, it is my hope
that scholars, researchers, leaders of interest groups,
and politicians in other countries will read this
outstanding monograph and draw their own conclusions
from the comparisons of Spanish experiences and problems
with the experiences and problems of their own countries. This book is a study of the case of Spain, but
the Spanish case is part of a much more general historical process that is ongoing in many countries and
therefore deserves the attention of not only those
interested in contemporary Spain. It is a model of
research that should stimulate replication in other
societies. At the same time, of course, Spaniards can
learn a great deal about their recent political social
history. Only works like this will allow the deepening
of our understanding of central problems of our time:
transitions to and consolidation of new democracies,
business and democracy, the organization of interests
and their participation in the political process, the
institutionalization of labor-management relations to
prevent destructive conflicts, and democracy, the market
and multinational society. In all these fields, this
book makes an outstanding and unique contribution.

Let me add a personal note. It has been a pleasure
to work with Roberto Martínez on a study that represents
a continuity with the research I did jointly with Amando
de Miguel on Spanish business over twenty years earlier.
I also want to add that I have met many of the persons
he interviewed in the course of this fieldwork and they
express their satisfaction with their encounters with
him, a fact that enhances the value of his survey data,
although not everyone in the business community has been
happy with some of his findings--a fact that attests to
the objectivity of his study. His work is an example of
what Max Weber meant by <u>verstehende Soziologie</u> in its
empathetic understanding of businessmen and leaders of
business organizations, but also of <u>wertfreiheit</u>, the
objective scholarly analysis.

Juan J. Linz

Acknowledgments

Indispensable among the many who helped me in this study are the hundreds of Spanish chief executives, leaders of employers associations, and the staffs at the Confederación Española de Organizaciones Empresariales (CEOE), Fomento del Trabajo Nacional (FTN) and other business associations. Without their generous and valuable time, the data could not have been collected.

The Social Science Research Council and the Fulbright Commission were my primary sources of funding. I received the strong support of Rafael López Pintor, then Director of the Centro de Investigaciones Sociológicas (CIS), and of Víctor Pérez Díaz and the Fundación Fondo para la Investigación Económica y Social. Their assistance facilitated data collection among chief executives and associations, respectively. I also acknowledge the efforts extended by CIS interview coordinators Margarita Gómez and María Pilar Solana.

DATA provided major infrastructural and moral support, as well as critical work space during my two years in Spain. I am indebted to the entire staff at DATA, and in particular to Manuel Gómez-Reino and Darío Vila. Manuel Ludevid's efforts afforded me an office to call home in Barcelona and infrastructural support at the Escuela Superior de Administración y Dirección de Empresas (ESADE).

My access to Spanish business elites and understanding of their problems was facilitated by Fernando Fernández Rodríguez of the Banco de Bilbao, José Antonio Gefaell of the Banco Industrial de Vizcaya, Professors Juan José Caballero Romero and José Castillo of the Complutense de Madrid, Professor Manuel López-Linares of the Escuela de Minas, and Antonio Garrigues Walker, then President of the Asociación para el Progreso de la Dirección. Professor David Cameron was the first one at Yale to express his confidence in my capability for research scholarship. Amando de Miguel and Fermín de la Sierra were particularly insightful on Spanish business. Carlos Ferrer Salat, then President of the CEOE, was instrumental in affording me access to the CEOE. Román Adrados of his staff and Juan Pujol Segarra at Fomento were key in the nuts and bolts of names, lists and phone numbers.

On a personal level, I am grateful to Nieves Fernández de Sevilla, Mercedes García-Soto, José María Pagés Font, Luis Ferrer Pagés, Xavier Pla Aubanell, Patricia Zahniser, Rocío de Terán and Houchang Chehabi. My friend and colleague Rafael Pardo Avellaneda collaborated in the associations survey. I have benefited immensely from his penetrating commentaries on Spain and on debates within the business sector during the ten years since completion of my field work. Robert Fishman was an almost daily source of support, advice and insight into the other side of the labor-management dialectic during the years in Spain and in the analysis of the data.

My parents, Hilda and Juan Martínez, have given their unflinching support in every endeavor I have ever undertaken. Their confidence in me never wavered for an instant during the years this study took to realize. They also worked extensively in helping prepare this manuscript for publication. It was not an easy task.

My wife's love has been a constant encouragement to bring this book to completion.

Nothing I can write would even begin adequately to express the degree of gratitude and the sense of esteem I hold for my teacher and the director of this study, Juan J. Linz. His devotion to the social sciences is complete. He is a person of great humanity. I have been extraordinarily fortunate to have had the opportunity of working with a man and scholar of such stature.

Abbreviations

AEB	Asociación Española de la Banca
AES	Acuerdo económico y social
AI	Acuerdo interconfederal
AMI	Acuerdo marco interconfederal
ANE	Acuerdo nacional de empleo
ANFAC	Asociación de Fabricantes de Automóviles, Camiones, Tractores y sus Motores
AP	Alianza Popular
AP/CD	Alianza Popular/Coalición Democrática
APD	Asociación para el Progreso de la Dirección
ASEFA	Agrupación Sindical Económica de las Fibras Artificiales y Sintéticas Cortadas
ASERPETROL	Asociación de Empresas Refinadoras del Petroleo
BDI	Bundesverband der Deutschen Industrie
CBI	Confederation of British Industry
CCC	Confederación Catalana de la Construcción
CCOO	Comisiones Obreras
CC-UCD	Centristas de Catalunya
CDC	Convergència Democràtica de Catalunya
CDS	Centro Democrático y Social
CEA	Confederación de Empresarios de Andalucía
CEB	Confederación Empresarial de Barcelona
CEIM	Confederación Empresarial Independiente de Madrid
CEOE	Confederación Española de Organizaciones Empresariales
CEPYME	Confederación Española de la Pequeña y Mediana Empresa
CEV	Centro Empresarial de Vizcaya
CGEV	Confederación General de Empresarios de Vizcaya

CiU	Convergència i Unió
CNC	Confederación Nacional de la Construcción
CNPF	ConfédeXcration Nationale du Patronat Français
CNT	Confederación Nacional del Trabajo
Confemetal	Confederación Española de Organizaciones Empresariales del Metal
COPYME	Confederación de la Pequeña y Mediana Empresa
CSUT	Confederación de Sindicatos Unitarios de Trabajadores
EC	European Community
ECSC	European Coal and Steel Community
EE	Euskadiko Ezkerra
EEC	European Economic Community
ERC	Esquerra Republicana de Catalunya
ESADE	Escuela Superior de Administración y Dirección de Empresas
ETA	Euskadi ta Askatasuna
FBI	Federation of British Industries
FEC	Federación de Entidades Empresariales de la Construcción de Barcelona
FTN	Fomento del Trabajo Nacional
FVEM	Federación Vizcaína de Empresarios del Metal
GDP	Gross Domestic Product
GNP	Gross National Product
HB	Herri Batasuna
INE	Instituto Nacional de Estadística
INH	Instituto Nacional de Hidrocarburos
INI	Instituto Nacional de Industria
IU	Izquierda Unida
OECD	Organization for Economic Cooperation and Development
PCE	Partido Comunista de España
PDC	Pacte Democràtic per Catalunya
PNV	Partido Nacionalista Vasco
PSA	Partido Socialista de Andalucía
PSC-PSOE	Socialistes de Catalunya
PSOE	Partido Socialista Obrero Español
PSUC	Partit Socialista Unificat de Catalunya
PYMEs	Pequeñas y Medianas Empresas
Sercobe	Servicio Técnico Comercial de Constructores de Bienes de Equipo
SU	Sindicato Unitario
UCD	Unión de Centro Democrático
UG	Unidad Galega
UGT	Unión General de Trabajadores
USO	Unión Sindical Obrera
VAT	Value Added Tax

BUSINESS AND DEMOCRACY IN SPAIN

1

Introduction

During the emergence of a democracy, the degree of identification by different sectors of society with developing democratic processes, institutions, and policy making can serve to aid in the consolidation of the new democratic system or contribute to destabilization. An appreciation of the impact of the positions adopted by key societal elites represents one means by which one can measure the success of Spanish democratization. We will assess how one such elite, the Spanish business elite, was affected by democratization and how they, in turn, influenced the evolution of Spanish democracy during the transition from authoritarianism and into the early years of a new constitutional order.

Economic elites are but one of several relevant components of society that can contribute to broad system stability. During a political transition and the early stages in the consolidation of democracy, it is difficult to identify fully the "stress threshold" that divides successful consolidation from crisis and potential breakdown. Economic prosperity can serve to buttress emerging democratic institutions. In an industrialized market economy such as Spain, the role of business elites and their participation in and identification with the nascent democratic system was a critical element. It would be futile to try to quantify their weight, nor can one divorce treatment of business from that of other societal groups whose interests and participation are similarly required for democratic consolidation. Nevertheless, it is clear that in capitalist societies, the business sector, given its control over capital and level of organization, makes

critical demands on political systems. The denial by
business of support can more rapidly result in the
demise of democracy than a similar withdrawal by other
sectors.

How did business perceive itself affected by the
transition to democracy? How did business influence the
consolidation of democracy, both through the aggregate
of individual business decisions and through its
collective interest organizations?

Business people are by nature pragmatic. As the
dénouement of the authoritarian regime neared and
business experienced an increasingly evident exhaustion
of the political system and the economic model it
represented, it was natural that most of them, as
individual citizens, would accept the development of
democratic institutions. Indeed, most important segments
of the business community welcomed the change. The
activities of their incipient collective interest bodies
reflected acceptance of the new political order and were
structured to maximize membership interests under
evolving circumstances. Just as the Franco system
adopted new economic policies to cope with the exhaustion of the autarchic economic model in the late 1950s,
a crossroads accurately documented in the valuable work
by Anderson,[1] so the early 1970s witnessed global
economic changes that would have repercussions within
Spain.

In the late 1950s, limited measures of economic
liberalization, starting with the 1959 Stabilization
Plan, were adequate to meet changing requirements
without necessitating political change. Nevertheless,
the Franquist economic policies of the 1960s, which
facilitated Spanish participation in the generalized
European boom of the period, led to a profound
transformation of society.[2] Exhaustion of that new
economic trajectory by the early- to mid-1970s required
a different political order concordant with new societal
realities, more responsive to demands now more fully
articulated by sectors of the working class, and that
could better situate Spain for increasing global market
interdependence and competition.

Changes in global economic relations, highlighted
by the oil crisis, marked the end of the period of easy
growth in Spain. The economic downturn in Europe ended
the easy market for Spanish goods and closed the doors
to guest workers, which until the mid-1970s had represented an important component in Spain's overall balance
of payments and a safety valve that alleviated some
potential social tensions that would have arisen from
high unemployment.

The Spanish transition to democracy, beginning with

Franco's death in November 1975, did not occur at the
most propitious moment in economic terms. Furthermore,
in addition to difficulties encountered as a consequence
of the coincidence of the political transition with the
oil crisis and the international monetary restructuring,
boom-period policies were deficient over the longer
term. Wide-scale industrial diversification was based
on unjustifiably high protectionist barriers. Antiquated
machinery could profitably be kept running. Investment
in research and development was extremely low, leading
to dependence on foreign technology. Inadequate attention was devoted to infrastructural development and
educational and vocational training reforms. The level
of capital intensity in industry was inappropriately
high for the labor-surplus economy. The deteriorating
trade balance after 1973 and reverse migration from
Europe were joined in the mid-1970s by saturation in the
tourist industry (which only after 1983 began to profit
via "qualitative" expansion).[3]

THE OBJECTIVE

We will empirically document the position of
business regarding questions posed by the introduction
of democracy and thereby attempt to measure the degree
of business support for the fledgling system. To what
degree did business perceive the need for change, given
the economic and political bottlenecks posed by the
institutions of the authoritarian regime? To what degree
did business support the changes that were produced and
the manner of their establishment? What level of
political participation in the democratic system do we
find among individual business people and their collective interest representatives? Were their activities,
as individuals and collectivities, consistent with
democratic requisites?

Given this objective, and the fundamental questions
posed by the transition to democracy, I conducted field
investigations at the levels of the individual company
and of the collective spokespieces of business, the
employers associations. One survey was conducted in 1981
among the chief executive officers of over 250 companies, and a second in 1982 among the top functionaries
of 115 employers associations, all of them affiliated
either directly or indirectly with the "peak" employers
association, the Confederation of Spanish Business
Organizations, the CEOE.[4]

TOPICS OF INQUIRY

To assess the perceptions of business regarding the
political transition and its own role in the process,
I addressed four broad areas of inquiry of major concern
to business: (1) changes in the labor relations structure; (2) the collective representation of business
interests; (3) direct political participation in the new
system; and (4) the enhanced viability of the then
potential integration in the European Community.

Labor relations had already been undergoing
substantial change during the closing years of the
Franco regime.[5] Workers' organizations had developed
through a combined strategy of increasingly vigorous
clandestine activity and through opposition within the
limited possibilities afforded by the official Sindicato
Nacional superstructures.

The Sindicato Nacional, also referred to as the
"unitary," "vertical," or "organic" _Sindicato_, was the
Franquist institution under which both employer and
worker interests were represented. The Sindicato was,
perhaps, the single most purely "corporatist" institutional element in the system. As such, it is perhaps not
surprising that long after the Falangists lost their
position as one of the bases in the configuration of
Franquist support, they remained at the helm of the
Sindicato. Separate _secciones_ within the Sindicato for
the representation of workers and employers at low
levels in hierarchical terms were not created until
1958.[6]

Opposition within the Franquist organic, vertical
union by significant segments of the labor movement was
achieved via participation in elections to "workers
councils" (_jurados de empresa_). Elections to the
jurados, which did not actually begin until 1966, were
the primary means used by the labor movement to oppose
the system from within. Not all worker organizations
participated in this strategy. The mostly Communist
union, _Comisiones Obreras_, that emerged as the top-
ranked union in the first free and open elections for
worker representatives for works committees (_comités de
empresa_) in 1978, actively pursued a strategy of
infiltrating the official Franquist structure. Indeed,
its very name, "Comisiones Obreras," or "Workers'
Commissions," was derived from its Franquist period
participation. In contrast, the Socialist union, the
Unión General de Trabajadores, or UGT, which ranked
second during the early years of democracy, had adamant-
ly opposed any participation in Franquist organizations.
The much less important Unión Sindical Obrera (USO),
which split from _Comisiones_ and which originally had

been influenced by progressive Catholic labor activists, also participated in the elections to the jurados.

The worker-employer relationship and the breakdown of the Franquist-era syndicalist model and its attempted suppression of conflict to an institutionalized conflictual model is a key area of change. The close of the Franquist era and the early transition period were marked by a skyrocketing increase in the number and intensity of labor conflicts as long-unheeded demands were voiced and the policies of repression dismantled. Naturally, employer responses followed suit. Notable effects on profit margins led to a rapid drop in investor confidence.[7] Attitudinal changes have subsequently occurred as experience with a more open labor relations system has been garnered.

Measurement of the perceived labor impact and employer positions regarding new legislation on employment and dismissal policies (such as the Workers' Statute, "Estatuto de los Trabajadores," of January 1980) is a concern of this research. This data measure the degree of legitimacy accorded unions and attitudes regarding the manner in which free unionization was realized. To what extent is a given employer willing to concede that the unions are the legitimate representatives of worker interests in his or her enterprise? What portion of the blame for declines in productivity and slow general growth do individual employers attribute to labor unrest and unionization? We might expect a high correlation between more traditional employers on labor-management issues and levels of identification with the previous regime, democratic institutions, and ideology.

The same April 1977 legislation legalizing the labor unions also opened the door to the development of the employers associations as they currently exist.[8] Reference to free associability for both workers and employers in the same legislation introduced a pattern that has been maintained on representational issues in the "world of work" throughout the democratic period, including in the constitution. On issues of collective representation, the pattern was established that both sides of the picture would be cited in the same legislation. Similarly, article 7 of the 1978 constitution guarantees the creation and rights of both labor unions and employers associations.

In addition to the legislation legalizing collective activity, the establishment of "peak-level" bargaining by the collective interest representatives of workers and employers in areas of wages and conditions of work has led to very visible protagonism by employers associations which continues to date. Such

activities by organized employer groups, initiated with
the UGT-CEOE bilateral agreement on collective bargaining and industrial relations of July 1979[9] and strengthened by the "interconfederal framework agreement" (AMI)
between these two peak organizations in January 1980,[10]
can benefit from the vantage point afforded by the
extensive literature on corporatism and by a consideration of Spain as a case of liberal or societal corporatism in the manner elaborated by Lehmbruch and
Schmitter.[11] However, whereas a dynamic analysis of the
post-Franco period would lead one to stress the impressive degree of consolidation achieved by the employers
associations both in representational terms and in their
role within the system, a static view would still have
to emphasize their limited control over membership.
Perhaps more important in a neo-corporatist assessment
of Spain are the extreme organizational weaknesses of
the unions, which constitutes an insurmountable obstacle
to real corporatist policy making. While I will document
the failure of our data to support a corporatist
classification, the corporatist literature does frame
a number of relevant questions for this research,
particularly in the treatment of the series of
peak-level, employer-worker agreements and of the
internal properties or characteristics that govern the
operations of the associations. The failure of the CEOE
and the unions to reach any wage agreement, after the
expiration of the "Economic and Social Agreement" (AES)
in 1986, further demonstrates the inappropriateness of
classifying the Spanish case as corporatist. Corporatist
classification of our case is not an objective of this
research. In fact, a good case for debunking corporatism
can be made based on the material I will present, which
fundamentally places in question a corporatist analysis
of the Spanish case.[12]

The organization of the collective interests of
business constitute a primary focus of this study and
will be dealt with extensively from the perspective of
individual chief executives who constitute the base
membership of the associations and of the leaders of
associations. The degree of allegiance and immediate
individual employer compliance with associational
directives is essential in the development of stable
patterns of association-labor union bargaining both at
the peak level and at the level of the local sectoral
association negotiating annual agreements. What objectives do individual employers hope to realize through
their membership and possible active participation in
the associations? Are the associations a primary means
of formulating demands or are other institutions or
informal channels perceived as more effective in

achieving tangible results? How do the associations pursue achievement of their objectives? Associations are key in aggregating interests. They participate in formal structures, but may depend to a greater degree in reaching desired ends through informal contacts or lobbying.

Our treatment of the operationalization of collective employer representation, its direct political import, and how it adopted current associational forms, parallels major studies done elsewhere in Europe, such as the contributions by Ehrmann on the Confédération Nationale du Patronat Français (CNPF), Blank on the Federation of British Industry (FBI), Grant and Marsh on the FBI's successor organization, the Confederation of British Industry (CBI), Braunthal on the Bundesverband der Deutschen Industrie (BDI), and the description of the political role of Italy's Confindustria by LaPalombara.[13]

The non-Europeanist, American reader is cautioned not to expect associational patterns of Spanish employers or their political expression to approximate those characterizing the United States. The position and perception of employers in society is very different (although important shifts began in the late 1980s), and so is their historical trajectory. The role of the state differs substantially, and Spanish employers still hold greater expectations of state support and intervention than do their U.S. counterparts, in part a legacy from Franquist days.

To illustrate one important difference, according to the strictures of the Workers' Statute, when an association has legally been deemed the legitimate spokespiece of business, paralleling similar designation (recognition) of a labor union (or unions), agreements signed by the organization are binding on all firms falling within its geographic and sectoral jurisdiction, with equal force to member and nonmember firms. The jurisdictional boundaries in such cases tend to be provincial and for a given sector or, more frequently, subsector. As such, the juridical position of a Spanish association is much stronger than that of U.S. business groups. Nevertheless, we find some parallels in assessment of the motivations that led to initial collective organization, as a reference in Chapter 3 to the work by James Q. Wilson will maintain.

How representative are the associations? The strong empirical work by Fishman on Spanish labor confirms that workers consciously select representatives more radical than themselves, recognizing that such individuals will more energetically exert pressure on their behalf.[14] Might there exist similar considerations among employ-

ers? Certainly, a number of major business leaders
(although definitely not all) characteristically used
rhetoric that was more ideologically charged than that
found among individual employers. As with workers, there
is a self-selection process at work, but I will not
delve here into the motivations leading individual
businessmen and women to become visible protagonists as
business leaders.

In the past, the literature on the rationale of
organizations has tended to investigate worker groups
to the detriment of our understanding of business
organizations. Some critical elements distinguishing
associational dynamics among business from that of
unions include: the greater autonomy at the disposal of
the "affiliated" employer (relative to that held by the
individual worker); the character of the base membership, which is that of chief executives managing firms
that already constitute organizational entities in of
themselves; and the fundamentally different relationship
between a chief executive and the factor of production
he controls, capital, versus the counterpart factor
controlled by workers, labor, from which they cannot
divorce themselves.[15] Lindblom correctly argues that one
of the natural political advantages held by business is
their organizations. Business can use its own enterprises as political organizations in a democracy.[16] The
organizational dimension characterizing the "base
membership" of employers associations (i.e., persons
already heading their own organizations) alters my
analysis of the dynamics of collective interest representation substantially in comparison to the principles
that hold for labor unions.

Further distinctions between worker and employer
associability arise from the juxtaposition of competing
market positions among firms that must be surmounted to
organize collectively. Nevertheless, as Bendix notes,
such conflicts of interest in the market can "give way
to an overriding unity by virtue of their common
encounter with a hostile social environment."[17]

In spite of the distinctions between workers and
employers, could it not be the case that employers
expect their leadership to stand further to the right
than they do themselves? Might they perceive a need for
their leaders to demonstrate a greater willingness to
maintain a high level of "defensive" rhetoric? How
successful are association leaders in influencing the
attitudes of business people? Michels' ever-present
"iron law" is an important consideration.[18] It will be
more likely that policies pursued will reflect the
concerns of the more active (and more "elite") among the
CEOE's constituency and, specifically, those concerns

of the leaders themselves.

Direct political participation by organized business groups is an entirely normal phenomenon in a pluralist society. There exist limits to the activities interest groups can undertake without violating the jurisdictions of political parties, which are better equipped to aggregate a wider spectrum of interests for representational purposes. The issue was controversial for Spanish business in the early 1980s as the CEOE attempted to identify its place and as some criticized its perceived role during the disintegration of the governing UCD party (Unión de Centro Democrático). Mistakes may have been committed by the Confederation, perhaps in part a consequence of misreading the positions of its base and affiliated association constituencies and in part due to simple human errors by top leadership—an element too often omitted from consideration by social scientists in explaining social reality. The most notable early example of misjudgment by the CEOE of individual chief executives postures may have occurred during the period of erosion in the then-governing UCD's position, particularly evident at the time of the important first regional elections for autonomous governments in Galicia (October 1981) and Andalucía (May 1982).

Political activity by business, as with all other key segments of society, must be analyzed not only in its collective manifestations, but also in terms of the electoral behavior of individuals. To what degree do business people differ from the population at large in their voting behavior? Do association leaders diverge from their employer constituents in their voting participation as individual citizens? Differences between the individual political attitudes of leaders and employers may contribute to erroneous judgments on the part of associations regarding the preferences of their base membership.

Inclusion of the issues posed by the Spanish bid for Common Market integration may at first appear to break with issues directly affecting the possibilities of democratic consolidation. However, the European Community (EC) issue was the single, primary international concern of the business community and constituted a priority international agenda item not only for all democratic governments (Suárez, Calvo Sotelo, González), but also for the Franco government. The EC issue was strongly politicized by both authoritarian and democratic governments, which viewed entry as bestowing legitimacy. In the wake of the collapse of Communism in Eastern Europe, the inclusion of the EC issue in a study on democratization is perhaps less in question, given

the evident intensity of interest in joining "Europe"
by the new governments in the East.

It is of interest that González later tied Spanish
integration in the EC with continuance in NATO in the
referendum of March 1986, thereby hoping to legitimize
the latter by association. While Europe could con-
veniently exclude Franquist Spain from membership
consideration given its failure to fulfill the political
requisites of the Treaty of Rome, the assumption of
adequate democratic political credentials, in theory,
automatically altered Spain's candidacy. The establishment of a democratic regime, changing Spanish prospects
with regard to EC integration, suitably measures
important political attitudes among business elites on
a priority policy issue. It records attitudes regarding
the Franquist period and the validity of the earlier
entry attempt relative to the final successful application.

For the CEOE and its affiliated federations and
associations, the Common Market issue served as a
fruitful means of gaining wider public exposure and
offered opportunities to provide membership with special
services that could raise organizational appeal and
contribute to their own consolidation. Hence, the topic
illuminates issues of collective goods versus selective
incentives, a critical component of Olson's seminal work
on the logic of collective action.[19]

SOME STRUCTURAL CONSIDERATIONS

Several factors can be expected to emerge as key
variables explaining social reality or as corollaries
to the central research concerns.

Given the time-dynamic nature of our research, continuity versus change or disjuncture among business
elites emerges as an important element. While Spain
possessed a significant industrial foundation prior to
the 1959 Stabilization and subsequent economic growth
period concentrated in the Basque and Catalan regions,
the substantial industrialization that transformed Spain
into a modern industrial state was achieved only in the
wake of the early 1960s. Furthermore, contrary to the
assessment of many, even academic, analyses of this
period, it is erroneous to depict Spain as a more
successful, lesser-developed or newly industrializing
country. Its level of industrial output, character of
inter-versus intra-sectoral trade, product specialization, and labor force sectoral breakdown, as well as its
available institutional mechanisms in the industrial
realm and historical evolution, place the problématique

of the country's industrial realities firmly among those of developed Western European states, constituting the standards against which to compare Spain. These are, incidentally, the standards to which Spanish policy-makers and industrialists refer. All such considerations are not to ignore the important sectoral and regional disparities in overall Spanish economic development, which also have their sociological manifestations and are partially a reflection of the country's relatively late development. From the EC perspective, the size of the Spanish economy placed its candidacy in a fundamentally different position from those of Greece and Portugal.[20] Nevertheless, the relative brevity of Spain's inclusion among the ranks of developed countries at the time of the democratic transition separated a large segment of the Spanish business sector, in sociological terms, from those in countries that industrialized earlier. Thus, it is not far fetched to describe some sectors of the business generation at the helm of industry in the 1970s and early 1980s as viewing themselves as the "builders" of a modern industrial state. Rapid economic growth left a strong psychological impact on those businessmen who had been successful in exploiting opportunities.

The tenures of the individuals contacted in our surveys reflect important differences on the issue of continuity versus change. Stronger political or sympathetic identification with the Franco system may partially be a consequence of having directly profited from the economic policies of the growth period (1959-1974) or having achieved one's professional goals during that period. Organizational continuity is also of interest. While the CEOE superstructure was a recent construct at the time of my fieldwork in the early 1980s, its component member associations were not always so. The forms of continuity vary. In regions with longer industrial traditions, most notably in Catalonia, continuity is present in the regional peak organization of employers, Fomento del Trabajo Nacional (FTN), and, at the "base" associational level, in numerous individual organizations that are direct descendants of guilds dating to Renaissance or even medieval times. Particularly on the issue of assessing the degree of organizational continuity versus disjuncture with Franquist-era groups, this study benefits from comparisons with the early work by Juan Linz and Amando de Miguel on employers, based on interviews conducted among 460 chief executives in 1960. The emphasis given to the collective representation of employers by the primary publication that resulted from their study, Los empresarios ante el poder público, is of particular

interest. Indeed, this early work documented the importance of continuity with pre-Franco collective interest
organizations.[21] Continuity emerges as closely inter-
twined with regional diversity, a result of the widely
differing regional patterns of industrial development.
With respect to issues relating to Francoism, the
regions with the greatest degree of historical autono-
mist-nationalist demands, Catalonia and the Basque
Country, were also fully industrialized prior to
Franco's assumption of power. Hence, in providing
explanations of economic protagonism, business in these
regions was less dependent on the economic policies of
the previous regime. Thus, regional nationalist sentiments coincide with a lower psychological--or real--
dependence on Franquist economic policies, a pattern not
without political and sociological consequences among
chief executives and association leaders.

The regional issue is present in topics other than
that of historical continuity. Although there exist
smaller concentrated areas of significant industrial
activity, Spain's three primary industrial regions are
Catalonia, the Basque Country, and Madrid, the last of
which developed only over the course of the last thirty-
five years and was strongly dependent on the economic
policies of the Franco period. At the time of the
transition, these three regions (eight provinces in all)
accounted for fully 49 percent of the gross national
product.[22] A fourth area with a significant industrial
base is the Levante, specifically the provinces of
Valencia and Alicante. The transition from a centralized
state to a multiregional structure that includes
significant autonomy for the major Basque and Catalan
regions has led to difficulties in the organization of
business interests and contributed to significant
variations in the "self-identity" of business people
along regional lines. As such, to document the regional
impact on employer attitudes, research for this study
was conducted in five provinces--Madrid, Barcelona,
Vizcaya, Valencia, and Sevilla--with total sample
companies divided among these five by their relative
provincial industrial weights. Hence, a high concentration of interviews in Barcelona and Madrid resulted.[23]
The map on the following page illustrates industry's
spatial distribution and the location of our sample
firms. The regional issue is critical in understanding
Spanish society, including the business sector, and
resurfaces throughout this analysis.

Each provincial sample of chief executives was
divided in thirds by size of firm, among "regular" size
companies of 50 to 199 employees, intermediate companies of 200 to 999, and large companies of 1,000 and

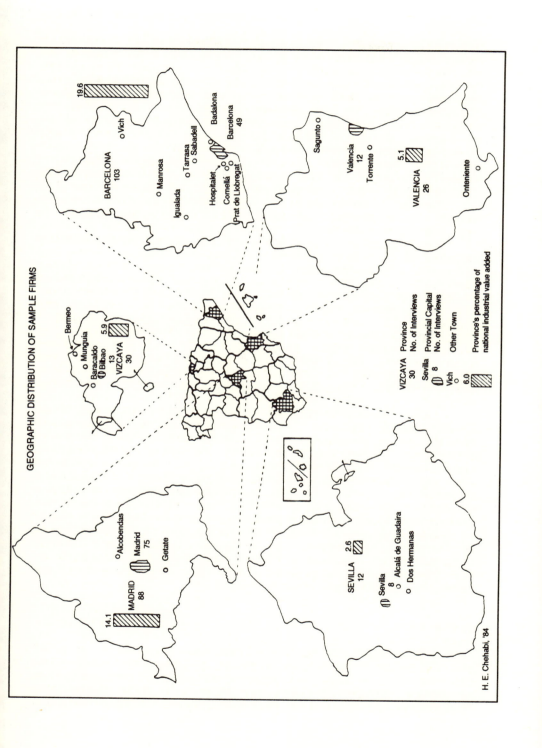

GEOGRAPHIC DISTRIBUTION OF SAMPLE FIRMS

H. E. Chehabi, '84

more employees.[24] Given the "elite" character of this
study, and the objective of assessing the impact of
business on democratic consolidation, it was legitimate
to exclude small companies (under fifty employees) from
the sample. This is not to deny the important role such
companies play in the economy. Resource limitations on
sample size meant that inclusion of small company chief
executives could not have adequately represented their
views and would have reduced the significance of what
we might say about larger company chief executives,
whose influence in the system and ability to organize
collectively far surpasses that of their smaller
colleagues.[25] Nevertheless, the three size distinctions
among the research group is critically important in
explaining attitudes.

Inclusion of "regular" size companies, which employ
between 50 and 199 persons, allows for inclusion in our
findings of the primary concerns of "small firm" chief
executives. There exists a high degree of consciousness
in Spanish business about the differing demands and
circumstances of the small and medium size company, the
pymes as they are widely called (pequeñas y medianas
empresas). Often, firms under 200 or 250 employees are
generally considered pymes for political purposes and
much rhetoric surrounds their role and position in the
economy. Hence, our "regular" category represents the
"elite" among this widely acknowledged special employer
group.[26]

Other characteristics strongly influence employer
views. Sector is one.[27] Differences similarly emerge by
the degree of foreign equity participation in a company,
separating those with majority foreign participation
from domestically held firms and, particularly, stressing important differences for those fully in foreign
hands.[28] Much analysis has been done elsewhere in Europe
on the sociological effects of the owner-manager
dichotomy among chief executives, following the treatment of this issue by Linz and de Miguel.[29] Unfortunately, while I can treat the effects of ownership of the
firm on chief executive views, the data fail to pick up
the richness of analyses which differentiate between
owner-founders and owner-heirs.[30]

OUR PLAN

Given the strong organizational nature of much of
the analysis, the first half of this study deals with
the collective interest representation of business. As
no major piece of research has yet elaborated the
structures of business representation, Chapter 2 is a

largely descriptive analysis of the peak employers confederation, the CEOE, and its hierarchy of directly and indirectly affiliated associations.

The dynamics of collective interest organizations can be viewed from the level of the individual chief executives who constitute the base membership, and from the perspective of the organizations themselves. Chapter 3 looks at the individual employer level, the logic of their collective representation, and their views regarding the associational hierarchy. Chapter 4 treats the same issues, but from the perspective of the leaders of the associations that constitute the CEOE's hierarchy. As this is an organizational view, correspondingly greater stress is placed on issues of internal operations, internal governing properties, and the degree of organizational consolidation.

The second half of this study treats the major thematic concerns of my research. Key to the understanding of business and democratic consolidation is consideration of direct political indicators, as done in Chapter 5, which also includes some information on the economic policy preferences of business. The satisfaction of economic problems and political guarantees of economic well-being contribute significantly to a lessening of uncertainty and a strengthening of investor confidence.

Many employer attitudes regarding the new political system were influenced by the impact of the legalization of labor unions and the right to strike. This was particularly true for the initial period of democratization. Chapter 6 assesses employer views of labor.

Chapter 7 on Common Market integration represents a case study of an ongoing policy priority that first emerged under the Franco period. This issue is a prime example of how an economic policy issue can register business attitudes against a backdrop of changing political circumstances.

NOTES

1. Charles W. Anderson, <u>The Political Economy of Modern Spain</u> (Madison: The University of Wisconsin Press, 1970).

2. Anderson stresses the failure of political liberalization to have followed the economic opening, the result of a certain pragmatic flexibility of Francoism that allowed it to endure as long as it did. In their analysis, García-Delgado and Segura note that

"reformist actions" in the economic realm, while responding to the pressures of circumstances, did not constitute concessions to any group, but were, rather, "awarded" or "granted" by deed. José L. García-Delgado and Julio Segura, Reformismo y crisis económica (Madrid: Editorial Saltés, 1977), 46-47.

From 1959 to 1973 Spain's real gross national product (GNP) grew at an annual rate of 7.3 percent, the highest average in the Organization for Economic Cooperation and Development (OECD) except for Japan and Greece. Per capita income increased from 25,655 pesetas in 1960 to 57,863 in 1973 (in constant 1964 pesetas). Having already largely substituted domestic consumer manufactures for imported goods by 1959, the government promoted expansion of intermediate goods production such as steel, cement, chemicals, and fertilizer. While overall effective rates of protection on manufactured goods fell significantly, and were lower than in the average lesser developed country by the late 1960s, they remained at levels significantly above those of the EEC or the United States.

Labor force participation in the primary sector dropped from 41.7 percent in 1960 to 23.1 percent in 1974. Tertiary sector employment correspondingly increased from 26.5 percent to 40.2 percent. Changes in the export mix were notable as food products fell from 57.2 percent to 29.3 percent of total exports and raw materials from 9.9 percent to 3.7 percent between 1959 and 1973. Capital goods, in contrast, increased from 3 percent to 23.2 percent and consumer manufactures from 9 percent to 20.7 percent. Eric N. Baklanoff, The Economic Transformation of Spain and Portugal (New York: Praeger Publishers, 1978), 57-69.

3. The best economic analysis of the growth period may be that by Manuel-Jesús González González, La economía política del franquismo (1940-1970) (Madrid: Editorial Tecnos, 1979).

4. La Confederación Española de Organizaciones Empresariales.

5. On changes in the labor movement towards the end of the Franco regime see José Maravall, Dictatorship and Political Dissent: Workers and Students in Franco's Spain (London: St. Martin's Press, 1978); Jon Amsden, Collective Bargaining and Class Conflict in Spain (London: London School of Economics and Political Science, 1972); and Fernando Almendros Morcillo, Enrique Jiménez-Asenjo, Francisco Pérez Amorós, and Eduardo Rojo

Torrecillo, <u>El sindicalismo de clase en España (1939-1977)</u> (Barcelona: Ediciones Península, 1978).

6.   On the structure of the Sindicato Nacional, see Carlos Iglesias Selgas, <u>Los sindicatos en España</u> (Madrid: Ediciones del Movimiento, 1965); and Manuel Ludevid, <u>Cuarenta años de sindicato vertical</u> (Barcelona: Editorial Laia, 1976).

7.   Which is not to attribute the significant drop in new investment by Spanish capital during the early democratic years entirely to changes in labor relations. While the direct economic effects of rising labor demands did strongly affect wage costs and damage productivity, the perception of labor demands probably left a greater imprint in attitudinal terms among employers than it did in real costs.
    Although affected, foreign investors did not perceive as great a threat from changing labor relations structures and labor strife as did Spanish employers, a logical extension of their experiences with more open labor relations systems elsewhere. One possible discrepancy between foreign and Spanish investors was extended by a Catalan industrialist heading the operations of two heavy equipment manufacturers, both of which are controlled by multinationals. He claimed to have insider knowledge that multinationals don't have full information. Simply put, he said, "multinationals don't know so much."
    Foreign investment almost doubled from 1979 to 1983, jumping from 80.1 billion pesetas to 158.2 billion. Banca Más Sardá data published in <u>El País</u>, Madrid, 21 May 1984. Long-term capital inflows boomed in the late 1980s, also reflecting official policy encouraging liberal views toward long-term operations. Organization for Economic Cooperation and Development, <u>OECD Economic Surveys: Spain 1987/1988</u> (Paris: OECD, 1988), 7, 21, 56.

8.   Law 19, of 1 April 1977, <u>sobre regulación del derecho de asociación sindical</u>.

9.   The "Acuerdo básico interconfederal."

10.   "Acuerdo marco interconfederal," or AMI. The third ranking labor union, the Unión Sindical Obrera (USO) also adhered to the AMI in February 1981.

11.   Gerhard Lehmbruch, "Liberal Corporatism and Party Government," <u>Comparative Political Studies</u> 10, no. 1 (April 1977); and Philippe Schmitter, "Still the

Century of Corporatism?," in Frederick B. Pike and
Thomas Stritch, eds., The New Corporatism (Notre Dame:
University of Notre Dame Press, 1974), 85-131.

12. Perhaps a fundamental flaw in the corporatist
literature when applied to the realities of politics is
its excessive dependence on formal structures. Great
differences exist between formal arrangements of
governmental-corporate body interaction and reality.
While the existence of numerous committees might "prove"
corporate body-bureaucratic interpenetration, severe
resource limitations affecting corporate intermediaries
mean that available staff is insufficient even were
corporate groups to attempt full participation. When
information is a key commodity in and of itself,
collective interest groups may willingly participate in
corporate arrangements, but are doing so in order to be
better equipped to pressure in more traditional lobby
manners or in more effective fora.
    Lehmbruch, himself, notes that "we are led to the
rather trivial conclusion that some institutionalization
of organizational participation in corporatist policy
formation is of course always to be found, but that no
specific institutional framework leads with necessity
to the emergence of corporatism." Gerhard Lehmbruch,
"Introduction: Neo-Corporatism in Comparative Perspective," in Lehmbruch and Schmitter, eds., Patterns of
Corporatist Policy-Making (Beverly Hills: Sage Publications, 1982), 24.
    Related to the inability of an overly formal
approach to describe a dynamic reality, Frank Wilson
points to the unpredictable role of leadership in
enhancing the position of a given collective interest
group. Indeed, the point is well taken and is an element
normally overlooked in static analyses. For some of our
organizations, the quality of leadership proves essential in describing the influence a given association
enjoys.
    The role of leadership is an area of study much
ignored in the social sciences relative to its importance. In the case of Spanish democratization, the
fortuitous presence of Juan Carlos and Adolfo Suárez
were of much greater importance in achieving successful
consolidation than many of the formal institutional
changes adopted by the different parties and elites. It
is difficult to adequately measure a seemingly ephemeral
personal quality such as leadership, but its role at
critical junctures should not be underestimated.
    For the French case, Wilson argues convincingly
that interest groups adopt corporatist practices as part
of covering all "points of access" in trying to make

their influence felt in the policy process: "[C]orpo-
ratist forms of interest group-government interaction
are no more than forms of action within the pluralist
pattern." The same is true for Spanish business. Frank
L. Wilson, "French Interest Group Politics: Pluralist
or Neocorporatist?," American Political Science Review
77, no. 4 (December 1983): 904-909.
    Elsewhere, Wilson points out that neocorporatist
writers suggest that a mix between pluralist and
corporatist forms of intermediation are normal in the
transition from pluralist to corporatist interaction.
I believe a mix is normal.

    13. Henry W. Ehrmann, Organized Business in France
(Princeton: Princeton University Press, 1957); Stephen
Blank, Industry and Government in Britain (Westmead,
England: D.C. Heath Ltd., 1973); Wyn Grant and David
Marsh, The Confederation of British Industry (London:
Hodder and Soughton, 1977); Gerhard Braunthal, The
Federation of German Industry in Politics (Ithaca, N.Y.:
Cornell University Press, 1965); and Joseph LaPalombara,
Interest Groups in Italian Politics (Princeton: Prince-
ton University Press, 1964).

    14. Robert M. Fishman, "Working Class Organiza-
tion and Political Change: The Labor Movement and the
Transition to Democracy in Spain." Ph.D. dissertation,
Yale University, 1985, 64-73, published as Working Class
Organization and the Return to Democracy in Spain
(Ithaca, N.Y.: Cornell University Press, 1990).

    15. This final point is elaborated in an article
by Claus Offe and Helmut Wiesenthal, "Two Logics of
Collective Action: Theoretical Notes on Social Class
and Organizational Form," Political Power and Social
Theory, 1 (Greenwich, Conn.: JAI Press, 1979), 67-115.

    16. Charles E. Lindblom, The Policy-Making Process
(Englewood Cliffs, N.J.: Prentice-Hall, 1980), 81.
Other important advantages held in comparison to other
interest groups, which Lindblom notes, include available
funds and, often, greater access to policy makers and
administrators.

    17. Reinhard Bendix, Work and Authority in
Industry (Berkeley: University of California Press,
1974), 199.

    18. Robert Michels, Political Parties: A Socio-
logical Study of the Oligarchical Tendencies of Modern
Democracy (New York: Dover, 1959).

19. Mancur Olson, <u>The Logic of Collective Action</u> (Cambridge, Mass.: Harvard University Press, 1971).

20. Elaborated in the excellent comparative work by Loukas Tsoukalis, <u>The European Community and Its Mediterranean Enlargement</u> (London: Allen & Unwin, 1981).

21. Juan J. Linz and Amando de Miguel, <u>Los empresarios ante el poder público</u> (Madrid: Centro de Estudios Políticos, 1966). See also Linz and de Miguel, "Asociaciones voluntarias. La realidad asociativa de los españoles," in Confederación Española de Cajas de Ahorros, <u>Sociología española de los años setenta</u> (Madrid: Confederación Española de Cajas de Ahorros, 1971).

22. Banco de Bilbao, <u>Renta nacional de España</u> (Madrid: Banco de Bilbao, 1977). Measured by value added.

23. See the methodological appendix. Barcelona, Madrid, Vizcaya, Valencia and Sevilla ranked first, second, third, fourth and eighth, respectively, among the fifty provinces by industrial value added. The five provinces accounted for 47.3 percent of Spanish industrial output. Madrid and Barcelona alone accounted for 33.7 percent. Banco de Bilbao, <u>Renta</u>, 73.

24. Percentages of industrial labor force for the universe of firms with fifty employees or above, per the industrial census of the National Statistical Institute (Instituto Nacional de Estadística, INE), are: 36.7 percent in firms of from 50 to 199 employees, 37.8 percent for the 200 to 999 employees size category, and 25.5 percent at firms with 1000 or more employees. INE, Ministerio de Economía, <u>Censo industrial de España—1978</u>, industrial establishments (i.e., workplaces).

25. The universe of large companies is substantially smaller than that of intermediate companies, which is substantially smaller than that of regular companies. Hence, further equal division among the three groups, knowingly, "biases" the overall analysis by giving correspondingly greater weight to the group of large employers.

26. Classification of the smallest size category as "regular," rather than "small," is an open acknowledgment of the failure of this sample to adequately represent the views of the very small company, which

requires separate empirical treatment. The term "regular" was also employed by Linz and de Miguel.

The essential elements of the problématique of the small and medium firms can be found in César Menéndez Roces, La marginación de la pequeña y mediana empresa (Madrid: Editorial Mañana, 1978); Manuel Rojo Alejos, Prosper Lamothe Fernández, and Enrique Moreau Moya, Financiación de la pequeña y mediana empresa (Madrid: Asociación para el Progreso de la Dirección, 1981); and Andrés Fernández Romero, El autodiagnóstico de la pequeña y mediana empresa (Madrid: Asociación para el Progreso de la Dirección, 1981).

27. Although not a criterion in sample selection, the method used for drawing the sample produced a representational sectoral distribution for manufacturing and construction firms. All firms listed in the provincial industrial registries (Ministry of Industry) for these five provinces were numbered after being classified by size. They were numbered for random selection in the same order as they are listed in the registry and every "nth" firm chosen, with a substitution procedure for companies that had gone out of business or which refused the interview. Given that the industrial registry lists firms by distinct subsectoral classifications, sector is fully included in a representative manner. Service sector firms were excluded as it was felt that their problématique differed somewhat and would reduce the significance and accuracy of what we might say about industrial and construction firms.

28. The degree of foreign participation in Spanish business is very high. As one might expect, the larger the company, the more likely a higher degree of foreign participation.

29. Juan J. Linz and Amando de Miguel, "Fundadores, herederos y directores en las empresas españolas," Revista Internacional de Sociología 81 (January-March 1963); 82 (April-June 1963); 85 (January-March 1964). English version, Linz and de Miguel, "Founders, Heirs, and Managers of Spanish Firms," in International Studies of Management and Organization (New York: International Arts and Sciences Press, Spring-Summer 1974, vol. 4, 1-2). See also Paolo Farnetti, Imprenditore e societá (Turin: Li/Ed L'impresa, 1970); Dean Savage, Founders, Heirs, and Managers: French Industrial Leadership in Transition (Beverly Hills: Sage Publications, 1979); and Harry Mark Makler, A Elite Industrial Portuguesa (Lisbon: Centro de Economia e Finanças, 1969).

30. On the transition, I also draw reference to the important survey work conducted among 123 top managers of large companies by de la Sierra, Caballero, and Pérez Escanilla. In comparison to our research, their work focused to a greater extent on the perceived internal impact of the transition within firms and on managerial-organizational considerations. As their field work was conducted in the first half of 1980, business attitudes are recorded during a somewhat earlier period.

De la Sierra et al. addressed the universe of industrial firms which had invoiced over a billion pesetas in 1975. Fermín de la Sierra, Juan José Caballero, and Juan Pedro Pérez Escanilla, <u>Los directores de grandes empresas españolas ante el cambio social</u> (Madrid: Centro de Investigaciones Sociológicas, 1981). As their title suggests, change was treated in a somewhat broader sense than in my approach, with less attention to the impact in firms of political change and democracy <u>per se</u>.

Businesswomen were a minor component in Spanish industry. The random selection process used in both surveys supports a contention that the Spanish business world was a male-dominated realm. Only one woman emerged among individual chief executives (in a regular Barcelona firm), although two other firms listed women as presidents but not chief executive (a regular Madrid and a large Valencia firm). It appears that women who are employers tend to head family-owned concerns. Two small base-level associations, one in Madrid and another in Vizcaya, had women leaders who were interviewed in the association survey. The Association of Women Entrepreneurs refused to allow an interview. The interview in question was to have been informal and open format given that the women's association was only an associate member of the CEOE and as such outside the universe of this research.

2

The Institutional Framework of Employer Associability

During our survey period in the early 1980s, CEOE membership claims of affiliated firms, constituting the foundation of its hierarchy, ran from 1.25 to 1.45 million in number, which represented, according to their own calculations, 80 percent of active labor force in 1981 and 75 percent in 1982.[1] Both in terms of the number of member firms and its role as a system actor, the CEOE has enjoyed a hegemonic position in the representation of business. Competing organizations exist, but over time the CEOE has further consolidated its membership base. Other employers associations are inconsequential in comparison to the CEOE, although under specific circumstances, in relatively unimportant sectors and within local contexts, they may play relevant roles.

EMPLOYERS ORGANIZATIONS OUTSIDE THE CEOE

In the early years of free employer associability, perhaps the most important division in the "employers movement," to use a misleading term, was that existing between the CEOE and the CEPYME, the Spanish Confederation of Small and Medium Firms. While the CEOE theoretically represented all firms, the CEPYME sought to defend the interests of smaller firms, a long, ongoing problématique in the Spanish context. However, despite its more particularized focus and rhetoric, the CEPYME never drew precise demarcations as to what constituted a small or medium firm. Furthermore, relations between the two organizations were complementary rather than adversarial, although critical postures vis-à-vis the CEOE were adopted on given issues. Certain employer groups (unfairly) criticized CEPYME as a "lackey" of the CEOE. Nevertheless, the CEOE's hegemonic position was significantly enhanced by the incorporation into its ranks in March of 1980 of CEPYME, which now occupies a unique position as neither a sectoral nor provincial or regionally defined intersectoral (territorial) affiliate, but, rather, as a state-wide peak affiliate for smaller companies. While the affiliation served to resolve the serious financial difficulties facing CEPYME, some highly placed segments of opinion within the organization criticized the integration as a diminution in its protagonism.[2]

Given its hegemonic position, I will focus my attention to the CEOE in analyzing the political representation of employers. In addition to the minor competing organizations to which reference has been made, employers combine in forms other than the associational model. The Círculo de Empresarios, founded in 1976 and directly modelled on the Business Roundtable in the United States, is composed exclusively of the chief executive officers of a number of larger corporations.[3] Originally the organization focused on lobby activities with the aim of influencing upcoming legislation. In the early years of the transition, the Círculo may have played an important contributing role in securing a constitutional guarantee of the free enterprise system. In the late 1980s, the group moved away somewhat from the Roundtable model and increasingly concentrated on more research-related activities similar to those of the Committee for Economic Development (CED) in the United States or the Keizai Doyuki in Japan, producing "white papers" with the hope of contributing toward framing debates on important policy issues. In part, one high-ranking Círculo functionary contends that while the group would prefer to focus on a lobby mode, a greater shift toward CED-type activities was necessary given the still embryonic channels for lobbying activities in Spain and the illegitimacy with which strict interest group lobbying is held. Besides the key role played in keeping elite chief executives informed regarding pending legislation, we can assume that the Círculo provides a forum for developing and maintaining a strong personal network among key actors in the business community. The organization appears economically well endowed and is an associate, that is; a nonvoting, member of the CEOE.

The Association for Progress in Business Administration (Asociación para el Progreso de la Dirección—APD) has for some thirty years conducted activities in the field of employer training (formación) and larger-scale information interchange among business people.[4] The leadership of APD, which is of a largely

honorary character, reads like a "who's who" of business sector politics (CEOE, banking sector, public
sector, etc.).

A number of smaller organizations play important
research, informational, and publication roles with
varying degrees of definite and direct business, as
opposed to solely academic, participation. Most prominent among these are the Barcelona-based Círculo de
Economía, which had a more activist image during the
Franco regime;[5] the Instituto de Empresa; the Fundación
Universidad-Empresa, which is housed in the same building as the Círculo de Empresarios; and the Fundación
Fondo para la Investigación Económica y Social, headed
by Enrique Fuentes Quintana, former vice-president for
economic affairs under the first constitutional government, and which publishes the quarterly Papeles de
Economía Española.

The semi-official system of Chambers of Commerce,
Industry, and Navigation (Cámaras de Comercio, Industria y Navegación) constitutes an additional channel of
organized employer activity. They are of particular importance in high-exporting regions and those with long
traditions of high-employer associability. The chamber
system provided a more notable forum for employer activity during the Franco period given its independence from
the cumbersome Sindicato Nacional and its unitary
structures.

The chambers of commerce have a "peak" organ (Consejo Superior) in Madrid and were originally recognized
toward the end of the nineteenth century as representative structures of commercial, industrial, and merchant
marine interests. The April 1886 legislation granting
the Cámaras official recognition described them as "con-
sultative bodies of the public administration" that
would be consulted on matters pertaining to projected
commercial treaties, tariffs, customs arrangements, commercial legislation, social legislation, and the like.[6]
As with employers associations, chambers of commerce in
Europe differ substantially from their American counterparts. Specifically, the primary distinctions arise from
the much more extensive governmental influence in their
development.[7] Modelled on the French system,[8] local
branches of the provincially defined Spanish Cámaras
system vary substantially in their degree of protagonism,[9] from relatively strong interest representation to
existence as mere bureaucratic artifacts.[10] In certain
ways, the semi-official Cámaras system parallels or
replicates a portion of the roles of the employers
associations. However, their semi-official status and
activity in more traditional and limited representational arenas serve to distance the Cámaras from associa-

tional roles.[11]

To exhaust the entire gamut of organizations, employers are also active in professional associations,[12] export organizations, producer trade associations, clubs, and so forth.

DEFINING CHARACTERISTICS OF ASSOCIATIONS

At the "macro" level, the CEOE plays the key role among employers associations. However, our data will confirm that among its primary clientele, the base of the employer hierarchy, composed of individual chief executive officers, the roles played by the CEOE's constituent affiliated associations proves more noteworthy in members' estimation than that of the peak itself. As the CEOE's own chart (on the following page) indicates, individual firms cannot be directly affiliated to the peak but can only belong via the affiliated sectoral or territorial (intersectoral) associations.[13] In 1981, the CEOE listed seventy-seven sectoral associations and forty-four territorial (intersectoral) associations as full members. Of the former, over 80 percent have their headquarters in Madrid,[14] with an additional 10 percent in Barcelona. Forty-two of the territorial associations extended over single provinces, and two—Fomento del Trabajo Nacional (active in the four Catalan provinces) and the Confederación Canaria de Empresarios (for the two provinces of the Canary Islands)—are regional rather than provincial in extension.[15] Membership figures for 1982 indicate ninety-two sectoral and thirty-nine territorial affiliates. CEPYME is a full member classed separately from the sectoral and territorial associations. With its eighty-three votes in the CEOE's General Assembly, the peak's governing body, CEPYME held roughly twice the number of votes held by the two major sectoral associations, Confemetal (forty-six votes), representing the metal industry, and the Confederación Nacional de la Construcción, the CNC (forty-one votes).

A precise classification of any association located within the CEOE requires hierarchically the identification of three characteristics. These are: (1) membership-order level, (2) affiliation, and (3) sectoral character. Membership-order level refers to the nature of the members of an organization. Those associations whose membership is composed of individual firms are termed "base associations." "Intermediate associations" are those composed of lower-ranking associations, which is to say that these are "associations of associations." The affiliation distinction classes organizations as either direct or indirect affiliates of the CEOE. The

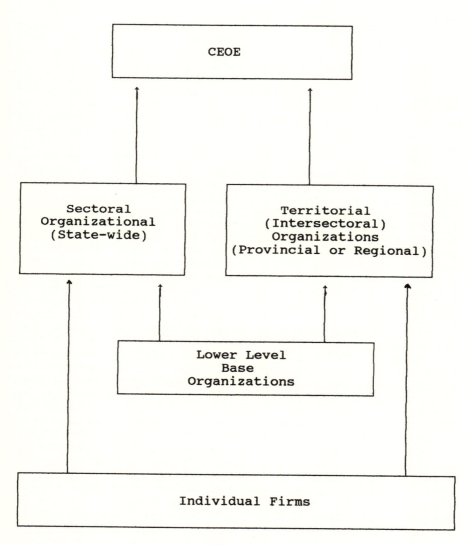

Chart I

Simple CEOE Organizational Chart

sectoral classification is simply the primary distinction drawn in Chart I separating the associations
defined along sectoral lines from the territorial
(intersectoral) associations.

A number of base associations, composed of individual firms, are affiliated directly to the peak.
Indeed, such organizations represent the majority of the
direct affiliates of the CEOE (65%), although none of
the seven or eight most influential member CEOE affiliates are base organizations, with the exception of
the banking association, the Asociación Española de la
Banca (AEB).[16] Likewise a number of intermediate associations, formed in turn by lower-ranking organizations,
are not necessarily themselves directly affiliated to
the peak. Associations such as the Motor Vehicles Manufacturers' Association (ANFAC),[17] or that of petroleum
refiners (ASERPETROL),[18] represent sectors composed of
only a few but relatively wealthy companies, among which
the organization of collective action appears exceedingly self-evident, given that the affiliation of each firm
to the group markedly increases the amount of the collective good accruing to the whole as a consequence
thereof, a process amply described by Olson. Given the
relative ease (and self-evident "logic") of organizing
interests collectively in such cases, and grouping an
entire sector at the national level with only ten or
twenty companies,[19] such associations affiliate themselves directly to the peak without any need for
intermediate organizations.

Despite the fact that neither ANFAC nor ASERPETROL
could be classified as among the handful of most influential member associations within the CEOE, they do provide examples of associations which are economically
vigorous, given the relative well-being and size of
their constituent member firms. As such, the associations play important lobby roles for their member firms
before the peak (as well as in relation to the unions
and the public administration). ANFAC and ASERPETROL,
not the only such associations, perhaps most closely
approximate the ideal type for the Spanish case at the
state-wide level and represent almost direct access to
the peak for each member firm.[20] Nevertheless, there are
a number of sectors which, despite being composed of a
much larger number of firms, possibly given a relatively
narrow spectrum in the economic activities realized by
member firms (i.e., high homogeneity), are affiliated
in base organizations that extend over the entire
country and that are then directly affiliated to the
CEOE. The association of insurance agencies, UNESPA,[21]
with over 600 member firms, is a case in point. Naturally, there exist limits to this model, given that it

would be exceedingly difficult to affiliate a sector composed of thousands of companies into a single country-wide association that in turn would be affiliated directly to the peak. While one cannot compute a single threshold in the number of potential member companies in a given sector that can organize effectively in a single national level organization without further differentiation, a case such as that of UNESPA is an outlier.

THE COMPLEX CEOE ORGANIZATIONAL CHART

As the description of the base-intermediate and direct-indirect dichotomies suggests, the reality of the organizational hierarchy of the CEOE is far more complex than the simple CEOE chart identifying the sectoral and territorial pillars would imply. The actual organizational reality is represented more accurately by the second chart appearing below. What emerges is a complex system of multiple representation of a single firm, and of multiple and, at times, overlapping associational levels, possessing varying degrees of organizational validity.

The issue of organizational "validity" involves making two primary determinations in a statistical treatment of associations. The figures I have extended regarding the number of (direct) affiliates in the CEOE are figures which have already consolidated those organizations that appear as two separate entries but are actually a single "valid" organization. Given that all direct sectoral affiliates were contacted for this study, and the vast majority were included, all such discrepancies were eliminated.

Two entries on the CEOE membership list are considered a single case for purposes of this study when they share the same bureaucracies, occupy the same offices, and have the same individual as secretary-general, as well as having the same firms as base members. A number of organizations share offices and a portion of personnel, but are distinguishable in not having complete congruence between the two. Common are instances when the offices and clerical staff of an intermediate direct CEOE affiliate are shared with one or more of its own member base associations, with the objective of reducing costs for the smaller associations. Such arrangements can be considered entirely valid in that the smaller association will have its own secretary-general and a completely separate group of elected leaders, and will have arrangements for, at least, nominal compensation via its own budgeted expenditures to offset some of the costs of shared staff or space. In instances when I treated two entries as a single association, budgets, generally, are not drawn up separately, and the secretary-general is the same individual, as is the staff. In these instances elected boards may appear to be composed of different business people, but reviewing lists a few years back reveals that they are drawn from the same pool of a limited number of active chief executives.

At the level of the CEOE itself, instances of this phenomenon include the cases of the associations of bus companies (FENEBUS—Federación Nacional de Transportes en Autobus) and that for urban transport (Asociación Nacional de Transportes Urbanos de Viajeros de Superficie); the flour producers association (Asociación de Fabricantes de Harinas de España) and that of flour exporters (Asociación Harinera de Mercado Exterior); and, producers of paper and cardboard (Asociación Nacional de Fabricantes de Papel y Cartón) and that of paper pulp manufacturers (la Asociación Nacional de Fabricantes de Pastas Papelera). These associations generally operate as two organizations because the same firms in a given economic activity have to deal with separate public administration structures and regulations for somewhat different ends; intercity versus city transportation, domestic versus foreign markets, or primary raw material transformation versus production of finished goods. In other countries, these somewhat different operations within the same sectors might be conducted by different groups of firms, albeit probably with some overlap. In Spain, the overlap or congruence among the firms involved in these sectors is complete or almost so.

The paper industry is interesting in that while the primary and secondary transformers of paper figure as "two" associations that are actually a single operation, another subsector of the industry, producers of corrugated cardboard and processed cardboard (for packaging) have two associations. These are a Madrid-based association, AFCO (Asociación Española de Fabricantes de Cartón Ondulado), which appears particularly defiant (as associations go) in defending the specific prerogatives of its narrower manufacturing niche in the face of the larger industry, and a Barcelona-based association, ASPACK (Asociación Nacional de Fabricantes de Envases, Embalajes y Transformados de Cartón y Materias Auxiliares) which, despite the "nacional" in its name, appears to derive its primary raison d'être as an organization physically and politically closer to the Catalan manufacturers that it represents at the CEOE. This identification need not be necessarily attributable to Catalanism, but is more probably just a consequence of the historical development of the organizations and of the industry. AFCO, the Madrid-base organization, having identified its relatively narrow niche of economic activity and being composed of a limited number of relatively well-off firms, approximates, in organizational terms, the ASERPETROL or ANFAC model described previously in which collective action is relatively easy and its "logic" very evident (although the firms involved are not of the size of those affiliated in those earlier examples).

The same phenomenon of duplicate entries for a single organization is found at the level of indirect affiliates as well. Among affiliates of Confederación Empresarial Independiente de Madrid (CEIM), the Madrid provincial intersectoral, one case is that of the association of aerial agricultural support (i.e., the use of airplanes for agricultural purposes; Asociación Empresarial de Trabajos Agrícolas y Forestales por Medios Aéreos) and of aerial photography (ASTOFO-- Asociación de Trabajos Topográficos y Fotogramétricos). The organizational differentiation here may reflect promotional efforts by member firms in the definition and attraction of clients.[22]

The second consideration in determining "validity" is somewhat similar and involves the identification of "paper" organizations. One such case is mentioned in treatment of Chart II (below) and involves the intersectoral provincial association of Barcelona, the Confederación Empresarial de Barcelona (CEB). All activities of the CEB are conducted by Fomento del Trabajo Nacional, the peak employers association for Catalonia. However, employers in the other three Catalan provinces, Gerona, Lérida, and Tarragona, operate valid intersectoral associations which make representations at Fomento and participate in the regional peak. While Fomento fully determines intersectoral employer policies for the Barcelona province, the employers of Barcelona required some organizational mechanism by which to legitimate their interest representation in those instances when issues arise involving intersectoral concerns on which common postures are desirable. In reality, that all concerned know that the CEB is a paper operation is of little consequence given the predominance of Barcelona within Catalan industry overall and given that the other three valid "provincials" operate with the purpose of meeting more local needs and not Catalan regional needs that all concerned willingly (usually) leave in the hands of Fomento anyway. There are numerous examples of such paper organizations. A number of intermediate associations, particularly those which are less important,

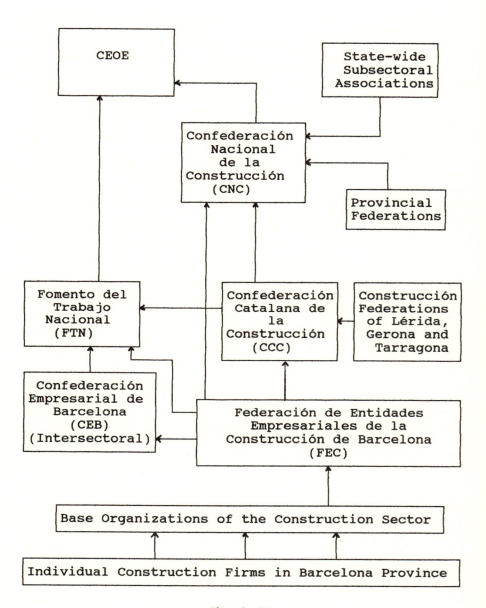

Chart II

Complex CEOE Organizational Chart

are slow in deleting the names of member base associations that have ceased to operate from their own organizational charts, for obvious reasons.

Referring to Chart II, the FEC, the Construction Federation of Barcelona (not a "base organization") is itself directly affiliated to the Confederación Nacional de la Construcción (CNC), the country-wide association for the construction sector, which, in representational terms, is one of the two most important CEOE sectoral affiliates. This FEC affiliation is in its capacity as a CNC provincial federation. Although not the case in large provinces such as Barcelona, many of the CNC's provincial affiliates will be base associations of the construction sector. In Barcelona, as indicated on Chart II, the FEC is a federation composed of smaller associational entities. Subsectoral, country- wide associations make up the other major component of the CNC. The Catalan Construction Confederation, the CCC, exists for purposes of constituting a region-wide interlocutor for the sector in Fomento del Trabajo Nacional, the regional intersectoral organization for Catalonia,[23] and for purposes of representing sectoral interests at the Generalitat, the Catalan regional autonomous government.

The CCC, as indicated, is composed of the provincial construction federations for the four Catalan provinces. In turn, we see that the FEC is affiliated directly to Fomento as well as to the CEB, the intersectoral territorial association for Barcelona province, essentially a paper organization that provides Fomento with what it might consider as necessary territorial representational symmetry in relation to the other three intersectoral and "valid" provincial associations of Catalonia. These individual intersectoral associations for the different Catalan provinces are also direct affiliates of the CEOE.

THE CEOE AS BUREAUCRACY

Chart III (next page) provides a simple outline of the internal organization of the CEOE as an institution. As one might imagine, much of the activity undertaken in the assembly, and even in the Fifty-seven-member board of directors, involves accepting or rejecting decisions reached previously by the Executive Committee or among smaller and changing collections of leaders of those organizations which stand to be affected most by a given CEOE policy choice. That is to say, the most interested parties on a given issue most influence the decisions reached, with the President's office, technical staff and Executive Committee playing important

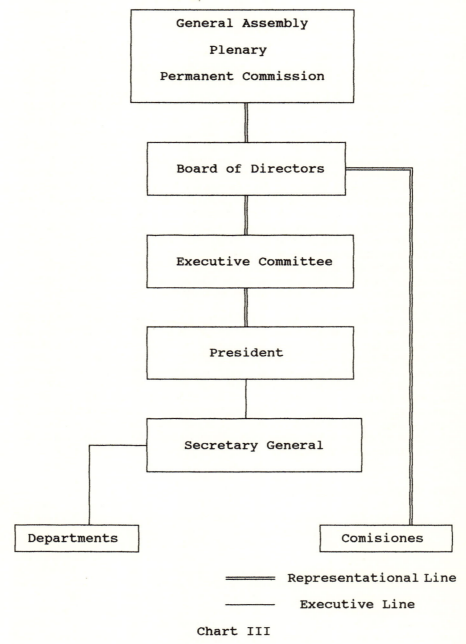

Chart III

CEOE Internal Organization

roles.

Much of the work focused on adopting public postures is done in the commissions, which are further
subdivided into committees. Each is headed by a well-
known chief executive, individuals on a number of
company boards in large firms who tend to hold strong
credentials in the functional areas of the commissions
or committees they chair. The major CEOE commissions
are: labor relations, economy, internal organizational
regulations, international relations, and professional
and interprofessional relations.

The executive bureaus (or departments) of the CEOE,
generally headed by career association managers,[24] are:
economic affairs, labor relations, international relations, communications, affiliate organizational relations, Common Market, research, and management and
administration. Competencies tend to blur across departmental lines as circumstances warrant and there are
occasional shifts among the subgroups listed under
different departmental rubrics.

The direct CEOE staff, including bureau chiefs and
excluding all the elected officials, stood at seventy-
five in mid-1982. 1980 revenues were slightly above 232
million pesetas (U.S. $2.9 million at the 1980 year-end
exchange rate). Slightly over half (53%) originated from
membership dues and an additional third (36%) was derived from special contributions.[25] Expenditures were
slightly lower than revenue, with a large proportion
allocated toward salaries (38%) and social security payments (8%) for staff. Important amounts went towards
travel costs (7%) and the CEOE's own payment of dues
towards the international organizations to which it is
affiliated (5%). As the budget director argued, with
almost half of expenditures targeted towards salaries
or other employee costs, analyses of budget spending in
the hopes of deciphering organizational priorities is
a "ludicrous exercise." The same individual longed for
the days of compulsory membership (the Sindicato) due
to its financial arrangements. He argued that quotas
paid within the totality of the associational hierarchy,
to all organizations, at all levels, would represent
from 10 percent to 12.5 percent in real terms in 1981
of that received by the Sindicato in 1975.[26] While the
total budget may appear small, we need to recognize that
the CEOE depends on work done by member chief executives
and their company staffs, that is volunteer work.

Having worked for five years in a prestigious U.S.
business association, I can attest to the fact that the
relative size of budgetary expenditures by issue area
is not necessarily a realistic reflection of an organization's priorities. In a given business organization,

which individual executive heads which committee and how
that individual leader chooses to work his issues, and
how much is expended directly by individual companies
on an issue (with coordination/communication by the association, but without funding through the association)
determines to a great degree how much association money
may be needed.

There are limits in a business organization to the
number of issues that can be followed by the peak's top
leadership, although leaders of a given committee may
choose to pursue additional efforts. The nature of certain issues, perhaps those requiring extensive legal
work, may boost expenditures over other issues that may
be more important. Similarly, interests opposed to the
business view are well organized or financed, expenditures by business need to rise, while issues facing less
opposition and less opposing funding may be more important. The level of expenditures in a given area remains
an important--but not fully accurate--measure of an
organization's priorities. Nonetheless, expenditures
skewed for too long a time towards areas other than
those few of priority concern can eventually damage
internal self-identity and cohesion.

The peak is not a huge bureaucratic apparatus.
Sufficient time had not elapsed since its founding. As
with organizational membership charts and the formal
internal organization chart, however, the reality of
CEOE finances cannot be explained merely by discussion
of formal financial arrangements. While not a wealthy
organization, the peak can depend on solid sources of
financial support to provide any extraordinary expenditures unforeseen at budget time and relies a good deal
on volunteer support.

FORMAL AND INFORMAL NETWORKS

Formal structures for interest representation notwithstanding, it is clear that major policy postures
adopted by the peak with implications beyond those of
a sectoral nature are determined by the positions of the
leaders of a handful of organizations. On all major
policy decisions, there are a group of perhaps six organizations whose positions will always be sought. However, another group of six to eight additional organizations can be considered to have a secondary, but
important, impact on policy choices. On policy issues
of a sectoral character, it is those organizations most
affected that appear most to influence decisions taken.
Hence, peak level support is extended for the positions
of sectoral affiliates. Similarly, when the interests

of two roughly equivalent member organizations are at odds, the CEOE as a whole is unlikely to adopt any posture.

That a handful of organizations should informally enjoy the "big say" on important issues is not much of a revelation given that even in formal terms, their pre-eminent roles are generally acknowledged, most obviously in the number of assembly votes held. Although roughly three-quarters of sectoral affiliates control only a single vote, the CNC and Confemetal each control over forty and CEPYME over eighty.[27] The CEOE's representa-tiveness in terms of numbers of companies is based on these three organizations. As one department chief put it: "Confemetal is another CEOE." A second CEOE bureau chief was more explicit:

> The instant that the CNC and metals [industry] disaffiliated, there would go the CEOE. It wouldn't result in CEOE bankruptcy, but it would take away all its meaning. If the CNC and Confemetal departed, the representativeness which the CEOE has would be eliminated.

The ten votes that the AEB controls in the assembly, equal to the votes controlled by ANFAC and ASERPETROL, fall far short of reflecting the banking sector's true weight. The AEB far surpasses its formal degree of strength given its large financial support of the peak organization and its prominent public role outside the hierarchy due to the importance of the sector it affiliates.

Only two territorial organizations contend with the major sectorals in influencing overall policy, the very important Fomento and the Madrid intersectoral, the CEIM.[28] The CEIM is an interesting example of the difference leadership can make in strengthening an organization beyond its formal role. Former CEIM presi-dent José Antonio Segurado used his position to promote the positions of his business constituency before the public at large, and thereby enhancing the role of the CEIM within the CEOE in the process. While a provincial organization like CEIM may develop province-wide "mini-accords" on salaries or working conditions with the unions, they do not play a direct role in collective bargaining, a crucial component in the consolidation of many sectoral associations. Lacking any strong histori-cal basis of strength within the region, as Fomento enjoys in its region, and lacking the direct collective bargaining role, the prominence of CEIM can be largely attributed to the incidence of its admittedly confron-tational, but protagonistic leadership.

A number of other organizations hold considerable sway at the CEOE (albeit at levels below those of the most prominent), simply as a function of the importance of the sectors they represent within the economy. The food and beverage industries (Federación Española de la Alimentación y Bebidas), textiles (Consejo Intertextil Español), mining and metallurgy (CONFEDEM--Confederación Nacional de la Minería y la Metalurgia), electrical utilities (FEIE--Federación de la Industria Eléctrica Española), and chemicals (FEIQUE--Federación de la Industria Química) all figure prominently.

While the agricultural sector is important within the CEOE, it pursues its primary objectives independently of the peak association to a greater extent than most. The large agrarian associations (most notably, la Confederación Nacional de Agricultores y Ganaderos), given their long traditions and the importance which agriculture continues to hold within the economy (and its electoral over-representation), deal directly with the relevant public authorities. Agribusiness concerns (such as the abovementioned Federación de Alimentación y Bebidas) participate more actively in the CEOE.

The measure of the strength of an organization is not determined exclusively by its position within the CEOE. Organizations that might not be in any way distinguishable from their peers within the hierarchy may nevertheless enjoy important roles on stages of greater priority for them, which are those arenas affecting their specific sectors. Individual heads of firms look more to their own sectoral association at a local level than to the peak. Hence, an association appearing insignificant in comparison to its peers within the CEOE may enjoy a considerable degree of consolidation among its membership. It may have achieved full recognition of its position by other actors relevant to its concerns, which may be localized and sectoral. Enjoying wide support among its constituent organizations in its primary political arena, the CEOE is afforded considerable leeway in the formulation of macro-policy. CEOE constituent organizations are much more concerned with the details of their more limited realms. This parallels the primary concerns of base member firms. Hence, the measure of an organization's strength from its own perspective may lie more with its constituency than with peak level politics. It is to treatment of associability among individual employers and associations to which we turn in the next two chapters.

NOTES

1.   The very high figure membership derives from the many self-employed or family outfits that balloon the ranks of employers. The CEOE can always count on its taxi driver members to help its "mass" image.

2.   Other minor confederations for small and medium enterprises have been created. The now defunct COPYME, Confederation of Small and Medium Firms, was led by Enrique Miret Magdalena and was inspired by Christian progressive and socialist influences. It was overwhelmingly composed of self-employed individuals and small family concerns, and was dominated by a single member federation, the FIPYME, the Independent Federation of Small and Medium Firms of Madrid.

In June of 1981, perhaps partially as a response to the integration of CEPYME into CEOE ranks, Fernando González Olivé, a Rioja employer, founded UNIPYME, the Union of Small and Medium Employers, Artisans and Self-Employed. It is of anecdotal interest to note that the central headquarters of the union is located in the same office space occupied by CEPYME prior to its affiliation to CEOE.

In addition to UNIPYME, a number of independent sectoral associations remain outside the CEOE rubric, although these are few in number and in no instance represent sectors of any importance in the economy. In the early 1980s, a few of the national sectoral associations, such as the Agrupación de Comercio (ACA), did not participate in the CEOE due to economic constraints. While in agreement with CEOE positions, a given sectoral might be unable to pay the required CEOE membership quota or to employ the personnel that would be necessary to truly benefit from membership in the peak, such as attending meetings, working as a liaison, and so forth.

3.   In theory, like the U.S. Business Roundtable, the Círculo denies its chief executive member the right to delegate his authority to lower-level associates for purposes of attendance at policy-level meetings or official representations, but exceptions to this rule appear to occur frequently. The Business Council on National Issues (BCNI) in Canada also follows the Business Roundtable model.

4.   Formerly led by Antonio Garrigues Walker, who departed the high-visibility position for more direct political activism, the APD was subsequently headed by Claudio Boada, former president of the Instituto Nacional de Industria (INI) and chief executive of the Insti-

tuto Nacional de Hidrocarburos (INH), the largest public
sector holding company. That Boada headed an organization overwhelmingly private sector in tone and complexion says something about the undifferentiated role
of the public sector in the Spanish business context.

5.   Officially founded in 1958, the Círculo de
Economía had as its three primary objectives: (1) the
achievement of a democratic political system, (2) a free
market economy, and (3) Spanish integration into the
European Community.   Composed of businessmen, econo-
mists, and technicians, the historian Jaime Vicens Vives
is considered by the Círculo to have been its early
decisive inspiration. Founded originally in the early
1950s as a sort of student club (indeed, a chess club),
the Círculo operated on the fringe of legality.   Carlos
Ferrer Salat, first president of the Catalan peak employers association, Fomento del Trabajo Nacional,
following the resumption of free associability, and of
the CEOE, was also one of the group's early activists.
Círculo de Economía, Círculo de Economía 1958-1983
(Barcelona: Círculo de Economía, 1983), 6-61.

6.   Enciclopedia jurídica española 1910 ed., vol.
4, s.v. "Cámaras de Comercio," 804-806.

7.   Carl J. Friedrich, Constitutional Government
and Democracy (Boston: Ginn and Company, 1950), 465.

8.   The 1886 legislation explicitly noted that it
would prove beneficial to follow the French model. The
first real chamber of commerce anywhere was officially
organized towards the end of the sixteenth century in
Marseilles, although it had been developing long before.
In Spain, forerunners of the Cámaras appeared in the
thirteenth and fourteenth centuries in the Balearics,
Catalonia, and among the merchant traders of Burgos.
Enciclopedia jurídica española, 806-809.
The Spanish organizations appear to have followed
a similar evolution to their French counterparts. As is
the case in Spain, Ehrmann states that the French
chambers have not frequently engaged in political or
pressure group activities, functions left to the CNPF.
The Spanish chambers play limited roles in more traditional forms of business interests, closer to the role
of trade associations. However, we will find numerous
employers associations within the CEOE that similarly
emphasize more traditional activities and de-emphasize
those of a more representational or political nature.
Ehrmann notes that, in comparison to the Paris Chamber,
some provincial chambers of commerce were more active

in the pursuit of political or pressure group objectives. The same might be true in certain Spanish provinces, particularly in some of the semi-industrialized provinces with only weak employers associations present. Ehrmann writes:

> Conflicts between them [the Chambers] and the employers' movement could easily have arisen where the Chambers, according to the statute of 1898, were called upon to present their views to the government as to appropriate means of promoting industrial and commercial prosperity and to advise the administration on all questions referred to them.
>
> By their constitution, by their membership, by the character of their financial means, and by their legally stipulated relationship to the public authorities, the Chambers were little suited to play the role of fully developed pressure groups in a modern state. Were it not for the comfortable niches in nineteenth century style which present-day France still offers to the nostalgic, they might have lost all of their status. As semi-official bodies the Chambers draw their income from certain taxes, and from state subsidies which make the Chambers fairly affluent but too dependent on the government to have all the desirable freedom to maneuver."

Ehrmann, 166-172. While I would not characterize the Spanish Chambers of Commerce as "nostalgic relics," the above description could otherwise apply to this case.

9.   Each province must have at least one Chamber of Commerce or Chamber of Commerce and Industry. Chambers might exist separately for each commerce, industry, and navigation (in maritime provinces), or these might be included within the same body. Local level chambers also exist.

10.   In relatively smaller but old industrial/commercial areas of Catalonia, such as Sabadell, Tarrasa, and Reus, the local chambers hold substantial roles as industry spokespieces. Obviously, this responds in part to their long history in the region. In the Basque Country, the _Cámaras_ system was promoted by the Basque Nationalist Party (PNV) in its pursuance of a specifically Basque autochthonous economic reality. The PNV formed the first autonomous government in Euskadi in 1980 and was in office until September 1986, when the former PNV president of the Basque regional government, Carlos Garaikoetxea, split from the PNV to form his own party, Eusko Alkartasuna (EA—"Basque Solidarity"). This led to regional elections 30 November 1986 and the formation of a minority Socialist government (PSE-PSOE) headed by José Antonio Ardanza.

11. In our survey among association leaders, the heads of base level associations, that is, the lowest level of association, with membership composed directly by individual firms, were asked to compare the associations with the _Cámaras_. Only 27 percent (N=84) responded that the associations were clearly better than the _Cámaras_. Four percent argued that the _Cámaras_ were better. Thirty-one percent believed the _Cámaras_ and associations to be equally positive within their respective arenas or to be complementary. An additional 11 percent drew more ambiguous assessments, generally more favorable to the associations, but also assessing the _Cámaras_ as important organizations. 12 percent considered the two types of organizations too dissimilar for comparison. Hence, there exists more sympathy than animosity among association leaders with respect to the _Cámaras_.

12. Given the relatively high proportions of employers holding professional degrees, no doubt important informal networks exist within professional associations that are used by business. As with some of the other groups listed, the _colegios profesionales_ provided important independent outlets for business contacts during the Franquist era and its mandatory unitary employer-worker structures.

13. Some firms can "belong" to the peak via "associate" affiliation, which means that they can be present directly at most functions as observers and receive the CEOE's periodic or special publications directly from the peak rather than via the sectoral or territorial associations. They cannot vote and are not "members" in any true sense of the word. However, the status of associate does permit the CEOE to receive their special contributions and allows certain large firms thereby directly to support the organization and manifest their business "solidarity." Undoubtedly, some chief executives feel they are benefiting from increased informational access and availability of contacts. All firms so associated to the CEOE must also be affiliated via normal associational channels. Even officially, membership quotas generally provide only somewhat over half of CEOE regular budget revenue, the special extra-quota contributions by member organizations and those of associates account for roughly 35 percent to 40 percent of income.

14. A very high proportion of these are housed either right in the CEOE building, in the northeastern section of Madrid, or within a ten-block radius thereof.

15. Although still embryonic in the early 1980s, 1982 witnessed the inception of a number of attempts in the development of associations that would operate at the level of the autonomous regions. Fomento, with its very long traditions and financial strength, is the prime model. The Confederación de Empresarios de Andalucía (CEA) initiated its public role with the approach of elections for the Andalucian parliament (May 1982). Early talks towards the formation of some formal structure for regular cooperation among the territorial associations of Castilla-La Mancha began in 1982. Organization of a confederation for the Basque Country was long obstructed by political differences within the employers' movement in the region, detailed elsewhere. Hence, while of minimal consequence in most areas, organizations targeted at regional issues may gain in ascendance if the "estado de las autonomías" endures, although the uproar over the expense of an additional layer of bureaucracy may eventually lead to some pullback.

One level down hierarchically, we might further expect a rise in sectoral associations of a regional, rather than provincial character as regional governments increase their protagonism. The Catalan Construction Confederation (Chart II), the CCC, is a case in point.

16. The AEB was composed of 126 member banks (1982) that represented the entire sector, a sector whose field of operation is well-defined and that was historically dominated in Spain by the seven largest banks. Mergers and acquisitions and the increased presence of foreign banks led to some fundamental changes in the industry in the late 1980s, including consolidations among the seven largest. The AEB is one of the most service oriented of the major associations (as one might expect given that it is a base and not an intermediate association) and the selective incentives provided by the organization in the form of vast amounts of financial, statistical, and legislative data may be of absolute necessity to all banks. Minor banks would be unable to provide such data as fully for themselves, practically ensuring affiliation by all potential members. While the larger banks may be capable of satisfying their own informational requirements, albeit at a higher cost, the very limited number of institutions (the universe of large banks) involved and the manner in which they controlled the sector on their own, guaranteed that the maximum amount of collective goods, in Olson's terms, would be provided. There is a concentrated interest of a few individuals that collective goods be produced and a self-evident knowledge that a

failure to participate (i.e., contribute) on the part
of any single of the major banks would markedly reduce
the amount of the collective benefits to be had by all.

17.   Asociación de Fabricantes de Automóviles,
Camiones, Tractores y sus Motores.

18.   Asociación de Empresas Refinadoras del
Petroleo.

19.   Indeed, in 1982, ASERPETROL was composed of
seven firms!

20.   The internal operations of such associations
are generally less problematic given the greater efficiency attainable by the reduced number and characteristics of member firms. Sectors composed of a greater
number of firms face serious obstacles in the process
of organizing interests collectively. This issue is
treated at length in Chapter 3.
In the case of the banking sector, direct affiliation of the AEB to the CEOE certainly provides almost
direct access of the larger banks to other elite sectors
of the business community. In this instance, however,
the issue is one of formal structures that serve to
channel and facilitate contacts that most certainly
would exist (and do) without and outside of organizational mechanisms, a situation different from that of
the larger employers affiliated to ANFAC or ASERPETROL.
In less frequent instances for these other affiliates,
informal networks may similarly exist. The very public
role of Rafael Termes, president of the AEB, both within
the CEOE as well as independently of it, as a spokes-
man for the banks, rivaled that of Carlos Ferrer during
the early 1980s, an indication of the weight of the
sector.

21.   La Unión Española de Entidades Aseguradoras
y de Capitalización.

22.   Ultimately many of the duplicate associations
at either level (direct/indirect) may possibly merge
into a single publicly recognized organization, as
occurred in 1981 between the intersectoral associations
of Alcobendas and San Sebastián de los Reyes (bordering
towns just north of Madrid).

23.   When originally organized towards the end of
the eighteenth century, the forerunner of the present
Fomento was open to the early industrialists of the
entire country, which explains the "nacional" in its

name. See Guillermo Graell, <u>Historia del Fomento del Trabajo Nacional</u> (Barcelona: Imprenta en Viuda de Luis Tasso, 1911). Fomento could be described as the "peak" organization for Catalan companies.

24. A number of bureau heads are themselves small business employers and practically all had private sector business experience before entering the CEOE. While a goodly proportion of the secretary-generals of member associations were in some way connected to the old Sindicato, such was not the case among department heads.

25. All member organizations are requested yearly to make contributions above quota obligations. Associate member contributions are included in this amount. Membership quotas are determined via a formula that takes into consideration the number of member firms in the organization, their gross value added, and employment. The components of this formula have been weighted differently at different points in time.

26. Indeed, he claimed that union leader support for compulsory membership had little to do with solidarity, but was due to resource shortfalls, and he commiserated. The budget director estimated that for 1981 6 to 7 billion pesetas would be collected for the totality of the associational hierarchy. By comparison, in 1975, the CBI's income stood at £2.4 million. Grant and Marsh, <u>Confederation</u>, 37.

27. While indicative of an important role for CEPYME, this is not to imply that CEPYME has twice the impact of its more important construction and metal industry counterparts.

28. One should not forget that the four Catalan provinces represented by Fomento, together with Madrid province, constitute 38 percent of Spain's total industrial value added. Banco de Bilbao, <u>Renta nacional de España</u> (Bilbao, 1980), 73.

3

Business and Collective Action

Two primary means by which to measure the degree of early consolidation that the CEOE achieved as an important, uncontested legitimate spokespiece within the democratic political system are assessment of how closely individual chief executives were integrated into their base associations and how closely these were linked into the CEOE.

While identification with the peak level among individual companies is important, the CEOE also requires that its affiliated associations be well consolidated. The CEOE draws on the strength of its affiliated organizations among the base membership. In looking at the consolidation of the associational hierarchy among individual companies, three fundamental questions arise: (1) How strong is the CEOE?; (2) How strong are its relationships to other relevant system actors, such as the government, the bureaucracy and labor?; and, (3) How much of its potential constituency has it successfully affiliated?

In focusing on internal dynamics, one must assess what legitimacy is accorded to peak and lower-level organizations by their base membership, the support these organizations can muster, and the role of the internal governing mechanisms they can command. System actors unable to deliver promised outputs following macro-level agreements will not long be entrusted with the unhesitant confidence of other actors. To what degree are the CEOE and other associational channels institutionalized and used by the base? Given the manner in which issues of economic and social policy were addressed over the transitional and early constitutional periods, the degree of consolidation achieved by major socio-economic

actors, such as the employers organizations and the
labor unions, played an important role in the development of Spanish democracy.

THE LOGIC OF ASSOCIATION

Much of the literature on employers associations
places emphasis on the "reactive" nature of responses
on the part of individual businessmen, leading to the
initial organization of the collective interest groups
of business. The work by Wyn Grant and David Marsh and
that of Stephen Blank for Britain, Henry Erhmann for
France, Lars Norby Johansen in Denmark, James Q. Wilson
on the National Association of Manufacturers in the
United States, and work on employer groups in other
European countries generally depicts employers as
"later" organizers than labor. Assessing the motivations
leading to the organization of collective interest
groups representing business forms an essential component of any analysis of their internal dynamics. From
time immemorial businessmen have joined forces either
conjunctionally or in a perdurable manner to further
their interests. Historically such combinations, at
times collusive in nature, have had <u>directly</u> market-
oriented objectives. In my treatment of employers as
"later" organizers and characterization of their primary
motivations as "reactive," I am limiting discussion to
employer entry into strictly non-economic realms or what
we might call "political markets." I am not dealing with
the issues posed by the representation of businesses as
producers, nor with attempts via cooperation at greater
control of market forces.[1]

Capital controllers hold a natural advantage over
groups representing other factors of production in economic markets. However, there may come a point when activities conducted through purely economic means no
longer produce desired outcomes. It is at this juncture
that employers organize to further their interests in
political markets.

> The operation of the market is based on the principles of self-interest
> and competition. But if competition hurts the interests of a firm, it need
> not restrict its activities to market-oriented action. Firms are political
> actors, whose returns, conditions of expansion, and possibilities for
> survival are to a great extent decided within the political system.
> Self-interest does not stop at the boundaries of the market. Particularly
> when a firm is threatened by loss or bankruptcy, its executives are likely
> to look for political solutions to economic problems.[2]

While not losing sight of the difficulty of

divorcing associational functions dealing with industrial relations, macro-level representation in relation
to the Government, or other examples of the political
representation of business from associational functions
dealing with market conditions, this analysis of the
CEOE focuses on "political entry." We are dealing with
the representation of business as employers-not as
producers. In economic markets, capital indubitably
enjoys a priori advantages relative to other factors of
production. In the political markets of a democratic
system, organized entry by employers is a normal
phenomenon, and employers will more often than not
continue to enjoy certain advantages. Without minimiz-
ing these advantages, however, political entry is an
externally induced, sub-optimum choice necessitated by
the failure in the wielding of purely market-oriented
instruments to achieve desired ends.

Grant and Marsh described the main appeal of the
Confederation of British Industry (CBI) for its base
membership as being its influence with the government
and as a counter-balance to the trade unions.[3] For its
predecessor, the Federation of British Industry (FBI),
Blank argues that whereas labor unions have perceived
their role as providing a vehicle for wider social and
economic reform, the FBI's employer membership has
always viewed their organization's function as purely
defensive in nature.[4] The Ehrmann study of the Con-
féderation Générale de la Production Française (CGPF)
describes the "wavelike pattern existing between business and labor organizations" that has "often led on
the part of employers to an imitation of trade union
developments."[5] Johnansen's research on Danish employer
federations emphasizes the "external, environmental"
factors that lead capitalists to organize for political, collective action.[6] Although American business
associations and the context in which they operate are
very different, for the early period of heavy industrialization, Wilson likewise wrote about the "threat-
oriented nature of general business association."[7]

To a certain extent, for Spain, this "wavelike,"
reactive characterization of business association explains part of the motivations leading to the initial
organization of the CEOE. Other factors are present,
however, particularly continuity with earlier collective interest organizations and the difficulties
arising from the existent representational multiplici-
ty. Such difficulties may in certain cases result from
the obfuscation between activities aimed at the representation of business as employers versus representation as producers, the latter reflecting more traditional perceptions of associational justification for

existence by significant sectors of the base membership.

In characterizing Spanish employer associability
as "reactive" and in treatment of "continuity," it is
difficult to isolate the impact played by labor. Without question, during the early years of the transition,
a good deal of the strengthening of the associations
resulted from employer concerns over the effects of
labor conflicts. Historically, however, the desire for
tariff protection has been an important inducement.
Indeed, this was the primary motivation that led to the
creation of the direct forerunner of Fomento del Trabajo Nacional in the early eighteenth century.[8]   Also,
perceived "state failure" during the transition went
beyond elimination of Franquist protection against
strike action and extended to other areas of protectionism, including from external competition, that
would similarly be threatened by a new democratic
government actively seeking to liberalize and to enter
the Common Market.

THE MOTIVATIONS LEADING TO ASSOCIATION

Surveyed chief executives were asked (open-ended)
to describe the primary reason that led to the affiliation of their company to a peak employers organization
(CEOE or CEPYME). All respondents who had indicated
membership in any organized employer group (N=236) were
addressed to register the image of the peak organization and measure its perceived role among the base
membership.

More than a quarter (26%) of employers indicated
political or external inducements. Such external inducements support a "reactive" characterization of
Spanish employers. They include: organization as a
response to the level of labor conflicts or earlier
labor organization; as a response to detrimental government politics, the growth of bureaucracy or regulation; or some form of "state failure" (i.e., the failure of the state to provide previously guaranteed
protection required in relation to domestic or international market threats). Of those classified under
external inducements items, nearly a quarter (of the
26%) felt that the peak association was needed either
to counter growing labor union force or as a spokespiece for dealing with the unions and/or the public
administration. However, over two-thirds of this group
expressly stated that the political transition to democracy necessitated the development of peak associations. Therefore, these employers recognized the need

for a legitimated spokespiece within the emerging pluralist system. Of the two sub-groupings described (as a counter to labor/public administration and due to the political transition), the latter, which can be considered as perceived "state failure," appears the more interesting. This second sub-grouping might partially be tied to the growth of labor unions and the rise of the level of labor conflicts, but alternatively might include a higher directly politically partisan component aroused by the rapid elimination of a series of benefits in the form of protection previously extended to business under the economic machinery of the Franquist system (of which the labor factor would be but one component, albeit a very important one).

Table 3.1 Initial Motivations for Joining a Peak Association

	Size of firm:			Province:*					
	R	I	L	M	B	VZ	VA	S	Total
Political or external inducements	19.7	17.1	40.5	36.4	24.5	23.1	4.2	27.3	26.3
"Logical/normal" or for selective incentives	5.3	15.8	23.8	16.9	18.4	3.8	12.5	9.1	15.3
Via personal contacts	7.9	6.6	6.0	10.4	3.1	7.7	12.5	0.0	6.8
Interest solely in base organizations	31.6	28.9	14.3	10.4	28.6	26.9	50.0	27.3	24.6
Organizational continuity or inertia	7.9	6.6	7.1	13.0	4.1	11.5	0.0	0.0	7.2
Non-membership	25.0	19.7	3.6	9.1	17.3	19.2	20.8	27.3	15.7
Don't know/no response	2.6	5.2	4.8	3.9	4.1	7.6	0.0	9.1	4.3
	(76)	(76)	(84)	(77)	(98)	(26)	(24)	(11)	(236)

* Throughout these tables, the sequence of columns labelled "R - I - L" stand for regular, intermediate, and large size companies.
"M - B - VZ - VA - S" stand for Madrid, Barcelona, Vizcaya, Valencia, and Sevilla provinces.

The "logical/normal" or selective incentives classification includes categorical responses that membership in the peak association was either the normal or logical route for all companies, or seem the obvious course to follow, accounting for over two-thirds of these. Direct references to various selective incentives account for a mere 3 percent. It is interesting to consider briefly the implications of these first two sub-groupings specified.

A closely related issue to that treated here was also dealt with by a parallel question in the second survey among association leadership. Fully 18 percent of the leaders of associations specified selective incentives as the primary attraction that had led firms to affiliate. This compares to 37 percent in the political/external inducements category and 28 percent responding that it was a combination of these two categories, external inducements and selective incentives. Looking at the higher percentages in these categories, keep in mind that the option of professed non-membership, with a very significant 16 percent here is not an option for participants in the second survey among associations. Furthermore, the 25 percent here who indicated that their interest is solely in base level organizations, and not in the peak, is clearly not an issue among association leaders. Indeed, many of the latter, as heads of base organizations, would be heartened by that datum.

What can be made of these figures that is pertinent to this discussion? I am analyzing here affiliation to a peak-level association, while the associational leadership (in the second survey) is responding to a consideration of affiliation to their own hierarchical levels. Three-quarters of the organizations in the second survey are base-level organizations, which, in general, are characterizable as service-oriented.[9]

Keeping the association survey in mind, those answering categorically among individual companies are, for the most part, not fully integrated into the associations. The mere 3 percent specifying selective incentives is partially related to the fact that the question addresses affiliation to a peak level. Yet, in light of findings from the second survey, it poses anew the problem of how to isolate selective incentives fully from collective goods. Measurement of the collective goods/selective incentives dichotomy can contribute to an understanding of the "reactive" characterization of business associability. A collective good can often serve the purposes of a selective incentive, however. Collective bargaining as it has developed within the framework of the Workers' Statute (Estatuto de los Trabajadores) is a case in point. In many sectors, as required statutorily, and as practiced, bargaining conducted by the associations and unions is binding upon all firms in a given sector, whether or not they are affiliated to the association.[10] Hence, any benefits from efforts expended in bargaining by associations accrue to all employers, regardless of whether they contributed to the organizational expenses incurred. This "free rider" predicament is faced by most large collective interest groups, as described in the seminal work by Olson.[11] Yet, consistently in both surveys, individuals placed great importance on the value of first-hand information regarding the bargaining process, about which they could periodically inquire only through association membership. This information is often valued even by small employers really powerless (in sectors dominated by a few large firms) to apply it usefully in any meaningful manner. Olson's later work recognizes the role of information about a collective good as a collective good in and of itself.[12] The packaging of this type of information as a selective incentive also is relevant, even if its utility function (on a rationality scale) is low for many of those interested in acquiring it.

The role of information should not be underestimated. Seemingly innocuous or apparently self-evident information can be marketed at a premium to the extent that one person has access to it and another does not. To hold information unknown by another is to control information. To this extent, information often is of value precisely to the extent that another does not have it or could not profit by it. Once public, it might no longer be of value. In short, information is power.

Almost 7 percent joined an association as a consequence of personal contacts or "obligations" (employers having a brother-in-law, for example, active at some level of association leadership), or personal invitations from association leaders.

A quarter of these chief executives, while possibly acknowledging their indirect membership in the peak association, claimed to have an interest only in their local association, be it sectoral or intersectoral. (Usually, interest was greater in the local sectoral than in the intersectoral association.) The affiliation of that association to a rung higher up the scale leading hierarchically to CEOE membership was of no concern and had not entered the calculations when their company affiliated. The overwhelming majority of firms will have their contact with the CEOE through similar local sectoral associations. Few firms will be in the position of those seven companies composing the petroleum refiners association (ASERPETROL), further undifferentiated, and with almost direct contact to the peak. Furthermore, few firms would have thought in terms of state-wide employer solidarity upon entering the local association. Yet it is highly significant that over a quarter of chief executives (the 26% in the first row) see beyond immediate contacts and assess the aggregate impact of individual employer decisions to affiliate among local base associations. It is similarly very significant that this other 25 percent were not interested in that aggregate impact and might not even consider themselves members of a peak organization. Such a phenomenon on this scale does not bode well for the achievement of stable and binding macro-level agreements. Clearly it remains for the CEOE to impress upon a significant portion of its membership that the hierarchical system of associations is more than incidental.

An additional 16 percent of individual heads of firms claim not to belong to a peak organization. Although some of these, indeed, do not belong, others may simply not be active participants in local base associations and are unaware of the affiliations of those local organizations. Undoubtedly, others were aware of the affiliation of their local organizations yet felt themselves in no way committed by the memberships of those organizations. Those categorized in the "continuity" category are individuals stating that the current associations are the same ones that have always existed, there having been no change or disjuncture. Regarding their company's membership, they state that they "have always been members." Such continuity is an important issue.

In summary, a significant proportion of employers clearly is interested in peak-level associability, constituting nearly a fifth of the total, but another more substantial 40 percent, is either interested exclusively in the base level association or denies affiliation to the peak. Hence, the magnitude of the task of consolidating its base remains an important one for the CEOE.

As could be expected, large firms recognize the political role of the peak (41%). Twice as many large as regular or intermediate size firms recognized political roles. Another significantly higher proportion of large firms falls into the logical or selective incentives category, representing firms most closely approximating rational actors undertaking cost/benefit analyses. The proportions are reversed by size for those categories where enterprises disassociate themselves from the peak. Thirty-two percent of regular and 29 percent of intermediate firms claim interest solely in the base organizations and 25 percent and 20 percent of these size categories, respectively, are among those disavowing membership. Thus, whereas the chief executives of 57 percent of regular firms and 49 percent of intermediate firms expressed marginal or no peak-level identification, only 18 percent of the heads of large firms responded similarly. The larger the firm, the more closely its chief executive is tied into the elite networks of business, which include the peak-level leadership.

REGIONAL DIFFERENCES IN THE MOTIVATIONS LEADING TO ASSOCIATION

As one might expect, higher proportions of the heads of firms in the politically conscious capital emphasize political motivations. Perhaps less expectable without a more detailed understanding of the economic dynamics and sociological and historical characteristics of the Levante region, Valencia emerges as an outlier in the opposite direction.

In controlling "motivations" responses by province, the large Madrid company is particularly conscious of the need to organize given the transition to a pluralist system and rising union strength. While the overall proportions in Barcelona and Vizcaya approximate the country-wide average, a review of Table 3.2 likewise indicates a higher consciousness of political factors among large firms. Nearly half of large Barcelona chief executives express political motivations. Two factors are relevant; the relatively high level of labor conflicts in the province,[13] highly concentrated in particular localized areas, and the strong roots of the Catalan peak association, Fomento del Trabajo Nacional (FTN), within the context of a more legitimized image of business in Catalonia than in the rest of Spain.[14]

Subsequent strong public attention focused on the activities of the CEOE in the electoral campaigns for the autonomous legislatures of Galicia (October 1981) and Andalucía (May 1982).[15] However, the first major campaign participation in post-transition Spain by an employers group was that by Fomento targeted toward elections for the regional parliament of Catalonia in March of 1980, out of which the regional government, the Generalitat, emerged. The FTN campaign generally focused on reducing abstentionism, while also declaring support for free enterprise and for a "Catalan option." The purpose served was to concentrate votes of the non-socialist center and right around the most viable Catalan bourgeois electoral coalition, Convergència i Unió (CiU). One analyst of the election, who depicts the FTN as instrumental in facilitating a CiU victory, emphasizes the primacy of the concentration of "useful votes" around the Catalan option most likely to succeed.[16] Among voters of the center-right or right, CiU,

Table 3.2 Initial Motivations for Joining a Peak Association by Province and Company Size

	Madrid			Barcelona			Vizcaya		
	R	I	L	R	I	L	R	I	L
Political or external inducements	38.1	25.0	43.8	10.3	11.7	48.6	20.0	14.3	33.3
"Logical/normal" or selective incentives	4.8	25.0	18.8	6.9	14.7	31.4	0.0	0.0	11.1
Personal contacts	14.3	8.3	9.4	3.4	2.9	2.9	10.0	14.3	0.0
Interest solely in base organizations	14.3	16.7	3.1	44.8	32.4	11.4	10.0	42.9	33.3
Organizational continuity or inertia	14.3	12.5	12.5	3.4	5.9	2.9	20.0	0.0	11.1
Non-membership	14.3	12.5	3.1	27.6	23.5	2.9	40.0	14.3	0.0
DK/NR	0.0	0.0	9.4	3.4	8.8	0.0	0.0	14.3	11.1
	(21)	(24)	(32)	(29)	(34)	(35)	(10)	(7)	(9)
			(77)			(98)			(26)

	Valencia			Sevilla			Total
	R	I	L	R	I	L	
Political or external inducements	0.0	16.7	0.0	50.0	20.0	0.0	26.3
"Logical/normal" or selective incentives	8.3	0.0	33.3	0.0	20.0	0.0	15.3
Personal contacts	8.3	16.7	16.7	0.0	0.0	0.0	6.8
Interest solely in base organizations	50.0	50.0	50.0	25.0	20.0	50.0	24.6
Organizational continuity or inertia	0.0	0.0	0.0	0.0	0.0	0.0	7.2
Non-membership	33.3	16.7	0.0	0.0	40.0	50.0	15.7
DK/NR	0.0	0.0	0.0	25.0	0.0	0.0	4.3
	(12)	(6)	(6)	(4)	(5)	(2)	(236)
			(24)			(11)	

a Catalan coalition, may simply have appeared as the most logical choice for a Catalan legislature.

Political entry by the FTN was not new, as a review of the Lliga party of the early part of this century confirms.[17] However, the same historical traditions that might explain the high percentage of large companies with political consciousness, arising from the activities of the peak Catalan association, might also partially account for the high percentage of regular-size firms (45%) whose sole interest is with base organizations. Just as FTN traces its roots back more than two hundred years, likewise a substantial portion of the Catalan hierarchical system of associations can do so as well. Many of the base level guilds (gremios) in traditional artisan or early industrial sectors have origins in medieval, renaissance or early modern times.[18] Although it continued to exist during the years of the vertical Sindicato Nacional, FTN activities during the Franquist period were minimal. However, such was not the case for many of the local guilds that continued to operate, almost entirely independently of the Sindicato, while adopting some form of de jure paper connection to the unitary Sindicato. It is this type of historical continuity that, for the Catalan example, might account for a certain "guild mentality" that manifests itself in little concern for more recent employer superstructures higher up hierarchically.

The work by Linz and de Miguel based on a survey among 460 chief executives in 1959-1960, at the start of the economic take-off, documents the existence of a system of parallel employer organizations largely independent of the vertical Sindicato Nacional, which while legally covered in some form under its rubric, approximated the functions of business pressure groups in more open societies (corroborated by my survey among associations.)[19] The Linz and de Miguel study included a review of the seventy-one entities which constituted the Unión Nacional Económica (UNE), the peak employers organization of the Second Republic.[20] Of these, twenty-six continued to exist at the time of their research (sixteen in Madrid, six in Barcelona, and four in the Basque Country). These correspond to intermediate-level associations affiliated to the UNE. Clearly, the numbers of "survivors" among small-base level associations would be great, which is my point regarding Barcelona.

Looking at the continuity issue for CEOE affiliation throughout Spain, the pre-1936 associations were not the only (de facto) independent organizations to exist during the Franco years. As Linz and de Miguel describe it, others arose during this period in "more or less tenuous relation" with the Sindicato, usually taking the legal form of a corporation ("sociedad anónima"), but realizing all the functions of pressure groups.[21] Survey-based research commissioned in 1966 by the OECD and the Spanish Planning Commissariat in Andalucía, headed by Eberhard Dülfer, similarly made reference to the extra-official collective interest bodies then active.[22] Dülfer describes the case of a "technical-commercial association" of manufacturers of automotive and other machine parts named Sercobe, which is now an important CEOE affiliate. Headquartered in Madrid, Sercobe then numbered about a hundred members, employing 100,000 workers. Essentially the organization exchanged information and maintained contacts with the public administration and with other industries domestically and internationally. (From our reactive characterization of associability, it is interesting that Dülfer argues that such collaboration among businessmen was not for purposes of rationalizing their firms or production but, indeed, to defend themselves from the need to rationalize as a consequence of increased competition! A good deal of Sercobe's activities were related to efforts to restrict imports.)

Although the legal means allowing for their continuing operations were "temporary," the professional associations (colegios profesionales) and the semi-official system of chambers of commerce (Cámaras de Comercio, Industria y Navegación) existed without major interruption throughout the Franco period. Indeed, some Falangist supporters of the organic Sindicato singled out these institutions for criticism given that they allowed for multiple representation of business not extended to labor.

Comparing the two largest provinces, Madrid and Barcelona both follow country-wide patterns, but only loosely. The provinces deviate in opposite directions. Size of firm proves much more important in Barcelona than in Madrid. For Spain overall, by size, the major break in the patterns of peak-level identification appeared between regular and intermediate firms versus the large firm. In Barcelona, this basic break is very great. The reverse is the case in Madrid, where the position of the regular and intermediate firms approximate those of the large firms. Relatively low percentages of the heads of regular and intermediate firms in Madrid have marginal or no identification with the peak and very high percentages extend political explanations, deviations all from the country-wide pattern.

In the case of Barcelona, connections between the Catalan large-firm business elites and those of the rest of the country explain a great deal. Among regular and intermediate enterprises, one must look at the strength of base-level organizations. The strength of FTN among large Catalan firms, its recent past political activity, and its important role in CEOE, may serve to link the top Catalan business elites into country-wide elite networks.[23]

In Madrid, the positions of the regular and intermediate firms more closely approximate those of large firm. Looking at respondents describing political or logical explanations and those expressing marginal or no identification with the peak, a pattern emerges quite different from that in Barcelona. Unlike Barcelona, the patterns by size of firm are not consistent in Madrid. Political-reactive respondents and logical-rational actor respondents increase consistently by company size in Barcelona, with the significant differences separating the large firms from the rest. Responses reflecting base organization strength and weak peak-level identification or non-membership drop consistently by size of firm in Barcelona. The size variable in Madrid fails to "perform" as adequately. In Madrid, only the non-membership classification shows a consistent size relationship.

Other characteristics, rather than the consistency of patterns by size, emerge as more interesting in Madrid. We already noted the relatively keen political consciousness in Madrid province. This consciousness is high among all sizes. Political roles are more apt to be described by those working in the capital than elsewhere and, in this light, the physical presence of the CEOE in Madrid cannot be denied as a factor, resulting in wider recognition of the peak's political role and greater awareness about the membership of one's base organization into the CEOE hierarchy. In fact, it is interesting to note the relatively high number of organizations physically located in the CEOE building and the very high concentration of employers organizations within a ten-block radius thereof. Ease of contact is assuredly greater.

Secondly, the Madrid organizations, with important exceptions, lack the base-level strength attributable to Barcelona organizations on the basis of history or heritage. Whereas Catalan industrialization long preceded the Franco regime, Madrid's industrialization was significantly enhanced by Franquist policies and the Madrid business class was more closely linked to the Franco system than was that in Catalonia. Thus, in Madrid, organizational continuity often implies organizational inertia with regard to active Sindicato-era "secciones económicas-turned-associations" (keeping the same leadership). Significantly, 60 percent of Madrid association leaders acknowledged the activity of their organizations during the Sindicato and in some way integrated in it versus 41 percent among Barcelona association leaders. Likewise only 12 percent of Madrid association leaders openly denied a Sindicato past, compared to 35 percent in Barcelona. The pattern of acknowledging integration in the Sindicato in Madrid relative to Barcelona holds true for both base level organizations and intermediate associations.[24]

MOTIVATIONS FOR ASSOCIATION OUTSIDE MADRID AND BARCELONA

Basque politics have been the most conflictual in democratic Spain. This most politically divided region is the only one with major region-specific divisions existing among labor unions. It is only logical that the divisions characterizing Basque society would extend to employers organizations, manifested in the competition during the early democratic years between two provincial intersectoral associations, the CEOE-affiliated Confederación General de Empresarios de Vizcaya (CGEV) and the Centro Empresarial de Vizcaya (CEV), which considered itself the descendent of the Centro Industrial de Vizcaya, originally founded in the nineteenth century with the rise of heavy industrialization in the Basque Country. Each of the provincial intersectoral associations defended somewhat different conceptions regarding the economic ramifications of the future autonomous development of Euskadi. Some issues of a sectoral nature were also involved. Although the CEV was not a CEOE member, its affiliate organizations were integrated into the peak association via their given national sectoral associations. The CEV supported the creation of the types of regional economic frameworks which had been promoted by then-Basque government President Carlos Garaichoetxea. Indeed, the Centro was generally considered close to the Basque Nationalist Party (PNV). The CGEV's top leader, Luis Olarra, in contrast, was close to Alianza Popular's leader, Manuel Fraga. CGEV affiliates had the double CEOE affiliation common in most of Spain. This associational division at the provincial level and its politicized component may account for the many intermediate and large companies not expressing an interest in any organization beyond the confines of the region.

Valencia proves the most interesting of our

provinces due to a combination of the strongest degree of membership and utilization of associations at the base levels with the weakest implantation of the CEOE. Half of Valencia's respondents expressed interest solely in local level associations with an additional 21 percent claiming not to be members of an association in turn affiliated to a peak organization. While this latter phenomenon is a characteristic of regular and intermediate-sized enterprises, half of the respondents of all size categories expressed interest solely at the base organization level.

Table 3.3 Membership in Employers Organization

	CEOE	Sectoral	Regional/ Provincial	Cámaras de Comercio
Madrid	73.9	69.3	25.0	55.7
Barcelona	71.8	77.7	37.9	56.3
Vizcaya	53.3	60.0	26.7	70.0
Valencia	57.7	88.5	46.2	84.6
Sevilla	50.0	66.7	16.7	66.7

A listing of various employer organizations was handed to each chief executive, introducing the associational topic in the interview. The highest level of achieved associational institutionalization for both sectoral and regional/provincial intersectoral associations was in Valencia. As would be expected, such organizations, closer hierarchically to the company, have stronger roots in Barcelona than in Madrid. The CEOE is strongest in the capital, but not surprisingly given the division among business organizations in the province, very weak in Vizcaya. Very significant in Valencia is the proportion of employers indicating membership in the chambers of commerce. Logically, the more export-oriented the province, the greater the protagonism by the Cámaras. Vizcaya's stronger export orientation relative to Madrid or Barcelona partially explains this strength. The autonomous PNV government's vigorous promotion of industry with a "Made in Euskadi" label also gave the Cámaras of the zone a prominence not found elsewhere in Spain.

Legally, all firms belong to the Cámaras, which are financed through the state by employer taxes. However, many firms do not contact them nor use their services. Cámaras in certain regions are more effective and active than in others. The same phenomenon of not recognizing actual membership, whether it be in the Cámaras or in the peak association, reflecting disinterest or apathy among important sectors of employer opinion, was also an important finding of the Linz and de Miguel work for 1959-1960. At that time, Sindicato and Cámara membership was obligatory for all companies, yet fully 21 percent and 29 percent, respectively, did not indicate membership in those two organizations.[25] The Linz/de Miguel study attributes a portion of this to alienation and hostility. The phenomenon today can partially be explained by a "defiant apoliticism," that politics should not enter the firm and that employers should be totally apolitical. It is partially in light of this more traditional view of non-entry by organized employers into non-market activities that the Valencia example should be analyzed. Valencia exemplifies the case of significant extension of traditional views, but similar problems of a failure of the CEOE to take root, albeit at lower proportions, appear in all the provinces.

Historical continuity by region is also substantiated by the Linz/de Miguel study. On their index of overall associability (combining membership in all types of associations by employers), the Levante region (Valencia and Alicante) scored the highest among the six regions they compared.[26]

Valencia stands out because of the strength of traditional associational views, which appears tied to a certain extent to political conservatism, reflected particularly on economic issues and regarding the Franco regime. Part of the rejection of modern forms of employer association might also be linked somehow to the cultural incoherence that is found in the Valencia-Levante region. A Catalan-speaking region, some describe the Valencian bourgeoisie as Castilian-leaning. There are, obviously, other important factors at work. In economic terms the region only more recently became industrialized by means of a tremendously export-led growth pattern. Politically, the hegemony of the left in the region and the presence of anarchists and communists is an additional element.

The ideological positioning of Valencian employers is also a factor contributing to their associational patterns. Strongly conservative in their ideology, 96 percent of Valencia's business people supported a free market system, compared to a Spanish average of 77 percent. While Valencia chief executives are, perhaps, only marginally more to the right politically than those in the other four provinces, political variables clearly indicate the highest percentage of far right employers. This pattern of the most significant far right component within an otherwise comparable "right" proportion for employers appears on the question regarding an overall assessment of Franco and on a ten-point left-right scale. In drawing an overall assessment of Franco's "legacy," Valencia does not reach as high an approval rating as Madrid (a minimal difference of 3%) but it remains above the total state-wide average and the existence of a relatively high level of total approval appears particularly significant (12% versus the 5% country-wide). The same pattern emerges in Valencia on the ten-point scale. Twenty-three percent of Valencian employers located themselves between eight and ten, compared to 13 percent in Madrid, 15 percent in Barcelona, and 8 percent in Vizcaya and Sevilla. A politically conservative business sector, with traditional views and a greater degree of identification with and activity within Franquist-era organizations, combined with a more aggressive and successful recent industrialization, will tend to adopt traditional associational views, disinterest or even rejection of a peak association in the modern mold, and more interest in promotion exclusively on a local level.[27]

More direct economic characteristics differentiating the Valencian firm and its employers from those elsewhere are probably the most important in explaining the motivations towards association. Valencia's unusual export-led growth seems to contribute the most to explaining associational patterns.

Thirty-five percent of Valencia firms export over

Table 3.4 Exports as a Share of Production

	R	I	L	M	B	VZ	VA	S	Total
Zero/minimal	51.8	27.1	20.2	39.8	26.2	30.0	30.8	50.0	32.9
1% to 24%	30.7	44.7	43.7	35.2	51.5	36.7	15.3	33.3	39.7
25% to 50%	7.1	15.3	24.7	16.8	16.5	16.7	19.2	0.0	15.8
51% to 80%	7.1	10.6	11.3	7.9	5.8	13.3	26.9	8.3	9.7
81% to 95%	3.6	2.4	0.0	1.1	0.0	3.3	7.7	8.3	1.9
Total exporting above 50%	10.7	13.0	11.3	9.0	5.8	16.6	34.6	16.6	11.6
	(85)	(85)	(89)	(88)	(103)	(30)	(26)	(12)	(259)

half of their production, compared to a 12 percent
average for all of Spain. By industrial sector, 61 percent of the Valencian consumer goods industry exports
over 25 percent of production and 60 percent of the intermediate goods sector exports over that 25 percent
level.   Significantly, these sectors account for 69
percent and 19 percent respectively of the provincial
sample. The only other provincial sample sectors in all
of Spain nearing these export levels are Madrid capital
goods (67% exporting above 25% of production) and Barcelona capital goods (50%). However, these sectors account for only 7 percent and 6 percent respectively of
their provincial samples.

Disaggregating further, 60 percent of Valencia
firms exporting between 25 percent and 50 percent of
production, and fully 89 percent of those exporting
above half of production either expressed disinterest
or rejected peak association membership. High-export
orientation partially explains the need for the
services provided by the Cámaras de Comercio, although
the role of continuity from the Franquist system is
also a factor in their provincial strength.

A REACTIVE CHARACTERIZATION OF SPANISH EMPLOYER ASSOCIABILITY

The reactive characterization in other European
countries and the issue of employers as later
organizers than labor are also true for Spain. In
assessing the overall behavior of unions, the more
critical, distrustful, or fearful, the more likely an
employer indicated politically or externally induced
motivations for association. The higher the level of
responsibility attributed to labor unions, indicating
less concern about union activities or less fear, the
higher the percentages, generally, not indicating an
interest in the peak association or disclaiming membership. In short, chief executives who consider the
unions to have acted irresponsibly cannot afford the
luxury of ignoring the peak-level association. The CEOE
played a very important macro-level role on labor
issues. Expressed non-membership or disinterest in the
peak are options only for employers not worried about
union activities.

Further questioning provided additional support
documenting a reactive characterization of associability. Employers were requested to rank, from most to
least important, five possible reasons that explain the
current affiliation of their companies to an
association, omitting non-relevant items.

Table 3.5 Reasons for Joining and Union Behavior

The unions have been:

	Very Responsible	Fairly Responsible	Not Very	Very Irresponsible	Total
Political or external inducements	16.7	16.5	31.9	44.1	26.1
"Logical/normal" or for selective incentives	11.1	16.5	13.9	8.8	14.0
Via personal contacts	11.1	7.7	6.9	5.9	7.2
Interest solely in base organizations	16.7	26.4	25.0	14.7	24.3
Organizational continuity or inertia	5.6	9.9	4.2	11.8	7.7
Non-membership	38.9	17.6	13.9	8.8	16.2
Don't know/no response	0.0	5.5	4.2	5.9	4.6
	(18)	(91)	(72)	(34)	(222)

In general, those items that can clearly be considered collective goods received significantly more mention than selective incentive items. The associations' role relative to the government and to labor are representational functions that, in general, produce benefits accruing to the entire sector, as opposed to technical services and employer formation (or training) items, which are selective incentives from whose benefits non-members are excluded. The fifth item, the international role, is more difficult to classify into a collective goods/selective incentives dichotomy. Precipitated dismantling of protective barriers or the failure to defend domestic industry in the face of newly emerging competitors (who might be competing unfairly) can most certainly be characterized as one form of "state failure." Indeed, this type of "State failure" may become an increasingly important propellent of the reactive associability previously more attributable to labor unrest. It reflects the basic domestic orientation of the Spanish economy, large portions of which only recently began to turn towards export promotion with Spain's entry into the Common Market and the scheduled 1992 creation of the EC's "internal market." In 1981, however, such a characterization of "failure" could not be made.

Rather, most respondents would have looked at this fifth role in terms of information on foreign markets, trade potential and assistance, and the like, placing the category firmly among selective incentives.

It is evident that the representational-collective goods functions are the overwhelming determinants of continued associability, with selective incentives playing a lesser, but significant, role for some, particularly smaller, employers.

Table 3.6 Reasons for Current Affiliation to an Employers Association

	Ranked:						Cumulative by Size:		
	1st	2nd	3rd	4th	5th	Total	R	I	L
Role in representing interests to Government/ Administration	75.0	13.1	1.7	.8	.4	91.0	84.2	96.2	92.7
Role vis-à-vis labor	11.9	50.0	6.8	0.0	3.8	72.5	70.9	71.7	74.4
Technical services extended to membership	6.8	12.3	14.4	3.8	1.3	38.6	48.7	38.5	29.0
Activities of employer formation/training	1.7	4.7	7.2	8.9	1.3	23.8	30.2	25.6	15.8
Role vis-à-vis business in other countries	.4	5.5	13.1	4.2	5.1	28.3	28.9	23.1	33.0
Other reasons	4.2	1.3	.4	.8	.4	7.1	3.9	3.8	13.4
	(236)	(236)	(236)	(236)	(236)	(236)	(76)	(78)	(82)
Percentages responding:	100.0	86.9	43.6	18.5	12.3				

A few figures should be cited, such as the great relative size of representational functions (91% and 73%) compared to the next closest item (technical services at 39%). Both these representational functions (role relative to Government and labor) support a reactive characterization of employer associability. Regarding these two, the role relative to the government was overwhelmingly chosen as the most important (ranked first) in comparison to labor. It is also interesting to note that 28 percent of the companies did not specify the labor role as a factor, which seems surprisingly high.

Most chief executives specified only two reasons. Selective incentive categories play a diminishing role in continued affiliation the larger the company. However, it should not be overlooked that technical services are considerations for roughly half of regular size companies and employer formation for roughly a third of these.

ORGANIZATIONAL UTILIZATION, CONTROL AND COMPETENCIES

To what extent are associational channels used by the base constituency? What properties of internal control can the organizations muster to guarantee implementation of macro-level agreements reached with other system actors? In what issue-areas does the base membership concede associational jurisdiction?

Does the emphasis in the literature dealing with interest groups and with corporatism prejudice investigators to overestimate the importance of peak-level associations? Two means by which to assess the Spanish situation are: (1) measurement of associational roles in policy formation; and (2) analysis of such roles in interest intermediation. The measurement of associational policy formation roles must include an historical analysis of the corporatist structures of the Franco period and discontinuity of those earlier institutions with post-transition instruments of policy formation, as well as careful analysis of the series of outcomes, the "quasi-corporatist" agreements that were achieved over the early years of the democratic regime. The second focus of analysis, the associational role as interest intermediaries, involves assessment of the degree of achieved consolidation, measured most appropriately through an analysis of the views of the base and working up hierarchically through the organizational levels. Assessments of the importance of the associations viewed from the base is a major component in the analysis of the roles of organizations in what may be described as neo- or quasi-corporatist arrangements. While Spain is clearly not characterizable as corporatist, there are corporatist tendencies present and the literature can be used to center discussion.

If the company were faced by economic difficulties, would the employer deem it more efficacious to address company difficulties directly to the competent public authority (ministry or other public organism or agency) or channel these concerns through the associations? Response by company size is as would have been expected: the larger the firm, the more likely direct contact with the official bodies are used, and the less likely one needs to rely on the associations.[28] Madrid and Barcelona responded similarly. Vizcaya reflects weaker employer organization, Valencia stronger.

When the issue involves presenting problems or addressing one's opinions to the associations on items other than procedural or routine in nature, responses by company size are reversed from those reflected in dealing with economic difficulties in the firm. On providing company viewpoints on non-routine matters, the larger the company, the more likely it uses the organizations frequently (77% among large firms, down to 68% among regular) although very high percentages across all firm sizes and provinces consider the associations appropriate fora (72% overall would provide opinions). However, the fact that one-fifth of large firms (22%) and one-third of regular firms would not offer opinions to the organizations, would have to be disconcerting to the associations if full consolidation is the objective.

What if legislation were pending that was potentially damaging to the firm? To which types of contacts could be the chief executive turn for information (Table 3.7)? A comparison of total results for the six possible information sources (a closed-ended list with multiple response) shows the great dependence on the associations, 80 percent compared to 36 percent for contacts in the ministries, the next most frequent response. The responses are, otherwise, largely as would be expected. The larger the company, the greater the possibility of having contacts in the ministries, Parliament, or other "personal" contacts who could reveal details on pending legislation. This same higher probability exists for firms headquartered in Madrid. Valencia has the highest response rate indicating associations and Cámaras. Table 3.8 also underscores the important relative position of associations. These multiple responses to a closed-ended list indicate the types of activities that the employer would support to defend against legally promulgated, anti-business legislation. Again, the highest response item requested that the associations apply pressure (74%). The next two most frequent responses, convening a meeting of businessmen (65%) and waging a campaign to inform public opinion (59%), are, significantly, activities that would most likely be conducted under an associational rubric and which in the opinion of the immense majority of chief executives fall under functions corresponding to association competencies (see Table 3.9).

In assessing consolidation of the democratic system, the findings are encouraging. The two clearly politically illegitimate options, failure to pay one's taxes or to execute legal norms, receive only minimal

Table 3.7 Contacts Used to Obtain Legislative Information

	R	I	L	M	B	VZ	VA	S	Total
Ministry contacts:									
Would contact	20.0	33.3	54.1	49.4	32.3	20.0	26.9	25.0	35.8
Would not	78.8	66.7	44.7	50.6	65.7	80.0	73.1	75.0	63.4
No response	1.2	0.0	1.2	0.0	2.0	0.0	0.0	0.0	.8
Associational contacts:									
Would contact	75.3	89.3	74.1	80.5	77.8	73.3	88.5	83.3	79.5
Would not	23.5	10.7	24.7	19.5	20.2	26.7	11.5	16.7	19.7
No response	1.2	0.0	1.2	0.0	2.0	0.0	0.0	0.0	.8
Contacts with parliamentarians:									
Would contact	2.4	2.4	12.9	10.3	3.0	6.7	0.0	8.3	5.9
Would not	96.5	97.6	85.9	89.7	94.9	93.3	100.0	91.7	93.3
No response	1.2	0.0	1.2	0.0	2.0	0.0	0.0	0.0	.8
Contacts with regional autonomous governments*:									
Would contact	2.4	11.9	17.6	6.9	12.1	30.0	0.0	0.0	10.6
Would not	96.5	88.1	81.2	93.1	85.9	70.0	100.0	100.0	88.6
No response	1.2	0.0	1.2	0.0	2.0	0.0	0.0	0.0	.8
Contacts with Cámaras de Comercio:									
Would contact	24.7	19.0	14.1	12.6	20.2	13.3	50.0	8.3	19.3
Would not	74.1	81.0	84.7	87.4	77.8	86.7	50.0	91.7	79.9
No response	1.2	0.0	1.2	0.0	2.0	0.0	0.0	0.0	.8
Personal contacts:									
Would contact	9.4	7.1	14.1	16.1	10.1	3.3	0.0	8.3	10.2
Would not	89.4	92.9	84.7	83.9	87.9	96.7	100.0	91.7	89.0
No response	1.2	0.0	1.2	0.0	2.0	0.0	0.0	0.0	.8
	(85)	(84)	(85)	(87)	(99)	(30)	(26)	(12)	(254)

* Only Catalonia and the Basque Country had operating autonomous governments at the time of the survey.

levels of support, 8 percent and 5 percent respectively. Depending on interpretation, the third of respondents who would be willing under hypothetical circumstances to support political sectors willing to undertake fundamental changes in the system can still be somewhat disconcerting, although this option is not necessarily anti-constitutional given the vagueness of its wording.[29]

Chief executives displayed a fairly discerning selection and rejection from a closed list of fourteen items of directly political items as inappropriate

Table 3.8 Collective Action against Anti-Business Legislation

	Yes, would support	No, would not support
Not pay taxes	8.2	90.7
Convene a meeting of businessmen to signal dissatisfaction to Government	65.4	33.5
Fail to execute legal norms	5.1	93.8
Invest outside of Spain	22.2	76.7
Undertake public opinion campaign	59.1	39.7
Request employers associations to pressure vigorously	73.9	24.9
Appeal for constitutional review	54.1	44.7
Promote a constitutional change which would prevent this type of legislation	23.7	75.1
Support political sectors willing to undertake fundamental changes in the system	32.3	66.5 (257)

arenas for associational activities. The five items receiving the least support, that is, those areas deemed the least appropriate for associational activities, are the five that would involve the most direct intervention in the political arena. Those items are: influence the candidate selection within parties, 27 percent; financial support for parties favorable to businessmen, 35 percent; campaigns in favor of pro-businessmen parties, 44 percent; campaigns against anti-private enterprise parties, 31 percent; and, campaigns in favor of pro-free enterprise parties, 46 percent.[30]

If one were to look at Table 3.9 by company size, the trend throughout the list of fourteen items, with two exceptions, is that the larger the company is the higher the percentage defining a given function as an appropriate associational function. Significantly, the two exceptions to this general rule are the two items that are the most directly market oriented. These are the third and eleventh items, commercial relations with other countries and attempts to organize the market. Here regular and intermediate firms express a desire for greater associational activity. However, two points are more important: (1) the general strong acceptance of associations among all size categories on all the non-political items; and (2) the significant direct relationship on the five more directly political items by company size, where the larger the firm, the more willing to allow for associational political entry.

Table 3.9 Appropriate Employer Association Competencies

		Yes	No	DK/NR	(N)
1.	Representation vis-à-vis Government	93.0	6.2	.8	(256)
2.	Relations with international organizations	88.7	10.2	1.2	(256)
3.	Commercial relations with other countries	52.6	46.6	.8	(251)
4.	Statistical studies	93.3	5.9	.8	(255)
5.	Information on domestic markets	79.8	19.4	.8	(253)
6.	Information on international markets	85.0	14.2	.8	(254)
7.	Influence candidate selection within parties	27.3	71.5	1.2	(253)
8.	Financially support parties favorable to business	35.4	62.6	2.0	(254)
9.	Campaign in favor of pro-business parties	43.7	54.3	2.0	(254)
10.	Campaign against parties unfavorable to private enterprise	31.0	67.5	1.6	(252)
11.	Attempt to organize the market	76.2	22.6	1.2	(252)
12.	Facilitate the meeting of business people to discuss problems	98.4	.8	.8	(254)
13.	Campaign in promotion of business	79.4	19.8	.8	(253)
14.	Campaign in favor of pro-free enterprise parties	46.1	52.4	1.6	(254)

Examination of responses by province reveals that on non-political items Valencia is the region where employers express the greatest hesitancy concerning associational jurisdiction. On these items, Vizcaya generally lies somewhat closer to Madrid and Barcelona. For the five most political items, Valencia and Vizcaya

are both highly critical of organized activity. A 93
percent rejection rate in Vizcaya of "inside party
influence on candidate selection" is especially striking. The significant difference between Madrid and Barcelona also appears on political items, with Barcelona
conceding the most leeway for organized entry, consistent with Fomento's postures during elections to the
Generalitat described earlier. The greater willingness
for political entry in Barcelona, particularly among
larger companies, also reflects the more established
position of the bourgeoisie in the region.

Table 3.10 Degree of Appropriate Associational Contacts with Political Parties

	R	I	L	M	B	VZ	VA	S	Total
Very close	12.9	11.4	4.8	14.3	12.4	0.0	3.8	0.0	10.2
Close	27.1	29.1	25.8	29.9	30.3	9.1	23.1	33.3	27.4
Informational only	30.6	41.8	43.5	40.3	37.1	36.4	34.6	41.7	38.1
None	25.6	16.5	17.7	10.4	16.9	45.5	38.5	25.0	20.4
Other answers	2.4	1.3	8.1	5.2	3.4	4.5	0.0	0.0	3.5
No response	1.2	0.0	0.0	0.0	0.0	4.5	0.0	0.0	.4
	(85)	(79)	(62)	(77)	(89)	(22)	(26)	(12)	(226)

In looking at the appropriate level of contacts
between associations and political parties (closed-
ended), consistent with the rejection of political activity, 59 percent overall responded either for "informational contacts only" or for "none." Barcelona and
Madrid responses are relatively similar. Vizcaya and
Valencia responses are more limiting for the associations, particularly in the former.

ORGANIZATIONAL CAPACITY AND JURISDICTION

More important from the corporatist perspective is
associational competence in areas characterizing the
types of agreements typifying corporatist arrangements,
such as on the issue of whether the associations and
unions had sufficient strength and legitimacy successfully to elaborate a wage/price package as seen in
Table 3.11.
A significant majority of chief executives believed that the associations possessed sufficient

strength to effect wage/price programs, particularly among the smaller companies. Although the Valencia and Vizcaya results were more limiting of associational functions elsewhere, employers in these regions were slightly more willing to accede to associational activity in "corporatist" arrangements. Furthermore, of the 42 percent who felt that the organizations did not have the capacity to conduct and implement agreements on wages and prices successfully, 65 percent believed it could be undertaken successfully on a tripartite basis, if the government were present.[31]

Table 3.11 Strength and Legitimacy for Associations and Unions to Structure a Wage/Price Program

	R	I	L	M	B	VZ	VA	S	Total
Yes, capable	69.0	50.6	48.8	51.7	58.2	60.0	61.5	50.0	56.1
Incapable	29.8	45.8	50.0	47.1	40.8	33.3	38.5	41.7	41.9
Other answers	0.0	1.2	1.2	0.0	1.0	3.3	0.0	0.0	.8
DK/NR	1.2	2.4	0.0	1.1	0.0	3.3	0.0	8.3	1.2
	(84)	(83)	(86)	(87)	(98)	(30)	(26)	(12)	(253)

Table 3.12 catalogs open-ended responses and reflects a relatively high degree of obligation by employers toward agreements reached between associations and labor unions. The type of agreement in question was not specified, and this item was not a follow-up to the wage/price example raised earlier. Although wages and prices were not specified, however, the AMI was probably the point of reference for most. We find a widespread willingness to observe agreements reached via collective interest groups. Indeed, the majority felt totally bound. One would expect important differences to emerge by size, with the largest being the least willing to respect the authority of associations. Such proves to be the case. There appears a striking falloff in the sense of obligation between those employers heading regular and intermediate firms compared to those in large firms. Collective bargaining is what would come to mind for most, given that the type of agreement was left unspecified. The large firm often has the ability to bargain with greater flexibility and can afford to pay for labor peace. Smaller firms are interested in achieving a relatively minimal or inexpensive floor, placing all firms on an equal footing. Their hope is that such conditions be respected--and

treated as ceilings--to limit undercutting by firms in more favorable market conditions. It is, nonetheless, noteworthy that a majority of large companies (55%) also felt either totally or generally obligated.

Table 3.12 Degree of Obligation Felt by Individual Heads of Firms toward Association-Labor Union Agreements

	R	I	L	M	B	VZ	VA	S	Total
Totally obligated	65.9	63.9	42.5	59.3	50.5	56.7	80.8	58.3	57.7
Generally obligated	14.1	9.6	18.8	14.8	16.2	13.3	11.5	0.0	14.1
Have reservations	12.9	10.8	15.0	11.1	14.1	16.7	3.8	25.0	12.9
Not obligated	7.1	15.7	23.8	14.8	19.2	13.3	3.8	16.7	15.3
	(85)	(83)	(80)	(81)	(99)	(30)	(26)	(12)	(248)
Collapsed rows:									
Totally/generally	80.0	73.5	61.3	74.1	66.7	70.0	92.3	58.3	71.8
Reservations/not obligated	20.0	26.5	38.8	25.9	33.3	30.0	7.6	41.7	28.2

Table 3.13 Associations Accorded the Most Importance

	R	I	L	M	B	VZ	VA	S	Total
Sectoral	48.1	48.8	45.5	52.6	43.9	45.8	34.6	75.0	47.5
Provincial/Regional	19.0	13.8	5.2	5.3	7.1	33.3	42.3	0.0	12.7
National Peak	30.4	32.5	42.9	32.9	44.9	20.8	23.1	25.0	35.2
Other answers	2.5	1.3	5.2	5.3	3.1	0.0	0.0	0.0	3.0
DK/NR	0.0	3.8	1.3	3.9	1.0	0.0	0.0	0.0	1.7
	(79)	(80)	(77)	(76)	(98)	(24)	(26)	(12)	(236)

By province, Valencia employers stand out as adhering strictly to agreements reached by the associations. Eighty-one percent feel "totally obligated." This level of respect in Valencia, as well the high level of respect garnered in Vizcaya, is generally attributable to the strength of lower level associations (Table 3.13). The peak level is comparatively weak in Valencia, as well as in Vizcaya, certainly partly due to the divisions then existing among employers associations in Euskadi, distancing the region from the dynamics of the CEOE. Size is fairly important. The peak level is accorded slightly more importance, and lower level organizations are definitely weaker the larger the company.

VIEW OF THE CEOE

Open-ended comments about the peak organization were aggregated by those believing the CEOE to be controlled democratically, undemocratically, or who were ambiguous in their responses (Table 3.14). A high level of criticism reflects the animosity in Valencia toward the peak. In no province, however, were as many favorable as unfavorable comments extended. Over a quarter of the chief executives responded in the "don't know" category.

Table 3.14 Control of the CEOE

	R	I	L	M	B	VZ	VA	S	Total
Democratically controlled	11.8	23.2	33.3	25.6	27.4	6.7	19.2	8.3	22.4
Criticisms as undemocratic	48.2	25.6	25.6	34.1	32.6	23.3	50.0	25.0	33.5
Responses open to interpretation	8.2	11.0	17.9	15.9	9.5	6.7	7.7	33.3	12.2
Don't know	28.2	34.1	20.5	22.0	27.4	53.3	23.1	16.7	27.8
No response	3.5	6.1	2.6	2.4	3.2	10.0	0.0	16.7	4.1
	(85)	(82)	(78)	(82)	(95)	(30)	(26)	(12)	(245)

Significantly, a fifth of large firm heads felt unable to comment. The divisiveness of employer politics in Vizcaya and the tenuous establishment of the CEOE in the Basque region is clear in that over half of these interviewees (53%) were unable to comment and an additional 10 refused refused to do so.[32]
Particularly outside Madrid and Barcelona, and among smaller firms, the CEOE needed to boost its image.

CONCLUSIONS

> In general, the data for the total employer sample reflect considerable
> apathy and lack of opinion, and, further, a fragmentation in the climate
> of employer opinion. Our task shall be to detail that first impression,
> which upon more thorough examination reveals more complicated and
> interesting nuances.[33]

The Linz and de Miguel study made an initial
description of employer associability for the early
economic take-off period in those terms. For Andalucía
in 1966, Dülfer arrived at a similar conclusion.[34] For
the transition and early constitutional periods, the
data still reflected a considerable degree of disinterest regarding collective organization, particularly beyond the sectoral level, although such apathy was probably not as extensive as in the Linz/de Miguel period.
This finding may simply be a function of the nature of
business people. Certainly, changed political circumstances have necessitated a much more actively involved
business community, given the rapid dismantling of the
series of Franquist restrictions that served to protect
business beyond those extended under liberal norms. The
general impression for the totality of the interviews
on the issue of employers associations, however, was
the existence of a clear demarcation between the genuine interest of a significant minority actively participating and the lack of opinion or vagueness of position expressed by much of the roughly half "non-active"
portion of employers. Similarly, on the issue of the
initial motivations for joining, a wide dispersion of
opinion or apathy in the associational hierarchy
emerges among significant sectors of employer opinion.
Yet this is compensated to a considerable degree by
high levels of active organizational participation and
the demonstrated strength of lower level associations,
particularly in certain regions and among local or provincial sectoral associations.[35] Among these individuals, opinions are quite clearly stated, although,
again, it is very important that analyses be conscious
of the level of association in question.
      In addition to the localized strength of the
associations among certain types of employers or in
certain regions, the data show the high degree to which
employers considered associational channels amenable to
potential use and effective, particularly when compared
to other networks and channels of contacts and information which the system had to offer. There is a general
willingness to participate in and respect peak-level
agreements between labor and capital and a diffused
perception of sufficient organizational capacity at the

peak levels to reach such accords. Additional data, for example, showed that 86 percent categorized the acuer-do-marco interconfederal (AMI) between the CEOE and the UGT as either very or generally positive. However, it is also important to keep in mind the quarter of the sample that does not feel obligated to respect these accords and the fact that a large minority still questioned organizational capacities to reach agreements and to make them binding. These tend to be larger firms and the minority in question is of significant size.

The weakness of the associations must be viewed within the context of a Spain in which the representational institutions of democracy had as yet to solidify. They have travelled much further down this road since these surveys were conducted. As such, the failure of the associations to have earned the confidence of business fully is comparable to the weak consolidation of the unions among labor. Indeed, the unions face a relatively weaker position, further aggravated by their more serious financial resource limitations. The political parties similarly have few militants. Furthermore, the level of citizen contacts with all institutions remains low, as do contacts among different institutions. These issues posed major problems for the consolidation of democracy. All forms of voluntary associations face problems of consolidation among association-resistant Spaniards.

In his analysis of the "Values" survey, Francisco Andrés Orizo concludes that among Europeans, Spaniards, together with the Italians and the French, are the least willing to associate themselves in voluntary organizations. It does appear that Spaniards express confidence in the basic social institutions (e.g., church attendance, marriage, the family, etc.) at levels comparable to those elsewhere in Europe and demonstrate comparable levels of confidence in what Orizo terms "instrumental institutions" (e.g., the Church, the armed forces, the legal system, the educational system, etc.). However, he qualifies this by stating that: "It is in the world of work, the entrepreneurial and economic realm, where, perhaps, we [Spaniards] locate ourselves outside the [European] order." This is to say, below European levels. In short, Spaniards are uninterested in voluntary associations and, particularly, in economic organizations.[36] While perhaps the impact of the desencanto (the "disenchantment") with democracy over the 1979-1980 period was overplayed in the Spanish media and in foreign academic circles, some argue that such disappointment with the meager "concrete" results from democracy may have contributed to a further alienation of many from the institutions and organizations of the new system.[37]

The majority of employer opinion favors limitations on organized political entry by the associations.
This clearly contrasts with the active campaigns by the
CEOE in the first Galician and Andalucian regional
elections, a more active entry that might have been
tied to the perception by certain employer sectors of
the disintegration of the center-right (particularly
the former Government party, the UCD) and the failure
of conservative (read AP) options successfully to face
the Socialist challenge. As one association leader described, the CEOE is like "a gas which will occupy all
the open spaces it can," and, as such, had to take up
the banner not being carried effectively by the political parties. Nevertheless, while an interest group in
a pluralist society must be permitted the promotion of
its public postures, limitations exist as to what is
appropriate, given the existence of a competitive party
system that is theoretically better equipped to serve
the purpose of aggregating interests. This was recognized by the base membership, and eventually by the
CEOE after its unsuccessful forays.

From the perspective of the base membership, with
the above description of competencies accorded to the
associations together with the recognition of the validity of a competitive party system having been made,
some would expect liberal corporatism to develop in
Spain in the style of Lehmbruch.[38] As time goes on,
that appears increasingly less likely. As that definition requires, the Spanish organizations are certainly
voluntaristic, but further development down this liber-
al-corporatist "progression," following a strict definition, depends on many factors, particularly on the
political fortunes of the left and on the future development of the labor unions and of their access to policy-making fora. The many years of "left" domination of
the Spanish political system may reflect an additional
factor Lehmbruch may not have foreseen in developing
his model--namely, the extent of accommodation with
free enterprise proclivities among socialist parties.
Possibly as important as the role of left parties and
the unions in Spain along some "pluralist-corporatist
continuum" is the issue of continuity with earlier
periods, particularly for employer groups, and how this
might influence their view of future neo-corporatist
arrangements.

In terms of the diversity and structure of its
hierarchy, there are certain problems the CEOE must
face in its organizational consolidation, both internally and as a system actor. Despite the incorporation
years ago of CEPYME into its ranks, the problem of the

small firm remains far from closed. It should be re-
called that the truly small firms, those under fifty
workers, remained outside this study. Although the
challenges posed by competing organizations may prove
of minimal importance, the lack of confidence in the
CEOE's hierarchy and leadership by small employers and
the numerical strength such employers represent in
Spain, may lead to further difficulties in the implementation of associational policies. Some of this
dissatisfaction emerges even among the regular size
firms included in this study.

The Estado de las autonomías with the concession
of autonomy to all regions of Spain and the rise of regional governments and bureaucracies could further the
strengthening of the territorial intersectoral pillar
of the CEOE hierarchy. However, retrenchment in autonomous development would also be reflected among business organizations. The victory of the left at the
local level in the municipal elections of April 1979
led to the strengthening of many intersectoral base
associations and the Socialist victory at the state
level in the October 1982 elections was not without its
consequences on the continued consolidation of the associations. Further development of collective bargaining along the lines established in the Estatuto de los
Trabajadores (Workers' Statute) will also contribute to
strengthened organizations. Likewise, the threat posed
in certain sectors as well as the simple need for increased services resulting from the continued liberalization of the economy and the ongoing EC process and
the rise of the Single Market are opportunities not
lost on the CEOE's leadership in relation to its affiliates and base membership. Although there remain many
organizational flaws and areas of limited recognition
of its role, the achievements of the CEOE among its
base membership have been considerable.

NOTES

1.   It is difficult fully to disentangle
market-oriented activities from those not directly
market-related. Indeed, information gathered in the
survey of the associational leadership suggests that a
number of organizations are quite market-oriented in
nature, or evolved from more market-oriented forms.
Even when they come together for more "political" purposes, it is only natural that two business people will
discuss market issues. Nevertheless, analysis of the
more political content of employer associability remains
an important problem for exploration.

2.   Gudmund Hernes and Arne Selvik, "Local
Corporatism," in Suzanne D. Berger, ed., Organizing
Interests in Western Europe, (Cambridge, U.K.: Cambridge
University Press, 1981), 110.

3.   Grant and Marsh, Confederation, 48.

4.   Blank, Industry and Government, 207.

5.   Precursor to the Conseil National du Patronat
Français, the CGPF was founded in 1919.   Ehrmann,
Organized Business, 123-124.

6. Lars Norby Johansen, "Organization of Business
Interests in the Danish Metal-working and Construction
Industries" (Paper delivered at the International Socio-
logical Association Conference, Mexico City, 1982), 3.

7.   James Q. Wilson, Politicial, 154.   The U.S.
case is an outlier in a study of the operations of business in society. Unlike other developed countries, the
vast majority of Americans do not question the economic
system. To understand the dynamics of European business
groups, an American reader must appreciate the much
broader and viable ideological spectrum that leads business groups to become ideological protagonists, usually
in defense of free enterprise and in favor of a loosen-
ing of the welfare state (on terms that simply would
never emerge in the U.S. context).

8.   Graell, Historia, 16.   The German Central-
verband Deutscher Industrieller (CDI), precursor of the
BDI, was founded in 1876 specifically to counteract "the
traditional national free trade policy."   In this respect, we note certain historical parallels between the
German and Spanish cases. Braunthal, Federation, 5.

9. To be precise, the composition of the second
survey is: 76 percent are base organizations (membership
constituted directly by companies), 20 percent are intermediate level organizations of some form (associations of associations), and 4 percent are a mixture of
the   two   (treated   throughout   as   intermediate
organizations).

10.   As article eighty-seven stipulates, for
bargaining beyond the scope of a single firm, unions
representing at least 10 percent of the members of the
enterprise committees within the geographic or functional perimeter implicated and employers associations representing 10 percent of affected companies are legiti-

mate negotiators for a binding document. For state-wide bargaining, the 10 percent figure again applies, except that unions and associations representing at least 15 percent of either the workers or firms of regions granted autonomous status are also legitimate negoti-ators. Separadas del Boletín Oficial del Estado, Estatuto de los Trabajadores, Ley 8/1980, de 10 de marzo, Madrid.

11. Olson, Logic, 16-44.

12. Mancur Olson, The Rise and Decline of Nations (New Haven: Yale University Press, 1982).

13. The higher level of labor conflicts in the province may simply be due to its heavier or earlier industrialization or a higher blue-collar component in comparison to the rest of Spain, excluding the Basque Country. For the sample firms in Barcelona, however, responses to the question of the degree of perceived responsibility of past labor union activities do not reflect greater concern among large employers versus the level of concern by the chief executives of smaller size firms. Indeed, there is a weak relationship on this issue in the opposite direction, the smaller the firm, the more critical of unions.

Two other indices in the survey that measure labor conflicts likewise failed to establish a relationship by size of firm for Barcelona. Employers were asked to classify the state of labor relations in their firms compared to what they perceive as the Spanish average. With a possible exception of Vizcaya, this failed to provide any interesting provincial breakdowns by size. Second, information was sought regarding the last strike (or work stoppage) experienced in the given firm. 53 percent reported such conflicts. The provincial break-downs by size of firms produces interesting findings for Madrid and Valencia and a significant and very strong relationship for Vizcaya. No significant relationship appears for Barcelona between reported labor conflicts and size of firm, however. In Barcelona, therefore, we may be dealing with higher class consciousness or generally diffused tension in the labor relations area, independent of company size.

14. It would be difficult to measure levels of "class consciousness," but there appears to exist a higher degree of acknowledgment by many Catalans in business that they belong to an entrepreneurial class. The historical development of Catalonia and, specifi-cally, of industry in the region, are undoubtedly at

the root of such self-recognition. While the degree of perceived labor-management tensions may be more diffused in Catalonia than elsewhere, it is also the case that a public role by business enjoys greater legitimacy, which increased in the later 1980s. Along these lines the dominant coalition in the region, Convergència i Unió (CiU), has a bourgeois character. A high proportion of its leaders have a business or banking background.

In a post-coup survey realized by DATA in March of 1981, 51 percent of Spaniards felt that "employers" had opposed the 21 February 1981 military coup attempt; 53 percent similarly believed the banking sector to have been opposed. By region, the highest proportions believing these sectors to have been opposed to the coup were found in Catalonia and 64 percent believed both employers and bankers to have opposed the attempt. Hence, we might argue that these sectors were perceived as legitimate and democratic.

In the DATA post-election survey conducted at the end of 1982 and early 1983, respondents (N=5463) were requested to describe their level of confidence in each of a number of different groups. A scale of zero to ten was devised. Zero indicated extreme hostility; five, neutrality; and, ten, great attraction. The averages derived among all Spaniards for different groups were: the Church, 5.94; the army, 6.07; the police, 6.43; the parties, 5.96; the unions, 5.58; and, large firm employers, 4.44. Hence, business scored low. Only inclusion of ETA (at 0.45) spared business from emerging as last on the list.

The de la Sierra study also treated the issue of the perception by company directors of the poor image of business among the public at large. de la Sierra et al., Los directores, 77-78.

15.   Conservative Alianza Popular (AP) won handsomely in Galicia in elections in which CEOE national leaders, including then-president Carlos Ferrer Salat, campaigned in favor of free enterprise. It was widely perceived that the CEOE was moving increasingly towards AP and distancing itself from the UCD.

In Andalucía a frontal attack against the PSOE by the CEOE and the regional employers confederation, the Confederación de Empresarios de Andalucía (CEA), backfired spectacularly. The associations learned that Andalucía was not Galicia. The sociological bases of AP support in Galicia were not a present in the south. The CEA had called on the electorate not to allow itself to be deceived. Allusions to the (then leftist) French Socialists were made in CEA posters and the PSOE was depicted as a "fist" holding an apple (representing Asturias) from which a worm emerged with a hammer and sickle. (A Socialist-Communist [PSOE-PCE] coalition had recently emerged in Asturias.) Elsewhere, back-to-back silhouettes of PSOE head González and second-ranking Alfonso Guerra were printed with the ominous words: "Which one should we believe?" (i.e., the moderate González or the radical Guerra behind him?). Indeed, the campaign called into public question associational activities and led to a review of the electoral law on political campaigning. The PSOE won overwhelmingly and the Andalucía debacle contributed significantly to the erosion of the UCD. See Bernardo González and Miguel Angel Noceda, "Campaña electoral sucia: Andalucía pierde," Mercado 49 (21-27 May 1982): 22-26; and CEA pamphlets, "Entérate bien y entérate a tiempo" and "Andalucía es empresa de todos" (May 1982).

16. Antonio Izquierdo Escribano, "Sobre la evolución electoral de los partidos políticos parlamentarios en las elecciones catalanas," Mientras tanto, 5 (1980): 108. The Izquierdo thesis was supported by interviews I held at Fomento.

17. A good historical analysis of the Lliga is that by Isidre Molas, Lliga catalana (Barcelona: Edicions 62, 1972).

18. Examples of such base organizations include the Instituto Industrial de Tarrasa, 1401; Gremio de Fabricantes de Sabadell, 1559; Colegio del Arte Mayor de la Seda, 1533; and the Gremio de Carpinteros Ebanistas y Similares, thirteenth century. The correct translation of the term gremio in Spain is "guild." In most of the Spanish-speaking Americas, gremios are unions of workers.

19. Linz and de Miguel, Los empresarios, 17-18.

20. On employers organizations during the Republic, see Mercedes Cabrera, La patronal ante la II República (Madrid: Siglo Veintiuno de España Editores, 1983).

21. Linz and de Miguel, Los empresarios, 18.

22. The research included a survey conducted among some 320 enterprises in all eight Andalucian provinces. Manufacturing and construction establishments (not necessarily corporate headquarters) were visited. The individual interviewed was not always the chief

executive. Eberhard Dülfer, <u>Problemática de colaboración y promoción industrial en Andalucía</u> (Sevilla: Ediciones del Instituto de Desarrollo Regional, 1975).

23.   The fact that former CEOE president Carlos Ferrer and AEB President Rafael Termes are both Catalans is not insignificant. These prominent figures reflect the integration of important Catalan concerns into the state-wide network. They were experienced business sector leaders who emerged from a region with a greater degree of legitimacy accorded to business and with the longest trajectory of organized collective activity in the country. In contrast, Catalans have not emerged as leaders of major nation-wide political parties and have not been supported electorally outside of their region. The spectacular failure by Miguel Roca to build a nation-wide centrist alternative in the 1986 general elections is a case in point.

24.   Among base organizations, 58 percent of Madrid association leaders admitted to past activity within the Sindicato, versus 42 percent in Barcelona. In Madrid 15 percent denied any past activity integrated in the superstructure versus 32 percent in Barcelona. Percentages for Vizcaya associations almost exactly match those for Barcelona.

25.   Linz and de Miguel, <u>Los empresarios</u>, 32.

26.   Juan J. Linz, "Asociaciones voluntarias. La realidad asociativa de los españoles," 336-342. The study encompassed thirteen provinces and the other regions were Andalucía, Asturias, Barcelona, Madrid and Zaragoza.

27.   Controlling "motivations" by Franquist sentiment for Valencia, 79 percent of those who extend favorable assessments of Franco either were interested exclusively in their base organizations or professed non-membership. Among the minority criticizing Franco (25%), only a third responded in these two categories.

28.   Of regular firms 31 percent can contact directly, while 49 percent of large firms would contact directly. Correspondingly, 64 percent of the regular firms would turn to the associations, while only 44 percent of the large would do so.

29.   Ambiguity in the question has disadvantages. However, having proffered an explicitly anti-system option, such as an open espousal of pro-coup arguments,

would have received almost no support. It may be more interesting to identify "soft" support for democratic mechanisms than to pick out a tiny handful willing to espouse openly anti-democratic positions.

30. Campaigns "against" receives even less support than campaigns in favor of parties given widely perceived counter-productive results. Yet the public as a whole appears surprisingly tolerant regarding open support, including financial contributions, on the part of employers associations to political parties. According to the DATA "Mentalities" survey of nearly 4000 Spaniards in the fall of 1983, 57 percent accepted the right of associations to support and contribute to parties; 31 percent opposed it; 12 percent failed to respond. Two-thirds of all Spaniards accepted such partisan activities by labor unions while 22 percent were opposed and 12 percent did not respond.

31. Such tripartite arrangements run counter to the societal corporatist model. Using a different question, the de la Sierra group queried company directors about the desirability of reaching socioeconomic agreements such as the Moncloa Pact or the AMI. The Moncloa Pacts were signed by the political parties. The AMI was the first peak level salary agreement between the CEOE and a peak level union, the UGT. The de la Sierra question does not treat the issue of organizational capacity. Of directors 95 percent considered such agreements either advantageous or, indeed, indispensable. Fully 89 percent believed that solely the associations and labor unions should participate, and only 4 percent believed that the government should be present. Not a single director felt that the political parties should ever play a role. de la Sierra et al., Los directores, 111.

32. At the time of the survey only one of the two Vizcaya intersectoral associations, the smaller CGEV, was affiliated to the CEOE. The intersectoral association of Alava was not affiliated and that of Guipúzcoa was affiliated but, according to a high-level CEOE source, paid little heed to peak level directives.

33. Linz and de Miguel, Los empresarios, 34-35.

34. The Sindicato Nacional, Dülfer argued, was not considered a suitable instrument for the promotion of business. Many, he felt, might look somewhat more favorably on the Cámaras. However, a number viewed them as too traditional. Asked to choose the person or institution which could most satisfactorily realize efforts

at association among firms, many of Dülfer's respondents were not very interested: 22 percent said the sindicatos; 17 percent the <u>Cámaras</u>; 29 percent other; 19 percent don't know; and, 10 percent no response. Dülfer attributed a good deal of organizational weaknesses to the "extreme individualism of Spaniards, especially Andalucians." He nevertheless felt that there existed a latent general willingness to participate in private business associations. Dülfer, <u>Problemática</u>, 38-60.

35. Other data, for example, show that roughly a third of employers had at some point participated in some capacity on a working or study group or committee, at some level of association.

36. In comparing the image of large firms and that of unions, 37 percent expressed confidence in the major companies (9% a "great deal" and 28% "quite a lot") and 31 percent did so in the trade unions (7% a great deal and 24% quite a lot). This compares with a European average among the thirteen countries surveyed of 39 percent expressing confidence in major companies (6% a great deal; 33% quite a lot) and 33 percent in the unions (5% and 28%). Within Spain, confidence levels expressed for other institutions were: 50 percent in the Church; 61 percent in the armed forces; 50 percent in the educational system; 48 percent in the legal system; 46 percent in the press; 48 percent in Parliament; and, 38 percent in the civil service. On the Spanish case, see Francisco Andrés Orizo, <u>La sociedad española en el umbral de los 80</u> (Madrid: Mapfre, 1984). The field work in twelve of the countries in the "European Values" survey was conducted between March and November of 1981 (coincident with our first survey). In Norway, it was realized over November and December of the following year. On the overall study see Jean Stoetzel, <u>Les valeurs du temps présent: une enquête européenne</u> (Paris: Presses Universitaires de France, 1983).

37. See Peter McDonough and Antonio López Pina, "Disenchantment and Dealignment in Spanish Politics" (Paper delivered at the conference of the American Political Science Association, Washington, D.C., August 1980), 63-69.

38. Gerhard Lehmbruch, "Liberal Corporatism and Party Government."

4

The Organizational Expression of Collective Action

The measurement of the consolidation and legitimacy of the hierarchical system and, particularly, of the CEOE, viewed from among its constituent member organizations, provides information for answering fundamental questions posed by the literatures on corporatism, interest groups, and pluralism. We are interested in the degree of legitimacy accorded to organizational levels further up, the support that the peak level enjoys among its affiliates, and the strength of the internal governing properties which are essential to the continuance of interest intermediation by employers associations and labor unions.

The interviews among the top functionaries heading each of the direct sectoral affiliates of the CEOE in Madrid, Barcelona, and Vizcaya, and the leaders of indirect affiliates drawn from the territorial inter-sectoral confederations in these three provinces allow me to address these fundamental questions. The distinction between direct and indirect affiliation to the peak will be emphasized, and this characteristic was an essential criterion in drawing the sample. There were seventy-one "valid" direct sectoral affiliates listed in the 1981 annual report of the CEOE that was used in contacting organizations.[1] Of these, sixty-six were headquartered in the sample area and fifty-eight (88%) interviews were realized. Data for the indirect affiliates was collected among member associations of CEIM (Madrid), the Barcelona provincial affiliates of Fomento (FTN), and from among the membership of both the competing Vizcaya territorial intersectorals, the CGEV and the CEV, as well as other indirectly affiliated organizations in the Basque province not affiliated to either the CGEV or the CEV.[2]

Although only thirteen interviews were conducted among Vizcaya associations, all active associations of any consequence were visited and associations for all the major regional industrial sectors are included. Industry is more highly concentrated on a sectoral basis in Euskadi than elsewhere in Spain, and overwhelmingly so in Vizcaya.[3] This is evident in contacting active employer organizations, and should be kept in mind when viewing the data. Whereas Madrid and Barcelona (especially the latter) have numerous small sector associations that are active, the phenomenon appears much less frequently in Vizcaya where industry is dominated by three or four sectors, which in turn are composed of only a very few firms of any consequence. There are correspondingly fewer consequential associations as well.

Although the number of cases in the entire sample of associations may appear small, its significance is indisputable. All of the elite organizations are included. For direct affiliates, we deal not with a sample, but rather with nearly all (88%) of the valid associations in the study area, representing 82 percent of the valid direct affiliates of the CEOE in Spain. For indirect affiliates in Barcelona and Madrid, with use of a substitution technique, over 40 percent of the valid associations are represented for each province. While for Vizcaya only thirteen cases are included and no random technique was used in drawing a sample, the state of flux in the province at the time must be kept in mind, as well as the elite nature of this study. Certainly, all provincial sectorals in Vizcaya of any consequence were included.

As mentioned as the outset, the primary distinction used to differentiate associations in the research design (once the sample area had been designated) was that between sectoral associations directly affiliated to the peak and associations affiliated indirectly, chosen from among members of the intersectoral, territorially defined direct provincial affiliates of the CEOE. A second obvious distinction that will appear is that between base organizations, whose membership is composed strictly of individual firms (constituting 76% of the organizations surveyed), and intermediate organizations, associations composed of lower level organizations ("associations of associations"). Referring to Chart II of Chapter 2, we could identify the FEC, CCC, CNC, and FTN as intermediate associations. As that chart also illustrates, an organization identified as intermediate is not necessarily affiliated directly to the peak. The base versus intermediate distinction has to do with the character of an organization's membership

--not its affiliation. Indeed, the majority of our direct affiliates are base and not intermediate organizations. Thus, we will refer to this distinction as organizational "membership-order level." (The specific classificatory term "intermediate organization" should not be confused with "intermediary" organization, a term with a generalized usage in the corporatist literature.)

THE LOGIC OF ASSOCIATION

The logic leading to initial organization viewed by the association leadership clearly will involve different assessments from those expressed by individual chief executives. Important numbers of chief executives stated either disinterest in the peak employers organization or claimed non-membership. The topic was queried in somewhat different terms among leaders of associations. Rather than referring to the peak organization, they were asked to comment as to why companies would affiliate themselves to their own organization. Obviously, the results will not be directly comparable to those from the employer survey. Disinterest and non-membership are not options. Nor will association managers make categorical, ambivalent statements about affiliation, that it was the "natural" or "logical" course of action to adopt. The logic leading to initial affiliation is an issue with which all managers of associations have had to grapple on a continuing basis.

There exist counter-poised stresses that place demands on the associations to play different roles. An association must provide for its membership but also play a role relative to the state. As a political system evolves, if a given functional domain is brought under a corporatist rubric, the stresses placed on associations increase. Member companies continue to demand that pressure be placed on the state for any of a number of objectives, while the state, in turn, demands that the associations provide base-level compliance in exchange for the access and recognition it grants to the associations as system actors. At issue is a characterization of the positions of associations and of the system in which they operate along a pluralist-corporatist continuum. The associations' primary role may be similar to that described in the literature on interest groups and pluralism or may, alternatively, have moved towards the development of a relatively static state-association relationship of cooperation. The Spanish example is closer to the former. Some corporatist aspects are present, given the evolution of collective bargaining and of the

series of macro-level agreements reached, but the
effects of this on forms of stable state-association
relationships remain to be established. Furthermore, the
unions are relatively weak. Were stable neo-corporatist
forms of policy-making to emerge in Spain--and they
still have not done so more than ten years since this
fieldwork--the implications would differ considerably
from one association to another. In a sector involving
few firms, by extension of Olson's logic, where each
individual employer's incentive to affiliate for purposes of collective action is high, independence of action relative to the state will likewise tend to remain
high. This is to say, that even with the standardization
of wage and price policy-making at a sectoral level, and
involving union, association, and state coordination,
a vast difference will continue to exist between the
sector having a strong association and that association
in another sector requiring state policies for the main-
tenance of a dominating, sectoral organizational role.
This may appear obvious, but such considerations often
are lacking in the corporatist literature when discussing business interest groups in a comparative perspective.

Most associations will not achieve a perfect
overlap between their actual membership and the entire
sector (actual versus total potential membership) within
their defined functional (i.e., sectoral or subsectoral)
and geographic organizational spaces. However, differences in organizational dynamics will be infinitesimal
between associations at near-complete overlap or affiliation, in terms of organizational consolidation over
their defined potential membership, and those associations enjoying total or perfect affiliation (complete
overlap between an organization's target and actual membership). It appears logical that organizations enjoying
complete or near-complete consolidation within their
defined geographic and functional perimeters will tend
to be in sectors or subsectors with fewer firms and with
a relatively high level of difficulty involved in entry
by new firms into the industry. Ease of entry by new
firms into a sector, on the other hand, clearly represents an obstacle to stable associational consolidation
and stable internal dynamics. However, factors other
than the number of firms in the sector influence associational consolidation. Building on the logic of this
reactive characterization of business association, a
sector that has faced higher levels of labor conflict,
greater government regulation, or intense state failure, perhaps due to structural reasons or to the complexion of its labor pool, may nonetheless be very
effectively consolidated despite encompassing a large

number of companies. An example could be a previously protected subsector that was deeply affected by market liberalization. The logic of collective action may appear blatantly manifest in such a case.

Two associations in different sectors, each at near complete consolidation and composed of few firms, despite parallel developments in their patterns of collective bargaining (falling under the same labor legislation) and equal access to equivalent official agencies, may differ significantly in their ability to pressure the government due to the characteristics of their member companies. Associations composed of companies with stable and roughly equal market positions differ from those in which capital-controllers must act in a more competitive fashion in their roles as producers (as opposed to their attempts at collective group cooperation on political matters). Associations composed of a few successful companies will have infinitely enhanced possibilities at pressuring the state compared to those composed of a few firms with declining profits. The latter, as is the case for a number of sectors in Spain, may be relying on special official recognition as affected industries requiring legislation for purposes of restructuring. Clearly these associations will not be in a position to pressure for much of anything, although market conditions may be such that maintained organizational consolidation may nevertheless be virtually guaranteed. Indeed, in certain cases, as in the "white line" subsector of kitchen appliances during the early 1980s, it was the state that attempted to develop an association and that guaranteed its complete consolidation because it required a "valid" interlocutor for purposes of formulating and implementing needed sectoral restructuring (reconversión) policies (its "industrial policy" plan).

For Spain, other instances in which sectoral characteristics largely determine associational patterns at higher hierarchical levels (direct affiliates of the peak) are also related to the size of the sector (i.e., the number of firms). Although complete consolidation may be impossible to achieve, the massive size of the construction or metal industries gives their respective sectoral peak confederations an independence of action and capacity for pressure beyond that of smaller, perfectly consolidated organizations.

Sectoral associations sharing non-overlapping memberships will cooperate in their relations with the state. Competing associations, each needing to extend demands, might benefit substantially by state recognition. In Spain, collective bargaining in the construction industry is conducted on a provincial level. In

many other industries, however, provincial sectorals
are cut off from this critical role that is often the
primary imperative for continuing affiliation by individual companies. For collective bargaining, the association of producers of corrugated cartons and packaging will be forced to negotiate under the rubric of,
and essentially in a subordinated position to, the
graphic arts confederation. In these instances, therefore, the conferment or denial of state recognition,
via the collective bargaining structure it erects, critically impacts upon associational consolidation (initial
or continued).

     Other factors are present that serve to counter-
balance state policies. For example, although state
policies strengthen construction sector provincial associations by conferring on them representation in bargaining, the sector is so massive that the political
weight of its sectoral peak (covering the entire country) is substantial independent of state recognition of
provincial bargaining. In comparison, although it is a
small sector, the corrugated cartons packaging sectoral
at the state level is composed of a relatively few but
well-off companies. In addition to being characterized,
therefore, as a sector with a high incentive to organize
for collective action, the sectoral peak organization
further compensates for its lack of collective bargaining protagonism by stressing services rendered to members.

     In short, to determine associational patterns both
sectoral characteristics and state policies must be
analyzed. Sectoral characteristics may in some cases
prove dominant in establishing associational qualities.
Elsewhere state policies may be dominant. Speaking in
general terms, the former pull toward pluralist forms
of interest group activities while the latter supports
corporatist forms of interest intermediation. The development and proper packaging of selective incentives
might place a great deal of protagonism in determining
self-development on the associations themselves. Indeed,
for many of provincial sectoral or local intersectorals,
the development of now indispensable legal, financial,
and labor counseling provided to small businesses is
crucial.

THE ASSOCIATIONAL PERSPECTIVE OF THE MOTIVATIONS
FOR INDIVIDUAL FIRMS TO AFFILIATE

     Responses to the question regarding the perceived
primary motivation for affiliation failed to provide
quite the range of answers, nor were they as interest-

Table 4.1 Motivations Leading Firms to Affiliate to the Association

	Affiliation:		Membership-Order Level:		
	I*	D	B	I	Total
Political inducements/collective goods	39.3	34.5	33.3	48.1	36.8
Selective incentives	16.1	20.7	18.4	18.5	18.4
Combination political and selective	30.4	25.9	31.0	18.5	28.1
Via personal contacts	1.8	0.0	1.1	0.0	.9
Organizational continuity	5.4	5.2	4.6	7.4	5.3
Other answers/NR	7.1	13.7	11.4	7.4	10.6
	(56)	(58)	(87)	(27)	(114)

* I and D indicate indirect and direct affiliates of the CEOE; B and I indicate base and intermediate associations. This sequence of column headings is used consistently in treatment of association leaders.

ing, among leaders of associations as among heads of firms. Generally, responses were more focused, but few significant patterns emerge in looking at the data. An overwhelming 83 percent responded either in terms of political motivations/collective benefits, selective incentives, or a combination of the two. As parallels responses among chief executives, results indicate a relatively large response in the political or collective goods row and fewer in the selective incentives category. Yet many association leaders, those answering a combination of political and selective incentives, could not ignore the role of selective incentives in attracting membership. Furthermore, in contrast to what one might expect, it was not necessarily those associations more distant hierarchically from the peak that stressed selective incentives. Only minor differences appear between indirect versus direct affiliates of the CEOE, base versus intermediate associations, or small versus medium versus large associations (measured by budget size). In fact, controlling the indirect/direct dichotomy by the membership-order level, an inverse relationship to the expected occurs. No pattern emerges for selective incentives. Base associations not directly affiliated to the peak do not stress selective incentives to a greater degree than the remainder of the sample.⁴ Furthermore, these indirectly affiliated base associations place somewhat greater stress on political inducements than do the direct base affiliates of the

CEOE. Likewise, indirectly affiliated intermediate organizations place greater stress on the political inducements than do the intermediate direct affiliates, which, we should note, represent the elite associations, including all the large sectorals playing the greatest policy roles in the CEOE (with the important exception of the bankers' association, the AEB, a base-level direct affiliate). One might have expected that organizations further from the peak level, closer hierarchically to the base, might depend to a greater extent on selective incentives. It may be the case that an important subgroup of small base organizations has politically conservative leadership for whom a reactive characterization of associability is particularly appropriate. We will explore this possibility further on.

Leaders of associations who expressed external, political motivations or collective goods to the exclusion of other factors as the primary determinant most closely parallel individual chief executives who can be characterized as "reactive."

Following the assumption that organizations closer to the firm, that is, base organizations, would be the most likely to stress selective incentives, one might expect significant findings differentiating these from intermediate organizations. Differences appear more marked on the base/intermediate dichotomy than on the indirect/direct affiliation characteristics, but there is no difference in the percentages indicating selective incentives. Rather, the important difference appears in the political inducements-collective goods category. Roughly half the leaders of intermediate organizations chose the external inducements category (political inducements/collective goods) to the exclusion of all other reasons. Whereas half of base association leaders mentioned selective incentives exclusively or in combination with political motivations/collective goods, only 37 percent of intermediate association leaders did so. Base organizations are more service-oriented. Attracting and keeping membership high devolves largely to them. Intermediate organizations will, as a rule, be more interested in political activities, both within the system as a whole as well as within the CEOE hierarchy. Naturally, the intermediates tend to be larger sectors whose own affiliates are either divided by functional subsector or defined geographic space. Slightly over a quarter of the intermediate associations are indirect affiliates of the CEOE, however. Similarly, about 44 percent of the base organizations are direct affiliates of the CEOE.

Regarding the two key intervening variables, three findings appear the most interesting: (1) Great differences fail to emerge between direct and indirect affiliates; (2) high proportions responding with political inducements-collective goods arguments fail to emerge consistently in moving up hierarchically; and (3) organizations closer to the base membership fail to stress selective incentives to any significantly greater degree than those hierarchically closer to the peak. Therefore, other organizational properties must be important in explaining these tendencies.

Regarding selective incentives, an important difference emerges between associations with collective bargaining roles versus those without. Sixteen percent choose selective incentives exclusively among leaders of associations that conduct collective bargaining versus 25 percent among associations without that critical role. Thus, a number of organizations develop services to compensate for lacking more prominent roles in the production of collective goods.

The only clear pattern that emerges by province is a larger exclusive emphasis on political motivations/collective goods in Barcelona (54%), which holds for both base and intermediate associations, compared to a lower level in Vizcaya (46%) and a significantly lower level in Madrid (29%).

Table 4.2 Motivations Leading Firms to Affiliate to the Association by Sector

	By sector:*			
	Mfg.	Serv.	Ints.	Total
Political inducements/collective goods	44.4	26.7	33.3	36.8
Selective incentives	14.3	26.7	0.0	18.4
Combination political and selective	27.0	28.9	33.3	28.1
Via personal contacts	0.0	0.0	16.7	.9
Organzational continuity	6.3	2.2	16.7	5.3
Other answers/NR	8.0	15.5	0.0	10.6
	(63)	(45)	(6)	(114)

* Sector refers to broad sectors of the economy: manufacturing (including construction), service sector, and intersectoral associations.

By size of an organization, among those who mentioned political motivations or collective goods items either exclusively or in combination, there is a steady but insignificant increase (small 62.5%; medium

63.3%; large 70.6%). Broad sectoral classifications, in comparison, appear to be of greater import. Leaders of secondary sector associations, which here includes construction, responded with political-collective goods arguments at a proportion significantly above that for tertiary sector association leaders (18% higher for secondary associations). Exclusive mention of selective incentives motivations was extended more often (12% higher) by tertiary than secondary association leaders. The critical factor is simply the severe economic difficulties constraining many of the older technology industries affecting Spanish industry, as is the case in much of the developed world. Several industries heavily affected by the international economic crisis of the 1970s and early 1980s, such as iron and steel, shipbuilding, textiles, and footwear, had all been important in the Spanish economy in the recent past. Construction was affected for many years by weakness in domestic demand (in vivid contrast to the speculative boom which followed in the late 1980s). The service sectors, on the other hand, did not feel the crisis to the same extent. As long established industries, it was also logical that more manufacturing sector leaders chose the continuity category than did service sector organizations.

GENERATIONAL–PROFESSIONAL COHORTS AND AFFILIATION

Grouping respondents by the number of years of activity in collective interests of business organizations (i.e., "generational-professional" cohorts) proves interesting. Those with six years or less of activity had worked in the field only since the death of Franco (recall that the survey took place in 1982). Those who indicated twenty-one or more years of activity (nearly a quarter of the sample) were already active in collective employer activities prior to the economic take-off period. The intermediate group of association leaders (seven to twenty years) began working in the field during the Franco period concurrently with or after the economic take-off period.

The importance of this variable is that the pre-1960 group (pre-economic take-off) represent those who worked in organizations representing established industries. Although their organizations may have had ties to the Sindicato Nacional, or may have developed them subsequently, the economic bases of the firms they represented were already established prior to the 1959 and early 1960s Franquist policies that facilitated the opening up of Spain and the substantial economic growth of the 1960-1974 period. This is not to say that their member companies did not benefit from those policies, but that they would tend to have a looser identification with Franquist economic policies given their pre-existing foundation. Those with six years or fewer of activity, naturally, did not have to interact with the Franco institutions and policies.

In looking at the leaders' perceptions of the motivation for firms to affiliate, it is not surprising that a very high 52 percent indicated external inducements exclusively among those in the intermediate generational-professional cohort, (of seven to twenty years). Only 24 percent of those in the post-transition cohort and one-third of those in the older cohort chose political inducements exclusively. Additionally, while roughly more than half of these two latter groups chose political inducements-collective goods arguments overall (either exclusively or in combination with selective incentives), over three-quarters of the intermediate cohort included political-collective rationales to some extent. The intermediate 1960-1974 cohort began their professional activity during the growth period facilitated by Franquist policies and represent a group probably identifying most closely with the regime in organizational terms, whose organizations tended to be most dependent, albeit indirectly, upon the regime's policies, and most threatened by the dismantling of its structures. The dependence on the regime is described as "indirect" in the sense that it was not necessarily institutional. Rather, these leaders constitute a professional cohort formed during the 1960-1974 growth period. Their attitudes may partially be explained by the socio-economic circumstances characterizing that important period in Spanish economic development. While not necessarily more institutionally or politically linked to the regime, the economic raison d'être of their associations may have arisen only during this period. The companies constituting their organizations may have emerged in response to the changed economic realities of post-1959 Spain. Alternatively, companies in the given subsectors may have reached a "critical" mass or achieved new-found wealth during the growth period. The 52 percent level extending political or collective goods arguments among the 1960-1974 cohort is the highest single proportion derived for any of the many manners by which we can group our association leaders. This result holds steady even when the cohort characteristic is crosstabulated as the dependent variable by affiliation (indirect/direct), membership-order level, or province.

Among all three generational-professional cohorts, we have leaders who acknowledge that their organizations previously participated within the Franquist Sindicato Nacional and others who deny that their organizations were in any way implicated in the vertical structure. Significantly, for the group entering organized employer activity during the 1960-1974 period, no difference appears in percentages choosing external/collective inducements by whether or not the leadership acknowledges association linkages to the Sindicato Nacional. Fifty-two percent chose political/collective goods arguments (exclusively) among those (in the 1960-1974 cohort) who described their organizations as in some manner integrated in the Franquist Sindicato Nacional versus 54 percent for those who deny that their associations were linked to the Sindicato. In sharp contrast, for both the group entering organized employer activity only after the democratic transition and the older generation already active prior to the growth period, the degree of integration in the Sindicato is significant in looking at the external inducements argument. For the post-transition cohort, 29 percent extended external/collective inducement arguments among Sindicato-linked organizations versus 19 percent for the non-Sindicato organizations. For the older leadership group, 40 percent chose external/collective inducement arguments among the Sindicato-linked versus 25 percent among those leaders of organizations denying a Sindicato heritage. In summary, we can say that for leaders whose organizational justification for existence were not dependent initially on growth period policies, an institutional identification with the Franco period partially explains the higher percentages choosing reactive characterizations of associability, whereas reactive characterizations can be drawn for those with an economic rationale based on the regime's economic policies regardless of institutional linkages with the Sindicato.[5]

The reactive characterization of employer associability is typical for initial association, but loses its meaning increasingly as the long term stability of a socioeconomic system becomes evident (and as a rationale for continued association). In this study, however, many individual employers perceived widespread uncertainties or had held such concerns in the recent past of the political transition. We have also noted the important role among employers played by representational and collective goods functions in maintaining associability. It is difficult to dissect how and when such functions cease being symptoms of the reactive characterization of business associability and assume utility on their own merits and are legitimated by the political system.

ORGANIZATIONAL CONTINUITY

Although overall only about 5 percent of leaders indicated that organizational continuity had been the primary motivation for affiliation by their member companies, the importance of continuity is evident elsewhere. Respondents had been requested to describe the degree to which organizations prior to the political transition had served as foundations for their current associations. Almost 60 percent described linkages either to activity integrated within the Franquist Sindicato Nacional (54%) or continuity based on an associational leadership that had been formed or emerged intact into new associations but was derived from Franquist-period organizations (5%). Twenty percent denied any activity within the Sindicato structure and 21 percent indicated that their associations were formed only following the political transition.[6] In short, 59 percent of association leaders essentially link their organizations to the Sindicato and 41 percent deny a Sindicato heritage. A number of those denying a Sindicato past could have been trying to avoid the stigma attached in many circles, although a number of other organizations may have been classified as linked to the Sindicato by their leadership out of an overly legalistic characterization, leading one to underestimate the degree of independence that an organization may have enjoyed or the degree of "pressure politics" it may have played during the Franco period. One thing is certain: An analysis of some of the more political attitudes (reviewed at length in the next chapter) shows that leaders linking their organizational history to the Sindicato are to the right of those denying it--not an earth-shattering finding.[7]

To summarize the Sindicato past, Table 4.3 provides a breakdown by affiliation to the CEOE (indirect/direct), membership-order level (base/Intermediate), province, and size of budget. As would have been expected, Madrid associations were the most integrated and Vizcaya the least. More organizations closer hierarchically to the peak tended to have had a life integrated in the Sindicato (higher for direct affiliates, higher for intermediate associations). This pattern does not extend to budget size, however, where only 47 percent of the wealthiest associations had had links versus 60 percent among small and 64 percent among medium size organizations.

Hence, whereas for affiliation the organizations higher hierarchically proved to have had higher participation levels in the Sindicato, an important caveat emerges in that those organizations economically best endowed had lower Sindicato participation rates. Given

that these richest formed the elite decision makers
within the CEOE, this finding is not inconsequential
during an uncertain period of democratic consolidation
in the country.

Table 4.3 Organizational Links to the Sindicato Nacional

	Affiliation:		Membership Order:		Province:			
	I	D	B	I	M	B	VZ	Total
Yes, linked	52.7	65.5	57.5	64.2	64.4	51.7	46.2	59.1
Deny links	47.4	34.5	42.5	35.8	35.6	48.3	53.9	40.9
	(57)	(58)	(87)	(28)	(73)	(29)	(13)	(115)

Size of annual budget (in millions of pesetas):

	0-7	8-30	31+	NR	Total
Yes, linked	60.0	64.0	47.1	50.0	59.1
Deny links	40.0	36.0	52.9	50.0	40.9
	(40)	(50)	(17)	(8)	(115)

ORGANIZATIONAL CONTINUITY AND THE POLITICAL TRANSITION

The topic of organizational continuity requires
emphasis in light of the political transition that is
a backdrop for this entire study. In understanding the
collective activities of business in democratic society, it is necessary to analyze their origins. To what
degree is continuity an important factor in the complexion of the employer hierarchy in Spain? How does
the high degree of continuity impact on the development
of democracy? If there is substantial continuity and
employer activity appears to have had an influence in
the evolution of the democratic system, has the transformation of the system via reforma pactada (or, alternatively, reforma pactada-ruptura pactada) allowed for
full (or sufficient) integration of business at the collective level so as to guarantee the system its continued support?
There exist a spectrum of associations. Within
this spectrum, however, there is an important group composed of more politically conservative organizations
that, generally, are those whose leaders, emotively and

institutionally, linked their associations to the Sindicato and to the Franco regime. While the conservative business association may ascribe a greater emphasis to political motives towards affiliation, this is due to a traditional view of business associability and is not reconcilable with modern views of the same. Traditionally, the motive for business associability was tied to a great extent to external inducements, the "reactive" arguments developed and maintained throughout. While such reactive arguments may satisfactorily characterize initial associability, they do not suffice in justifying continued organizational existence.

The modern organizational view favors active--but appropriate--political activity within a democratic system in which groups compete freely with one another, defending legitimate interests. This is not to overlook advantages that certain groups may continue to enjoy, nor does it exclude the corporatist dimension, which is not really pertinent at this point. The traditional view may likewise favor political entry, but, in Spain, the implications are quite different. For many sectors, the dismantling of the series of protections afforded by the Franquist period, most significantly the lifting of restrictions on labor, together with the process of political liberalization (threatening the economic status quo) and the promise of continuing substantial economic liberalization in the future, signify that components of the "reactive" arguments have been present very recently in the past. In terms of organizational <u>raison d'être</u> for employers associations, a system in transformation, like the Spanish one of the early 1980s, is quite different from that of societies with long-established democratic political systems. This is not to say that those holding traditional views set the agenda within the hierarchy of employers associations. For the most part, they did not. But these individuals and organizations did constitute an important component of the hierarchy.

Traditional leaders of business associations will tend to obfuscate the distinction between the representation of business as employers versus that of business as producers. Among individual employers (Table 3.9), it was not surprising that the smaller the firm, the greater the percentage indicating more closely market-related activities as appropriate associational functions. Likewise this market-oriented view of associational activities is evident among leaders of associations. Those organizations headed by individuals formed professionally during the 1960-1974 period or with past activity integrated in the Sindicato, smaller organizations (by budget size), those lower down

hierarchically (indirect affiliates of the CEOE), or
base associations, all favored market fixing as an
associational objective. While the ideological
identification of these individuals very much includes
a defense of the free market system, this must be viewed
more in ideological terms as defending political
conservatism than as promotion of open markets and
economic competition. In short, the traditional organization leader can be characterized as a political
conservative threatened by competitive forms of capitalism and, in associational terms, more likely to
support market collusion openly. He favors political
entry not so as to play a role as negotiating bargaining agent within a changing system, but rather as a defender of the legal and market status quo. In this
sense, many association leaders, as well as individual
chief executives, in a manner similar to that uncovered
by Dülfer in Andalucía in 1966,[8] are interested not in
rationalizing production to conform to changing market
exigencies but rather to protect themselves from having
to undergo rationalization. These individuals are not
necessarily a threat to the democratic order, but do
form a constituency of the CEOE, and an issue with which
it needs to deal. Given the economic reality of declining industries and the continued institutionalization
of democratic bargaining between capital and labor at
various levels (company, local, provincial sectoral,
sectoral peak, national peak), this traditional component has slowly continue to diminish in size as time
has progressed.

THE ORGANIZATIONAL CONSOLIDATION OF BASE AND
INTERMEDIATE ASSOCIATIONS

The overwhelming majority of associations (86%)
are inclusive organizations, which is to say that all
companies falling inside their defined geographic and
functional "space" (putting aside the intersectorals)
are considered eligible for membership (i.e., constitute potential membership). An additional 9 percent
had memberships that were, indeed, more than inclusive
in that they also either allowed businessmen to become
members as individuals (not binding their firms),
straddling the role of employers association and professional organization (5%), or counted among members
firms outside their geographic or functional space (4%).
These latter were older associations founded to affiliate a wider geographic or functional jurisdiction
within the limits of which competing organizations subsequently arose. While ceding to those new associations

the authority to affiliate firms within a portion of their earlier wider geographic-functional space, they allowed already affiliated companies to remain. Only 4 percent of the organizations were not inclusive, placing membership restrictions beyond those of defined geographic and functional space.

Restrictions not included above in descriptions of the inclusiveness of associability are those regarding the granting or denial of participation to public sector and multinational firms. For the former the issue in certain sectors can be particularly perplexing and the issues involved in analysis focusing on public sector participation in private sector associations can prove a pandora's box.

Forty percent of associational defined geographic/functional spaces to include public sector firms. Of this 40 percent of these associations with potential public sector membership (in terms of defined space), roughly 60 percent (not quite one-quarter of all associations) actually had member companies in public sector hands.[9] However, the proportion of public to private sector firms among the memberships failed to reach 5 percent in two-thirds of these cases. Nevertheless, although few in number, the two or three public sector enterprises within the defined associational space can often be massive in size. In the defined spaces of a few organizations, the public sector is dominant. However, in no instance did these companies control the formal leadership. It appears, rather, that informal agreements allowed membership (in public-sector dominated spaces) but placed restrictions on or, indeed, fully excluded them from formal leadership.

Two-thirds of those leaders of associations having public sector membership state that they could detect no difference between public sector and private sector companies in terms of internal associational matters (as opposed to external, market activities) and almost 60 percent of these same associations stated that they found no theoretical incompatibility between the affiliation of public sector versus private sector firms. Furthermore, for the 40 percent of associations whose defined spaces included public sector firms, but whose actual membership did not, only 50 percent actually had stated organizational prohibitions against public sector membership (roughly 8% of all associations).

In considering the scope of this public sector participation issue in Spain and the attitudes held by association leaders, three considerations are important. OECD data for 1978 showed 2.9 percent of the Spanish labor force employed in public enterprises (exclusive of the public administration), compared to 7.3 percent

in France, 6.6 percent in Italy, 7.2 percent in the
Federal Republic of Germany, and 8.1 percent in Britain.[10] This data should not be interpreted to imply a
weak role for the state in the economy in Spain. The
state plays a paramount role. But, we suspect that the
level of employment in state-owned industrial companies
affects private sector perceptions of the public sector.

Second, from a comparative perspective, the relative brevity of free associability at the time in Spain
points to less evolution. The private/public representational dimensions characterizing some systems with
longer periods of development have not had time to
emerge here.[11] The same patterns need not necessarily
evolve in Spain. The evolution in the role the public
sector plays in the economy may prove the determining
factor. Continued dismantling of state enterprises and
the boost provided private investment under González
policies probably means that this dichotomy would remain
a non-issue for most associations.

Third, current employer organizations have emerged
from representational and market conditions in which the
distinctions between public and private were less clear
and less important and where official policy, generally,
failed to delineate rigid distinctions.

The issue of the participation by multinational
companies is quite different given the very large presence of such companies in Spain. Almost 60 percent of
these associations included companies with important
multinational participation among potential membership
as defined by geographic/functional spaces. Among this
near-60 percent, only 4 percent did not have multinational company members and only one association explicitly excluded them. Thus, over half of all associations
have multinationals as members.

In about 28 percent of the near-60 percent of
associations with potential multinational firm membership the proportion of foreign capital firms to domestic firms exceeded 10 percent of membership, although,
as in the case of public sector firms, the multinationals will tend to be large and a number of associational
spaces are dominated by them. Almost 20 percent of those
with potential multinational membership admitted that
there could exist incompatibilities between the organizational objectives pursued by these companies and
those of domestic companies. This represents about 11
percent of all associations. The multinational dimension
is, therefore, an issue for more associations than is
the public sector issue but their economic importance
is such generally to guarantee them access to association participation. In contrast to the somewhat diminishing role of public sector enterprises in the economy

over the 1980s, European integration has resulted in continued expansion of interest in Spain by foreign capital. As such, the importance of the multinational issue in the associations has followed a different trajectory from that of public sector companies.

An additional special "sector" important in measuring the level of achieved consolidation is the integration of small- and medium-size companies (pymes) into the associations. Obviously, in some specific industries this will be more important than in others, but the weight of small and medium enterprises in the economy means that the incorporation of the concerns of such firms should be a priority for the CEOE. Leaders were asked if they perceived differences in the roles played by pymes within their own organizations. Not surprisingly, the leaders of indirectly affiliated associations proved more conscious of the need to distinguish a different role for small and medium enterprises within their associations (58%) than did those heading directly affiliated organizations (45%).

By dividing the budget size into five categories, the study uncovers the degree to which smaller associations are, indeed, more sensitive to the needs of smaller companies than are the large associations. A significant relationship exists by size and a steady decline is revealed. Sixty-one percent of the smallest associations (5 million pesetas or less annual budget) perceive a different role for smaller companies within the association, compared to only 31 percent among the wealthiest organizations (at above 40 million pesetas). Also, not surprisingly, the smaller the association, the more likely its leader was able to specify criteria by which to define a small- and medium-size enterprise. All this has important implications for the CEOE given the influence of the largest within its ranks in policy making. Our findings appear to support the claims extended by smaller companies and their representatives regarding the inadequacies by the CEOE in responding to their concerns.

The problem of the small and medium firm is a complex one in Spain. As in the United States, much rhetoric is bantered about over it, and such firms are often strapped financially by credit limitations and by the little real influence afforded them in many business circles. They nevertheless constitute an important segment of the economy and of the CEOE's base membership, and represent an overwhelming majority of employers. The extent to which they are successfully incorporated into the system may contribute substantially to the consolidation of the associations and their hierarchy.

The percentage of potential membership actually

affiliated to an association is important not only in terms of the consolidation achieved by the association but also in influencing how an association interacts with the CEOE. It seems that associations that have succeeded in affiliating less than two-thirds of potential membership will tend to be more critical of the peak's representativeness and that those suffering from particularly weak consolidation (under 50% of potential membership actually affiliated) will be significantly opposed to complying with peak-level agreements with which they disagree.

Table 4.4 Actual versus Potential Affiliation

% actually affiliated:	Number of companies in the defined space:				
	1 to 100	101- 500	501- 2000	above 2000	Total
Under 60%	24.2	35.0	27.3	43.8	31.5
61 to 90%	33.3	45.0	36.4	31.3	37.8
91 to 100%	39.4	20.0	36.4	18.8	28.8
Other/N.R.	3.0	0.0	0.0	6.3	1.8
	(33)	(40)	(22)	(16)	(111)

In reviewing how the number of companies in an associational jurisdiction is reflected by the percentages of this specified space actually affiliated, patterns are inconclusive. However, it tends to be easier to achieve complete or near complete affiliation among smaller potential memberships than among larger. Whereas nearly 40 percent of those associations representing a jurisdictional space of fewer than a hundred firms have achieved nearly complete or complete affiliation by potential members (91-100%), less than 20 percent have achieved it among groups of above 2,000 firms. Furthermore, over 40 percent of groups of above 2,000 potential member firms have achieved less than 60 percent actual affiliation.[12]

Additional data reveal that over a third of those associations affiliating under 60 percent of potential firm membership nevertheless represent over 60 percent of the labor force in their defined spaces, reflecting a greater tendency for non-affiliation by smaller firms. Likewise, an eighth of associations at between 61 percent and 90 percent affiliation also represent above 90 percent of the active labor force.[13] Thus, looking at firm affiliation level is insufficient to gain a full picture of actual consolidation. The incidence of lower participation by smaller firms emerges as it did in the employer survey.

It is impressive that 29 percent of all associations have achieved above 90 percent affiliation. Significantly, over 40 percent of these fully or near-fully consolidated associations have memberships of a hundred firms or fewer. Nine percent have over 2,000 member firms. However, nearly a third of our associations have consolidated less than 60 percent of their potential membership.[14] Hence, the CEOE includes a significant constituency composed of weakly consolidated organizations in terms of sectoral position or prominence.

Despite the weak consolidation of some organizations, only 12 percent of the leaders stated that their associations actively sought to increase membership by means of incentives or promotional campaigns. Over two-thirds of the leaders mentioned that membership levels were maintained and increased through personal contacts among employers and between association leaders and employers rather than through promotional policies.

The collection of dues appears generally not to represent an obstacle for most associations. Nearly half claim to collect 100 percent of their dues regularly. Nevertheless, a quarter of the associations collect dues regularly from fewer than 90 percent of their members, and for a few of these organizations, collection of dues is a problem. It was on the question of dues payment that a few leaders reminisced about the old period of automatic and compulsory membership. Although in practice a problem restricted to a minority of associations, fully 42 percent of the leaders stated either that nothing could be done regarding the non-payment of dues or that although procedures existed on paper for expulsion, they were never and could not really be enforced. Another 13 percent stated that limited measures could be applied against delinquent member companies, but that expulsion was not a viable ultimate threat. Forty-four percent mentioned expulsion as an ultimatum for the non-payment of dues.

The inability to deal adequately with the non-payment of dues is a significant problem in terms of organizational consolidation. However, both those associations that are forceful in demanding dues payment and those with an expressed inability to do so had high proportions (above 50% for each of these two groups) that could not guarantee full compliance by member firms in the application of agreements or decisions adopted democratically and by large majorities among their memberships. This is certainly a key ele-

ment in assessing associational consolidation. It impacts upon the ability of the CEOE to operate successfully and has important and negative implications for
neo-corporatist arrangements.

In simple economic terms, there are a number of
weak associations. In discussion of dues and of enforcement, however, we must not overlook that a number of
associations are characterized by the dominance of a
limited number of firms with an active interest in collective action, a situation fully described by Olson.
Fewer than 10 percent of the associations have dues
schedules that do not weigh payments by size. For the
vast majority, the large firms pay a greater share of
the cost, thereby ensuring production of the collective
good.

Despite the economic weakness of many associations, only a third of the associations admitted to
relying partly on services rendered voluntarily by member firms to maintain operations. Associations relying
on voluntary services are not necessarily the most in
need. Certainly, many thereby more actively involve
their memberships. Manufacturing associations (40%) and
associations that had affiliation rates under 50 percent
of potential membership (41%) appeared to rely to a
greater extent on voluntary services. No organization
admitted to receiving economic assistance from the CEOE,
although a couple of the smallest associations were
planning to petition the peak for subsidy.

ORGANIZATIONAL DEVELOPMENT AND COLLECTIVE BARGAINING

The ability to provide collective goods is critical in consolidating membership. Our reactive characterization of business associability among individual
employers stresses the role of the level of labor conflicts plays as an impetus toward collective action.
The first domain to be entrusted to neo-corporatist
arrangements is that covering issues of employer-worker
bargaining. Hence, there is a primary distinction to be
drawn between associations conducting collective bargaining and those without that role. Lower level associations (indirect, base, or small and medium) tend to
play more prominent roles in bargaining, although for
no category of association do fewer than half conduct
bargaining.

Controlling association affiliation level (indi-
rect-direct CEOE affiliation) by membership-order level,
the role of lower-level organizations in collective
bargaining emerges as an important one. Among the
hierarchically lowest of the four categories repre-

sented, indirectly affiliated base associations, 90 percent conduct collective bargaining.

Table 4.5 Associations and Collective Bargaining

	Affiliation, Membership-Order Level, and Budget Size							
	Affiliation:		Membership-Order:		Annual Budget (million pesetas):			
	I	D	B	I	0-7	8-30	31+	Total
Yes	87.7	56.9	74.7	64.3	70.0	82.0	58.8	72.2
No	12.3	43.1	25.3	35.7	30.0	18.0	41.2	27.8
	(57)	(58)	(87)	(28)	(40)	(50)	(17)	(115)

	Affiliation Controlled by Membership-Order Level						
	Base associations:			Intermediate associations:			Total
	I	D	Subtotal	I	D	Subtotal	Sample
Yes	89.9	55.3	74.7	75.0	60.0	64.3	72.2
No	10.2	44.7	25.3	25.0	40.0	35.7	27.8
	(49)	(38)	(87)	(8)	(20)	(28)	(115)

     No significant difference in collective bargaining appears by sector of the economy (manufacturing, service, intersectoral) or by province. We would expect that associations that conduct bargaining would have an edge in consolidating their membership. Yet, no relationship emerges between the percentage of potential membership affiliated and role in collective bargaining. Only a slightly higher percentage (5% higher) of those conducting bargaining have achieved complete or near-complete affiliation among potential membership (above 90%) compared to those without bargaining roles.
     This may simply mean that to assess the impact of labor in inducing employers to collective action, one has to control by the level of labor conflicts, which, unfortunately, is unavailable for this survey of association leaders. It may be the case that collective bargaining roles are a factor in consolidating membership for associations located in highly conflictual industries or regions, whereas those with bargaining roles but located in low conflict areas and sectors simply face the typical free-rider dilemma. We previously established the importance of perceived labor unrest in influencing collective action among individual heads of firms.

Associations with collective bargaining roles tend to be organizations whose membership affiliation represents larger proportions of the active labor force. Perhaps associations not conducting bargaining have failed to incorporate some of the leading firms in their geographic/functional spaces within their membership ranks. Whereas 83 percent of those with bargaining roles have affiliation representing above 60 percent of active labor force (and 41% at above 90%), only 70 percent of those without roles have membership affiliations totalling to above 60 percent of active labor force (with 30% at above the 90% mark). It is the large firm, naturally, that will generally (although not always) prefer to maintain maximum flexibility and avoid, when possible, inclusion under mandatory bargaining mechanisms. The economic weight of the large firm often allows it to purchase labor peace, exceeding the collective agreements that must take into account the positions of the weakest companies. The phenomenon of lower proportions of "affiliated" labor force among associations not conducting bargaining could be partially linked to such circumstances.

It may be as important simply to emphasize the very large proportion of associations overall with a role in collective bargaining (72%). Of these, nearly two-thirds claimed to have full compliance by members on negotiated labor contracts. An additional quarter of those associations conducting bargaining claimed general compliance, and only 10 percent complained of any significant difficulties in gaining employer compliance with signed labor accords.

Possibly the most important indicator of the level of achieved consolidation--fundamental in strengthening the peak's position as a system actor--is the capacity of lower level organizations to enforce membership compliance with associational decisions. All the hierarchical links must be able to enforce decisions if employers associations are to enjoy the unhesitant confidence of other system actors. The primary enforcement level is that of the base association. Assessment of the organizational capacity to make majority, democratically reached decisions binding reveal that full consolidation still had a considerable distance to go. Roughly half of the associations lack sanctions by which to deal with the failure on the part of a dissenting member to comply with decisions supported by a large majority. Intermediate organizations, with 57 percent having sanction measures, appear somewhat stronger than base organizations with 47 percent. But it is at the base level where the ability--or inability--to deal with noncompliance has the most relevance. Twenty-seven orga-

nizations admitted to having faced the dilemma posed by
non-compliance. In thirteen cases, it led to expulsion,
in five, to compliance; and in seven, to an inability
on the association's part to enforce the decision or
expel the dissenter.

THE ORGANIZATIONAL CONSOLIDATION OF THE PEAK ASSOCIATION

Regarding the degree of obligation toward capital-labor agreements, 58 percent of individual chief
executives felt totally obligated to respect capital-
labor agreements and an additional 14 percent felt generally obligated, a total of 72 percent favorably disposed towards compliance with collectively achieved
agreements. Because individual employers were not asked
to specify the hierarchical level of association, the
unspecified capital-labor agreement could be at the
macro level or at the given employer's provincial
sectoral--the usual collective bargaining agent. Certainly a number of employers must have had the macro-
level agreements in mind when assessing the degree of
obligation they felt toward capital-labor accords given
the media play given early agreements such as the AMI
or ANE. Nonetheless, the willingness expressed to respect such agreements is surprising. Nearly 65 percent
of the leaders of associations that conduct bargaining
claimed full compliance by member firms and an additional 25 percent general compliance. This may seem high-
flown, but the leaders are not way off from the expressed obligation extended by individual employers.

Table 4.6 Degree of Obligation Felt toward Agreements Reached by the CEOE among Leaders

| | Affiliation: | | Membership-Order: | | Province: | | | |
	I	D	B	I	M	B	VZ	Total
Totally obligated	43.9	31.6	37.2	39.3	31.9	55.2	30.8	37.7
Generally obligated	12.3	12.3	11.6	14.3	9.7	17.2	15.4	12.3
Have reservations	17.5	21.1	17.4	25.0	23.6	13.8	7.7	19.3
Not obligated	21.1	31.6	27.9	21.4	30.6	13.8	30.8	26.3
Other/don't know	5.3	3.6	5.9	0.0	4.2	0.0	15.4	4.4
	(57)	(57)	(86)	(28)	(72)	(29)	(13)	(114)

Within the hierarchy, leaders are more cautious in claiming immediate adherence. The data indicating the level of unhesitant support that the CEOE can call upon from among its affiliates show a propensity for leaders to emphasize their own flexibility and independence of action over immediate compliance.

While nearly 72 percent of individual employers are favorably disposed towards compliance, only half the leaders are so disposed. Nearly half do not have a sense of obligation, and, significantly, over a quarter feel themselves not at all obligated by peak-level agreements. Small associations feel slightly more obligated toward the peak than average, and medium associations slightly less so. While overall somewhat less obligated by CEOE agreements, large associations distribute themselves toward the extremes, either feeling fully obligated (41%) or not at all (41%). In terms of CEOE posturing and the strength of its agreements, all the large organizations that do not feel obligated prove to be base associations. The most influential and elite associations are not among the 41 percent who feel uncommitted by peak agreements. It would be a more serious matter were the handful of organizations most influential in determining CEOE policy not to feel bound by it.

Limited comparisons can be drawn to patterns among individual chief executives in that the smaller the firm, the greater the belief in the capacity of associations to negotiate and the greater the sense of obligation towards resultant agreements. This emerged despite a more critical posture by regular and intermediate firms regarding the CEOE and the greater distance from the network of contacts. A similar pattern emerges for the survey of leaders wherein those less integrated into the "elite" (the leaders of the indirectly affiliated and of the smallest associations) hold a greater sense of obligation to capital-labor accords reached higher up in the hierarchy.

We also find a strong tendency towards compliance among Barcelona leaders, quite striking when compared to the levels for Madrid. This probably results from the more consolidated position of employer collective activity in Catalonia. Further, the striking results obtained in comparing Barcelona to Madrid are not due to the high number of direct affiliates in the Madrid sample.

For the eighty-three associations that conduct collective bargaining, there is some correlation between the level of achieved consolidation by member associations and the sense of unhesitant confidence (obligation) they in turn entrust to the CEOE. As such, organizations that can count on total adherence by member

affiliates to collective bargaining agreements signed
with labor unions are more likely to express allegiance
to accords negotiated by the peak. The more consolidated
an organization is itself, the more likely it will contribute to strengthening the CEOE's consolidation. This
substantiates the thesis that consolidation of the CEOE
requires consolidation of each of its hierarchical
levels. Weakness at any point weakens the structure.

Table 4.7 Degree of Obligation to the CEOE among Leaders by
the Level of Member Firm Compliance to their Own Labor Contracts

Degree of obligation to the CEOE:	Level of compliance with collective bargaining agreements:		
	Full	Less than full	Total
Totally/Generally obligated	55.5	42.9	51.8
Reservations/Not obligated	37.1	53.6	42.2
Other	7.4	3.6	6.0
	(54)	(28)	(83)

Data indicating level of consolidation by the
percentage of potential membership actually affiliated
(based on defined geographic and functional space) support the same conclusion. The CEOE has severe problems
in assuring compliance among its least consolidated affiliates. Almost 70 percent of those associations that
have achieved less than a 50 percent actual affiliation
level for potential membership either hold reservations
(27%) or do not feel obligated (42%) by macro-level
accords. The figure for all associations is 46 percent
(those holding reservations plus the not obligated). It
is interesting to note the severe difficulties that the
CEOE could conceivably face among these least consolidated in light also of the strong unwillingness among
its wealthiest affiliates (with 12% holding reservations
and 41% not obligated). These two groups of organizations constitute nearly 40 percent of all associations
and there is absolutely no overlap between the two
categories. Recall the very important caveat, however,
that the non-compliant wealthy associations are all base
organizations and do not include the most "elite" of
this group. Obviously, the strategy implemented by the
peak in winning over the allegiance of the weakly consolidated perforce must differ from that used to induce
the remaining wavering wealthiest into full compliance.

THE NATIONAL EMPLOYMENT AGREEMENT

        Turning   to   an   actual   macro-level   agreement
reached,   the   acuerdo nacional de empleo   (ANE--the
National Employment Agreement of June 1981), those lower
in the hierarchy prove more critical. With a proportion
of 18 percent unfavorable overall, 25 percent of the
indirectly affiliated are unfavorable, as are 21 percent
among base associations, and 28 percent among small
associations. It may, be more important to emphasize the
high proportions of all categories responding favorably
in their assessment of the ANE (59%) which, unlike the
acuerdo marco interconfederal of January 1980 (AMI),
received considerable public criticism from many organized business sectors. Among base associations, we find
important levels of unfavorable responses outside of
Madrid. Nearly a third of Barcelona respondents criticized the ANE. In this, the province follows the pattern
that appears for affiliation and size. The indirectly
affiliated and the smaller associations had indicated
greater willingness to abide by peak-level agreements
and yet proved to have larger minorities holding critical opinions regarding the ANE compared to those higher
up the scale. Likewise, larger proportions of Barcelona
leaders relative to those in Madrid felt an obligation
toward meeting peak-level agreements. Yet we now see,
for base association leaders, more critical postures
adopted in Catalonia. Vizcaya responses regarding associational obligation were roughly equivalent to those
for Madrid, but, as one would expect, the Basque prove
the most critical (46% unfavorable).
        Whereas the high 59 percent drew favorable over-
all assessments of the ANE, overall percentages are reversed in commenting upon the agreement's potential in
employment creation. Over 60 percent stated that they
considered the ANE ineffectual as an instrument in com-
bating unemployment. (They were right!) Logically, business supported the ANE primarily for its role in supporting a framework for limiting wage demands and for
contributing to labor peace. The employment creation
feature was correctly perceived as a concession to labor
by the government.

CONTACT NETWORKS

        As among chief executives, leaders were asked to
indicate all the channels available to combat forthcoming, potentially damaging legislation. A comparison of
the responses of chief executives and leaders shows
strikingly similar figures on three items and important

Table 4.8 Contacts Used by Association Leaders to Obtain Information on Pending Legislation

	Affiliation:		Province:			Budget size:			
	I	D	M	B	VZ	0-7	8-30	30+	Total
Ministry contacts:									
Would contact	41.1	79.3	68.5	53.6	30.8	42.5	69.4	88.2	60.5
Would not	58.9	19.0	30.1	46.4	62.2	57.5	28.6	11.8	38.6
Don't know	0.0	1.7	1.4	0.0	0.0	0.0	2.0	0.0	.9
CEOE contacts:									
Would contact	83.9	74.1	78.1	75.0	92.3	87.5	75.5	64.7	78.9
Would not	16.1	24.1	20.5	25.0	7.7	12.5	22.4	35.3	20.2
Don't know	0.0	1.7	1.4	0.0	0.0	0.0	2.0	0.0	.9
Contacts with other employers associations:									
Would contact	14.3	20.7	16.4	25.0	7.7	5.0	18.4	41.2	17.5
Would not	85.7	77.6	82.2	75.0	92.3	95.0	79.6	58.8	81.6
Don't know	0.0	1.7	1.4	0.0	0.0	0.0	2.0	0.0	.9
Contacts with parliamentarians:									
Would contact	23.2	27.6	24.7	35.7	7.7	10.0	30.6	52.9	25.4
Would not	76.8	70.7	74.0	64.3	92.3	90.0	67.3	47.1	73.7
Don't know	0.0	1.7	1.4	0.0	0.0	0.0	2.0	0.0	.9
Contacts with regional autonomous governments									
Would contact	37.5	15.5	12.3	53.6	46.2	22.5	24.5	47.1	26.3
Would not	62.5	82.8	86.3	46.4	53.8	77.5	73.5	52.9	72.8
Don't know	0.0	1.7	1.4	0.0	0.0	0.0	2.0	0.0	.9
Contacts with Cámaras de Comercio:									
Would contact	21.4	19.0	16.4	28.6	23.1	10.0	24.5	35.3	20.2
Would not	78.6	79.3	82.2	71.4	76.9	90.0	73.5	64.7	78.9
Don't know	0.0	1.7	1.4	0.0	0.0	0.0	2.0	0.0	.9
Personal contacts:									
Would contact	8.9	17.2	13.7	14.3	7.7	2.5	14.3	35.3	13.2
Would not	91.1	81.0	84.9	85.7	92.3	97.5	83.7	64.7	86.0
Don't know	0.0	1.7	1.4	0.0	0.0	0.0	2.0	0.0	.9
	(57)	(57)	(73)	(28)	(13)	(40)	(50)	(17)	(114)

divergences on three others. Table 4.8 lists seven items compared to six in the chief executives survey. Chief executives were asked merely to identify associations among their informational channels. Leaders of associations were asked specifically to identify the CEOE and

other associations separately as informational channels.
Ignoring the option "contacts with other associations,"
we find parallels between chief executives and leaders
on reviewing the non-political contacts among the remaining six options. Eighty percent of chief executives
identified associational contacts. Seventy-nine percent
of leaders identified the CEOE (specifying the CEOE more
closely approximates associational contacts among individual employers as in each instance one is referring
to contacts upwards hierarchically). Nineteen percent
of employers chose contacts with the Cámaras, as did 20
percent of leaders. Ten percent of chief executives mentioned personal contacts, versus 13 percent here.
     For the more directly political contact groups,
we find the associations much better connected. Whereas only 36 percent of individual chief executives could
call upon ministries, 61 percent of associations could
do so. While the figure is significantly higher, it is
surprisingly low for associations given the nature of
their business.[15] Over a quarter of association leaders
have contacts in parliament, more than four times the
level among individual chief executives. Over a quarter
of leaders also had contacts in the regional autonomous
governments, compared to slightly more than 10 percent
among the heads of firms. Paralleling the data for chief
executives on these three political contacts, the larger
the organization, the higher the percentage indicating
the possibility of contacts. Among the largest associations, those with annual budgets of over 30 million pesetas, 88 percent have ministry contacts, and roughly
half have contacts with parliamentarians or in the
autonomous governments.
     Contacting the CEOE appears to compensate some-
what for the lack of "political" contacts among the
leaders of small and medium associations, indicated particularly by the high 88 percent of the leaders of the
smallest associations identifying the CEOE. What is more
striking, however, is the 80 percent who mentioned the
CEOE compared to the parallel figure contacting employers associations among individual heads of firms. Relative to the frequency of other contacts in the employer
survey, the near-80 percent was very high and a positive
sign of consolidation for the   associations. In the
associations survey, on the other hand, the near-80 percent identifying the CEOE as an informational source
could indicate weakness. A fifth of all leaders did not
specify the CEOE. This is particularly significant in
that over a quarter of those directly affiliated to the
peak failed to mention the CEOE as an informational
source. For the largest associations, over a third do
not rely on the CEOE for informational needs. It is log-

ical that the elite organizations would be well integrated into various informational networks, but exclusion of the CEOE by such a large proportion is a serious
flaw in its consolidation.

An additional indication of weakness is the
failure of over 80 percent of leaders to indicate contacts among their colleagues in other associations. It
is interesting in this light to note that roughly
equivalent (but slightly higher) percentages mentioned
the Cámaras de Comercio as mentioned other associations.

In a reversal from the employer survey, Barcelona
has the highest percentage indicating parliamentary contacts. Large numbers of both Barcelona and Vizcaya association leaders tend to have contacts with their respective regional governments. Both Convérgencia (CiU)
and the then regionally dominant Basque Nationalists
(PNV) can be characterized as bourgeois parties, unhesitant in their strong and open linkages to the business
sector. This contrasts with Madrid-based parties. Suárez
lacked rapport with the business sector and many in
business perceived his policies as inimical to their
interests. While objective reality might have been
otherwise, these attitudes came to have an important
impact on the fortunes of the UCD. The very high 92
percent of Vizcaya associations that would contact the
CEOE is very interesting in light of the divisions among
employers in the province and may possibly be partially accounted for as a result thereof in that many of the
region's associations sought added legitimacy as the
valid spokespieces in relation to the peak.[16]

ORGANIZATIONAL COMPETENCIES

As in the chief executives survey, association
leaders were asked to choose from a closed-ended list
those functions appropriate for employers associations
to undertake. As with responses by individual heads of
firms, the five items receiving the least support were
those most directly political in nature: influence candidate selection within parties, 44 percent; financially
support parties favorable to business, 60 percent; campaign in favor of pro-business parties, 64 percent; campaign against parties unfavorable to private enterprise,
53 percent; and, campaign in favor of pro-free enterprise parties, 70 percent. The difference between the
two surveys is in the levels of support these items received. Significantly higher percentages supported political activities among leaders than among individual
chief executives. Another parallel between the two surveys emerges, however, if one ranks these five items

Table 4.9 Appropriate Employer Association Competencies

	Yes	No	DK/NR
1. Representation vis-à-vis Government	92.2	7.0	.9
2. Relations with int'l organizations	96.5	2.6	.9
3. Commercial relations with other countries	79.1	20.0	.9
4. Statistical studies	97.4	1.7	.9
5. Information on domestic markets	93.9	5.2	.9
6. Information on international markets	94.8	4.3	.9
7. Influence candidate selection within parties	43.5	55.7	.9
8. Financially support parties favorable to business	60.0	39.1	.9
9. Campaign in favor of pro-business parties	64.3	34.8	.9
10. Campaign against parties unfavorable to private enterprise	53.0	46.1	.9
11. Attempt to organize the market	80.9	18.3	.9
12. Facilitate the meeting of businessmen to discuss problems	98.3	.9	.9
13. Campaign in promotion of business	95.7	3.5	.9
14. Campaign in favor of pro-free enterprise parties	69.6	28.7	1.8 (115)

from the least level of support to the most. Although the levels of support for political activities is higher among leaders, the five most political items receive the least support, and a ranking of the items from least to most results in exactly the same ordering as among individual chief executives, influencing candidate selection (item seven) proving the most discredited arena for association activity, followed by items ten, eight, nine and fourteen (Table 4.9).

For both surveys, after the five most political items are eliminated from the list, the next two items receiving the highest proportions rejecting organized employer activity are the two most directly market-related functions, commercial relations with other countries (no. 3), followed by attempts to organize the market (no. 11). Relative to the political items, however, these market items receive significantly more support. Among the leaders, only 20 percent consider such activities inappropriate for the associations.

Disaggregating by province, Vizcaya proves the most "rejectionist" on the political items, as it did among chief executives. Furthermore, the highest provincial rejection level was recorded among Vizcaya respondents on the issue of influencing candidate selection within parties (77% rejection). Barcelona appears slightly more pro-political than Madrid, although on item ten (campaigns against parties unfavorable to private enterprise) a significantly lower 41 percent "yes" percentage was recorded for Barcelona respondents in comparison to the 58 percent Madrid level. In the chief executive survey, this was the only one of the five political items in which support among Barcelona chief executives was lower than among Madrid chief executives. This may constitute a higher level of consciousness about the possible counter-productive repercussions of such an activity in a region with otherwise established participation by employer groups during political campaigns. Recall the more limited nature of Fomento's campaign during the regional elections to the Generalitat, which contrasts sharply with the openly anti-socialist character of the campaign waged in Andalucía in 1982 by the CEOE and the Confederación de Empresarios de Andalucía (CEA).

Again running parallel to findings for the chief executive survey, Vizcaya registers higher proportions favoring association activities for those activities identified as most directly market-oriented in nature compared to the figures for Barcelona and Madrid. Eighty-five percent of Vizcaya leaders favor commercial relations with other countries, compared to 79 percent state-wide recall Vizcaya's higher export-orientation and 92 percent favor "organizing" the market, compared to the overall average of 81 percent.

The leaders of intermediate associations favor political entry to a greater degree than those of base associations, although by size (measured by annual budget) roughly equivalent proportions favor political entry. The exception is of campaigns against parties and campaigns in favor of pro-free enterprise parties where significantly higher proportions of the leaders of the smallest associations gave "yes" responses. A significant relationship by size appears on item eleven

(organizing the market) with small association leaders
registering the highest (93%) favorable response, again
paralleling the size variable among individual chief
executives (medium associations, 74%; large associations, 71%).

Leaders had been asked earlier during the interview to specify those fields of politics in which employer association activity is legitimate (Table 4.10).
As in Table 4.9, very large proportions of the leadership of intermediate associations favor political entry.
It may be important to emphasize in the responses to
this open-ended question that the second category, "only
economic/labor policy," may be open to interpretation
when compared, particularly, to the total rejection of
political activities. We could consider these respondents as favorable to political activities, but sensitive to the need that only those activities be conducted
that are appropriate to collective interest groups and
legitimate in the context of a democratic system with
a competitive party system.

By size of organization it is the leaders of small

Table 4.10 Legitimate Political Activity by Employers Associations

	Affiliation:		Membership-Order:	
	I	D	B	I
All of politics	42.1	36.2	34.5	53.5
Only economic/ labor policy	31.6	37.9	36.8	28.6
No areas	24.6	19.0	23.0	17.9
Other	1.8	6.9	5.7	0.0
	(57)	(58)	(87)	(28)

	Province:			Size of budget:			
	M	B	VZ	0-7	8-30	31+	Total
All of politics	41.1	44.8	15.4	42.5	40.0	23.5	39.1
Only economic/ labor policy	24.2	34.5	38.5	35.0	34.0	47.1	34.8
No areas	20.5	17.2	38.5	20.0	24.0	17.6	21.7
Other	4.1	3.4	.7.7	2.5	2.0	11.8	4.3
	(73)	(29)	(13)	(40)	(50)	(17)	(115)

and medium associations who most favor entry into all political arenas. Large association leaders strongly support appropriate activities (input into economic and labor policy), but reject unrestricted activity. To assess the importance of this, one would have to determine which organizations take the lead in formulating CEOE policy. Indeed, in many instances only a few organizations will be involved and these will set the tone for collective employer activity. As mentioned previously, we can identify important sectors of traditional associations. Leaders in the traditional mold tend not to shade or nuance political options, leading in the aggregate to a certain failure to distinguish between appropriate and inappropriate political activities.

The leaders of the largest associations are the most limiting on political entry among base and intermediate associations. The leaders of large base associations are the least favorable to unlimited political activity (controlling budget size by membership-order). We could conclude that there may be more careful assessments drawn by the leaders of the largest and most influential associations. These leaders tend to draw distinctions between appropriate and inappropriate activities. Leaders of smaller associations or in the traditional mold may not do so.

More traditional leaders linked to the Sindicato Nacional favor unrestricted political activity to a greater extent than the non-Sindicato group (43% versus 34%). However, we also found a higher rejection rate for any political entry among those with a Sindicato legacy, 27 percent versus 15 percent. As one would expect, the province most critical of political entry is Vizcaya and the most pro-political is Barcelona.

INTERNAL DEMOCRACY AND THE CEOE

In assessing the CEOE as either democratic or undemocratic in its internal operations, we find two important findings: (1) A relatively important proportion of affiliates, nearly two-thirds of association leaders, regard the peak as democratic; but, (2) important groups are critical.

The greater the hierarchical distance from the peak (indirect affiliates, base associations, and small and medium associations) the higher the proportions of critical or "don't know" respondents. Furthermore, we derive a very strong relationship by province. Whereas a low 19 percent replied "no" in Madrid, Barcelona recorded 31 percent, and Vizcaya 54 percent.

Significant findings appear when the view of the

Table 4.11 View of the CEOE as Internally Democratic

		Affiliation:		Membership-Order:	
		I	D	B	I
Yes		59.7	69.0	59.7	78.6
No		26.3	25.9	27.6	21.4
DK		14.0	3.4	11.5	0.0
NR		0.0	1.7	1.1	0.0
		(57)	(58)	(87)	(28)

	Province:			Size of budget:			
	M	B	VZ	0-7	8-30	31+	Total
Yes	72.6	69.0	7.7	60.0	60.0	82.4	64.4
No	19.2	31.0	53.8	27.5	30.0	17.6	26.1
DK	6.8	0.0	38.5	10.0	10.0	0.0	8.7
NR	1.4	0.0	0.0	2.5	0.0	0.0	.9
	(73)	(29)	(13)	(40)	(50)	(17)	(115)

CEOE by province is controlled either by membership-order level or by affiliation. While no differences emerge among intermediate associations, among base associations we find twice as many critical responses among the leaders of Barcelona organizations as in Madrid. Vizcaya is striking due not only to the extremely high level of critical responses (54%), but also to the very high 39 percent expressing insufficient knowledge about the CEOE to respond adequately, a pattern that emerges for Vizcaya throughout these CEOE assessment variables and that parallels the findings among individual chief executives. Asked to comment regarding control of the CEOE, individual employers in Vizcaya had response rates of 23 percent criticizing the peak as undemocratic and 53 percent in the don't know category (and 10% no response). Controlling province by affiliation produces findings roughly equivalent to those for membership-order level. In summary, the obvious may be that Madrid leaders are the closest to peak activities and partake of the most direct access.

It is the leaders of base associations that are less favorable and more critical, with the leaders of indirectly affiliated base associations somewhat less favorable and more critical than those heading direct-ly affiliated base associations. This group of indirectly affiliated base associations is the most distant hierarchically from the peak.

Respondents were queried as to the adequacy for their own associations of the representation available

Table 4.12 View of the CEOE as Internally Democratic: Province Controlled by Membership-Order Level

	Base associations:			Intermediates:		
	M	**B**	**VZ**	**M**	**B**	**Total**
Yes	70.9	63.2	7.7	77.8	80.0	64.4
No	18.2	36.8	53.8	22.2	20.0	26.1
DK	9.1	0.0	38.5	0.0	0.0	8.7
NR	1.8	0.0	0.0	0.0	0.0	.9
	(55)	(19)	(13)	(18)	(10)	(115)

Table 4.13 Adequacy of Current Representation in the CEOE

	Membership-Affiliation:		Order:	
	I	**D**	**B**	**I**
Satisfied	49.1	68.4	55.2	70.4
Intermediate	21.0	21.1	23.0	14.8
Dissatisfied	19.3	8.8	13.8	14.8
Don't know	8.8	1.8	6.9	0.0
No response	1.8	0.0	1.1	0.0
	(57)	(57)	(87)	(27)

	Province:			Size of budget:			
	M	**B**	**VZ**	**0-7**	**8-30**	**31+**	**Total**
Satisfied	65.3	58.6	23.1	50.0	57.1	70.6	58.8
Intermediate	22.2	20.7	15.4	22.5	24.5	17.6	21.0
Dissatisfied	8.3	17.2	38.5	20.0	14.3	5.9	14.0
Don't know	2.8	3.4	23.1	7.5	4.1	5.9	5.3
No response	1.4	0.0	0.0	0.0	0.0	0.0	.9
	(72)	(29)	(13)	(40)	(49)	(17)	(114)

in the CEOE. To what degree did they feel that the opinions or postures of their association were adequately represented and received due consideration? For affiliation, membership-order, and budget size, the closer one draws to the peak, the higher the proportion of leaders who feel adequately heard and represented; the lower the association hierarchically, the greater the proportion of respondents who consider themselves inadequately represented. The consistency of the relationships on these three characteristics is undeniable. Controlling affiliation by membership-order produces the expected results. Nearly three-quarters (74%) of the most "elite" of the four categories produced, the leaders of directly affiliated intermediates, responded that their organizations received adequate representation, compared to fewer than half (47%) among the leaders of the lowest organizations hierarchically, indirectly affiliated base associations.

By province, Vizcaya, again, proves the most critical (39% unfavorable and 15% in the intermediate category) and registers the highest proportion of don't know responses (a very high 23% compared to the 5% total average). Controlling province membership-order level, equal proportions of Barcelona and Madrid intermediate-level respondents indicated that their associations are adequately represented (roughly 70% "satisfied" for each), whereas there are significantly fewer favorable and more critical responses among Barcelona base association leaders in comparison to their Madrid colleagues (favorable: Barcelona, 53%; Madrid, 64%; unfavorable: Barcelona, 16%; Madrid, 7%).

CONCLUSIONS

For this relatively early period in the process of democratization, the data reveal a peak association considerably consolidated among its affiliates given the short duration of its existence, but with specific areas of weakness. Weaknesses among member affiliates detract from the consolidation of the peak. The CEOE could identify difficulties among its weakly consolidated affiliates, for example, those failing to consolidate significant portions of their potential membership, those economically weaker, and those lacking in the capacity to provide collective goods, most notably the important collective bargaining role.

Both specific sectoral or subsectoral traits and state policies toward a given sector impact upon the type of association that arises. Market conditions and state policies share in a reactive characterization of, at least, initial employer associability for a given group of companies. The number of companies in a given sector; the number, role, and prominence of the leading companies; and market conditions determine whether the rise of collective action is "almost inevitable," as Olson might describe. The most critical state policy contributing to associational consolidation is the conferment or denial of a collective bargaining role. Policies related to subsidization or incentives or exemptions awarded by the state are also primary determinants in the consolidation of a limited number of associations. Obviously, policies pursued by leaders themselves can significantly strengthen the organizations and, indeed, often are key to understanding an association. Some policies adopted by leaders include the development of selective incentives and promotional campaigns to increase membership focusing on those least likely to affiliate, such as small and medium firms. Public protagonism in the defense of business by an association leader can also serve to attract and maintain membership.

Some of the data betray CEOE weaknesses at the affiliate level. Nearly half of CEOE affiliates hold reservations or do not feel obligated to assume accords reached at the peak level. Particularly important in this regard are serious shortcomings among the weakly consolidated affiliates, those with their own compliance difficulties on collective bargaining contracts, and an important segment of the largest associations. Fortunately for the CEOE, most of its affiliates do not face serious difficulties in assuring compliance with their own labor contracts and the most influential among the wealthiest few appear generally compliant, mitigating somewhat the previous statement. Another point of weakness is the one-fifth of association leaders who failed to identify the CEOE as a contact on potentially damaging legislation. Were its machinery and networks held in higher esteem, one would not derive as large a group in the "would not contact" category. Over a quarter of association leaders believe that the CEOE operates undemocratically and fewer than 60 percent feel that their organizations are adequately represented.

Serious deficiencies are identifiable among certain large groups of association leaders and, significantly, track findings among chief executives. The CEOE faces considerable difficulties in affiliating small and medium enterprises. The collective representatives of such firms tend also to be significantly more critical of the peak than are the leaders of large firm-dominated associations, although we also find that these individuals continue to afford the peak their support in its attempts to achieve accords with other system actors. This confidence by the leaders of smaller associations parallels that entrusted to the associations by the smaller firms interviewed in the first survey.

The regional dimension is one to which CEOE leadership must dedicate attention. Certainly, the peak is well consolidated among its direct sectoral affiliates, which together with the affiliated intersectorals, are the organizations voting in the CEOE's general assembly. It also appears evident that the associational hierarchy is well established in both Barcelona and Madrid. Barcelona findings will generally be valid for Catalonia as a whole, a crucial economic zone of Spain, with long established patterns of collective employer activity, and with an important bourgeois class. Looking at Vizcaya, all indications point to serious weaknesses for the CEOE, and collective employer activity as a whole, in the entire Basque area, another crucial economic zone. Were the CEOE to prove weak in Zamora or Avila is not of major import. However, similar findings for Euskadi implicate an important segment of Spanish industry and labor force. Naturally, the unique character and divisiveness in the Basque business community reflects similar circumstances throughout Basque society, also mirrored in electoral and public opinion data. The organized labor picture in Euskadi similarly constitutes a departure from the labor dynamics in the rest of Spain. The consistency of parallel findings between the two surveys in this study leads one to think that findings among Valencia employers are an indication of strong associational activity coupled with "excessive" independence in relation to the peak for many Levantine provincial sectorals.

The legacy of the past represents a segment of both individual employer and leadership opinion not always concordant with patterns of collective action within a pluralist framework. Thus, we find that linkages to the Sindicato or, alternatively, leadership formation during the growth period (dependent, therefore, on Franquist economic policies) contribute significantly to views regarding the rationale for collective action and to political activities by business groups, although the latter is somewhat more difficult to document. The more conservative groups are almost fully characterizable as reactive in terms of initial associability. Segments of these groups may continue to defend collective activities deemed inappropriate for associations by more "modern" segments of business opinion (both among individual chief executives and associations) as well as by actors and observers elsewhere in the political system. Such ill-suited operations might include both activities in political arenas more appropriate for political parties and attempts at market collusion, arising from a failure to distinguish between the representation of business as employers versus that as producers by the more traditional leadership. However, leaders carrying traditional baggage are not the only proponents of direct political action and, as detailed, other associational features can contribute to a more complete explanation of such inclinations.

Continuity can also contribute to a strengthening of the peak. The long-established legitimacy of collective employer activity in Catalonia combined with the important roles played, particularly, by Fomento and other segments of Catalan business in the CEOE, assure important levels of strength in the region. Proximity to the peak's networks facilitates the same among many Madrid associations.

The degree of similarity between this survey and that of individual chief executives may constitute the single strongest indication for potential full consolidation. The leadership of associations reflects the opinions of its constituents in a number of critical areas. It is logical that the leadership will favor associational activities to a greater extent than individual employers and that the organizations will tend to be better connected to other networks available in the political and economic system. Even more striking is the consistency in the patterns between the two surveys, such as the parallels regarding appropriate functions for employers associations, contacts used, and agreement regarding aspects of bargaining, as well as the frequent similarities by province, particularly for Barcelona and Vizcaya, and, to a lesser degree, by size of organization.

Part of the explanation for the similarities between the sample groups is certainly due to a relatively high proportion of leaders who are, themselves, individual employers. Recall that the survey deals with the actual managers who run the associations, about four-fifths of whom are secretary generals or managing directors, and not the elected leadership who will always be employers, accounting for under one-fifth of the interviewees.[17] Yet fully 41 percent of these leaders are also either directors or owners of individual firms. Relatively high concentrations of "employer" leaders are found among the leadership of indirect affiliates (46%), Vizcaya leaders (69%), and in small associations (65%), groups more distant from the peak in hierarchical terms and more similar personally to the base membership given their own employer status.

The short duration of the CEOE at this time might

partially account for similarities between the surveys. Unlike the case in other European countries, we are not dealing with an entrenched business bureaucracy. The leadership of the CEOE was not yet as "professionalized" as elsewhere, thereby contributing to proximity between individual employers and their representatives. In other European countries one often finds employer association functionaries resembling their counterparts in the public bureaucracy to a greater extent than their employer constituency.

Hence, we find encouraging possibilities for the CEOE in its future evolution. Important segments of the association leadership not fully committed to the peak can be identified. These are compensated for by a majority of association leaders willing to pursue consolidation of the system of representation for themselves, contributing thereby to that of the peak, and favoring a deepening of the patterns of interest intermediation with labor and government that have often characterized the operation of Spanish democracy to date in certain economic policy-making domains. Further important opportunities for a strengthening of the system exist due to the willingness of employers to invest their confidence in the capacities of the organizations. The important public and generally moderating role of the elite organizations cannot be overlooked. Much of our data indicate a trend toward increasingly stable and legitimated patterns of employer interest representation that can have salutary effects for the political system as a whole.

NOTES

1. A few, although listed, had either ceased to exist or discontinued membership in the peak. In two instances, two sets of "mirror" organizations were listed (comprising four entries), where one real organization is listed twice given subsectoral roles relative to different government regulations for different stages of the production process. When two such organizations overlap entirely in membership, staff, and leadership, they were treated as a single association. See Chapter 2.

2. See the methodological appendix. Although the CEV was not affiliated to the CEOE, its member associations were CEOE members via their affiliation to state-wide sectoral confederations, such as FVEM. The FEVM, affiliated to the CEV, was also affiliated to CEOE via Confemetal. In both number of affiliated firms and

percentage of active labor force represented by its member companies, the FVEM was the provincial sectoral
association of most consequence. Indeed, the sectoral
dimension of the divisions in the employer picture in
Vizcaya arose from the divisions existing within this
crucial sectoral organization. Without FVEM participation, the CEV would not have reactivated, nor would it
have been a noteworthy enterprise. The company headed
by the controversial president of the CGEV, Luis Olarra
Ugartemendía, was also in the metal industry. A few
subsectoral associations in the metal industry left the
FVEM and maintained their CGEV affiliation.

Of the thirteen Vizcaya associations visited, 62
percent were affiliated of the CGEV and only 15 percent
were CEV members. The massive metal sector federation
(FVEM) was among the latter, however. Twenty-three percent were affiliated to neither of the two provincial
intersectorals, but were affiliated to the CEOE via
their sectoral peak federations (encompassing all of
Spain).

3.   The dominant position of Vizcaya within the
Basque economy is evidenced by considering that the
province represents 54.5 percent of total industrial
value added and 52.9 percent of total active labor force
for the three province region (Guipúzcoa, 31.8% and 35%;
Alava, 13.7% and 12.1%).

An index of industrial concentration can be
constructed using Banco de Bilbao data for nine manufacturing sectors. In Euskadi, 79.3 percent of total
value is produced in the leading three manufacturing
sectors. In Vizcaya, the comparable figure is 83.6 percent. This compares with 65.4 percent in Madrid, 69.2
percent in Barcelona, 56.9 percent in Valencia, and 74.5
percent in Sevilla. The figure for all of Spain is 64.8
percent.

Although the accuracy of the INE's (Instituto
Nacional de Estadística) 1978 industrial census is ques-
tionable, it is suitable (particularly for medium and
large enterprises) for general patterns of industrial
composition. As an indicator of the concentration of
sectors into fewer companies, Vizcaya firms of fifty
workers or more employ 78.7 percent of active industrial
labor force (including construction), compared to 68.5
percent in Madrid, 65.9 percent in Barcelona, 53.3 percent in Valencia, 61.8 percent in Sevilla, and 59.8 percent for all of Spain. The same data indicate 39.5 percent of Vizcaya labor force in companies above five
hundred workers, compared to 32.2 percent in Madrid,
21.6 percent in Barcelona, 18.6 percent in Valencia,
26.4 percent in Sevilla, and 23.1 percent for all of

Spain. See Banco de Bilbao, Renta nacional de España, Madrid, 1977 and Instituto Nacional de Estadística, Censo industrial de España (Madrid, 1979).

These figures highlight the paramount leadership role of Vizcaya within Basque industry. The province far surpasses Guipúzcoa and Alava in its impact on aggregate numbers. Our recognition of the prominence of Vizcaya within Euskadi, however, should not be misinterpreted as a defense of the province's representativeness for the Basque region. Fundamental economic differences distinguish each of the three provinces. On the configuration of its companies, while Vizcaya is noteworthy (relative to all Spanish provinces) for the huge size of its dominant industrial establishments, small and medium size industrial firms play a much more important role in Guipúzcoa. The smaller, more agricultural, and more lightly industrialized Alava is in a third category.

Important political differences, particularly in the degree of Basque self-identification, also characterize the three provinces, particularly as a consequence of the varying patterns of industrial development and differing demographic trajectories. On the question of the divisiveness of Basque nationalism see Juan J. Linz, Conflicto en Euskadi (Madrid: Espasa Calpe, 1986); Juan J. Linz, "La crisis de un estado unitario, nacionalismos periféricos y regionalismo," La España de las autonomías, vol. 2 (Madrid: Espasa Calpe, 1981); Juan J. Linz, "Peripheries within the Periphery," in Per Torsvik, ed., Mobilization in Center-Periphery Structures and Nation-Building (Bergen: Universitetsforlaget, 1981), 335-389; Juan J. Linz, "The Basques in Spain: Nationalism and Political Conflict in a New Democracy," in W. Phillips Davison and Leon Gordenker, eds., Resolving Nationality Conflicts (New York: Praeger, 1980), 11-52.

4.   Indirectly affiliated base associations constitute the lowest hierarchical rung.

5. Regarding an overall assessment of the Franco regime, equivalent percentages of the growth period and older cohorts drew generally favorable appraisals (57% and 61%, respectively, versus 36% for the post-transition group). For the three groups, however, the growth period group registered the highest level of support for market fixing--an important reflection of unease over the dismantling of Franquist economic protectionism. Over 60 percent fully or partially supported market fixing versus 39 percent among the older cohort.

6. To detail, 48 percent acknowledged integrated activity within the Sindicato. (This figure includes 30% of the total sample who emphasized that their organizations had emerged "intact and unchanged" from the Sindicato.) An additional 6 percent indicated that their organizations dated prior to the Franco regime but had been integrated fully into the Sindicato. To reiterate from the text, an additional 5 percent indicated that the leadership had emerged from Sindicato organizations, although the associations were new.

Nine percent were organizations formed during the period of the organic union, but whose leadership claim operated independently of it, a phenomenon documented by the Linz and de Miguel research. In some instances these "independent" organizations may have had some de jure affiliation to the Sindicato or may, alternatively, have had legal status as private corporations but conducted collective activities. Ten percent were organizations founded prior to the Franco regime that claim to have maintained de facto independent operations during the forty years, and there is one organization founded prior to the Sindicato that closed down operations and was inactive until its reestablishment following the transition. As indicated in the text, 21 percent of the organizations were founded after the transition to democracy.

7. In looking at continuity, individuals who had described their organizations as integrated in the Sindicato were grouped with those claiming to head "new" organizations, but acknowledging that their leadership group had been formed and emerged from the previous unitary structures. Likewise, those denying a Sindicato link were grouped with those claiming to head organizations dating only to the post-Franco period. There were two main rationales for grouping these into two categories; the primary one was theoretical.

Those claiming to head new organizations with Sindicato organization leadership are individuals standing essentially together with colleagues acknowledging fully integrated Sindicato activity. Generally at issue are organizations whose structures were changed given the transformed political system and whose legal status was newly registered, but whose leadership and membership simply moved from the unitary hierarchy into the system of free associability. The case in Spain for most industrial sectors, particularly for the vast majority of sectors represented by a limited number of firms, and, in particular, of a few dominant firms, is one where the institutional rubric is not the unifying standard of identification. Rather, ongoing organiza-

tional momentum is sustained by the personal network of
individual contacts. A leadership group, which necessarily will be small for employer organizations, will
carry the bulk of its active membership with it from one
body to the next. This is not to overlook the compulsory
nature of the Sindicato and the debilitating effects
voluntarism had for particular organizations.

Combining those denying a Sindicato link with
those who could not have had one seems an easier
grouping to justify if, as is the case, the distinction
that is being drawn is that of participation versus
non-participation in the Sindicato.

Second, it was apparent that those whose
"leadership" was formed in the Sindicato fell together
with the "integrated" organizations and that those denying a Sindicato past coalesced with the post-Franco
associations. In terms of patterns of responses, this
split was particularly strong among the latter. While
a clear-cut division did not appear for all dependent
variables, it did appear for a number of them. Regarding
the motivations question, the division into two groups
was particularly clear. For those making a favorable
assessment of the Sindicato the pattern also emerged.
Other responses justifying the division of this independent variable into two categories include: the
assessment of the Franco regime in that the "integrated"
and "leadership" sub-groups were both more favorable and
less critical than the "non-integrated" and "post-
transition" sub-groups; regarding a preferred economic
system, there was a very strong relationship for each
matched set of sub-groups; and, the voting records for
the 1977 and 1979 parliamentary elections revealed
Alianza Popular/Coalición Democrática (AP/CD) to have
been strong among those in the first two sub-groups
while having virtually no support among those in the
second set of sub-groups. Furthermore, persons in the
"integrated" and "leadership" sub-groups were more
likely in the 1979 elections to have abstained or cast
a blank ballot. Individuals in the non-integrated and
post-transition sub-groups were more likely (roughly
twice as likely) to support regional party options (PNV
and CiU) than those in the integrated or leadership sub-
groups. Needless to say, on other important variables,
the split pattern described did not materialize. Some
such interesting variables include those regarding a
then-future potential socialist government, the issue
of the reforma pactada, and views regarding the CEOE.
In short, the groups emerged as logical clusters on
those variables related to the previous regime and on
some other political topics.

8. Dülfer, _Problemática_, 44-45.

9.   The Americanist business reader is not to confuse the "public," that is, state-owned, versus private _sector_ dichotomy with the distinction between publicly traded versus privately owned companies.

10.   OECD data reported in "The State in the Market," _The Economist_, 30 December 1978, 40.

11.   Which is not to say that similar patterns emerge consistently with longevity. In Italy, separate peak associations exist, Confindustria (private) and Intersind (public). In 1965, at its inception, the Confederation of British Industry limited public enterprises to associate membership status, but four years later granted full membership.

12.   It is true that for groupings of 101 to 500 firms only 20 percent have achieved complete or near-complete affiliation, a proportion insignificantly higher than that for groupings of more than 2,000 firms. However, fully 65 percent of these have at least achieved above 60 percent actual affiliation, compared to 50 percent for groupings of above 2,000 firms. Logically, the number of potential member firms increases consistently as does budget size and is greater for direct than indirect CEOE affiliates. The relationship between potential membership and the membership-order level is particularly high, which is not surprising.

13.   Nine percent of those affiliating over 90 percent of firms represent less than 90 percent of active labor force for their defined spaces, indicating non-participation by important firms in these cases.

14.   Nearly a quarter of the sample (24%) has consolidated less than a half of potential membership. Recall the caveat that a third of these weak associations, in numbers of firms, nevertheless affiliate the more important firms and represent above 60 percent of the active labor force for their defined spaces. For some associations dominated by a few firms that also dominate the sector (space), having an association operating as a lobby and conducting collective bargaining may fully satisfy them. Expanding membership may not constitute much of a priority.

15.   Ministry-association contacts work both ways. LaPalombara described his concept of _clientela_ in the Italian case by reference to the relationship between

the Ministry of Industry and Commerce and Confindustria.
From the bureaucracy's viewpoint, the relationship had
become essential to the work of the ministry itself. An
empirical analysis of this relationship in Spain would
certainly be a welcomed complement to this study.
LaPalombara, Interest Groups, 264 ff.

16. Similarity in social background and origins
is important in considering the availability of contacts
between business and the bureaucracy. For the Franquist
period see Kenneth N. Medhurst, Government in Spain: The
Executive at Work (Oxford: Pergamon Press, 1973), 172.
On the effects of such contacts in the energy sector see
Thomas D. Lancaster, Policy Stability and Democratic
Change: Energy in Spain's Transition (University Park:
The Pennsylvania State University Press, 1989), 129-152.

17.   Seventy-two percent of respondents are
secretary generals; 10 percent are managing directors
or directors generals; 17 percent are presidents; and
two individuals (2%) are executive vice-presidents in
associations having honorary presidents. These last two
categories represent instances in which elected and
managerial functions resided in the same person.

5

The Business Sector and Political Change: Apertura, Reforma, and Democratic Consolidation

It is difficult from the vantage point of the booming Spain of the 1990s to appreciate the achievement represented by the successful democratic consolidation begun in the mid-1970s. From the perspective of the 1970s, following forty years of Franquist rule in a country with a relatively limited democratic heritage, successful implantation of a democratic system was not inevitable. Moderation did not have to defeat radicalism or retrenchment--but it did, in large part because of the role play by moderating societal elites, the fortuitous historical incidence of very able leadership, and the cooperation and support of the vast majority of Spaniards, who were willing to defer less pressing, narrower interests, for the greater good.

Many specific factors contributed to the peaceful democratization of Spain: moderation by the major political parties and their leaders, moderation by important sectors of the society, including labor and business; moderation by important segments of regionalist sentiment and by the electorate overall; and a positive international climate. The support of economic elites within Spain was essential to the success of the transition. In attempting to democratize a modern, industrial, market-economy country such as Spain, the role of the business community, through its collective interest organizations and through the aggregate of individual business decisions, can be crucial. Given their control over capital, business represents a considerable force within the system. Loss of confidence by the business community in a market system can contribute substantially to the potential for strain, breakdown, or failed consolidation. Governmental policies supported

by the majority, but resulting in a loss of confidence
and capital evasion, constitute a threat to an emerging
democracy. During a political transition and the early
stages of democracy, it is difficult to identify fully
the "stress threshold" that separates successful consolidation from crisis and breakdown. Economic prosperity
can buttress emerging democratic institutionalization.
How did Spanish business perceive itself affected by the
transition to a democratic political system? How did
business, in turn, participate in and contribute to
democratic consolidation?

At the time of Franco's death in 1975, Spain was
in economic terms not a more successful lesser-developed
country but a more industrial state, albeit with major
underdeveloped lacunae in sector and regional terms
(with their concomitant sociological ramifications as
well). Such an appreciation of Spain's economic reality
is essential to understanding the role business played
during the transition. Had a modern economy not existed,
had Spain not fully participated in the boom years of
the 1960s, and had fewer people amassed a stake in continued economic well-being and stability, the likelihood
of successful democratization would have been considerably lower because the political behavior at the mass
level during the years of democratization would have
been substantially different. The Spain of the mid-1970s
was far removed economically and sociologically from the
Spain of the mid-1930s.

> In the mid-1970s the new political class confronted the same basic
> cleavages that had played a disruptive role in the past. But, with the
> passage of time, changes had occurred that served in some cases to soften
> and in others to exacerbate these historic divisions. The socioeconomic
> development of Spain over the preceding three decades had profoundly
> altered many aspects of its social structure, mitigating somewhat the
> divisive potential of class conflict. Insofar as high levels of literacy
> and urbanization and the existence of a large middle class are
> prerequisites for a stable democracy, these changes have contributed to
> the new regime's chances for success.[1]

The high degree of contact by individual Spaniards
with other Europeans, via tourism in Spain, tourism by
Spaniards, academic exchanges, and activity abroad by
business people and by large numbers of guest workers
in democratic Europe, could only serve to increase
Spanish consciousness about the lack of coherence between Spain's level of economic achievement and its political underdevelopment. In this regard, many Spaniards would have acknowledged the manifest logic of
supporting a political system consistent with their
level of economic well-being.

A West European economic status constituted the correct objective standard against which to compare Spain. Perhaps more importantly, had Spanish indus- trialists viewed themselves in a different light, and compared themselves to, say, a Latin American standard, or to the Spain of the 1930s, their activities during the transition and responses to developments during those years would have been very different, as would have been the outcome for the system overall. It mat- tered little that large segments of Spain, like Extre- madura, had as much in common with underdeveloped parts of Latin America as with the rest of Europe. The parts of Spain that counted most, including the economic elites, were looking toward Europe.

Full economic development is not a sufficient "cause" for democracy. Some will argue that it is not even a contributing cause. Nevertheless, full economic development provides conditions that can be conducive to democratic political development by increasing the demands and consciousness of society while also moder- ating the competing demands tabled by segments of the society holding stakes in its continued well-being. Economic growth at intermediate stages of development can actually serve to destabilize a democratic poli- tical system.[2] However, I contend that economic con- ditions in developed countries, particularly where economic decision-making and control are fairly decen- tralized, can serve to foster increased demands for a similarly decentralized political order, while also moderating the manner in which such demands are made.

The conditions required for successful democratization are many, and the successful outcomes, such as in Spain, are not predetermined and, even with hindsight, were not unavoidable. Despite all the favor- able conditions present in Spain during the mid-1970s, successful democratization was not the only course that could have been realized, notwithstanding the best in- tentions of the vast majority of Spaniards and of most of their leaders. The fortuitous incidence of moderate and skillful leadership, particularly the presence of King Juan Carlos and Adolfo Suárez, moderation by the labor unions and business, and, at least, acquiescence (and quiescence) by more conservative forces in the so- ciety, did not all necessarily have had to result in successful democratic consolidation. There were ingre- dients present that could have changed moderation into revanchism or radicalism on the part of right and left.

Dahl argued that "The higher the socioeconomic level of a country, the more likely that its regime is an inclusive or near-polyarchy"; and that "If a regime is a polyarchy, it is more likely to exist in a country

at a relatively high level of socioeconomic development
than at a lower level."[3] Dahl did not argue causality.
Nonetheless, pluralism in Spain was consistent with its
achieved level of economic development.

The role of business in democratizing an
industrialized, market economy is critical as a social
element, in terms of the broad "business community,"
through the organized spokespieces of business, and by
means of the aggregate impact of individual business
decisions. Given its control over capital, business represents a considerable force within the system. Linz
notes that:

> In addition to being responsive to the demands of a broad electorate and
> to the party membership, democratic governments cannot ignore the demands
> of key well-organized interests whose withdrawal of confidence can be more
> decisive than the support of the electorate.[4]

Indeed, Linz chose the business sector as an example of
where government might institute policies favored by
the majority but resulting in capital evasion, thereby
eroding regime stability. In Spain, one also must re-
member the privileged position held by business during
the Franco period.[5]

The extensive literature on corporatism holds that
collective interest groups can assume management over
a portion of policy making, normally in collaboration
with counterpart labor organizations. As in our own,
such analyses also underscore the importance of the
business sector. In pluralist contexts, the activities
of the same organized business groups essential to the
corporatist analysis can be viewed more in terms of
lobby or pressure groups. Some neo-Marxist analyses of
democratization, such as that on southern Europe by
Poulantzas, similarly emphasize the role of business
elites.[6]

Individual business people and organizations can
play important roles as financial contributors to
political parties. The political activities of individual businessmen and women as citizens are also important. An adequate analysis of the Spanish business
sector and the consolidation of democracy has to assess
the economic impact of individual appraisals of confidence, expressed primarily through market activities,
and the manner in which political postures are adopted
by the collective interest organizations and how these
attempted to form (and manipulate) business political
activity, both as actors in neo-corporatist arrangements and as pressure groups. Entry into political
markets by business is a normal phenomenon in a democratic society, and in Spain was partially attributable

to the democratic transition, as we have already confirmed.

> Many elements contributed to the peaceful transformation of the regime,
> among them a favorable international climate, the generally acquiescent
> posture of "los poderes fácticos" (the powers that be--armed forces,
> Church, business community), a widely shared desire among both elite and
> the masses to avoid the bitter confrontations of the past, the positive
> role played by the monarch, and the modernization of Spanish society. All
> of these were influential in contributing to the emergence of democratic
> politics.[7]

In treatment of democratization in Spain, many
commentators, even the most objective, have felt com-
pelled to adopt the use of the term "poderes fácticos"
to describe "the powers that be," that is, those forces
in society that constitute menacing powers behind the
scene, ever prepared to strike the system down should
it falter. Always included among its components are the
military, the Church (especially Opus Dei), and, almost
invariably, the business community, or, at least, "la
gran banca." Far from being an analytically meaningful
concept, it is difficult to understand what is meant by
poderes fácticos and, certainly, impossible to analyze
empirically. The way the term has been used has implied
an almost conspiratorial tone among the suspect groups.
No empirical evidence has yet suggested actual com-
plicity among the elites in question, however. Invari-
able inclusion of la Banca among its components serves
to acknowledge widely perceived dissatisfaction within
the sector with democratization and is indicative of
mistrust on the part of many segments of democratic
opinion of the financial elites. While we do not touch
upon the military or the Church leadership, the data
reveal strong support for the democratic system on the
part of business and confirm the willingness of the
overwhelming majority within the business sector to accept the manner in which the transition was achieved,
along with the existence of sectors of strong business
support for change. While, indeed, segments of undemocratic, anti-system opinion persisted, the poderes
fácticos arguments themselves for the business sector
do not stand up specifically to scrutiny.

With all its limitations, the data at least
represent an attempt to deal empirically with the position of business regarding the emerging democratic system. Unfortunately, much of what has been written on
emerging democratic systems has failed to gather the
necessary data to portray accurately the positions of
the different relevant sectors of society. Much work
remains at too high a level of abstraction for valid

analyses of empirical reality. Even many modest efforts in conceptual or theoretical terms fail to go to the field and acquire facts for analysis. Hard data to substantiate many statements extended on business elites are simply not there and the proponents of various views do not bother to collect them. Our task is to assess the degree of support among business for the previous regime and the level of acceptance of the political opening (apertura) and the consolidation of democracy.

The brevity of a newly established democratic system is a natural disadvantage toward its own consolidation. Linz stresses the importance of the formulation of the initial agenda of a new regime.[8] The emergence of Spanish democracy coincided with a prolonged and severe economic crisis, and perceived failures to deal adequately with the crisis may have tainted the new system somewhat among certain sectors of business opinion.

> To many, the worst shortcoming of the Suárez government was its failure to face up to the serious economic situation. Politics had an almost obsessional priority. The government, fearing their impact on an electorate about to vote for the first time, refused to implement the austerity measures the Spanish economy urgently needed. The economic situation continued, therefore, to deteriorate in 1976 and 1977. The stock exchange fell dramatically. Investment ceased. Inflation ran at almost 30 percent; unemployment reached unprecedented levels. All this, as we have seen, was in large part a Spanish edition of the world crisis triggered off in 1974. Yet the government's passivity exasperated economists, entrepreneurs and workers alike.[9]

The perceived failure of the Suárez government to devote sufficient energies to economic issues was widely commented upon during business interviews in the early 1980s, and was even more pronounced during the pilot survey conducted in late 1978 among the chief executives of thirty-two large Madrid and Barcelona firms. Despite widely expressed dissatisfaction, however, the data reveal that business people as individual citizens supported the transition by "reforma pactada," overwhelmingly voted in favor of the Constitution, and gave a large share of their vote to Suárez's centrist Unión de Centro Democrático party (UCD) in both 1977 and 1979 and not to more conservative and democratically ambivalent options. Few in business adopted reactionary postures during these critical years.

Criticism of Suárez derived from comments by business people, and from the above citation from Carr and Fusi, illustrates the perceptions of a segment of business opinion and should not be misconstrued as this author's view.[10] In fact, many in business criticized the prime minister yet gave him their vote. In a July 1983 interview with a founder of the UCD, Richard Gunther was told that:

> Political life [at that time] had such dynamism; the opposition was so strong; the attacks on the very process (of transition to democracy) were very serious. In those days, time, for me, was not a matter of months, it was a matter of seconds.[11]

There was little time to devote to non-political matters when the crucial task at hand was to build broad political consensus and to eliminate opposition to the change. It most certainly was not unreasonable to expect that economic matters would take a back seat. An overloaded transition would not have succeeded.[12] While many in business slighted the government for a lack of efficacy or efficiency, the data reflect the widely held legitimation of the political framework of democracy by business.

THE FRANQUIST HERITAGE

A priori, one would expect to find more pro-Franco sentiment within the business sector than in the Spanish population overall. Indeed, in comparing the data with that collected by investigators from DATA and Ohio State, I find significantly higher proportions of business people drawing favorable assessments of Franco. Those stating total approval of Franco are significantly fewer than in the population overall, however, and, although substantially smaller among business than in the population, the proportions generally unfavorable are nevertheless important numerically, representing roughly 30 percent of individual chief executives and of association leaders.

Business will tend not to discredit Franco totally, given the important economic growth experienced during the economic liberalization of Spain. That total business rejection of Franco that does emerge is centered among the Basque and, to a lesser extent, Catalans in smaller companies, and among those association leaders whose organizations had not participated in the unitary Sindicato Nacional or whose personal length of professional activity was under seven years (at the time of the survey), and who had therefore commenced their professional careers after the transition had begun.

It is not surprising to find relatively high

levels of favorable assessments among those in Madrid, given that the region was not an important industrial zone prior to Franco's regime and that many businesses established there in response to economic policies of the Franquist period favoring such investments. Further more, the high concentration of the headquarters of public sector firms in Madrid contributes to the high proportion of favorable assessments given that the heads of these firms overwhelmingly supported the system (80% gave favorable assessments of Franco).

Table 5.1 Evaluation of Franco

	DATA 1978	DATA 1979	State 1979	Ohio Chief Executives 1981	Chief Leaders 1982
Total approval	10	9	17	5	6
Qualified approval	19	21	9	52	44
Intermediate	11	13	24	13	17
Qualified disapproval	25	21	10	18	22
Total disapproval	31	25	38	9	10
Don't know/no response	5 (5898)	11 (5499)	- (5439)	3 (258)	1 (115)

The Barcelona business sector emerges, logically, as less favorable and more critical of Franco than that in Madrid, but surprisingly the differences are not as great as one would have expected. The heads of regular-size companies in both Madrid and Barcelona prove less Franquist than those heading larger-sized companies. Forty-one percent of regular firms in Madrid and 37 percent in Barcelona disapprove of Franco. At roughly 72 percent each, the heads of intermediate and large Madrid firms register a relatively high level of approval for Franco, whereas intermediate and large Barcelona firms, at roughly 61 percent each, are not as favorable overall. Hence, in Barcelona, it is the regular firm that is most critical. Lower favorable response rates among the heads of intermediate and large firms in the province compared with Madrid intermediate and large firms leave Barcelona with a lower level of pro-Franquist sentiment overall. Two points stand out: (1) The still relatively high levels of favorable sentiment in intermediate and large Barcelona firms; and, (2) the very high level of anti-Franco feeling among

Table 5.2 Business Evaluation of Franco by Province

	Chief Executives					1st	Leaders			2nd
	M	B	VZ	VA	S	Total	M	B	VZ	Total
Total approval	1.1	5.9	3.3	11.5	8.3	4.7	8.2	3.4	0.0	6.1
Qualified approval	63.6	50.0	20.0	50.0	66.7	51.9	49.3	31.0	46.2	44.3
Intermediate	10.2	15.7	13.3	11.5	16.7	13.2	16.5	24.1	7.7	17.4
Qualified disapproval	17.0	17.6	33.3	15.4	0.0	18.2	19.1	24.1	30.8	21.7
Total disapproval	6.8	9.8	16.7	7.7	8.3	9.3	5.5	17.2	15.4	9.6
DK/NR	1.1	1.0	13.3	3.8	0.0	2.7	1.4	0.0	0.0	.9
	(88)	(102)	(30)	(26)	(12)	(258)	(73)	(20)	(13)	(115)

Table 5.3 Evaluation of Franco by Leaders
and the Sindicato Nacional

Association formerly integrated in Sindicato:			
	Yes	No	Total
Total approval	8.8	2.1	6.1
Qualified approval	54.4	29.8	44.3
Intermediate	11.8	25.5	17.4
Qualified disapproval	20.5	23.4	21.7
Total disapproval	4.4	17.0	9.6
No response	0.0	2.1	.9
	(68)	(47)	(115)

the heads of regular Madrid firms.

The most striking levels of rejection are registered in Vizcaya, where half of individual employers and nearly half of association leaders made unfavorable evaluations, although it is more striking, perhaps, to find the very high 46 percent of the latter drawing qualified favorable responses. The favorable responses

appear related to the organizational divisions in Vizcaya among organized employer groups in the early
1980s, and the proximity of one of the two competing
provincial territorial confederations to Alianza Popular and positions favoring the economic unity of Spain.

Among leaders, the strongest determining factor
was whether or not the association had been integrated
in the Sindicato. The proportions of favorable responses among the leaders of previously Sindicato-
integrated associations, at almost two-thirds, was
nearly twice that among the leaders of associations
that had never participated in the old Sindicato, at
under a third. Similarly, the level of unfavorable
criticism among the latter was close to twice as high
as among the former, and with a significant and high
pro-portion of total disapproval of Franco.

THE REFORMA PACTADA

Following Franco's death and the king's reappointment of Arias Navarro as head of government, Spain
experienced a period of great uncertainty regarding the
future direction of the political system. Would Juan
Carlos prove to be a continuator of "Francoism without
Franco"? Statements made by Arias in early 1976 heightened expectations regarding the possibility of a cautious opening of the regime, through what was labelled
"bestowed democracy."[13] It grew increasingly apparent,
however, that Arias' trepidation about the Franquist
bunker precluded his undertaking necessary reforms. A
strategy of ruptura pactada (negotiated rupture) on the
part of the regime's opposition was initially declared
by opposition figures in the spring of 1976, pressuring
for negotiations with the government so as to install
a "democracy without adjectives," that is, a democratic
system without qualifications.[14] A clean (but, possibly, negotiated) break with the past was sought by the
opposition and, further elaborated, would include the
naming of a provisional government and a referendum on
the issue of monarchy versus republic.

The summer of 1976 brought Adolfo Suárez, formerly
minister of the Movimiento Nacional, the single Franquist pseudo-party, to the position of prime minister.[15]
It was from this vantage point of authority that Suárez implemented his change from above, the reforma
pactada, achieved via negotiations with the Socialists,
and later on, also the Communists and Catalan centrists. Rather than negotiate concessions to the
bunker, as Arias Navarro had attempted, Suárez isolated
the hard right bunker by a strategy of gaining consen-

sus support for his policies from the much wider spectrum of the opposition, immediately touching base with Felipe González and, later, other opposition leaders and the illegal labor unions. The transition was brought about via the legal instruments of the Franquist system itself and with the massive support of the governed (by means of the December 1976 referendum that overwhelmingly approved the political reform), weakening the arguments of Franquist hard-liners and pressuring toward the cooperation of opposition forces. Donald Share has described the process of reforma pactada, or alternatively, reforma pactada/ruptura pactada, as "transition by transaction."[16]

The issue of political change through reform and the validity of such a course of action at the time of the transition was addressed in chief executive and association interviews. Had viable alternatives to the reforma existed at the time of the transition? Overwhelming majorities of both chief executives (70%) and leaders (65%) rejected the possibility of political options other than the reforma.

Table 5.4 Belief in the Existence of Viable Alternatives to the Reforma by Province

	Chief Executives					1st	Leaders			2nd
	M	B	VZ	VA	S	Total	M	B	VZ	Total
Yes	26.1	26.2	20.0	24.0	27.3	25.3	27.4	27.6	15.4	26.1
No	71.6	68.9	70.0	76.0	63.6	70.4	61.6	69.0	76.9	65.2
DK	2.3	2.9	3.3	0.0	0.0	2.3	6.8	3.4	7.7	6.1
NR	0.0	1.9	6.7	0.0	9.1	1.9	4.1	0.0	0.0	2.6
	(88)	(103)	(30)	(25)	(11)	(257)	(73)	(29)	(13)	(115)

We find similar proportions of Madrid and Barcelona chief executives and association leaders who believed that viable alternatives to the reforma existed at the time of the transition. Slightly over a quarter of Madrid and Barcelona chief executives (26%) and of association leaders in the two provinces (27%) fall into the category. Asked to elaborate, however, a much higher proportion of such individuals in Madrid described non-democratic options in comparison to those in Barcelona. Among those chief executives who believed other paths could have been followed, 35 percent of those in Madrid extended arguments supporting greater continuity with the previous regime, compared to 17 percent in Barcelona. Thirty-one percent of those in

Barcelona expressed preferences to the left of the
reforma, either "ruptura" or options leading to a more
profound transformation of the system. Further, 14
percent of those in Barcelona retracted somewhat by
stating that although alternatives had existed, they
recognized that the reforma path had been the best
possible. The parallel figure for Madrid was 9 percent.

Table 5.5 Political Alternatives to the Reforma Proffered
by those Chief Executives Who Believed Viable Alternatives Had Existed

	M	B	VZ	VA	S	Total
"Ruptura" or greater transformation	13.0	31.0	50.0	16.7	0.0	23.9
Others existed, but reforma optimal	8.7	13.8	16.7	0.0	0.0	10.4
Reforma, but taken at a slower pace	21.7	24.1	16.7	50.0	0.0	23.9
Anti-democratic	34.8	17.2	0.0	16.7	33.3	22.4
Other/DK/NR	21.7	13.8	16.7	16.7	66.7	19.4
	(23)	(29)	(6)	(6)	(3)	(67)

Although it is difficult to interpret those in the
don't know/no response category, some of these individuals might have more limited identification with the
democratic political system. In this regard, it is of
interest to note the higher Madrid percentages. In summary, however, it is more important to note the extremely low levels of support for expressly anti-
democratic, continuist postures. Only 6 percent of all
chief executives clearly supported continuist or other
non-democratic options, with an additional 6 percent
supporting reforma, but at a slower pace. Even in "less
democratic" Madrid, only 9 percent supported anti-
democratic alternatives (and another 6% favored a
slower reforma). These extremely low levels of
opposition to peaceful democratic change represent the
single most important finding.
     Vizcaya stands apart from the other provinces.
Significantly, among both chief executives and leaders,
the Basque province had the lowest percentage of respondents expressing a belief in alternatives to the
reforma. Among chief executives in Vizcaya, it is also
very significant that among those professing a belief
in alternatives (20%), not a single individual chose an
option classifiable as undemocratic.

As one might expect, attitudes on the <u>reforma</u> are closely related to sentiments regarding the previous regime. Among chief executives, 87 percent of those preferring less of a break with the past were also favorable towards Franco, as are 92 percent of this group among leaders. However, we should note that not all of those favorable to Franco who believed alternatives to the <u>reforma</u> existed preferred anti-democratic options in its stead.

In his survey among workplace union leaders in Madrid and Barcelona, conducted in the same year as the chief executive survey (1981), Robert Fishman found that a clear majority of the workplace leaders, 56 percent, believed that the employer in their own company had accepted the transition, without necessarily having favored it as a matter of principle. Eleven percent believed their employers had fully supported the transition by <u>reforma pactada</u>. In total, therefore, nearly 68 percent of workplace leaders argued that their employers either had accepted or supported the <u>reforma</u>, a figure strikingly similar to the 70 percent of the chief executives who themselves actually stated that viable alternatives to the <u>reforma</u> had not existed. Thus, Fishman argues, drawing reference to my business data, the perceptions of workplace leaders were essentially accurate. The questions in the two surveys are not fully mutually re-enforcing. Fishman's interpretation of his data is of interest, however. He argues that responses by labor leaders reflect that employers were not perceived as delegitimizing their own status during the transition. "No generalized delegitimation of employers existed in 1977-1978, and the reconstruction of the union movement would have to rely on other sources for the activation of workers, activists and leaders."[17] In this regard, labor's perception that business accepted a change that was not unambiguous or without risks could have served to facilitate further moderation by labor. Elsewhere our data show that business conceded a surprising amount of good faith to labor in the manner labor conducted itself (see Chapter 6). Hence, both social forces aided in contributing to the democracy's legitimation through their perceptions of each other's posturing.

THE 1977 ELECTIONS AND THE LEFT-RIGHT CONTINUUM

Voting is the single most important political act a citizen makes in a democracy. In both the first (1977) and second (1979) parliamentary elections, high proportions of chief executives and association leaders participated and strongly favored the UCD. Parties to the left of the UCD did not attract business voters, and conservative Alianza Popular (AP) was the only other state-wide competitor for business sector voters, ranking a distant second. Convergència and the Basque Nationalists (PNV) garnered important degrees of support in their respective regions.

Leaders of associations in the aggregate emerge as more conservative than their constituents. Discounting those who refused to respond, higher proportions of those in business (59% among chief executives and 53% among association leaders) voted UCD compared to the Spanish population overall (34%). Significantly higher proportions in business supported Manuel Fraga's AP than did the electorate overall (20% among chief executives; 28% among the more conservative leaders; and, 8% among all voters). The most significant finding among business overall was the strong approval Suárez received in his first popular test, particularly relative to Fraga, given that the social complexion of AP's basis of support should have attracted greater numbers of business supporters. However, AP did draw more than twice the level of support among chief executives as it did in the electorate overall.

Business may have perceived Suárez as better able

Table 5.6 The 1977 Parliamentary Elections

Party	Chief Executives	Leaders	All Spanish Voters % Valid Votes
Partido Comunista de España (PCE)	1.1	1.2	9.2
Partido Socialista Popular (PSP)	2.2	0.0	4.4
Partido Socialista Obrero Español (PSOE)	2.7	2.4	28.9
Unión de Centro Democrático (UCD)	59.0	53.1	34.0
Equipo Democristiano	3.2	1.2	.9
Alianza Popular (AP)	19.7	28.4	8.0
Pacte Democràtic per Catalunya (PDC)	7.6	10.6	2.8
Partido Nacionalista Vasco (PNV)	2.7	3.5	1.7
Others	1.5 (228)	1.2 (114)	10.1

to complete a transition successfully and without inci-
dent and may have sensed that Fraga was too far to the
right to represent a viable option. By the June 1977
elections, Suárez had already gained the acquiescence
of the last Franquist Parliament in accepting his model
of reform, through manipulation of Franquist-era legislation, reflected in the November 1976 Cortes (Parliament) approval of the Law for Political Reform by a wide
margin.[18] Subsequently, Suárez won overwhelming popular
approval for his blueprint via the referendum on the
political reform (December 1976), successfully legalizing the political parties, including a gamble to
legalize the Communist Party (PCE) in April 1977. Suárez
succeeded in changing the system in a non-threatening
manner, using the legal institutions available under the
Franquist regime.[19] To have supported perceived im-
mobilism under Fraga, however justified or not such a
depiction might be, would have been unlikely for
business. In general, by the mid-1970s, business
recognized the need for change and the exhaustion of the
earlier model. In support of change, moderate stability,
represented by Suárez, was preferable to unreconstructed
conservatism.

In addition to such a pragmatic analysis, the UCD
may also simply have been ideologically better suited
to business than was AP. Amazingly, in looking at self-
location by chief executives and leaders along a ten-
point left-right scale, the mean for all chief executives as for all association leaders is exactly the
same, 6.29. This was a good fit with the UCD.

Our data was collected in 1981 and 1982. Straight
comparisons with population data collected in other
years need to be qualified. Nonetheless, in comparing
business' 6.29 self-location with the location attributed to each of the four major parties in 1979 by the
electorate overall, we find that business was much
closer to the 6.44 location attributed to the UCD than
it was to the other major parties: PCE, 2.50; PSOE,
3.89; AP-CD, 7.97.[20] Business was only 0.15 distant from
UCD, but a full 1.68 distant from the perceived position
of AP-CD. UCD's perceived position may have been moving
somewhat to the right between the first and second
parliamentary elections. However, it also seems clear
that AP's position at the time of the first elections
was further right than in 1979. For example, Madrid
voters in 1977 located UCD at 6.22 and AP at 8.36. A
1978 population survey located UCD at 5.96 and AP at
8.46.[21] Hence, while the distance between business
voters and the UCD may have been somewhat greater in
1977 than it would be in the elections of March 1979,
it is also highly probable that AP was an even less

acceptable option to a significant portion of the business vote given the manner in which it was perceived as even further to the right in the first democratic parliamentary elections.[22]

In looking at business and a left-right scale, it comes as no surprise that the right is more acceptable than the left. "Eight" constitutes a legitimate position for many (14% of chief executives; 12% of leaders), while "three," its equivalent left of center counterpart, is inconceivable for almost all (1% of chief executives; no leaders).[23]

Province is of interest. Given its anti-centralist sentiment and rejection of the Franquist system, we would expect Vizcaya to emerge somewhat to the left of other provinces. Indeed, for leaders of associations, Vizcaya does prove marginally more to the left than either Madrid or Barcelona. Among individual chief executives, however, Vizcaya stands to the right of Madrid (6.24 versus 6.18). Barcelona registered higher proportions of far right employers than did Vizcaya,[24] and its overall mean (6.31) is insignificantly to the right of that for Vizcaya (6.24). But Barcelona employers stand clearly to the right of those in Madrid. This reflects the fact that the regional- nationalist axis runs separately from ideological left-right positions (and is reflected in the social bases of PNV support, which includes the middle and upper classes, and in the conservative political positions of Convergència and its markedly bourgeois character). Valencia peaks at two points (six and eight) and can be classed as further to the right overall, although its location is insignificantly to the right of Barcelona (6.32 versus 6.31). However, Valencia clearly has the highest proportion of far-right employers. Twenty-seven percent of Valencia employers located themselves between eight and ten, compared to the overall average of 15 percent. As one would fully expect, leaders of associations that participated in the Sindicato are more conservative than those that did not (6.47 versus 6.05).

THE CONSTITUTION

Both chief executives and association leaders participated in the referendum on the constitution (December 1978) at levels far exceeding the population at large. Over nine-tenths of each group (91.7% of chief executives and 90.4% of leaders) voted, compared to a national participation level of about two-thirds (67.7%). The highest abstention levels in Spain were recorded in the Basque Country and Galicia. The FOESSA study characterizes Spanish abstention in general as partially attributable to ignorance, which was joined, particularly in Galicia, by socio-cultural factors, and in the Basque Country by what must partially be interpreted as a rejection of the legal framework of the state.[25] It comes as little surprise that among the four provinces for which we interpret our data, the Basque province registered the lowest participation level among chief executives, although at 82.7 percent, it was almost double the participation rate for all Vizcaya voters (43.9%). The level of participation among leaders in Vizcaya replicated that among heads of firms with a rate of 83.3 percent. Support for the constitution was strong among chief executives, at roughly the same level as the Spanish population as a whole, but it garnered less enthusiasm among leaders, although still overwhelmingly in the "yes" category. Eighty-seven percent of the chief executives voted "yes," as did 78 percent of association leaders. Just below 87 percent of all voters approved the document. The proportion of "no" voters among heads of firms (7.7%) was marginally lower than in the population overall (7.9%),[26] while that among the leaders of associations was higher (12.6%).

The constitution appears to have drawn roughly equivalent proportions of supporters in all company-size categories and in all five provinces, although we find higher percentages of opponents in Valencia and Sevilla. Not surprisingly, all the "no" voters in Valencia and Sevilla expressed approval of Franco and are on the right of the political spectrum (at "seven" or more on the left-right scale).

Excluding foreign chief executives, almost all the heads of companies with any level of foreign equity holdership participated in the referendum. All those heading companies with majority or complete foreign capital ownership (N=29) participated and all of them endorsed the constitution.

All the heads of public sector companies also participated in the referendum. A very high 27 percent of them were opposed, however. This compares to an extremely low 6.6 percent no vote among the heads of private sector companies. Public sector opponents of the constitution could have been individuals who had been well-connected politically during the Franquist regime and were more closely identified with it. All those heading public sector firms who voted against the constitution also expressed generally favorable assessments of Franco.

Among associations, size of organization appears very important in determining leader support for the Constitution. The more elite the association, the closer

hierarchically to the CEOE leadership, the more likely
one finds "yes" voters, the less likely "no" voters. The
emphasis placed by the architects of the transition on
a consensual approach negotiated at the elite levels may
have been a contributing factor to the strong support
among the most elite of the leaders for the new legal
framework.

As among heads of firms, Barcelona association
leaders emerge as more favorable to the constitution
than Madrid leaders. This is consistent with the overall
electorate in that Catalan voters approved the constitution at a rate (90.4%) exceeding the national average
(86.8%).

Table 5.7 Constitution Vote among Association Leaders

| | Budget size: (millions of pesetas) | | | Province: | | | |
	0-7	8-30	31+	M	B	VZ	Total
Yes	65.7	80.4	86.7	74.2	88.9	70.0	77.7
No	17.1	13.0	6.7	16.7	3.7	10.0	12.6
Blank	5.7	2.2	0.0	3.0	0.0	10.0	2.9
NR	11.4	4.3	6.7	6.1	7.4	10.0	6.8
	(35)	(46)	(15)	(66)	(27)	(10)	(103)

In discussing Basque chief executives and leaders
the most significant departures from what one would have
expected are the very high relative participation rates
(82.7% and 83.3%, respectively) that were almost double
the overall rate for Vizcaya province (43.9%). The then
regionally dominant Basque Nationalist Party (PNV)
supported abstention. In part, the traditionally
stronger identification of the upper bourgeoisie in the
Basque region with the Spanish state may partially
account for our higher participation rates. Small
entrepreneurs, outside this sample, would have expressed
greater sympathies with regional-nationalist aspirations.

THE 1979 PARLIAMENTARY ELECTIONS

Among business voters in the March 1979 general
elections, as in the electorate overall, the UCD increased its share of the vote slightly relative to 1977.
Support for the UCD increased by roughly 6 percent among
individual chief executives and over 4 percent among

association leaders. Fraga, now running under the Coalición Democrática rubric (AP/CD), suffered reverses among business supporters, as he did in the electorate generally.[27] His vote share among chief executives fell by over 2 percent and among the more conservative associations leaders, by over 5 percent.

Table 5.8 The 1979 Parliamentary Elections

Party	Chief Executives	Leaders	All Spanish Voters % Valid Vote
Partido Comunista de España (PCE)	.5	0.0	10.8
Partido Socialista Obrero Español (PSOE)	2.8	3.6	30.5
Unión de Centro Democrático (UCD)	65.0	57.8	35.1
Alianza Popular/Coalición Democrática (AP/CD)	17.3	22.9	6.1
Convergència i Unió (CiU)	9.5	12.1	2.7
Partido Nacionalista Vasco (PNV)	3.3	3.6	1.7
Others	1.5 (229)	0.0 (114)	13.1

Growing implicit support for AP by important sectors of the CEOE's peak leadership beginning in 1980 and accelerating over 1981 and 1982, which contributed significantly to the erosion of the UCD, and the press attention received by CEDE posturing, would lead one to assume that there existed a great reservoir of AP supporters among individuals in business. Our data show otherwise. Although levels of support for AP stand at well over twice their levels among the general population, the UCD was a pole of attraction far exceeding AP. In this respect, CEOE strategy in 1980 backfired, probably partially due to a lack of information regarding the political preferences of their lower level leaders and, more so, of their base constituents. Indubitably, large numbers of business voters must have defected to Fraga in the 1982 elections. It would appear, however, given prior voting records and the image of political leaders by business, discussed below, that AP was not widely perceived as a viable and natural alternative by business during the early years of the democratic regime.

The CEOE's distancing from the UCD in the early 1980s should not be underestimated in having contributed to the erosion in the UCD's foundation that led to its

October 1982 electoral debacle. However, it is difficult
to assess the degree of importance that the CEOE's
posturing played relative to others, particularly the
internal ideological incoherence of the UCD itself and
the gradual deterioration in the continued relevance of
its initial justification.[28]   The role of clashing
personalities also played a major role in the UCD's
collapse--as it did subsequently in the near-collapse
of the Communist Party during the mid-1980s and the
splits in the late 1980s within AP and PNV. Most
certainly, it would be entirely incorrect to assess
declining CEOE support in 1980-1981 as in any form of
collusion with "poderes fácticos" interpretations. The
very public actions and statements of the major business
and financial leaders following the failed February 1981
military coup attest to their unwavering support of the
democratic system. Nonetheless, their increasingly
public denial of support to the UCD hurt the government.
Individuals closer to the Suárez faction within the UCD
(i.e., "suaristas") never forgave the organized business
sector for its postures during the period. During a
visit to the United States in 1983, Suárez himself said
that the business sector's abandonment of the government
stemmed from the strength of the banking sector, which
had opposed his 1980 liberalization easing the entry of
foreign banks into Spain.
   There are reasons that would explain the increasingly pro-AP posture of the CEOE. The primary reason
was the evident erosion in UCD support among a spectrum
of groups. Given an unfavorable prognosis, the CEOE
naturally turned to the other party whose platform was
consistent with conservative business values. It is also
significant that AP had higher levels of support among
leaders of associations and that the UCD, while still
the dominant party among association leaders, garnered
significantly fewer votes among leaders than among
individual heads of firms. Because their own networks
of secretary-generals and director-generals of affiliated organizations tended to be somewhat more pro-
AP and slightly less pro-UCD than the base membership,
the peak CEOE leadership drew a slightly distorted
picture of business sector preferences. We should also
note the role of a handful of specific leaders in the
peak organization itself holding relatively open
sympathies for the AP option, particularly José María
Cuevas, its number two, who eventually succeeded Carlos
Ferrer Salat as CEOE president. Along these lines, there
was also marginally more support for AP among the
leaders of directly affiliated versus indirectly
affiliated associations. The leaders of the largest,
wealthiest associations, however, those at above 30

million pesetas annual budget, voted overwhelmingly for the UCD in 1979 (71%, versus none for AP). Active association involvement in the old Sindicato Nacional and greater length of professional activity in collective interest groups of business are significant in explaining AP support.[29]   Other data confirm a deterioration in Calvo Sotelo's support among leaders, which progressively eroded over the course of 1982, and an extreme decline in credibility by Suárez among individual chief executives in 1981. Hence, the CEOE may not have been that far off the mark in assessing a shift of individual business sentiment against UCD by the early 1980s. Finally, as Suárez himself contends, disapproval of government policies by the important banking sector may also have played a role in the peak's evolution, particularly in light of the banking sector's great influence within the CEOE.

CHARACTERISTICS OF PARTY VOTERS

     In treating the party preferences of business, it appears that most can be characterized into two major types with a number of additional important minority currents. The FOESSA lists four primary sources of support in analyzing the circumstances that gave rise to the UCD in the first place and a good portion of business opinion is quite adequately characterizable by the first of these four. The FOESSA contends that in 1977 there existed a wide sector of the population which, without identifying itself with the previous regime ideologically, had either given Francoism only passive support or was completely depoliticized. Given the objectives of the Franquist system, such depoliticization contributed to the regime's longevity. The issue of depoliticization or passive support is an important component in understanding the dynamics of authoritarian regimes. Depoliticization can in part be understood as a consequence of the dominance of "mentality" over ideology in such regimes. Alternatively, we might prefer to refer to the absence or weakness of ideology in authoritarian regimes. Successful depoliticization of the business sector was a part of the generalized depoliticization achieved by the Franquist regime. Linz noted that "in some [authoritarian] regimes, the depoliticization of the mass of the citizens falls into the intent of the rulers, fits with their mentality, and reflects the character of the limited pluralism supporting them." Furthermore, as applicable in the case of Spain, Linz states that "authoritarian regimes that emerge after a period of competitive democratic par-

ticipation that created an unsolvable conflict in the
society opt for depoliticization and apathy, which is
felt by many citizens as a relief from the tensions of
the previous period."[30]
     Depoliticized individuals were not attracted by
the ideological or programmatic postures of the opposing
parties.[31] Indeed, these are among the most apolitical
of Spanish voters. At points closely related to this
first group are those who might more appropriately be
classified by Amando de Miguel's label of franquismo
sociológico.[32]   These also generally maintained the
Franquist system passively, but identified more closely
with the regime. The greater clarity in their political
identification distinguishes them somewhat from the
earlier "apoliticals," although, again, we may not
necessarily be dealing with active proponents of the
previous regime. A goodly proportion of business people
might find themselves among these first two groups.
     There are two other more minor, but nevertheless
important, components of business opinion. Those
employers who are more progressive on economic issues,
whom we might identify as social democrats, emerge
relatively clearly in looking at economic preferences.
Nineteen percent each of chief executives and
association leaders expressed support for social or
mixed market approaches to the economic system.[33]
     Convergència and the Basque Nationalist Party,
representative of conservative interests at the level
of the regions or minority nationalities, accounts for
another major portion of political identification among
Spanish business. Given the nationalities issue, these
parties are spread over a wider left-right spectrum than
are the state-wide parties, although, obviously, among
Catalans and Basque parties, they represent the bourgeois options.[34] Overall, the UCD stands very slightly
to the right of Convergència, with the PNV somewhat
farther to the left. Contrary to the anti-capitalist or
anti-entrepreneurial general climate of opinion in the
rest of Spain, a "legitimated" bourgeois class in
Catalonia allows for a relatively open pro-CiU stand
regionally by a good portion of business opinion. This
allows Convergència to appear on the economic front as
the defender of Catalan business interests.
     The very high degree of religious self-
identification among business sector respondents as
practicing Catholics indicates the potential existence
of a Christian democratic component of business opinion.
Although this group in another country would have been
Christian democratic, in Spain they voted UCD, in part
due to the weak articulation of the Equipo de la
Democracia Cristiana in 1977. Paralleling findings among

the Spanish population as a whole, higher levels of
religiosity are expressed by AP than UCD business
voters.

Table 5.9 Religious Self-Identification of Chief Executives by 1979
Party Vote

	UCD	AP/CD	CiU	PNV	Total
Practicing Catholic	41.1	58.1	35.3	100.0	39.3
Irregularly practicing Catholic	33.0	22.6	17.6	0.0	28.9
Non-practicing Catholic	14.3	9.7	35.3	0.0	14.7
Indifferent	8.0	3.2	0.0	0.0	7.6
Atheist	1.8	0.0	0.0	0.0	2.4
Others	1.8	6.5	11.8	0.0	7.1
	(112)	(31)	(17)	(6)	(211)

Levels of religiosity among both chief executives
and association leaders prove lower than figures for
Spain as a whole. This may be due to the fact that the
business samples are drawn from industrialized Spain
(with the debatable and minor exception of Sevilla) and
represent a "modern" segment of society. The religious
self-identification of business, one of the main props
of the UCD, contributes to our understanding of the
former government party as having occupied an electoral
space dominated elsewhere in Europe by Christian democratic parties.

The ideological physiognomy of the UCD reminds us of European Christian-
democratic parties: the party of Catholic masses, which received the
support of employers and wide sectors of the middle and working classes.
A party which incorporates, to a certain extent, the social doctrine of
the left and defends human rights. I admit, nevertheless, that the
ideological physiognomy of the UCD is sufficiently disconcerting and, to
a certain degree, original so as to make any identification problematic.[35]

Referring to the AP before the 1982 elections,
information presented in the FOESSA study allows one to
characterize AP as liberalism tainted by Catholicism,
disallowing easy comparative classification in relation
to European counterparts occupying similar spaces on a
left-right continuum.

It is difficult to locate AP within a comparative international context and this explains the difficulty in a homologation comparable to those for the PCE, the PSOE and even the UCD at the European level. To the right of the UCD, without the Christian-democratic component, it is not comparable to the great European center-right parties such as the Italian DC, the German UCD, the Austrian OVP, the Belgian PSC-CVP, etc. Given that it is not the hegemonic party at the right of the political spectrum, it also is not comparable to the British Conservatives, which the AP's leader probably holds as a model. Nor does it occupy, given the Catholic character of its electorate, the place of the small liberal right Italian, Dutch or Belgian parties, which are distinguished by their lay and 'liberal' positions on matters such as education, divorce, etc. By its decidedly constitutional position and identification with democracy, AP is also distinguishable from the neofascist parties.[36]

Although among individual chief executives AP emerged as more "Catholic" than the UCD, the same is not the case among association leaders. Among leaders, half of UCD voters are practicing Catholics, compared to about a third (32%) of AP voters. However, for the sum of the first two categories, regularly and irregularly practicing Catholics, the overwhelmingly Catholic character of AP remains clear. Ninety percent of AP voters described themselves in these first two categories, as did 79 percent of those who voted UCD (in 1979).[37]

Table 5.10 Religious Self-Identification among Leaders by 1979 Party Vote

	UCD	AP/CD	CiU	PNV	Total
Practicing Catholic	50.0	31.6	30.0	100.0	40.0
Irregularly practicing Catholic	29.2	57.9	30.0	0.0	32.6
Non-practicing Catholic	14.6	10.5	30.0	0.0	17.9
Atheist	2.1	0.0	10.0	0.0	4.2
Others	4.2	0.0	0.0	0.0	5.3
	(48)	(19)	(10)	(3)	(95)

Hence, for the business sector, we derive very high levels of self-identification as Catholics (and practicing ones) for both UCD and AP, with slightly higher proportions overall for AP describing themselves as Catholics and fewer "secularized" individuals. However, the ideological conservatism of AP serves to better distinguish its voters from those supporting UCD, reflected, particularly, in attitudes regarding the

Franquist regime, although a number of other variables further differentiate the two groups. Religiosity operates in the expected direction in distinguishing between UCD and AP business voters, but not to the same extent as it does among the population at large. Factors reflecting conservatism on political issues and in the labor relations realm, as well as educational background, serve to better distinguish AP from UCD voters in the business sector.

While among both chief executives and association leaders, the UCD stands as a center-center-right option, AP/CD was a right option. The mean placement on the left-right scale for chief executives who voted UCD in 1979 was 6.09, compared to 7.18 for those voting AP/CD. Association leaders who voted UCD located themselves at 6.22, versus 7.06 among those voting AP/CD. Significantly, only 7 percent of chief executives and 9 percent of leaders voting UCD located themselves at eight and none further right. Among AP/CD voters, 45 percent of chief executives and 27 percent of leaders located themselves at eight, and 7 percent and 9 percent of each group, respectively, located themselves at nine. A good deal of the strong ideological conservatism of chief executives voting AP may be due to the high proportion of these who are at least part owners of the firms they head. Fifty-nine percent of the heads of firms voting AP are owners, compared to a considerably lower 44 percent among those voting UCD. Among leaders, 37 percent of AP voters are also owners of firms compared to 27 percent among UCD voters.

Opinions held regarding an assessment of Franco strongly demarcate UCD from AP voters. Views regarding the previous regime are probably the strongest single distinction between the two groups. Nearly six-tenths (58%) of the chief executives who voted UCD extended favorable comments of Franco, as did 46 percent of leaders voting likewise. Among AP voters, however, the proportions were 81 percent for chief executives and 90 percent for leaders. These figures are generally in line with those drawn for the Spanish population in 1978: 49 percent of UCD voters favorably disposed toward Franco and 89 percent similarly disposed among AP voters.[38] Even among UCD voters "inclined towards AP" (meaning that AP would be their second choice), the FOESSA findings revealed significant differences from AP voters sympathetic toward UCD (1978), wherein proportions among the former favorably disposed to Franco were significantly lower and the levels of critical remarks significantly higher than among the latter.[39]

Table 5.11 Assessment of Franco by Party Vote (1979 Elections)

Chief Executives:	UCD	AP/CD	CiU	PNV	Total
Total approval	6.2	3.2	0.0	0.0	3.8
Qualified approval	52.2	77.4	23.5	33.3	54.5
Intermediate	15.9	9.7	17.6	0.0	13.7
Qualified disapproval	20.4	9.7	23.5	33.3	19.0
Total disapproval	4.4	0.0	35.3	33.3	9.0
	(113)	(31)	(17)	(6)	(211)
Leaders:	UCD	AP/CD	CiU	PNV	Total
Total approval	0.0	21.1	0.0	0.0	4.2
Qualified approval	45.8	68.4	0.0	33.3	46.3
Intermediate	22.9	0.0	20.0	33.3	17.9
Qualified disapproval	25.0	10.5	40.0	0.0	22.1
Total disapproval	6.3	0.0	40.0	33.3	9.5
	(48)	(19)	(10)	(3)	(95)

For business voters, the point to be drawn is the strength of identification with the Franco regime in explaining party vote, closely paralleling the findings of the FOESSA study. We should note the significantly later date of our surveys, by which time Fraga was launching a new strategy and regaining assertiveness in light of the exhaustion of the governing UCD. For leaders, in particular, the later 1982 date of their survey and the further erosion of the UCD contributes to a stronger attraction in assessing the basic identification with the Franquist system, although one must also recall the generally slightly more conservative stand adopted by leaders than chief executives.

Logically, AP voters tend to be more critical of the "reforma pactada." Higher proportions expressed a belief that viable alternatives had existed. As with most other political variables, leaders of associations again stand further to the right than their constituents. The most notably conservative group are those leaders who voted AP in 1979, among whom an overwhelming majority (60%) believed that viable alternatives to the <u>reforma pactada</u> were available in 1976.

Table 5.12 Existence in 1976 of Alternatives to the Reforma Pactada by Party Vote (1979)

| | Chief Executives: | | | | 1st | Leaders: | | | | 2nd |
	UCD	AP/CD	CiU	PNV	Total	UCD	AP/CD	CiU	PNV	Total
Yes	24.1	33.3	29.4	16.7	23.7	21.7	60.0	11.1	0.0	29.1
No	75.9	66.7	70.6	83.3	76.3	78.3	40.0	88.9	100.0	70.9
	(112)	(30)	(17)	(6)	(207)	(46)	(15)	(9)	(3)	(86)

Closer scrutiny (of Table 5.12) reveals a more important distinction to be drawn between UCD and AP voters who believed that viable options other than the reforma had existed in 1976. A strong preference for undemocratic alternatives emerges for both employer and leader AP voters, particularly among the latter. Among chief executives who believed alternatives existed, 41 percent of UCD voters argued for alternatives to the left of the reforma, calling for a more profound transformation of the system (including proponents of ruptura), and an additional 22 percent subsequently clarified their position by stating that alternatives existed, but of the possibilities, the reforma pactada was the best path. Only 15 percent extended arguments against the breadth of the reforma, favoring less of a break with Francoism. In contrast, among heads of firms voting AP, the breakdown in alternatives was 10 percent for greater change, 40 percent that others existed but the reforma pactada was optimal, and 30 percent undemocratic (twice the level recorded among chief executive UCD voters who believed such options existed in 1976). In short, 10 percent of all AP voters among chief executives supported less of a break with Francoism compared to fewer than 4 percent among UCD voters. Among leaders voting UCD and AP, the demarcations are stronger. Twenty percent of the UCD voters who believed options to the reforma existed argued in favor of a more profound transformation, 60 percent in favor of the reforma, and 20 percent undemocratic (4% of all leaders who voted UCD). Among those voting AP, 11 percent thought that the reforma path was the best one possible, and fully 89 percent (53% of all the leaders who voted AP) argued for greater continuity with the Franquist regime. Thus, the strong conservatism of leaders is particularly prominent for those voting AP and emerges most clearly on attitudes regarding Franco and the reforma pactada, two issues that reference the previous authoritarian system. The particularly high identification of AP voters among leaders with the

Franquist system is attributable to the very high
levels of active participation by these same individuals with employers organizations integrated into the
Franquist organic unitary Sindicato.

Table 5.13 Integrated Past in the Sindicato for
Associations by the 1979 Party Vote of their Leaders

	UCD	AP/CD	CiU	PNV	Total
Yes	58.3	89.5	30.0	33.3	61.1
No	41.7	10.5	70.0	66.7	38.9
	(48)	(19)	(10)	(3)	(95)

A good portion of the UCD and AP voters among
associational leaders could be categorized under the
term franquismo sociológico. Not all those voting UCD
or AP and heading organizations have been more ideologically committed than the "apolitical," the more passive sector of opinion described earlier. Yet it does
appear that a good portion of them had a more than passive identification with Francoism and that such individuals were an important component of both the UCD and
AP business support, but overwhelmingly so in the case
of AP. Nearly nine-tenths of AP voters headed associations that had been integrated in the Sindicato. For
organizations whose leadership voted UCD, there is a
very strong, major proportion of associations having a
Sindicato heritage, but at a significantly lower 58
percent. Eighty-one percent of leaders voting AP expressed favorable general assessments of the Sindicato,
compared to 54 percent among UCD voters. More telling
of the significantly closer fit (including ideological
affinity) between leaders voting AP versus those voting
UCD, however, is that nearly a quarter of AP voters
(24%) believed that the old Sindicato system performed
better than the existing associations versus a minimal
5 percent holding this view among leaders voting UCD.
Furthermore, while 45 percent of the latter claimed
that the existing associations better represent the
interests of business, not a single AP supporter felt
likewise.[40] For the business sector as a whole, the
relative proportion of the franquistas sociológicos to
the apolitical component as a basis of UCD support is
higher than in the population as a whole, particularly
in the industrialized Spain with which we are dealing.
However, AP business voters are distinguishable by
their even closer affinity to the Franco regime (as
holds for the electorate overall).
    The existence of a relatively important social

democratic segment of UCD support may also be a component of the UCD vote in the business sector. While the
nexus may not be entirely clear, 21 percent of chief
executives voting UCD favored a mixed or social market
economy rather than a completely market economy. The
similar group represented only 10 percent of AP voters.
Among leaders, 19 percent of UCD voters favored a social or mixed economy compared to 5 percent among those
voting AP.

WORKING WITH THE SOCIALISTS

Our data document the overwhelming degree of support in the business sector for the legal framework established for the democratic system. One of the earliest lobby activities of the CEOE was directed toward
constitutional recognition of the free market system,
successfully achieved in article 38 of the constitution.[41] Business support for the document might possibly not have been as widespread had business lobby
efforts not achieved this open victory, particularly
after the amount of press attention the effort received. However, the victory was somewhat attenuated by
the fact that the same short article also recognized
the possibility of public planning as economic exigencies might warrant. The right for state intervention in
the general welfare and public sector initiative is
further elaborated in article 128.[42] Article 131 permits state planning to meet collective needs and
regional and sectoral harmonization, as well as for
income growth, and even for the achievement of redis-
tributive objectives.[43]
Other data from our surveys indicate that although
business voted at levels above those in the population
overall, other expressions of full political participation by business people as citizens had not yet taken
root. The types of political activities and level of
contacts that normally characterize relationships between constituents and their elected representatives in
other pluralist societies had not yet developed in
Spain by the early 1980s. For example, only 23 percent
of chief executives had on some occasion contacted a
senator or deputy regarding a specific problem in their
own company. The Spanish parliamentary system, as it
has evolved, does not lend itself easily to the
development of strong constituent-representative contacts. The lack of single-member constituencies may be
primarily responsible. A large proportion of chief
executives and association leaders reside in large
cities that have several deputies and lack single-

member district lines. Non-preferential voting lists
further weaken the prominence of individual candidates
to parliament.[44] The mechanics of the parliament and
the parties have further weakened the role of individual elected deputies. Unlike elsewhere in Europe,
where one finds stronger, livelier parties, Spanish
parties suffer from low levels of affiliation and
active militancy.[45] Strong party control diminishes the
maneuverability available to legislators. Indeed, parliamentary presentations and rebuttals are printed
prior to delivery. Finally, in the early years of
democracy, business-legislator contacts that developed
in individual cases could very likely have been eliminated by the great sea changes produced in general
elections. The UCD, along with most of its deputies,
disappeared after the October 1982 elections. Yet, over
this period there was even a relatively high turnover
among the ranks of PSOE parliamentarians.

In theory, the UCD governments (1977-1982) were
closer ideologically to the business community than the
Socialists. In practice, the UCD itself was not an
ideologically defined party and PSOE government policies have in most instances proven markedly more pro-
business than were the Centrists. Furthermore, the
subsequent duration and extent of PSOE electoral domination of Spanish politics at national, regional and
local levels means that there has probably been some
increase in "personnel" stability among both elected
leaders and public administration technocrats. As such,
we might expect that the frequency and ease of busi-
ness-ministerial (and other official) contacts may have
increased in the late 1980s.

The Linz and de Miguel work of the early 1960s
does not distinguish between ministerial contacts and
those with the old Franquist parliamentarians, the
procuradores. However, it does provide a breakdown in
the frequency of direct contacts between chief executives and a series of individuals in the various interest bodies that then existed (e.g., chambers of commerce, Sindicato Nacional) and in banks, as well as for
the entirety of official contacts. They found that 25
percent of chief executives contacted individuals holding official positions with a relative degree of frequency (either "daily," 3%; "frequently," 10%; or
"sometimes," 12%).[46] The 23 percent we found in 1981
was not much changed.

Yet despite the relatively low proportion of chief
executives who had contacted their representatives, a
majority (53%) felt they could contact an elected representative of a party on the Left if their company
faced economic difficulties.[47] In addition to this sub-

stantial willingness on the part of chief executives to deal with political leaders of the left if the need arose, investigation discloses substantial majorities of both company executives and leaders of associations not fearful about the impact of a then-future, potential monocolor (single party, homogenous) Socialist government. Among chief executives, only roughly a third (35%) believed that an absolute majority PSOE victory would actually lead to extensive socialization of the country (including important nationalizations). This proportion dropped to under a quarter of association leaders by the following year (23%). The later survey date (first half of 1982), and with it a longer stretch of moderation and movement toward the center by the PSOE, undoubtedly contributed to a lessening of fears about an increasingly likely Socialist victory. The lower level of "fear" expressed a year later by association leaders is particularly significant given extensive indications elsewhere that leaders were more conservative than their constituents.

Those in the second and third rows of Table 5.14 expected the PSOE either to adopt a line similar to that of the German social democratic party (SPD) or act similarly to the UCD, and did not fear the economic consequences of an absolute PSOE parliamentary majority. Recall also that "SPD" in 1981 brought to mind the moderate and well-regarded Helmut Schmidt for most respondents. Over half the chief executives (53%) are among those who did not feel that a PSOE victory would lead to significant changes in the economic system. Furthermore, "other responses" include a certain proportion who were not worried about a possible future PSOE electoral victory.[48]

By province, 60 percent of those in Vizcaya did not fear a PSOE victory. Significantly greater concern (over 10% greater) of the PSOE was expressed in both Madrid and Barcelona than in Vizcaya. The PSOE has played a moderate role in Euskadi, a zone that certainly has experienced truly extremist political behavior. In interpreting Basque data, however, the perceived moderation of the PSOE should also be balanced with its generally more centralist image compared to the UCD and to the not insignificant numbers of Basque Nationalist sympathizers among heads of firms in the province. In looking at Basque chief executives who did not fear a monocolor PSOE Government, 61 percent of voters of state-wide parties in the 1979 parliamentary elections (either UCD or AP) and only 17 percent voted for Basque parties (either the moderate Basque Nationalists, the PNV, or the abertzale Herri Batasuna, HB). In contrast, among those who believed that the PSOE

would introduce strongly socialist measures, including
important nationalizations, 38 percent were PNV voters
and an additional 25 percent either cast spoiled
ballots or abstained, which in Euskadi must partially
be attributed to weak identification with the Spanish
state. Only 13 percent of the "fearful" were UCD
voters. Eight percent of those voters of state-wide
parties feared the consequences of a PSOE victory,
versus 43 percent among voters of Basque parties.
Therefore, we can assume that the Socialists' centralist image, particularly when compared to the UCD's
"regionalization" of Spain, did contribute to concern
among some Basque business.

Table 5.14 Expected Impact of a Future "Monocolor" PSOE
Government by Chief Executives

	R	I	L	M	B	VZ	VA	S	Total
Relatively advanced socialism, including nationalizations	35.3	39.3	30.3	37.5	37.3	26.7	34.6	16.7	34.9
Social democratic à la German SPD	54.1	42.9	48.3	48.9	45.1	56.7	50.0	50.0	48.4
Would be similar to UCD Government	4.7	7.1	2.2	2.3	3.9	3.3	11.5	16.7	4.7
Other/DK/NR	5.9	10.7	19.1	11.4	13.7	13.3	3.8	16.7	12.0
	(85)	(84)	(89)	(88)	(102)	(30)	(26)	(12)	(258)

Among Vizcaya chief executives, in general, those
who identified more strongly with the Spanish state did
not fear a PSOE victory, while those with a weaker
Spanish identification faced the same prospect with
greater trepidation. However, the question focused on
potential economic changes resulting from a PSOE victory and did not refer to changes in the political climate. Had the question focused on political rather than
economic changes, the "Basque parties voters-state parties voters" distinction might have been even more pronounced, although it performed very strongly even in
dealing solely with the economic realm. But clearly the
center-periphery axis runs separately from the left-
right continuum in the minority nationalities regions.
    Owners were somewhat more concerned about the
potential impact of Spanish Socialism than were managers. Roughly 40 percent versus 30 percent expected extensive nationalizations. Public sector employers were
particularly open-minded regarding a future Socialist

government. Fully 90 percent of these expected the PSOE to perform in a social democratic manner or similarly to the UCD Government.

While the top CEOE leadership did not campaign directly against the UCD Government, it would not be incorrect to say--as stated before--that their widely perceived dissatisfaction with the Centrist government and, in particular, with Adolfo Suárez, contributed to the generalized deterioration in UCD support over the course of 1980 and to the time of Suárez's resignation in February 1981. The peak's leadership subsequently opted to favor Manuel Fraga and his more conservative alternative in the face of the continued erosion of the UCD under Leopoldo Calvo Sotelo, the party's growing internal crisis, and an evidently increasing inability to govern effectively. The setting of the initial agenda can be crucial toward satisfaction of the interests of given sectors of society following the establishment of a new democratic system. Such a period will be one of tremendous demands, as various groups compete for a piece of the pie. It appears that from the outset of the transition, segments of the business community were dissatisfied over the perceived low priority accorded to economic policies compared to the extensive political maneuvering taking place, that is, the "obsessional priority" accorded by the Suárez Government, as described by Carr and Fusi. The 1976-1977 period was marked by extremely high inflation and a massive wave of strikes. Suárez, as such, failed to attract strong potential business support and, indeed, was largely discredited among large segments of business opinion, as we will note below.[9] During a series of pilot interviews conducted by the author in the autumn of 1978, one chief executive described Suárez's economic policies as "una política de goteo," which meant that policies were adopted "drop by drop," that is, piecemeal, to patch-up the small, most critical aspects of given problems, rather than developing comprehensive strategies to confront them head-on. The opening of Spain to foreign banks, allowing them to participate in a full range of banking services, a policy introduced by Suárez in 1980, served to antagonize the very important banking industry. (Hence their eternal condemnation into the ranks of the "poderes fácticos.") The financial industry, obviously, plays a critical role in the economy and also is a (if not "the") primary economic support of the CEOE through the participation of its association, the AEB (Asociación Española de la Banca), as a financial contributor to practically all the territorial affiliates of the peak, as well as to the CEOE directly.

It was during the period of the continued evident erosion of the UCD government, in part attributable to its internal struggles, and the ineffectiveness of the Calvo Sotelo government (the first half of 1982), that the survey of associations was undertaken. While the ineffectiveness of the political center certainly was not pushing business to the left, it is possible that the PSOE, specifically, as well as AP, appeared as an increasingly coherent political alternative that might at least represent effective government.

Table 5.15 Expected Impact of a Future "Monocolor" PSOE Government by Association Leaders

	Province:			Size of budget: (millions pesetas)			
	M	B	VZ	0-7	8-30	31+	Total
Relatively advanced socialism, including nationalizations	20.5	17.2	46.2	37.5	14.0	5.9	22.6
Social democratic à la German SPD	39.7	51.7	23.1	27.5	52.0	52.9	40.9
Would be similar to UCD Government	12.3	13.8	15.4	20.0	10.0	5.9	13.0
Other/DK	27.4	17.2	15.4	15.0	24.0	35.3	23.5
	(73)	(29)	(13)	(40)	(50)	(17)	(115)

The 1982 date of the association survey contributed to diminished fears of PSOE government—particularly evident, as stated before, in that less fear was shown by a segment of business opinion that was unquestionably more conservative than the individual chief executives. The increasing signals of PSOE strength and its ever more vocal moderation might account for the significantly fewer respondents expecting that an absolute PSOE parliamentary majority would lead to extensive nationalizations. Hence, while over a third of chief executives (35%) expected the implantation of a truly socialist program, under a quarter (23%) of the more conservative leaders agreed. On the other hand, although fear of a strong socialist program was markedly lower among leaders, the difference in totals on comparing these to chief executives is made up by the significantly higher proportions of leaders in the "other or don't know" category. Fifty-three percent of chief executives believed the PSOE would act either along social democratic lines or would simply pursue policies similar to those of the Centrists. These opinions represented 54 percent of leaders.

For the bulk of association interviews (92%) conducted between February and June of 1982 (N=106), we find a progressive steady rise in the proportions of leaders responding with the social democratic or Centrist arguments, with the single exception of April, when only four interviews were conducted.[50] Forty-seven percent of those interviewed in February responded with moderate expectations, increasing consistently, with the April exception, to 60 percent by June. No pattern whatsoever emerged among chief executives over the ten-month duration of their 1981 survey.

Further indication of a mirror-image erosion of support affecting the UCD among leaders of associations is evidenced by looking at assessments of Calvo Sotelo over the same period, February through June of 1982. Among leaders, 60 percent drew favorable assessments of Calvo Sotelo in February and not a single individual expressed disapproval. By June, after consistent changes over the intervening period, equal proportions of leaders, 27 percent, drew unfavorable as favorable assessments of the prime minister. In summary, over of the course of 1982, our association survey documents the decline in support for the UCD government along with increasing acceptance that a PSOE government did not represent a threat to the economic system.

THE IMAGE OF POLITICAL LEADERS

In assessing the image of the PSOE, it is also interesting to view the very favorable image of Felipe González among chief executives, particularly when compared to Adolfo Suárez or Manuel Fraga. Among five political figures, only Calvo Sotelo fares better than Felipe González. Recall the timing of the chief executives survey. Given the erosion in the approval rating for Calvo Sotelo among the more conservative association leaders as 1982 progressed, we can assume he would similarly not have managed to garner a more favorable overall response among chief executives than González one year later. In 1981 many chief executives were willing to give Calvo Sotelo the benefit of the doubt, given his short tenure in office. He arrived at the prime minister's office with solid credentials and following the attempted military coup, highlighting the need to support the democratic head of government.[51] Unfortunately, an image of mediocrity and ineffectiveness subsequently came to dominate. The fact that in 1981, following the abortive coup, business saw the

need to express support for the democratically chosen
head of government, but apparently withdrew its support
from the governing UCD one year later, can be interpreted as business support for the democratic system,
while increasingly questioning the efficacy specifically of the party in power.

Table 5.16 Views Regarding the Conduct of Calvo Sotelo
over 1976-1981/2

	Chief Executives	Leaders
Total approval	24.9	3.5
Qualified approval	51.3	40.4
Intermediate	10.9	40.4
Qualified disapproval	1.6	12.3
Total disapproval	1.2	1.8
Don't know	5.8	0.0
No response	4.3	1.8
	(257)	(114)

In 1981, high proportions of chief executives in
the "don't know" row reflects the short period of Calvo
Sotelo's tenure in office at the time of the survey.
Many wished to wait before extending judgments. As
noted, substantial differences emerged in the image of
Calvo Sotelo by the time of the association survey the
following year. We have already confirmed the manner in
which support for Calvo Sotelo eroded among leaders
over the first half of 1982.

Among political figures, amazingly, only Carrillo
was as discredited among chief executives as Suárez.
González drew 30 percent more favorable assessments
than did Fraga. Assessments of Fraga among chief executives must have improved over the course of 1982 due to
the deterioration of the UCD and the CEOE's implicit
approval of AP.[52] Nevertheless, it is unlikely that it
would greatly have decreased Fraga's image gap relative
to the very favorable image then enjoyed by González.

González does well in all the provinces and all
company sizes. Disaggregating for both these characteristics simultaneously, only among large Valencia
companies do fewer than half the respondents (43%) extend favorable assessments and do unfavorable assess-

ments rise above a quarter (29%). In Vizcaya, favorable assessments increase consistently by company size from 58 percent to 78 percent.

Table 5.17 Chief Executive Views Regarding the Conduct of Various Political Leaders over the 1976-1981 Period

	Carrillo	González	Suárez	Calvo Sotelo	Fraga
Total approval	1.9	8.2	1.9	24.9	3.1
Qualified approval	23.4	59.5	30.0	51.3	34.2
Intermediate	16.3	14.0	22.9	10.9	26.1
Qualified disapproval	16.0	9.0	27.3	1.6	25.7
Total disapproval	36.2	3.1	12.5	1.2	5.1
Don't know	2.3	1.9	1.2	5.8	1.6
No response	3.9	4.3	4.3	4.3	4.3 (257)

Fraga does best among regular companies in Valencia, with 58 percent favorable and 17 percent unfavorable. However, González did considerably better among the same group (75% favorable, zero unfavorable). Large Valencia firms registered the same proportions of approvals and disapprovals for Fraga as they had for González (43% approvals; 29% disapprovals). Among the other three major provinces (Madrid, Barcelona, and Vizcaya), Fraga fares best among large Madrid companies (47% favorable) and poorest among small Vizcaya companies (17%), reflecting Basque regional-nationalist rejection of the Spanish centralist right.

The extent in the lack of support among business for Suárez and the significant success enjoyed by González relative to Fraga are further demonstrated in reviewing a disaggregation of chief executive views by their 1979 voting record. Even among UCD voters, one finds as many individuals drawing unfavorable as favorable assessments of Suárez,[53] and, amazingly, González does twice as well as Suárez. Only among the PNV voters does Suárez emerge reasonably well (50% approval). Suárez efforts towards the development of the estado de las autonomías accounts for the relatively favorable assessment drawn by PNV voters.[54] In comparing González and Fraga, González performs slightly better even among AP supporters in that 58 percent of these commented favorably on González compared to 55 percent for Fraga.

Table 5.18 Chief Executive Views Regarding the Conduct of Various
Political Leaders over 1976-1981 by 1979 Party Vote

| | G=González; S=Suárez; F=Fraga | | | | | | | | |
| | PSOE voters: | | | UCD voters: | | | AP/CD voters: | | |
	G	S	F	G	S	F	G	S	F
Approvals	80.0	20.0	20.0	75.7	37.4	33.9	58.1	16.1	54.8
Intermediate	0.0	20.0	40.0	8.7	23.5	27.8	25.8	9.7	32.3
Disapprovals	20.0	60.0	40.0	13.0	37.4	35.7	16.1	74.2	12.9
		(5)			(115)			(31)	

| | CiU voters: | | | PNV voters: | | |
	G	S	F	G	S	F
Approvals	70.6	17.6	23.5	83.3	50.0	16.7
Intermediate	11.8	29.4	17.6	16.7	33.3	33.3
Disapprovals	11.8	41.2	52.9	0.0	16.7	50.0
		(17)			(6)	

CONCLUSIONS

Business represents a conservative sector of Spanish society that overwhelmingly endorsed the break with Francoism. Despite strong and vocal criticism of the Suárez government by important segments of business opinion and by certain business leaders, partially attributable to a perceived failure of the government to deal adequately with economic problems, the UCD maintained a very strong electoral position among business people at least until the 1979 elections. Business was also still willing to extend Calvo Sotelo a reasonable amount of flexibility in 1981 and into early 1982.

By and large, most of business was a prime example, in great measure, of a source of passive, non-ideological support for the Franco system. The strong position of the UCD as compared with the AP among business must be partially attributed precisely to the fact that support for the previous system was apolitical. Although the degrees of approbatory assessments extended regarding Franco are very high throughout the business sector, high levels of absolute approval are found only among AP supporters or individuals more closely implicated in the regime, such as among association leaders who had been active in the Sindicato. Along party lines, only among AP business voters was there overwhelming approval of Franco without any significant level of criticism. In summary, it appears that the old regime managed to achieve a depoliticization of this sector of society, as it did among a number of others--a mechanism exploited in guaranteeing its amazingly long duration.

In addition to voting almost exclusively for pro-system parties and, specifically, for center-right moderate options, business was willing to deal with the left. A year to two years before coming to power, González and the PSOE had achieved a significant level of confidence and good will. Business was not unduly concerned about the implications of a possible PSOE assumption of government.

On the debit side, there still existed an important minority of chief executives who might turn to anti-system measures of transforming the political order were they to feel their interests threatened. Furthermore, whereas there was a considerable openness to deal with a wide range of political leaders and institutions, there also appeared relatively scant confidence that desired objectives could be achieved.

While important segments of business sentiment must certainly have shifted toward AP with the pending demise of the UCD, one must not forget the more moderate overall position of the business sector compared to existing perceptions of Fraga's party. There was clearly an important segment of business opinion that would not support AP--at least not as configured during the early and mid-1980s. The situation in the 1990s would be considerably different.

In summary, conservatism and moderation typified business political positions during the transition and the early constitutional periods. Business supported the consolidation of the new system and has subsequently been reaping the economic and political rewards therefrom.

NOTES

1. Richard Gunther, Giacomo Sani, and Goldie Shabad, Spain After Franco: The Making of a Competitive Party System (Berkeley: University of California Press, 1986), 7.

2. On Argentina, see Guillermo A. O'Donnell, Modernization and Bureaucratic Authoritarianism (Berkeley: Institute of International Studies, University of California, 1973).

3. Robert Dahl, Polyarchy (New Haven: Yale University Press, 1971), 206-207.

4. Juan J. Linz, <u>Crisis, Breakdown, and Reequilibration</u>, vol. I of Juan J. Linz and Alfred Stepan, eds., <u>The Breakdown of Democratic Regimes</u> (Baltimore: The Johns Hopkins University Press, 1978), 20.

5. The complexion of the Franquist elite was not static. Franco juggled various elements in the foundation of his system to reflect the differing needs of changing times. Individuals with business and banking connections increasingly rose to important positions in the government and bureaucracy as the regime endured. By the 1970s, the Council of Ministers overwhelmingly consisted of such individuals. Richard Gunther, <u>Public Policy in a No-Party State</u> (Berkeley: University of California Press, 1980), 7-10. On the privileged position of business under the authoritarian regime, see also Manuel Román, <u>The Limits of Economic Growth in Spain</u> (New York: Praeger, 1971), 93-94; and Thomas D. Lancaster, "Regime Change and Public Policy: The Political and Macroeconomic Decision-Making of Spanish Energy Policy," Ph.D. diss., Washington University, St. Louis, 6-8 and 77-86.

6. Analyzing the factors that led to the establishment of democracy in Greece, Portugal, and Spain, Poulantzas stressed the critical importance of the domestic bourgeoisie in the overthrow of dictatorship. Distanced from foreign capital relative to the position of the "comprador bourgeoisie," although still ultimately dependent on it, the domestic bourgeoisie aligns itself with the interests of the popular and working classes in bringing about democratization. Poulantzas argues that this does not imply any advancement towards "national independence" [from the international capitalist economic order], but rather merely a "rearrangement of the relationship between the domestic bourgeoisie, foreign capital and the comprador bourgeoisie, in favor of the domestic bourgeoisie, but still in the longer term under the renegotiated hegemony of the comprador bourgeoisie."
The domestic bourgeoisie is more favorable to political change given its desire to acquire political credit and more closely approximate economic reality by allowing valid worker interlocutors for purposes of bargaining. The domestic bourgeoisie is interested in an endogenous industrialization that, due to previous structural deficiencies, requires effective organizations for the representation of worker interests. Poulantzas argues that this somewhat more independent entrepreneurial sector hopes to gain the support of the popular masses and the working class in their own strug-

gle against a "comprador-agrarian" bloc. While the out-come will temporarily strengthen the position of the domestic bourgeoisie, Poulantzas argues in favor of this alliance "with the devil" to further the process of de-mocratization, given the increasingly evident failure of a telescoped transformation of the southern European systems from dictatorship to systems at once democratic, socialist, and independent.

The growing interdependence within the developed world and the greater distribution of economic wealth internationally makes strict distinctions between do-mestic versus comprador bourgeoisies increasingly anachronistic and irrelevant. When capitalists in impor-tant countries historically identifiable as major capi-tal recipients, such as Spain or Canada, are themselves important sources of capital in Third World countries, a good deal of revisiting is necessary adequately to revise work by authors such as Poulantzas. Nevertheless, this work illustrates the essential role in the process of democratization attributed to capital controllers in an analysis very different from our own. Nicos Poulantzas, _The Crisis of the Dictatorships_ (London: Humanities Press, 1976), 41-67.

7. Gunther, Sani, and Shabad, _Spain after Franco_, 2.

8. Linz, _Crisis, Breakdown, and Reequilibration_, 21.

9. Raymond Carr and Juan Pablo Fusi Aizpurua, _Spain: Dictatorship to Democracy_ (London: George Allen & Unwin, 1979), 219-220.

10. Even under the king's first government in early 1976, headed by Carlos Arias Navarro, business was already distressed about the lack of policies to deal with what was perceived as a massive economic crisis. Carr and Fusi, _Spain: Dictatorship_, 210-211.

11. Cited in Gunther, Sani, and Shabad, _Spain af-ter Franco_, 101.

12. A related issue for workers was simultaneous achievement of social justice and political democracy. A worker might slight Suárez for not having effectuated a more equitable distribution of wealth with the argu-ment that a unique historical moment was at hand. At-tempts to have met the divergent economic demands of workers and business would have lessened the probability of successful democratic consolidation.

13. Carr and Fusi, Spain: Dictatorship, 209.

14. Carr and Fusi, Spain: Dictatorship, 214.

15. On the Movimiento, see Juan J. Linz, "From Falange to Movimiento-Organización: The Spanish Single Party and the Franco Regime 1936-1968," in S. Huntington and C. Moore, eds., Authoritarian Politics in Modern Societies: The Dynamics of Established One Party Systems (New York: Basic Books, 1970).

16. Donald Share, "Two Transitions: Democratization and the Evolution of the Spanish Socialist Left," paper presented at the American Political Science Association annual meeting, Chicago, September 1983. On the manner in which Suárez negotiated with the opposition parties, see Donald Share, The Making of Spanish Democracy (New York: Praeger, 1986). "Reforma pactada/ruptura pactada" was the manner many on the left referred to the transition. Essentially, this served to justify in their own minds supporting a process that was in fact much more "reforma" than the "ruptura" they had originally sought.

17. Robert M. Fishman, "Working Class Organization and Political Change: The Labor Movement and the Transition to Democracy in Spain" Ph.d. diss., Yale University, 1985, 356.

18. On the process of Cortes approval, see Share, The Making of Spanish Democracy, 107-115.

19. Suárez's reform of the Franquist system was entirely legal--and, therefore, legitimate--under the legal/political framework of the Franquist structures. On the legal system of the Franquist regime, including the so-called "leyes fundamentales" or "leyes constitucionales," and the operations of the referendum law, see José Zafra Valverde, Régimen político de España (Pamplona: Ediciones Universidad de Navarra, 1973).

20. Gunther, Sani, and Shabad, Spain After Franco, 263.

21. Juan J. Linz, Manuel Gómez-Reino y Carnota, Francisco Andrés Orizo, and Darío Vila Carro, Informe sociológico sobre el cambio político en España 1975-1981 (Madrid: Fundación FOESSA, 1981), 363-367. Referred to henceforth as the "FOESSA" study.

22.   The self-location of UCD and AP/CD voters themselves in 1979 was in both instances to the left of their parties' location by the total electorate: UCD voters, 5.90; AP/CD voters, 7.09. Gunther, Sani, and Shabad, Spain after Franco, 273. In this regard, AP could have been a bit more attractive to business voters than the comparison drawn in the text.

23.   Ten percent of individual chief executives and 14 percent of leaders either refused to answer, argued they were apolitical, or otherwise rejected the scale. This is consistent with the 14 percent in the same category among a general survey of the 1979 electorate cited by Gunther, Sani, and Shabad, Spain after Franco, 275.

24.   16.7 percent of Barcelona chief executives chose from eight to ten, versus 9.3 percent among those in Vizcaya.

25.   FOESSA, 311.

26.   FOESSA, 312.

27.   Fraga's parliamentary group went from sixteen seats to nine.

28.   On the UCD, see Carlos Huneeus, La Unión de Centro Democrático y la transición a la democracia en España (Madrid: Centro de Investigaciones Sociológicas, 1985), and Antonio Navalón and Francisco Guerrero, Objectivo Adolfo Suárez (Madrid: Espasa Calpe, 1987).

29.   A quarter of the leaders of associations with a Sindicato past voted AP/CD in 1979, compared to a minimal 4 percent among those without a Sindicato heritage. 10 percent of leaders with six or fewer years of professional activity voted AP/CD, compared to 19 percent for those with seven to twenty years, and a quarter of those with more than twenty years of activity in collective interest groups.

30.   Juan J. Linz, "Totalitarian and Authoritarian Regimes," in Fred I. Greenstein and Nelson W. Polsby, eds., Handbook of Political Science, vol. 3 (Reading, Mass.: Addison-Wesley, 1975), 264-271.

31.   FOESSA, 463.

32.   FOESSA, 457.

33. Seventy-seven percent of chief executives and 80 percent of leaders espoused support for the free market system.

34. See Gunther, Sani, and Shabad, <u>Spain after Franco,</u> 372-381.

35. Luis García San Miguel, "Las ideologías políticas en la España actual," <u>Sistema</u> 40 (January 1981): 65.

36. FOESSA, 461.

37. Those categorized as "practicing Catholics" include 2 percent of chief executives and 3.5 percent of leaders who chose to describe themselves as "very good Catholics," a separate closed-ended option. The FOESSA study, using the same question, was able to find a significantly higher selection of this option among AP supporters than among UCD and, in all probability, accurately describes such prideful religious declarations as reflective not so much of a Christian attitude as of a "social self-identification congruent with an ideological and political position, that of the national Catholicism crusade of the forties." FOESSA, 499.
Given the strong position of the UCD relative to other parties for the business sector, the relatively small numbers of individuals in the samples, the very low incidence of "very good Catholics," and the fact that these were spread over all the parties, nothing interesting could be said about them and any analysis would not have been significant. As such, it appeared logical simply to combine these with practicing Catholics.

38. The FOESSA attributes the significant shifts between 1978 and 1979 to a disenchantment with the difficulties of democracy among UCD voters leading these to be less critical of the past. However, the more important change resulted from the shift in party image by AP to CD. Hence, some of those on the right-wing of the party may have switched to extreme right options (which markedly increased their vote in 1979 relative to 1977) and some may simply have opted to abstain. Coalición Democrática (CD) represented a change in image by AP that accompanied the incorporation of an opposition figure (José María de Areilza) into its ranks and attempts by the AP to distance itself from linkages to its Franquist past, which its strategists perceived as detrimental. FOESSA, 473. On the reasons for the

failure of AP strategists in their attempt to broaden the group's image, see Gunther, Sani, and Shabad, Spain after Franco, 170-177, 266-267, and 290-292.

Findings for the Spanish population in 1978 and 1979:

Evaluation of Franco:	1978		1979	
	UCD	AP	UCD	AP/CD
Total approval	15	43	18	22
Qualified approval	34	46	36	48
Intermediate	19	5	16	11
Qualified disapproval	20	4	17	14
Total disapproval	8	0	5	2
Don't know/no response	4	2	8	3
	(1573)	(381)	(1486)	(162)

39. Among UCD voters inclined towards AP one found 77 percent favorable and 8 percent unfavorable on Franco, versus 91 percent and 3 percent, respectively, among AP voters inclined toward UCD. Twenty-five percent of the UCD people were described as inclined toward AP, and 62 percent of AP voters would similarly have chosen UCD as a "second-best." FOESSA, 473.

40. Comparisons by association leaders of the Sindicato and current associations:

	UCD	AP/CD	CiU	PNV	Total
Associations better	45.2	0.0	66.7	66.7	36.9
Both are the same	23.8	23.5	0.0	33.3	21.4
Sindicato better	4.8	23.5	11.1	0.0	9.5
Not comparable	26.2	52.9	22.2	0.0	32.1
	(42)	(17)	(9)	(3)	(84)

41. On CEOE efforts on this issue, see Manuel Ludevid, Los protagonistas en las relaciones laborales en la España contemporánea: las organizaciones empresariales (Barcelona: ESADE), 13-21.

42. Article 128 reproduces article 44 of the Republican Constitution of 1931. Massimo Morisi, "Aspectos esenciales de la relación entre estado y economía en una Constitución de la crisis," in Alberto Predieri and Eduardo García de Enterría, eds., La Constitución española de 1978 (Madrid: Editorial Civitas, 1981), 382.

43. Article 131 is also of interest from a neo-corporatist perspective given its provision for the creation of economic and social councils through which labor unions and business associations would contribute to the planning process. This constitutional mechanism copies similar provisions in the French Constitution of 1958 and the Portuguese Constitution of 1976. Morisi,

"Aspectos esenciales," 394. While an economic and social council has never been created, the Socialists resurrected discussion of such a possibility in 1984 and the topic resurfaces periodically.

In summary, Morisi emphasizes the tension that exists between constitutional planning provisions, which are well defined, and the recognition of a market economy. He argues that public sector initiative is obliged to respect the rules framing a market economy. Morisi, "Aspectos esenciales," 392. In this regard, business won more than it gave up.

44.   Spain uses the D'Hondt electoral system, under which seats are allocated on the basis of lists of candidates and the use of the "highest average." When a seat is allocated to a given party, it is awarded to the person next on the party's list. Along with the existence of many small districts, the D'Hondt system also serves to penalize all but the largest party or the two largest parties in each district. On the electoral law, see Gunther, Sani, and Shabad, Spain after Franco, 43-53, and Mario Caciagli, Elecciones y partidos en la transición española (Madrid: Centro de Investigaciones Sociológicas, 1986), 78-121.

45.   This is also the case for many voluntary institutions in Spain, including the labor unions and employers associations.

46.   Linz and de Miguel, Los empresarios ante el poder público, 156-157.

47.   The exact wording of the question was:

In other countries, when a problem is faced by an economic sector, employers turn not only to those deputies or parties most favorable to business, but also attempt to obtain the cooperation of deputies or parties representing workers. Do you believe that you could address a deputy of such parties with a problem affecting your firm or sector?

Admittedly, the phrasing of the question encouraged open-minded responses by chief executives.

48.   A survey conducted in early 1982 by Mercado, a business magazine, and Emopública on the issue of imminent Socialist party government concluded that there was little fear among business of a PSOE victory. Of the 367 top managers interviewed, 24.5 percent expected favorable economic consequences from a PSOE triumph; 24.8 percent were indifferent; and 45 percent expected unfavorable consequences. However, only 28.4 percent

expected an unfavorable impact in their own companies
(24.3% unfavorable; 4.1% very unfavorable). Rafael Rubio
and Norberto Gallego, "¿Quién le teme?" and "En 1983,
Felipe González en la Moncloa," Mercado 3, 38 (5 March
1982): 39-49.

49.   While his historical treatment is weak and
his emphasis on undemocratic forces among entrepreneurs
overstated, the political analysis by Aguilar Solé of
the relationship between the CEOE and the UCD makes a
number of valid points. The earliest period of UCD
government, 1977 and early 1978, was marked by a great
deal of anti-UCD rhetoric by business leaders. Among
them, both José Antonio Segurado of CEIM and Alfredo
Molinas of Fomento criticized the UCD as a "government
of the right" effecting "policies of the left," opinions
that were relatively diffused among business.
      Aguilar divides the CEOE-UCD relationship into
three phases. The first phase of anti-UCD rhetoric was
followed by a period of cooperation over most of 1978
and 1979, marked particularly by the appointment of
Rodríguez Sahagún, a CEOE vice-president and former
president of CEPYME, as minister of industry and energy
in February 1978 and the dismissal of Enrique Fuentes
Quintana and his replacement by Joaquín Abril Matorell
as economic vice-president of the government. The dismal
performance of AP in the 1979 general elections
reinforced cooperation with the UCD given Fraga's
evident electoral inviability. The final stage began in
1980 as the fabric of the UCD began to unravel, a
development supported by important segments of the CEOE
and of business opinion. Salvador Aguilar Solé,
"L'empresariat i les seves organitzacions" (Paper
delivered at the conference of the Associació Catalana
de Sociología, Barcelona, June 1983), 18-21.

50.   Due to an interruption in interviews corresponding to the Semana Santa and Easter Week period.

51.   This same thesis of CEOE support for Calvo
Sotelo is extended by Carlos Huneeus. Calvo Sotelo had
been involved in business for many years and had close
family ties to the business elite. Huneeus also pointed
out that in 1981 Agustín Rodríguez Sahagún, a former
CEPYME vice-president, was serving as UCD president.
Huneeus, La Unión, 368-369. However, Rodríguez Sahagún
was also a suarista.

52.   The early 1982 Mercado-Emopública survey
found that only 25.6 percent of top managers expressed
a favorable assessment of UCD leaders, compared to

favorable assessments by 43.3 percent for PSOE leaders
and 53.1 percent for AP leaders. Rubio and Gallego,
"¿Quién le teme?", 46.

53. Not surprisingly, among Spanish voters overall, the DATA 1982 post-election survey found that
voters of Suárez's CDS party (Centro Democrático y
Social) were more critical of business than were those
who voted in 1982 for the by-then truncated UCD. On the
zero-to-ten confidence scale (extreme hostility to great
attraction), UCD voters averaged a 5.32 confidence level
in business compared to 4.91 among CDS voters (AP
voters, 6.36; PSOE, 3.64; and PCE, 2.09).

54. Suárez also did relatively well among the
foreign chief executives with a similar 50 percent
approval rating. Did they have a better appreciation for
what Suárez had achieved for Spain?

6

Business and Labor

Our study of the chief executive officers of Spanish firms alternatively refers to the individuals in question as heads of firms, employers, or chief executives, or, less frequently, as controllers of capital. Each term reflects a different facet of the same person. This chapter concentrates on chief executives in their role as employers, in their relationship to labor.

For business, the changes in labor relations that accompanied the political transition from authoritarianism were one of the most notable economic ramifications of democracy, particularly the legalization of labor unions and the recognition of the right to strike. No doubt, a number of employers would have preferred not to have had to deal with freely organized unions empowered with the valuable strike weapon. However, the more common employer complaint focused more narrowly: Workers had been freed from Franquist restrictions against strike action, yet paternalistic aspects of Franquist labor legislation prohibiting free dismissal continued to be enforced. Nevertheless, despite strong legal restrictions and continued repression, strike levels in Spain by the 1960s were equivalent to those found elsewhere in Europe.[1] As such, many employers, in their more tranquil moments, would have agreed that official recognition of strike activity and the strike instrument were preferable to legal non-recognition of increasingly organized and active worker unrest, albeit while supporting recognition of the need to update the remaining broad body of labor legislation.

The first two years or so of constitutional government were marked by considerable tension between labor and capital, and a good deal of resentment was harbored by many employers who believed workers in general and union leaders in particular were acting irresponsibly. While most of the decline in strike levels for 1980-1982 can be attributed to economic factors, the peak-level agreements reached may have at least served the purpose of leading to a perception by employers that the labor picture was being brought under control and that a new structure for changed, but ordered, labor relations was being constructed. The Workers' Statute, with all of its flaws from the employer standpoint,[2] served a similar purpose. A good deal of the credit that Adolfo Suárez could have expected from business sectors for his able handling of the political transition never materialized, however, due to a perceived failure to confront economic issues, among which a failure on labor issues, specifically, figured prominently.

In the 1978 pilot study conducted by the author among the chief executives of thirty-two of the country's largest firms,[3] the degree of consternation in relation to the potentially debilitating repercussions of labor action and the uncertain future trajectory of labor relations were considerably higher than those registered in 1981. Fully 77 percent of those interviewed in 1978 indicated that increasing labor costs were damaging their firms' competitiveness. Sixty-one percent acknowledged having suffered specific strike actions since the start of the transition.[4]

In 1978, the head of a large, money-losing shipbuilding company (the last two being essentially synonymous) attributed his company's diminishing economic position to excess capacity abroad, problems of tight credit, and to the widespread, and erroneous notion among workers that "democracy consists in not working." A "lack of conscientiousness" among workers was a fairly typical complaint among many employers. As another company president stated in 1978:

> There exists, in general, a clear lack of conscientiousness concerning the rights and obligations of each of the sectors which constitute the firm, which results, also in general, in decreases in overall productivity, which translate to the detriment of all.

A FIRST APPROACH TO LABOR-MANAGEMENT ISSUES

It is important to appreciate the depth of labor's weakness in Spain to assess properly its role relative to management. As such, to deal with labor issues from the perspective provided by the extensive literature on corporatism, including in its hyphenated manifestations, is largely inappropriate for Spain. Although the

literature poses a number of interesting questions, it
fails to provide adequate explanations. To describe the
corporatist analysis as inadequate is not to deny the
existence of certain corporatist features. However,
even to deal with the series of peak-level agreements
signed between business and labor in purely corporatist
terms would be misguided. Even today, there remains a
long way to go in organizational terms by both labor
and business before the type of relations correctly
labelled as corporatist could emerge.[5] The continued
division between competing labor confederations and
very low levels of union affiliation, within the
context of very high official unemployment and a
substantial submerged economy, make truly corporatist
arrangements impossible. Stable collective bargaining
relationships in other Western countries involve a good
amount of mutually acquired personal experience on the
part of both workplace union negotiators and management
teams. Such knowledge is essential in any long-term
bargaining relationship in a single firm and it can be
an important element in reducing the level of conflicts.[6] Each player learns when to push and when to
give. Each learns the real absolute limits to which the
other can be pushed, as opposed to public rhetoric for
the sake of the rank and file or of shareholders.[7] In
the Spain of the early 1980s, the period of time that
had elapsed was insufficient for development of such
relationships at either the level of the individual
company or among interest group representatives. It
would have been particularly misdirected to expect
stable relationships to have been defined between the
collective interest groups of labor and business in a
period during which each was attempting to influence
the very structure of collective bargaining on those
terms most beneficial to their respective constituencies.

The collective organizations of labor and business
may have somewhat reduced the "problem load" for the
state (in the corporatist sense) to a limited extent.
However, there has been little of the mutual penetration of state bureaucracies and large interest organizations essential for the rise of liberal or societal
corporatism.[8] Indeed, we noted the limited degree even
of contacts between business interest organizations and
the Ministries. On the labor side, an essential structural precondition for the development of corporatism
is missing--that of organizations that are non-compe-
titive--in that they do not recruit among the same
group of potential members.[9] Under conditions where it
was estimated that unions affiliated only from 10 to 15
percent of the active labor force,[10] and competed among

themselves, and where employers appeared unwilling to accept fully the larger communist union (<u>Comisiones Obreras</u>), serious structural weaknesses confront efforts at the "integrated societal guidance" in the sense used by Etzioni,[11] which is at the base of corporatism.

Despite more recent, significant economic advances, the labor market picture has remained difficult as Spain has progressed through its industrial restructuring (<u>reconversión</u>) and domestic and international market liberalization under the PSOE Government. The situation for the socialist UGT union has been particularly difficult given the relatively pro-growth policies of the PSOE that have accelerated the impact of change in many old-line traditional industries where union affiliation would tend to be somewhat higher than in newer industries. This is an important obstacle to strong public collaboration with business associations, particularly under the aegis of the government and particularly for the UGT.[12]

CEOE rhetoric notwithstanding, with a steadily increasing unemployment rate since prior to the transition, and standing at over 18 percent by early 1984 and above 20 percent in the late 1980s, it appears evident that the human economic hardships resulting from slack labor market conditions were a prime determinant of the lower level of strike activity. Although peak-level agreements lessened tensions by facilitating the institutionalization of bargaining and by providing a framework for the negotiation of agreements at individual companies or by lower ranking interest organizations, it cannot be argued that these agreements were the sole or even primary factor in reducing labor unrest. CEOE publications, naturally enough, fully credit the macro-accords with having produced the reductions.[13] Ashenfelter and Johnson modified more traditional views of bargaining by recognizing that strikes that might not appear economically reasonable could be understood as a consequence of political dynamics within unions. Over the longer term, however, they maintain the basic economic equilibrating function of the strike.[14] Synder brings contextual sensitivity to country-specific institutional settings that might appropriately be extended to Spain. He proposes two competing models of strike action by country: (1) the bargaining approach to industrial conflict characterized as primarily economically determined; and (2) the collective action approach and its organizational/political arguments.[15]

To the extent that national labor relations systems move toward increased size and stability of union membership, institutionalization of collective

bargaining and political integration of labor, the determination of strike
fluctuations shifts from a primarily political to an economic process.[16]

Given the weaknesses of the competing Spanish
unions in the context of a not fully institutionalized
system of bargaining, one might expect that Synder's
collective action model would be a more important element in Spain than more economically determined models.
Our data will also suggest that an additional criterion
included in the Synder's "collective action" model is
pertinent to Spain. In outlining the assumptions required for an analysis of the effects of economic fluctuations on industrial conflict (basically, the bargaining approach to conflict), Synder contends that for
France and Italy one would have to reject the framework
that logically follows. He argues that employers who
are unwilling to negotiate with unions (particularly
the communist ones) often will not honor signed agreements, and that "unions are not always (or primarily)
concerned with short term economic costs and benefits."
Union membership has not been large or stable in either
country. Hence, assumptions developed on the basis of
earlier studies realized with North American or north
European data have to be thrown out in the French and
Italian cases.[17] Spanish union membership has not been
large, and our data will demonstrate an aversion by
some employers to deal with the communist union. Combine the traditional weaknesses of union affiliation
with an economic crisis as severe as the one characterizing Spain in the late 1970s and early 1980s and we
can expect a lower incidence of strikes than would
otherwise have prevailed as fewer workers prove willing
to risk their employment for either wage or political
ends.[18] This combination of factors makes for a difficult classification of Spain.
        In short, a proper overview of labor-management
relations in this study requires appreciation of the
features of increasing institutionalization, with certain, at least nominally corporatist features present,
under conditions of continuing change and in which weak
unions compete in political as well as economic terms
while facing strong labor market difficulties posing
important obstacles in their organization of worker
interests.
        The impact of labor on business' perception of
democracy should not be underestimated. As noted by
Gunther, Sani, and Shabad, many of those in more conservative sectors of Spanish society feared a collapse
of law and order during the transition period.[19] While
the work by Fishman empirically documents that labor
moderated its economic demands to aid political

democratization, perceptions, in this case those of business, are also an important element--and labor unrest made a big impression. However, important countervailing factors compensated for a natural fear of instability by many in business. The business sector already had known levels of strike activity equivalent to the generalized European experience during the Franco years. Although not of the magnitude experienced over the transition period, widespread strike activity was therefore not new.[20] Furthermore, surprisingly, while uneasy regarding the perceived political impact of massive labor unrest, most employers were considerably less anxious over their own "micro-situation," that is, unrest in their own companies. Indeed, most stated that their firms had experienced increases in labor productivity for the 1973-1981 period as a whole. Business also generally perceived an increasing exhaustion of the Franquist economic model. Lastly, moderating elites played a critical role in promoting continued confidence in transition by reform.

LABOR AND PRODUCTIVITY

Despite the widespread fears expressed by employers interviewed in 1978, three years later roughly two-thirds stated that the productivity of their employees had registered growth over the 1973-1981 period. Indeed, 30 percent noted "high" increases in labor productivity for the period as a whole.[21] Less than a fifth (17%) said they had suffered declines in overall labor productivity in their firms.

Table 6.1 Changes in Labor Productivity over 1973-1981

	R	I	L	M	B	VZ	VA	S	Total
Large increase	29.4	25.9	34.9	37.5	33.0	13.3	26.9	0.0	30.1
Some increase	36.5	38.8	36.0	26.1	40.0	36.7	50.0	66.7	37.1
No change	15.3	16.5	10.5	20.5	8.0	16.7	11.5	16.7	14.1
Some decrease	9.4	12.9	10.5	6.8	12.0	20.0	7.7	16.7	10.9
Large decrease	8.2	4.7	4.7	5.7	5.0	13.3	3.8	0.0	5.9
Other response	1.2	1.2	3.5	3.4	2.0	0.0	0.0	0.0	2.0
	(85)	(85)	(86)	(88)	(100)	(30)	(26)	(12)	(256)

The length of the reference period must have substantially increased the proportion of those identifying an increase in the productivity of the labor factor. It would be difficult to imagine a great number of companies unable to register some growth in labor productivity over an eight-year period that was not entirely marked by recession. It may have been more interesting to have documented changes in labor productivity for the 1976-1981 period. Nevertheless, it remains surprising that 30 percent of firms registered important increases in labor productivity. On a provincial basis, Vizcaya registered the smallest proportions of positive assessments; only half of the province's chief executives reported increased productivity (and only 13% claimed high increases).

Had the question made reference to a shorter number of years (1976-1981) and used an alternative phrasing, a wider spectrum of responses with more comparable, harder numbers may have emerged. Nevertheless, our data document that employers appear to divorce more "political" issues involving workers and labor unions from the measurement of productivity. With the exception of a small minority of employers who identified large productivity decreases (6%), employers facing productivity falloffs were not more likely to be resentful of organized labor activity or to attribute their declines in productivity to the unions. Of those employers who suffered decreased productivity, 49 percent described labor union actions as somewhat or strongly irresponsible. This compares to 47 percent among those employers who registered increases.

Table 6.2 Degree of Responsibility Accorded Union Actions by the Change in Productivity over 1973-1981

Union actions characterized as:	Changes in productivity:					
	Increases:		No	Decreases:		
	Large	Some	change	Some	Large	Total
Very responsible	8.5	3.3	14.3	19.2	6.7	8.6
Fairly responsible	46.5	41.3	28.6	46.2	13.3	39.1
Fairly irresponsible	28.2	38.0	37.1	11.5	40.0	32.5
Very irresponsible	16.9	10.9	14.3	19.2	40.0	16.0
Other/DK/NR	0.0	6.5	5.7	3.8	0.0	3.7
	(71)	(92)	(35)	(26)	(15)	(243)

Indeed, among the five groups of employers classified according to changes in productivity (from large increases to large decreases), the highest proportions of high levels of responsibility were accorded to unions by those whose firms had registered some decline in labor productivity. Sixty-five percent of such employers characterized the unions as either fairly or very responsible, versus 55 percent among those who had noted important productivity increases.[22] While it is very important that unions were not blamed for productivity problems in one's own company, that fact that a high overall 49 percent drew unfavorable assessments of union responsibility is also important.[23]

Yet despite the favorable micro-economic assessments of the evolution in labor productivity and the fact that for most employers the unions specifically did not get blamed for productivity problems, when asked (open-ended) to specify those factors that could most significantly boost overall productivity in their industry, changes in the labor realm received the most mention.

Table 6.3 Proportions Who Specified Factors
which Could Most Augment Productivity by Major Area

Changes in the area of:	Employers	Leaders
Labor	60.6	37.4
Sector/firm-specific factors/market factors	55.0	52.2
Managerial/Organizational	9.7	3.5
Public/State policies	8.1	23.5
General/other	2.7	8.7
	(258)	(115)

Six-tenths of chief executives were able to specify changes dealing with the labor factor that would prove beneficial. Association leaders emphasized labor issues to a significantly lesser extent, probably due to the additional year of a slack labor market (1982 versus 1981), accompanied by markedly decreasing levels of labor conflicts, more experience in the institutionalization of labor relations, and the fact that many associations do not deal directly with workers. On management issues, individual employers appear similarly

more concerned than leaders, albeit in substantially
reduced proportions than on labor matters. On the other
hand, on issues involving the state or public sector
policies, almost three times as many association leaders as individual employers expressed concern. It is
the association that most directly deals with the
state, from which individual companies feel more distanced.

Disaggregating to look at specific items, the similarities are striking between chief executives and the
leaders of associations. Very high and roughly equivalent proportions of each group specified allowing free
dismissal (flexibilización de plantillas) exclusively
among labor issues as the single policy that would most
contribute toward increasing productivity, followed by
equivalent proportions mentioning the need for an im-
provement in the labor climate generally and the need
for greater conscientiousness on the part of workers
toward their work. Although the question allowed for
the possibility of multiple response, over half (52%)
the chief executives mentioned only a single factor. In
turn, over half of these individuals (51%) mentioned a
factor in the labor realm, with an important majority
specifying the need for free dismissal. Indeed, among
employers who mentioned only a single factor for increasing productivity (under all major headings combined), 31 percent mentioned free dismissal. Over a
third of all employers identifying factors mentioned
free dismissal either exclusively or in combination
with other issues. Hence, among employers we find acute
concern with labor issues and an important concentration of interest exclusively on the issue of free dismissal.

The larger the company, the more likely labor concerns were voiced. Three-quarters of the heads of large
firms cited labor factors, compared with less than half
(48%) of the heads of regular firms. As one might expect, those employers who had experienced declines in
labor productivity over 1973-1981 were more likely to
mention labor factors than those whose companies had
experienced growth, 74 percent among the former versus
58 percent among the latter. This contrasts with the
failure for differing assessments to emerge regarding
the degree of responsibility demonstrated by the unions
(where one's own labor productivity experience did not
predict a response regarding the view of the unions).
Barcelona emerges as the province with the most concern
on labor issues, particularly among the heads of intermediate (71%) and large (71%) rather than of regular
firms (63%). Vizcaya ranks second.[24] In Vizcaya, size
is of critical importance. Whereas only one-third of

regular firm employers mentioned labor issues, two--
thirds did so among intermediate firms, and nine-tenths
among large firms. Among the leaders of associations,
Barcelona and Vizcaya also emerge as numbers one and
two in the proportions concerned with labor productivity factors. Most employers (59%) stated that productivity growth among white-collar workers did not
differ significantly from that among blue collar.

Table 6.4 Changes in Productivity and Strike Action

	Productivity: Increases	No change	Decreases	Total
Acknowledge having had a strike:				
Yes	51.2	50.0	60.5	52.4
No	47.6	50.0	39.5	46.9
NR	1.2	0.0	0.0	.8
	(170)	(36)	(43)	(254)

     The level of strike activity may have affected
overall productivity, although definitive conclusions
are difficult to draw. With an average 52 percent of
all firms acknowledging having suffered disruptions
caused by strikes,[25] we find that a higher proportion
(61%) of those firms that suffered drops in labor productivity had experienced strike action. Roughly half
of those with either increased productivity or without
productivity changes experienced strike activity. But
57 percent of those registering large productivity increases suffered strikes while a smaller 53 percent of
those having suffered large decreases experienced
strike activity. Hence, the pattern is inconsistent,
although we might safely conclude that strike activity
contributed to productivity problems in a number of
firms but cannot be blamed for decreases as opposed to
increases in most. Further substantiating this final
point, among those firms having enjoyed either some or
large productivity increases and which were struck, 82
percent of the employers (for both categories combined)
stated that a majority of the firm's employees had adhered to the strike in question (i.e., the most recent
strike).[26] An equivalent 81 percent of the employers of
firms registering some productivity decrease and having
been struck similarly stated that the majority of
workers had participated in the strike action. However,
a significantly smaller 71 percent of the strikes

against the largest productivity losers were majority, worker-supported strikes.[27] Hence, for the group registering the greatest decline in labor productivity, we derive a relatively lower incidence of strike action, and smaller proportions of the strikes garnered majority worker support.[28] This phenomenon may partially explain why unions specifically did not get blamed for productivity problems, although the data are inadequate to make a firm determination.

LABOR-RELATED PROBLEMS FACING THE FIRM

In reviewing specific labor-related problems facing employers in their own firms, although considerable, directly conflictual problems between worker and employer were not necessarily the most important. Of equal or greater importance are problems more directly related to productivity, labor market conditions, and, very notably, free dismissal. While unions and individual workers, naturally, may extend demands in areas affecting productivity or attempt to obstruct changes in dismissal policies through political means, recognition of such labor items as problematic by an employer need not imply a higher level of conflicts in the given firm.

From a closed-ended list of fourteen types of labor-related problems, employers were asked to rank the three of greatest concern in their own firms. Technical and labor-market issues were interspersed with others that might logically be expected to contribute to greater conflictivity or that treated various forms of conflicts as problems in and of themselves.

The single most outstanding feature of specified items is the very high proportion identifying the lack of free dismissals as a serious problem, replicating the findings about the factors that could most contribute to increasing productivity. Twenty-nine percent of employers chose free dismissal as their number one priority labor concern, more than twice the proportion for the second most mentioned item, low output, that was singled out by 14 percent. Furthermore, more than half of all employers (57%) specified the lack of free dismissal as one of their top three concerns. Poor output again ranked second highest (38%).

The specific aspects of the labor dimension indicating the highest conflictual potential from among the fourteen listed are: conflicts with unions, disciplinary problems, strikes or work stoppages, and conflicts between employers and supervisors (numbers 4, 5, 8, and 10 in our tables). Adding these four most directly conflictual labor aspects, large companies emerge as more conflictual than either regular or intermediate companies. Vizcaya employers expressed roughly twice as much concern regarding conflictual issues as did those in Barcelona, the second most conflictual province.

Table 6.5 The Three Most Serious Labor Problems in the Firm

The three most serious labor problems by province (PART A): *

	M	B	VZ	VA	S	Total
1. Excessive turnover	4.7	2.1	10.0	11.5	8.3	5.2
2. Accidents	2.4	6.3	0.0	11.5	33.3	6.0
3. Lack of company loyalty	10.6	7.4	3.3	3.8	16.7	8.1
4. Conflicts with unions	7.1	9.5	10.0	3.8	0.0	7.7
5. Disciplinary problems	11.8	17.9	23.3	7.7	16.7	15.3
6. Absenteeism	21.2	33.7	23.3	26.9	41.7	27.8
7. Low output	30.6	38.9	46.7	38.5	50.0	37.5
8. Strikes/work stoppages	8.2	6.3	26.7	3.8	0.0	8.9
9. Lack of qualified personnel	25.9	14.7	10.0	7.7	41.7	18.5
10. Conflicts between workers and supervisors	4.7	5.3	10.0	7.7	8.3	6.0
11. Methods, hours, incentives	20.0	16.8	10.0	30.8	16.7	18.5
12. Lack of interest and initiative	35.3	24.2	20.0	50.0	25.0	30.2
13. Lack of free dismissal	57.6	63.2	50.0	50.0	41.7	57.3
14. Lack of promotion opportunities in the firm	17.6	12.6	20.0	19.2	0.0	15.3
15. Other/don't know	35.3	29.5	33.3	26.9	0.0	30.2
	(85)	(95)	(30)	(26)	(12)	(248)

* Percentages indicate the total proportion of each group which specified a given labor problem in any of the three positions (priority, second or third most important). As not every employer indicated three items, the columns do not add up to 300%.

Table 6.5 continued:
The three most serious labor problems by size of firm (Part B):

	R	L	L	Total
1. Excessive turnover	3.5	4.9	7.4	5.2
2. Accidents	8.2	4.9	4.9	6.0
3. Lack of company loyalty	9.4	7.3	7.4	8.1
4. Conflicts with unions	8.2	4.9	9.9	7.7
5. Disciplinary problems	12.9	17.1	16.0	15.3
6. Absenteeism	29.4	26.8	27.2	27.8
7. Low output	45.9	37.8	27.2	37.5
8. Strikes/work stoppages	7.1	6.1	13.6	8.9
9. Lack of qualified personnel	24.7	17.1	13.6	18.5
10. Conflicts between workers and supervisors	5.9	6.1	6.2	6.0
11. Methods, hours, incentives	18.8	22.0	14.8	18.5
12. Lack of interest and initiative	27.1	34.1	29.6	30.2
13. Lack of free dismissal	44.7	63.4	64.2	57.3
14. Lack of promotion opportunities in the firm	18.8	11.0	16.0	15.3
15. Other/don't know	22.4	30.5	38.3	30.2
	(85)	(82)	(81)	(248)

In Vizcaya, the heads of regular firms were more likely to have identified one of the more conflictual problems as their priority labor concern. However, intermediate and large-firm employers singled out such items with greater frequency as their second and/or third most serious labor problems. In contrast to this overall Basque distribution, a more intense level of conflicts in Barcelona relative to the state-wide average was due to the significantly higher selection of conflictual items by the heads of large firms. Nearly a quarter of large-firm Barcelona employers selected conflictual problems as their top labor concern, twice

the provincial average. Seventeen percent chose a conflictual item as number two, compared to the provincial
average of 14 percent. About a fifth chose conflictual
issues as their third most consequential problem, compared to roughly an eighth doing so for the province as
a whole. In Madrid, conflictual labor problems were
evenly distributed by company size.

Table 6.6 Totals Selecting the Four Most Conflictual Labor Problems

Province:				Size of firm:			
	Cumulative*	Priority	(N)		Cumulative	Priority	(N)
Madrid	31.8	11.8	(85)				
				Regular	34.1	14.1	(85)
Barcelona	39.0	12.7	(95)				
				Intermediate	34.2	8.5	(82)
Vizcaya	70.0	23.3	(30)				
				Large	45.7	14.9	(81)
Valencia	23.0	3.8	(26)				
				TOTAL	37.9	12.4	(248)
Sevilla	25.0	8.3	(12)				

* Totals of employers selecting one or more of the four most conflictual labor con
cerns in any of the three positions (priority, second and third most important).
The four items in question are: conflicts with unions, disciplinary problems,
strikes/work stoppages, and conflicts between workers and supervisors.

One might expect that the union controlling a
given firm's works committee (comité de empresa) might
affect the level of labor conflicts. While this may indeed be the case, it is only partially reflected in the
selection by employers of their most important labor
concerns. Employers heading companies with committees
controlled by Comisiones, the mostly communist union,
tended more frequently to chose one or more of the four
most conflictual labor concerns among their top three
in comparison to those heading socialist UGT-dominated
companies (40% to 32%). However, limiting ourselves exclusively to the single priority labor item, somewhat
more UGT-firm employers than those heading Comisiones--
dominated firms selected one of the four most conflictual labor concerns as their top priority (18% in UGT
versus 15% in Comisiones-dominated firms). Hence, other
aspects of labor relations should be considered in an
analysis of the impact of different unions on employer
attitudes.

LABOR UNION CONFIGURATION

The effects of the control of works committees by different unions is basic to this analysis of union activities from the employer perspective. Given that each establishment will have its own committee, the heads of multi-establishment firms having more than a single committee were asked to identify which union was in control of the majority of committees. Works committees categorized in our tables as Comisiones Obreras (CCOO) include firms where all worker representatives belonged to this, the mostly communist, union as well as those where it was merely the majority union. These tables likewise treat the UGT, the socialist union, linked to the PSOE, and independents (which included the non-affiliated). Grouped under the heading CCOO/UGT are those companies where committees had no union with an absolute majority but in which both the major unions were present, with or without the presence of third (and fourth, etc.) unions or non-affiliated representatives. "Other groups and combinations" include some firms having either minority Comisiones or UGT representation, but not both, together with other majority or minority unions. It is difficult, if not impossible, to interpret those grouped under this category given that we run the gamut from the Maoist Confederación de Sindicatos Unitarios de Trabajadores (the CSUT) or the Sindicato Unitario (the SU) to anarchist CNT (the Confederación Nacional del Trabajo) to USO (the Unión Sindical Obrera) originally influenced by Catholic and socialist union activists and for a time prior to the 1980 elections for works committee representatives appeared to be financed by the UCD, as well as a number of other primarily ideologically defined unions, and the spectrum of regional-nationalist unions such as the Basque Solidaridad de Trabajadores Vascos, ELA-STV (moderate), and the Langille Abertzale Batzrdeak, LAB (abertzale: radical separatist).

Whereas for the country as a whole the UGT then ranked a close second to Comisiones, with each having garnered roughly a third of total vote share,[29] several factors substantially reduced the UGT's proportional share among this study's firms. Gaining an absolute majority in the works committee of a given firm is fairly demanding for any union. While in the aggregate the UGT stood less than two percentage points behind Comisiones, any firm in that the two met head on and which reflected their relative strengths state-wide would lead to a Comisiones victory, amplifying its distance from second-ranking UGT. A treatment of union strength by looking at control of works committee rather than total vote share amplifies the position of the overall relative victor. In emphasizing industrial Spain, the <u>overall</u> balance of the provinces in this sample favors <u>Comisiones</u>, as does our having derived the number of interviews in each province on the basis of their relative industrial capacities, further favoring Madrid and Barcelona, provinces in which <u>Comisiones</u> emerged relatively stronger than its country-wide average. The UGT is relatively stronger in some less-industrialized areas of the country, such as the Castillas (excluding Madrid). The single strongest distortion may have resulted from our exclusive selection from among industrial (and construction) firms, however, excluding banking and tourism enterprises and other service sectors in which the UGT did better. In Spain as a whole, the UGT tended to do better the higher the skill level of the employee and better among white-collar than blue-collar workers. It is not surprising, therefore, to find that the socialist union did best in energy sector firms than elsewhere among our firms, controlling 29 percent of the companies' works committees and standing in minority representation with similar status minority CCOO representatives in 57 percent of the cases. The UGT did poorest among construction firms (7% majority control). <u>Comisiones</u> did relatively well in all our major industry categories, with the exception of the numerically small energy sector, and did particularly well in Barcelona, especially in the important industrial regions of the Baix Llobregat and Vallès Occidental, and in Valencia.

Table 6.7 Unions Controlling Works Committees

	<u>R</u>	<u>I</u>	<u>L</u>	<u>M</u>	<u>B</u>	<u>VZ</u>	<u>VA</u>	<u>S</u>	<u>Total</u>
CCOO	33.7	30.1	37.9	31.0	42.9	6.7	46.2	25.0	34.0
UGT	14.5	14.5	13.8	12.6	15.3	13.3	11.5	25.0	14.2
Independents	12.0	4.8	6.9	10.3	6.1	13.3	3.8	0.0	7.9
CCOO/UGT	9.6	28.9	34.5	31.0	16.3	26.7	30.8	25.0	24.5
Other groups/ combinations	14.5	10.8	5.7	5.7	11.2	30.0	3.8	0.0	10.3
No committee	14.5	8.4	1.1	9.2	7.1	3.3	3.8	25.0	7.9
DK/NR	1.2	2.4	0.0	0.0	1.0	6.7	0.0	0.0	1.2
	(83)	(83)	(87)	(87)	(98)	(30)	(26)	(12)	(253)

EMPLOYER PERCEPTIONS OF THE UNIONS

The CEOE preferred the socialist union over <u>Comisiones</u>. In earlier years, CEOE policies were directed toward strengthening the UGT relative to <u>Comisiones</u> by ascribing to the socialists a greater willingness to negotiate and general protagonism while depicting the communist union as obstructionist. The series of annual macro-level agreements were initiated by the UGT-CEOE bilateral agreement on collective bargaining and industrial relations of July 1979, followed by the much more important <u>acuerdo-marco interconfederal</u> (AMI) of January 1980, that grew out of talks at which <u>Comisiones</u> initially had been present. By negotiating with the peak employers confederation, the UGT risked its position relative to its own constituents. Just as an association will perforce have to deal with the state and other system actors in attempts to maximize concessions, unions and associations both have to settle for the achievable. While having to cooperate with the state or the unions the association must also appear to defend the interests of its constituency and not collaborate with actors which by their very nature stand for competing demands (i.e., the state or unions). The unions, obviously, face the same dilemma, having to cooperate with the state and business while maintaining the support of workers. In entering negotiations and signing an agreement with the CEOE, the UGT ran the risk of alienating more radical sectors of its constituency.[30]

In light of subsequent developments, the gamble by the UGT paid off. It bettered its position relative to <u>Comisiones</u> between the first (1978) and second (1980) union elections, substantially narrowing the edge held by the communists.[31] While a number of factors contributed to the change in their relative shares of worker support, the signing of the 1979 understanding and, more so, of the AMI in 1980, contributed to the UGT's strength. In explaining the strength of the communist union in the first union elections, one should recall that <u>Comisiones</u> had participated as an opposition force both within and outside of the Franquist vertical union (contesting seats to the <u>jurados de empresa</u>, as USO similarly had done) and had become particularly active as of the late 1960s, whereas the UGT only resumed significant activity with the impending demise of authoritarianism. A large part of CCOO's success in the first union elections could have been due simply to the brevity of the interval since the death of Franco during which the UGT attempted to reestablish operations.[32] As the work by Fishman emphasizes, however, the variation in support received by the different unions in the 1978 elections cannot be imputed solely to consideration of loyalty on the part of workers to workplace leaders who had already proven themselves during the Franco regime. A number of other characteristics of the workers themselves needs to be taken into consideration.

It is interesting that among other factors, Fishman stresses the possible political gain achieved by Comisiones in more clearly supporting the Moncloa Pact (Pactos de la Moncloa) of October 1977, that drew up inflation targets in part by placing restrictions on wage demands. The Moncloa Pact was negotiated and signed by the political parties, and not by representatives of business and labor. However, the support of Comisiones for the pact was the strongest of any of the unions. Hence, Fishman argues that many workers were willing to limit wage demands so as to contribute to an easing of the transition to democracy.[33] Thus, a first wage restraint was defended by a union, Comisiones, that would later refuse to negotiate for the acuerdo marco (AMI). In an analysis of the postures adopted by the workers themselves, it was a positive element for the system that those unions perceived as taking the most responsible position politically, helping to assure the continued stability of the political system, first Comisiones, at the juncture of the Moncloa Pact, and then the UGT, with the AMI, benefited by increasing their level of support among individual workers. Because the representatives of employers and workers had not produced the Moncloa Pact, both the CEOE and the UGT criticized the agreement as an imposition by political sectors against the rights of labor and capital to negotiate freely and to satisfy their own requirements.

Perhaps the best measure of the success of the UGT's strategy was the fact that Comisiones entered negotiations for the subsequent peak-level agreement, becoming a signatory to the ANE in 1981. It is not surprising given the UGT's willingness to negotiate limitations on wage demands with the CEOE and the CEOE's own policy depicting the socialist union as the honest partner that many employers perceived the UGT as a more responsible associate in business undertakings.[34] In fact, the high degree of good will held toward the UGT relative to CCOO, as documented by our data, is arresting.

The acknowledgment of a strike by employers heading firms with Comisiones and UGT works committees are at relatively close levels, although there was a higher incidence of strike activity in those firms with Comi-

<u>siones</u> committees.[35] Fifty-nine percent of firms with
<u>Comisiones</u> committees had had at least one strike, as
had exactly half of UGT committee firms.[36] On the other
hand, whereas <u>Comisiones</u> was able to win the adherence
of the majority of workers for only three-quarters of
its strikes, the UGT was able to do so in 87 percent of
its cases.[37]

    Despite the relatively minor differences in the
existence of strike activity by union control between
CCOO and UGT (recalling again the inadequacies in this
data), which is somewhat compensated by the higher success in levels of worker support in UGT strikes, the
respective images of the two unions differ substantially. Roughly two-thirds (66%) of all employers considered the UGT to be the most responsible of all the
unions. Only 6 percent chose <u>Comisiones</u>.[38] Furthermore,
of employers heading firms with UGT-majority works
committees, nearly four-fifths (79%) identified the UGT
as the most responsible union. In <u>Comisiones</u>-dominated
firms, only about a tenth of employers considered CCOO
as the most responsible union. Hence, employers who had
to deal with the UGT were overwhelmingly pleased with
their circumstances compared to an overwhelming majority of employers unhappy with having to deal with their
CCOO-dominated works committees.[39] In the highly

Table 6.8 Union Considered the Most Responsible by the Union
Controlling the Works Committee in the Firm

Most responsible union:	Works committee:				Other		
	<u>CCOO</u>	<u>UGT</u>	<u>Indep'ts</u>	CCOO /UGT	groups/ combinat.	No comité	<u>Total</u>
None	4.9	5.9	5.6	6.8	8.3	10.5	6.3
CCOO	9.8	2.9	0.0	3.4	8.3	5.3	5.9
UGT	63.4	79.4	66.7	62.7	58.3	68.4	65.7
USO	4.9	0.0	0.0	1.7	8.3	0.0	2.9
CCOO/UGT	4.9	2.9	5.6	3.4	0.0	5.3	3.8
UGT/USO	1.2	0.0	5.6	1.7	8.3	0.0	2.1
UGT/Others	0.0	0.0	0.0	3.4	4.2	0.0	1.3
Others	6.1	2.9	5.6	15.3	4.2	5.3	7.5
DK/NR	4.9	5.9	11.1	1.7	0.0	5.3	4.6
	(82)	(34)	(18)	(59)	(24)	(19)	(239)

politicized UGT-PSOE government debates of the late 1980s, business perceptions of the UGT may have changed dramatically.

Table 6.9 Union Considered the Least Responsible
by the Union Controlling the Works Committee in the Firm

Least responsible union:	Works committees:					
				CCOO	Other groups/	No
	CCOO	UGT	Indep'ts	/UGT	combinat.	comité	Total
None	2.6	9.4	5.9	8.8	12.5	0.0	6.1
CCOO	66.7	50.0	41.2	59.6	37.5	47.4	55.7
UGT	3.8	0.0	0.0	0.0	0.0	0.0	1.3
LAB	0.0	3.1	0.0	5.3	16.7	0.0	3.5
CNT	6.4	12.5	5.9	3.5	4.2	10.5	6.5
SU	1.3	0.0	5.9	5.3	4.2	10.5	3.5
CSUT	1.3	3.1	0.0	5.3	8.3	5.3	3.5
CCOO/ Others	0.0	3.1	5.9	0.0	0.0	0.0	.9
Others	11.5	6.3	23.5	12.3	4.2	10.5	10.9
DK/NR	6.4	12.5	11.8	0.0	12.5	15.8	8.3
	(78)	(32)	(17)	(57)	(24)	(19)	(230)

More telling of **Comisiones'** difficulties in winning the hearts of employers (admittedly, not the union's primary concern) are data regarding the union considered least responsible. Over half of all employers (56%) considered **Comisiones** the least-responsible organized representative of worker interests. While only half of the employers heading UGT-dominated firms so cited CCOO, two-thirds of those dealing with **Comisiones** in their own companies considered the union as the least-responsible option. In contrast to this striking degree of criticism by CCOO's associated employers, among those employers heading firms dominated by the socialist union not a single individual specified the UGT as the most irresponsible union.[40] Many employers outside of Euskadi probably limited themselves to the two major unions as the only relevant actors, dismissing minor unions given their minimal presence. Despite uncertainty as to the proportion who restricted themselves in this manner, the indictment of Comisiones is very significant.

An important distinction in dealing with works committees controlled by different unions (or by independents) was extended by employers in assessing the motivations leading their workers to vote as they did. While over half (54%) of those employers with CCOO committees expressed the belief that workers tended to vote with greater attention to the personality and experience of the candidate rather than his or her union, only 42 percent of the employers with UGT committees agreed. Fifty-three percent of the heads of UGT-dominated firms said workers voted more for the union than the candidate, versus 42 percent among Comisiones-dominated firms.[41] If accurate, such an assessment could be employed in supporting the more diffused, generally accepted arguments about the first union elections that Fishman qualifies in his analysis, that is, that a good portion of CCOO's initial success may have been due to having candidates whose dedication to worker interests had already been tested during the Franco regime. Some of this could have persisted to the second union elections of 1980 (the ones uppermost in the recollections of the employers interviewed in 1981). Employers tended closely to link Comisiones to the totally unacceptable Communist Party (PCE). As such, a number of them would be unwilling to recognize worker support for the union as acceptance of all of its ideological ramifications. Indeed, for many workers voting for Comisiones, as well as for UGT, such a close identification with a party line can be refuted. Nevertheless, employer perceptions of the motivations for worker support for Comisiones are distorted to a greater degree by ideological considerations than are their assessments of support for UGT.

THE EFFECTS OF THE COMPOSITION OF WORKS COMMITTEES ON EMPLOYER ATTITUDES

A number of conditions affect the manner in which employers view labor relations. Given strong differences among employers marking CCOO from UGT, one expects that the union with which an employer deals in his own company might significantly alter attitudes on a number of labor relations issues. While the data generally support this supposition, an employer's dominant union "partner" is not uniformly the most important distinguishing characteristic in predicting attitudes on all labor-related issues. On many issues it fails to hold any explanatory power. Nevertheless, despite the striking differences in the perceptions of Comisiones versus the UGT and the manner in which this influences opinions on certain labor matters, it remains more important to highlight the broad basic acceptance of union activity overall.

Perhaps most telling of how unions affect an employer's perception of labor are the more critical attitudes adopted towards the unions in general by those employers having to deal with Comisiones-dominated works committees. Whereas 57 percent of the heads of UGT-dominated companies considered that union actions (unspecified) could be described as responsible (either "very" or "fairly" responsible), only 45 percent of Comisiones-dominated company chief executives felt likewise. It may be more important to note that over a quarter (28%) of the latter condemned union actions as very irresponsible compared to fewer than a tenth (9%) among employers dealing with UGT-dominated works committees.

Both observations parallel our findings regarding which unions were considered most and least responsible. In looking at the union considered most responsible, Comisiones already emerged in a strongly unfavorable light relative to UGT, a perception further emphasized in turning to the issue of the least responsible union. In assessing the degree of general union responsibility, employers with Comisiones committees were less likely to hold favorable views toward union actions in general than those with UGT committees. The contrast is even more pronounced among employers holding strongly critical attitudes. In looking at the most/least responsible union and at union actions in general, however, it is important to note the existence of a very small core of employers whose dealings with Comisiones workplace leaders evidently were satisfactory. While Comisiones was reprobated left and right, a third of those employers having to contend with CCOO committees did not specify the communist union as the least responsible,[42] and roughly a tenth considered Comisiones as the most responsible union. Disaggregating responses on the degree of responsibility accorded union actions, with Comisiones marred much more seriously than their socialist competitors overall, still and all a larger proportion of employers with Comisiones committees attributed the highest degree of responsibility (i.e., very responsible) to union actions than among the heads of companies with UGT committees (11% versus 6%).[43]

Generally, the less strained labor relations are in the company, the more likely an employer will prefer

to conduct collective bargaining at the firm level
rather than the subsectoral, sectoral, or peak levels.
Bargaining at the sectoral and peak levels, in particular, implies little need on the employer's part to
participate in negotiations, merely requiring acceptance (or rejection) of finalized documents for implementation. Consequently, those employers who considered
the unions responsible actors, a vision strongly influenced by experiences within one's own enterprise, also
tended to indicate a greater willingness to conduct
collective bargaining within the firm. While almost a
third of those depicting union actions favorably preferred to conduct their bargaining within the firm,
only about a quarter of those critical of the unions
expressed the same preference. Those preferring to distance potentially tense bargaining from the firm,
deferring negotiations to their sectoral or peak representatives, rises from a third among those who considered union actions very responsible to 56 percent among
those most censorious.

Our findings hold implications for any introduction of neo-corporatist patterns of negotiations for
Spain. The union most willing to enter such negotiations, then second-ranking UGT, is also the one perceived as most responsible. CCOO is perceived as contributing to a more conflictual work climate and has
also been less willing to enter peak-level negotiations
with employers associations. A larger proportion of individual employers who deal with UGT committees, per-
ceiving their own workplace leaders as more coopera-
tive, prefer to conduct their collective bargaining
within their own firms. With a decrease in tensions in
the firm, it would appear that larger proportions of
Spanish employers would prefer assuming fuller control
over agreements with labor. What becomes, then, of
peak-level agreements? The model may be that of agreed
guidelines proffered by peak employer and worker organizations with the nuts and bolts of collective bargaining left to companies or to subsectoral organizations at the local level.

In negotiations conducted at levels higher than
those of the individual firm, the UGT possessed a small
edge over their Comisiones counterparts, as one might
expect among an associational leadership influenced by
CEOE policies. Among associations, a higher frequency
of contacts with the UGT relative to other unions may
serve to facilitate interactions for the socialist
union. Excluding those associations without collective
bargaining roles (27% of associations) and those associations maintaining only minimal contacts with labor
unions (52%), 97 percent of association leaders main-

tained contacts with UGT leaders compared to a smaller
85 percent having contacts with Comisiones individuals.
Five percent of these association leaders limited their
contacts entirely to UGT representatives, a phenomenon
not recorded at all for Comisiones.

Significant differences are found by province. One
would expect that Barcelona associations would have to
be better connected to Comisiones given the union's relatively stronger position in Catalonia. Indeed, such
is the case. All those Barcelona association leaders
who maintained union contacts did so with both Comisiones and UGT representatives. It was in Vizcaya and
Madrid that potential contacts with Comisiones were
forgone by a number of associations." We might further
note significant industry differences. While a total
average of 15 percent of associations with union contacts did not report having exchanges with Comisiones,
the corresponding figure for service sector associations was 22 percent, expected given the relative weakness of the communist union in the sector noted earlier. It is of interest that neither of the energy sector
associations with union contacts maintained contacts
with Comisiones, again a reflection of the union's
electoral weakness in the industry, similarly documented among individual companies. Hence, while CEOE
peak-level attitudes may have had some influence in
postures with regard to the union contacts of member
associations, reason appears to have the upper hand.
Given its greater willingness to negotiate with the
peak and its perceived moderation, the UGT may have
successfully developed channels of communications to
associations even in those sectors where its position
is subordinate to that of CCOO. On the other hand, it
appears that wherever Comisiones is dominant, channels
will be maintained by pragmatic associations. In many
instances when a denial of access to the communists is
inconsequential, however, association leaders do not
invest the effort required for exchange.

It comes as little surprise that in comparing responses regarding the relative difficulty in reaching
collective bargaining agreements with workers in 1981
versus the situation that existed in 1975, a larger
share of employers with UGT committees compared to
those dealing with CCOO committees indicated that the
conduct of bargaining was easier and fewer of these
felt that negotiations were more difficult. In analyzing the degree of difficulty encountered in 1981, it is
probably more important that the majority (55%) found
it more difficult to conclude negotiations successfully
with the unions in comparison to the secciones sociales
of the defunct vertical Sindicato Nacional. Relatively

few employers (17%) considered it easier to reach agreement than in 1975. Twenty-three percent of those heading firms with socialist works committees believed agreements were easier to achieve compared to 19 percent among those heading Comisiones-dominated firms. While 56 percent of the latter believed negotiations more difficult to conclude, slightly less than half (49%) of the heads of UGT-dominated companies felt similarly.

Despite the discrepancy in assessing the arduousness in bargaining, no difference appears between employers dealing with the two unions on whether it is the organization or the individual at the bargaining table that is of relatively more importance in negotiations. Equivalent proportions of employers working with Comisiones works committees as with UGT committees considered the organizations involved on labor's side as more important in affecting the tenor of the negotiations than the attitudes of the individuals actually conducting the bargaining. Roughly less than half of each group emphasized the organization over the individual.[45]

We might surmise that the perceived importance of the union organization at the bargaining table in firms with Comisiones committees would work to the detriment of the given chief executive's interests, due to the misgivings the vast majority of employers had about the communist union. In contrast, given the UGT's favorable image one would expect that organizational strength at the bargaining table would contribute to moderation and "professionalism" from the employer's viewpoint. Although the tendencies appear to run in the expected directions, our data fail to confirm this hypothesis fully. In analyzing only those firms with Comisiones committees, roughly equivalent proportions of those who considered union actions in general to have been responsible as those labelling them irresponsible stressed the importance of organizations over individuals in collective bargaining. Among employers dealing with the UGT, we derive differences in the expected direction. Half of those assessing union actions as responsible considered the organization as more important than the individual in bargaining, compared to only 42 percent among those assessing union actions as irresponsible. Hence, the importance of organizational affiliation in negotiations involving UGT may serve to facilitate bargaining, but our data are inconclusive.

In summary, the favorable disposition toward the socialist UGT affected other labor-related issues such that union activity generally was looked at with greater tolerance and collective bargaining was some-

what eased in cases where the works committee was controlled by the UGT. The public image of the UGT con-
formed to this perception, and CEOE policies, which
were reflected to a certain degree among individual associations, reinforced these attitudes. While not statistically significant, we find a higher probability
among employers with Comisiones committees to specify
the more conflictual labor related problems as relevant
to the labor concerns of their companies. In all of
this, however, while the general direction is very significant, one must not overlook the existence of a
small group of employers expressing good will toward
the communist union, the relatively high general tolerance of union activity, and the generalized separation
of union activity from perceptions about productivity.

UNION STRENGTH

     Spanish unions, relative to their European coun-
terparts, are weak. By levels of affiliation, Spanish
unions fall far below the percentages of union-affil-
liated labor force in Italy, the United Kingdom, or the
north European countries, and are probably at levels
lower than those of France. Indeed, the level of affiliation is probably the lowest of any west European
country, standing at between 10 and 15 percent.[46] The
duration and depth of the economic crisis over the late
1970s and early 1980s may have weakened the unions'
ability to unite workers given overriding fears about
job security.
     Despite this weakness, it is clear that there
exists widespread worker sympathy for the unions, and
large numbers are willing to lend their support to
strikes or other job actions at the behest of the
unions in the defense of worker interests. Additionally, voter turnout for the elections of workplace leaders for works committees is generally good, and union
options receive the bulk of worker votes--another indication of their appeal. Yet, the system of collective
bargaining channels the fruits of union efforts to all
workers, and the pernicious effects of the free rider
phenomenon are experienced even more acutely among
unions than associations.
     Employers table numerous complaints against un-
justified worker demands and the organizational activity of external elements within the confines of their
own purview. But despite the extent of these anxieties
and the existence of a significant minority of employers who recognize substantial union strength in their
own firms, chief executives are sufficiently discerning

to realize that in most cases the unions, as such, cannot be considered strong within their enterprises. Not surprisingly, and correctly, in assessing union strength for the country as whole, employers attribute greater substance to the unions relative to that found in their own companies.

Differing assessments of union strength by employers, first in their own companies and then for Spain, accurately portray reality in that our questioning did not specify different measures of union strength. While in considering his immediate environs, the employer will think of the organizational presence of the unions, affiliation level, or the ability adequately to formulate and extend demands, in which he might detect weaknesses given that his own firm is the point of reference, at the macro level few will consider issues such as affiliation levels in a comparative perspective or the amalgam of the organizational presence in individual firms. Rather, employers look at the representation of workers at industry levels, where given unions are the officially recognized and legitimate spokespieces conducting and signing collective bargaining agreements, and at the peak level, where top union leaders are the established and authoritative labor counterparts to the peak business confederation leadership. Media coverage of important strikes and the ever-present threat of diffuse strike action may also influence many to consider the unions powerful despite the knowledge that effective strike action in their own firms would be untenable.

Table 6.10 Assessment of Union Strength in their Own Firms by Employers

	R	I	L	M	B	VZ	VA	S	Total
Very strong	11.9	6.0	17.4	10.2	15.3	13.3	3.8	8.3	11.8
Strong	21.4	33.3	36.0	25.0	32.7	43.3	23.1	33.3	30.3
Neither strong nor weak	32.1	36.9	24.4	35.2	24.5	23.3	53.8	25.0	31.1
Weak	16.7	14.3	11.6	19.3	10.2	10.0	15.4	16.7	14.2
Very weak	17.9	9.5	9.3	10.2	16.3	10.0	3.8	16.7	12.2
Other	0.0	0.0	1.2	0.0	1.0	0.0	0.0	0.0	.4
	(84)	(84)	(86)	(88)	(98)	(30)	(26)	(12)	(254)

Considerably fewer than half (42%) the employers considered unions to be strong in looking at their own companies. Over a quarter (26%) described them as weak or very weak.

The larger the firm, the higher the incidence of chief executives recognizing union strength. By province, Vizcaya emerges with the greatest proportion of strong unions in the companies, with Barcelona a prominent second. Valencia proved to have the lowest frequency of employer attribution of strength to the unions. The assessment of union strength by employers is highly correlated with the perceived level of conflicts, as indicated in previously presented material. Hence, from the union perspective, one might stress the importance of the threat of job actions and the abeyant or potential ability to mobilize workers in advancing demands, measured by employers in terms of their conflictual import, rather than the "harder" figures of worker support in elections to works committees or dues-paying affiliation. Obviously, both are important union strategic objectives.

For Spain as a whole, probably with the aforementioned considerations in mind, a significantly higher 57 percent of employers considered the unions strong (11.5% very strong; 45.6% strong), and a relatively minor 14 percent considered them weak. Indeed, only 1 percent described them as very weak.

Logically, experiences in one's own company impact on generalized assessments. In addition to macro considerations, most employers compared the situation in their own companies to the vaguer perceptions of circumstances elsewhere. The attribution of a greater degree of union strength for Spain as a whole is due primarily to the large proportion of employers who, having described the unions in their own firms as simply "weak" or as "neither weak nor strong," described them as stronger for the country overall. A particularly large proportion of employers with very weak unions in their own firms ascribed them greater strength overall. A high 38 percent of those employers who described the unions as very strong in their own companies soberly assessed them as weaker elsewhere. Similarly, roughly a fifth of those labelling the union as "strong" in their own firms located them at weaker levels for the country as a whole. As one might expect, responses to the two questions were highly correlated.

Objectively, unions are very weak. Recognition of their weakness by employers further damages the possibility of stable neo-corporatist arrangements. Roughly half (52%) attributed an equal degree of strength to the unions in Spain as in their own firms. Over a third (35%) consider the unions stronger overall than in their firms. Only 13 percent extended the inverse argument.

In terms of the actual union that controls the works committees, those employers with UGT-majority committees tended to ascribe greater strength to the unions both within their own company and for Spain compared to the levels of strength attributed by employers with <u>Comisiones</u> committees. Understandably, in relative terms, unions were considered weakest among those employers with firms where works committees were composed of independent majorities.

THE EFFECTS OF INTER-UNION COMPETITION

Employers were asked to consider the effects of the competition among unions on five aspects of collective worker interest. Not surprisingly, almost all (95%) agreed that as a consequence of the competition among unions there existed unions that extended demagogic demands to gain worker support. <u>Per contra</u>, one suspects that an overwhelming majority would nonetheless agree that there also existed unions that, although weaker, behaved in a more responsible manner so as to gain the confidence of labor. Yet, while slightly over two-thirds (68%) agreed, more than a quarter (28%) of employers did not accept such a statement. Particularly high concentrations of employers rejecting a recognition of more reasonable posturing by certain unions were found outside of Madrid and Barcelona, with a strikingly high figure of 44 percent detected in strife-torn Vizcaya.[47] While employers with CCOO committees (with 68% "yes" and 23% "no") roughly approximated the total average, significantly higher proportions (41%) of the heads of UGT-dominated firms refuted the statement.[48]

In treating the effects of disunity among workers in the actual strength of their unions, six-tenths of employers believed that the unions were weakened by competition among themselves. Sixty-one percent believe that the lack of unity in declaring strikes facilitated their resolution and 59 percent believed that competition reduced union strength. Again, Vizcaya is our outlier. The convulsions suffered by Basque business as a result of labor strife, much of it politically motivated, was reflected in the high 58 percent of Vizcaya employers who refuted that the unions had been weakened and the remarkably high 72 percent who believed that the disunity in strike action had not diminished the difficulty in reaching agreement. Indeed, on both statements, only in Vizcaya did we register majority opinions refuting the statements as posed and claiming that the unions were not weakened by the competition

among themselves. Valencia emerged strongly in the
opposite direction. Over two-thirds of employers (69%
on each question) believed that competition weakened
the unions, figures surpassed only by the overwhelming
nine-tenths of Sevilla employers in agreement.

In comparing employers who believed that collective bargaining agreements were more easily achieved in
the early 1980s than in 1975 to those of the opposite
view, no differences emerge. Nor are there discrepancies between those dealing with UGT versus CCOO works
committees. However, we find that higher proportions of
those employers who preferred to conduct collective
bargaining in their own firms appeared to exploit the
advantages of perceived easier agreement resulting from
labor disunity. Two-thirds of those preferring firm-
specific bargaining believe that disunity among unions
in strike action facilitates reaching agreements (versus 54% for those favoring bargaining at the sectoral
level and 56% at the peak level).

Further substantiating the generalized view that
union competition had not been detrimental to business,
slightly more than half (53%) did not believe that
union competition had led to higher wage settlements.
Forty-two percent believed that wage increases had
risen more than they would have in the absence of union
competition. As before, Vizcaya employers stand in
stark contrast to the majority. Among the Basque
employers, 56 percent believed that wage increases had
been higher than they would have been without union
competition.

THE STATE OF LABOR RELATIONS

What, then, can be said to summarize the state of
labor relations from the management side? What degree
of "normalcy" characterizes this aspect of business?
Complete normalcy in labor relations in a European setting cannot be achieved under the conditions of roughly
20 percent unemployment and the institutional union
weaknesses in Spain. Such conditions continued even under a Socialist government in the late 1980s and into
the 1990s, manifestly evident in union-government tension.

That the unions were weak may both have contributed toward and resulted from the persistence of an
important minority of firms that either failed to conduct elections to works committees in 1980 or in which
only a minority of employees cast ballots. Eight
percent of the employers claimed not to have held
elections or not to have registered any worker partici-

pation whatsoever. We suspect that this phenomenon was even more pronounced among the smallest firms excluded from our study. The highest proportions of "zero" votes for works committees, 15 percent, was in regular-size companies, compared to 6 percent among intermediate and 3 percent among large companies, a clear indication of the trend against the holding of works committee elections as size diminishes. Some of this could have been attributable to union difficulties in fielding candidates the smaller the firm, an issue dealt with extensively in Fishman's work. However, although larger numbers of regular-size companies did not conduct union elections, for the group of companies that did hold elections a higher share of regular-size firms achieved complete or near-complete worker voting participation. In nearly a quarter (24%) of regular firms, more than 95 percent of the employees cast ballots, compared to 11 percent in intermediate firms and a much reduced 6 percent in large firms. It seems logical that in a smaller company with a good working climate, all or nearly all would participate in elections. Over three-quarters of employers reported that the majority of their workers cast ballots for representatives to works committees, but only 13 percent could report complete or near-complete (above 95%) employee voter participation.

Table 6.11 The Proportion of "Normal Strikes" in Spain by the Degree of Union Responsibility

% of current Spanish strikes which can be considered "normal" given the conflict of interests between labor and management:	Unions overall described as:				
	Responsible:		Irresponsible:		
	Very	Fairly	Fairly	Very	Total
None/zero	28.6	9.6	6.3	17.9	12.0
1-19%	4.8	13.8	22.8	35.9	19.0
20-49%	4.8	11.7	26.6	17.9	17.4
50-95%	33.3	31.9	16.5	10.3	22.7
96-100%	19.0	18.1	11.4	7.7	14.0
Other/DK/NR	9.5	14.9	16.5	10.3	14.9
	(21)	(94)	(79)	(39)	(242)

A higher proportion of employers (24%) reported over 95 percent employee participation among those chief executives who considered union actions very responsible. A higher 13 percent zero-worker participation was found among those accusing the unions of being very irresponsible. Nevertheless, in summing up the percentages at above 80 percent employee-voter participation, the 36 percent registered in companies headed by the most critical employers was not far below the 43 percent reporting above 80 percent participation among the companies of those most favorably disposed toward the unions.

On a second index of the degree of normalcy in labor-management relations, we find that attitudes held regarding union actions influenced employers' more specific views on strike action. Almost half of all employers (49%) believed that only a minority of strikes was "normal" given an unavoidable or natural conflict of interests between labor and capital. In the Spanish context, a good proportion of business criticized strike action as politically motivated, which is to say, as having objectives resulting from the machinations of forces outside the firm. "Normal" strikes are those conducted with purely economic objectives (such as salary demands) in mind, objectives that could be satisfied within the firm. We can assume that a good proportion of the roughly one-eighth of employers who considered that no normal strikes were being waged believed that to speak of "normal strikes" is a contradiction in terms.

While an important 14 percent of employers assessed all or nearly all (above 95%) strikes as normal given genuine conflicts that should be expected between labor and management, the proportion of all those considering a majority of strike action as such (50 percent or more) was only slightly above one-third of employers (about 36%). Those who condemn union actions, as expected, tend to be less tolerant of strike actions in general. The level of acceptance of strike action diminishes consistently as the level of union criticism increases for both those in the 50 to 95 percent and the above 95 percent categories. While over half (52%) of those who consider union actions very responsible accepted a majority of strikes as normal, only 18 percent of those in the very irresponsible group concurred. Yet we find a single, but major, inconsistency in the pattern in that over a quarter (29%) of those least critical of union actions were thoroughly intolerant of strike action.

While those who acknowledge having suffered strike action are marginally less tolerant, the differences are not at all significant. Neither are differences between CCOO- and UGT-dominated firms significant, although, again, the marginal differences are in the expected direction, with employers dealing with Comisiones committees slightly less tolerant of strike action. Although the level of rejection of strikes is high among those who registered substantial productivity declines, the patterns by shifts in productivity over the period of the preceding eight years was inconsistent.

On the other hand, we derive significant differences by province and very significant differences by firm size. Conservative Valencia, as well as Sevilla, emerges as very intolerant of strike action. Fewer than a fifth (19%) of employers in Valencia accepted that a majority of strikes were normal, and none of these was in the category extending complete or near-complete (over 95%) approbation. Vizcaya and Barcelona both approximated the state-wide average and were strikingly similar to one another. Madrid employers extended a surprisingly liberal view. Over a fifth (22%) assented to nearly all strikes as normal, with a roughly equivalent proportion (19%) conceding tolerance in a smaller but majority share of strikes (the 50 to 95% category).

Table 6.12 The Proportion of "Normal" Strikes in Spain by Size of Company and by Province

Percentage of current Spanish strikes
which can be considered "normal"
given the conflict of interests:

	R	I	L	M	B	VZ	VA	S	Total
None/zero	9.6	11.9	16.9	15.9	11.7	10.3	15.4	0.0	12.9
1-19%	27.7	15.5	11.2	14.8	16.5	17.2	30.8	30.0	18.0
20-49%	18.1	21.4	14.6	14.8	17.5	13.8	26.9	40.0	18.0
50-95%	22.9	23.8	21.3	19.3	25.2	27.6	19.2	20.0	22.7
96-100%	8.4	8.3	23.6	21.6	12.6	10.3	0.0	0.0	13.7
Other/DK/NR	13.3	19.0	12.4	13.6	16.5	20.7	7.7	10.0	14.8
	(83)	(84)	(89)	(88)	(103)	(29)	(26)	(10)	(256)

Nearly two-thirds (66%) of the heads of large firms earlier had recounted specifics on their "most recent" strike, compared to 41 percent of regular and 51 percent of intermediate firm heads did so. Yet, we find much higher tolerance of strike action among large-firm employers. The proportions in the responses of regular- and intermediate-firm employers bear a strong resemblance one to the other. The heads of large firms display a considerable degree of tolerance. While fewer than a third of either regular- (31%) or intermediate-firm (32%) employers considered the majority of strikes "normal," 45 percent of large employers were willing to do so. Although an important 17 percent of large firm employers rejected all strike action, the total of the heads of large firms in the two most critical categories (28%) approximates a proportion similar to that among intermediate-firm employers (27%), which is significantly lower than among the heads of regular firms (37%).

It appears that a number of characteristics of large firms may contribute to the greater liberalism of large-firm employers, without any single trait determinant. Controlling the attitude regarding normal strikes simultaneously by the acknowledgment of having suffered a strike and size of company, we find an important difference between large-company employers who escaped strike action and those who reported strike action in their firms. Fifty-three percent of the former accepted that a majority of strikes were normal versus 39 percent of the latter. While this discrepancy is substantial, however, the 39 percent among large-firm employers who had suffered strikes yet accepted a majority of strikes as normal compares to 33 percent among the similar group of intermediate-firm employers and 29 percent among regular-firm employers. Indeed, the 39 percent reflects higher tolerance among the strike-affected large-firm employers than the proportions of employers in intermediate firms (33%) and regular firms (33%) who failed to report a strike in their companies.[49]

One would expect managers to be more liberal than owners. Yet, for all employers, no significant difference emerged between the two groups. One might expect that those who had studied or worked abroad might prove more tolerant of strikes. Yet, again, the characteristic fails to perform as expected.

Increases in educational level is a significant factor favoring liberalism. The very high levels of tolerance of strike action noted for those few who have had some graduate study has important implications for size of firm given that 72 percent of those with graduate study headed large firms.[50] In controlling education simultaneously by size of company, however, significantly higher tolerance of strike action is noted for large-company employers at all levels of education in comparison to regular- and intermediate-company employers. If we look at those who accepted that a majority of strikes were normal, for the group having only a high school education or less a third of large-firm heads held liberal views compared to roughly a tenth of regular and of intermediate-firm heads. For the "some college" group (which includes those with two-year degrees, such as peritos industriales or profesores mercantiles), 40 percent of the large-firm employers were in the tolerant group versus 14 percent of regular and 18 percent of intermediate. For those with university degrees, 46 percent of large-firm heads were in the tolerant group compared to 37 percent of regular and 38 percent of intermediate.

Table 6.13 The Proportion of "Normal" Strikes in Spain
by the Educational Level of the Employer

	High school or less	Some college	College	Some graduate work	Total
None/zero	26.7	11.6	10.9	12.5	12.9
1-19%	26.7	27.9	16.3	6.3	18.0
20-49%	10.0	25.6	16.3	21.9	18.0
50-95%	10.0	9.3	27.2	25.0	22.7
96-100%	6.7	11.6	12.9	28.1	13.7
Other/DK/NR	20.0	14.0	16.3	6.3	14.8
	(30)	(43)	(147)	(32)	(256)

While large-company employers at all educational levels prove more tolerant than their peers in smaller enterprises, we derive greater tolerance as educational level advances for large firm (from 33% among the high school or less, to 40% for "some college," to 46% college, to 52% for those having done graduate work). Hence, given the greater concentration of the well-educated in large firms, this emerges as a significant factor.

CONCLUSIONS

In an article on French interest groups, Frank Wilson summarized some perspectives provided by the proponents of neo-corporatist theories regarding the transition from pluralist to neo-corporatist forms of interaction. He suggests that the majority of such authors contend that the period of transition is characterized by a "mix" between the two forms of interaction.[51] I contend that a mix is always the norm. Our data suggest that in the labor-management arena, the functional area most likely to manifest neo-corporatist phenomena, Spain is not an appropriate specimen for neo-corporatist dissection.

Unions enjoy wide sympathy among their worker base. During a process of institutionalization of collective bargaining mechanisms, within the context of the development of the new political system itself, one would expect unions to concentrate their efforts on organizational and political matters, particularly in light of many years of repression. However, we might describe many union actions as more appropriately understood in terms of damage limitation. Agreements reached with employers on wage ceilings and the falloff in strike levels over the late 1970s and early 1980s can in large measure be attributed to economic determinants.

By the early 1980s, employers were coming to accept the legitimate role of unions, although important lacunae persisted in employer tolerance. Nevertheless, it appears positive that the majority of employers during this early period of democracy divorced political or organizational union activities from shifts in the productivity of their own companies. I also note an apparently increasing acceptance of a certain level of strike activity as a normal phenomenon in the interplay between capital and labor, although, naturally enough, this may in large part be attributed simply to the fact that strike levels diminished so markedly. It is likewise important to note that this increased tolerance of the strike weapon was notably higher among the "elite" of business: large-firm employers. Secondly, tolerance by employers of strike action was somewhat comparable to evident worker endorsement of moderation on the part of their unions. Hence, each side was playing the game.

Obstacles to complete formation of a stable collective bargaining framework remain. Continued resistance on the part of the peak (and a number of its affiliate associations) and the then-top ranking communist union to enter negotiations fully with one another in good faith is a factor. Each may be responding in part to ideological criteria and the data strongly document the resistance and distaste on the part of a large majority of individual employers towards Comisiones. We further noted the effects unfavorable views of the communist union had on attitudes towards different aspects of collective bargaining and the activities of unions in general.

Increased willingness to negotiate, greater experience with the mechanisms of bargaining, and an upturn in union fortunes, which are strongly linked to economic recovery, are prerequisites to the establishment of stable labor-management relations in Spain.

NOTES

1.   José Maravall, <u>Dictatorship and Political Dissent</u>, 32-33. It is a curiosity and inconsistency of the Franco era that despite the prohibitions against strikes, relatively reliable strike data was published officially.

2.   Including continued prohibition of free dismissal.

3.   All the companies ranked among the 200 largest. Twenty-two companies were visited in Madrid and ten in Barcelona. The interviews were conducted from late August to mid-September 1978.

4.   A proportion strikingly similar to that registered in 1981, as noted further ahead. While the 1981 overall average is 53 percent, the proportion of large-firm employers who acknowledge having suffered strike action was 66 percent. All the firms visited in 1978 were in the large firm category.

5.   By which time most social scientists probably will no longer be much interested.

6.   Reder and Neuman place particular emphasis on the role of acquired knowledge of the other bargaining agent in their study of the United Sates. Over time, bargainers learn what are the "minimum payoffs" that cannot be avoided. They also establish implicit protocols that ease negotiations, such as the time and place of meetings; the authority and organizational titles of representatives; specifications of the circumstances under which a previous contract will continue to apply after its expiration pending agreement on its replacement; provisions for the introduction of mediation or arbitration; and the benefits, rates and methods of compensation and work rules for each category of worker. Indeed, they argue that so tight a relationship can be developed that the negotiations of a new contract will reduce to the application of formulae. Melvin W. Reder and George R. Neuman, "Conflict and Contract: The Case

of Strikes," Journal or Political Economy, 88, 5
(October 1980): 868-871.

The Spanish examples should not be understood as
in the process of developing formulae. The situation is
too different from the American to expect hard and fast
protocols. There has been an elimination of certain
issues from mutual challenge, however, as collective
bargaining has been increasingly institutionalized.
Contesting the authority or legitimacy of the other
party has largely disappeared. Pérez Díaz argues that
employers have learned to live with the unions and that
workers have increasingly accepted the legitimacy of the
firm and of the administrative role of the employer.
Víctor Pérez Díaz, "La doble cara del neocorporatismo,"
112-113.

While not expecting automatic processes to
develop, the above items are legitimate considerations
that are often unstated assumptions of the type of long
term relationship required for corporatist forms of mediation. In Spain, acquired knowledge has been increasing, but it is far from becoming a dominant element.

The fact that a long-term relationship is in
question during contract negotiations need not imply a
reduction in conflicts. Indeed, during the earlier
stages in the development of such relationships the inverse may be more likely. Both parties may act more con-
frontationally than they might otherwise given a reali-
zation that "respect" gained over the short term can
contribute towards enhancing their relative position
for the duration of the longer term relationship. As
Reder points out,

> the gain from better terms during the duration of the contract under
> negotiation may obviously be insufficient to justify the strike; however
> the gain is not confined to the life of the contract being negotiated,
> but is reaped over the whole future period of bargaining relations, in the
> form of better contract terms and general day-to-day treatment than could
> otherwise be obtained. The cost of the stoppage may thus be considered an
> investment, amortizable over the whole future history of union-company
> relations.

M. W. Reder, "The Theory of Union Wage Policy,"
Review of Economics and Statistics (February 1952): 39.
Inclusion of such a consideration in Spain, where practically all companies (and their workplace leaders)
were in the throes of establishing bargaining relationships in the early 1980s, can have very important
aggregate effects.

7. Ashenfelter and Johnson assume that management actions coincide with shareholder interests (a big assumption) while stressing the need to acknowledge three actors in collective bargaining: management, the union leadership, and the union rank and file. Orley Ashenfelter and George E. Johnson, "Bargaining Theory, Trade Unions, and Industrial Strike Activity," The American Economic Review (March 1969): 36-39.

We are leaving much unsaid on the issue of divergence between the interests of management and shareholders. In truth, their interests can run counter one to the other. The classic work on the United States is that by Adolf A. Berle, Jr., and Gardiner C. Means, The Modern Corporation and Private Property (New York: Commerce Clearing House, 1932). Coincident with the hostile takeover environment of the 1980s and the shareholders' rights issues of the 1990s, this controversy has reemerged as an important unresolved issue in the United States. The increasing role of pension and mutual funds and other institutional investors as key players in U.S. equity markets further complicates the relationship. The boom in management leveraged buy outs posed further questions, particularly as regards to fiduciary responsibility and insider knowledge.

8. Gerhard Lehmbruch, "Liberal Corporatism and Party Government," 93-94.

9. For a treatment of corporatism under conditions of a multitude of interest groups and decentralized societal sectors, see Lars Norby Johansen and Ole P. Kristensen, "Corporatist Traits in Denmark, 1946-1976," in Gerhard Lehmbruch and Philippe Schmitter, eds., Patterns of Corporatist Policy-Making (Beverly Hills: Sage Publications, 1982), 189-218.

Under an entirely different set of circumstances from those found in Spain, Pempel and Tsunekawa provide an analysis in corporatist terms of a situation where labor is insufficiently represented relative to government and business. T. J. Pempel and Keiichi Tsunekawa, "Corporatism Without Labor? The Japanese Anomaly," in Schmitter and Lehmbruch, eds., Trends Towards Corporatist Intermediation (Beverly Hills: Sage Publications, 1979), 231-270. The danger in a broadly differentiated or dynamic approach to corporatism is in falling prey to interpreting everything as corporatist. Corporatist elements can be present in a case that cannot be classified as corporatist. In Spain, the weaknesses of corporatist players in their most-travelled realm, economic policy-making, means that policy is determined elsewhere.

10. Pérez Díaz states that in its 1980 congress, the socialist UGT claimed 1,375,000 members. In 1981, <u>Comisiones</u> claimed 1,123,640. His own surveys among workers documented a drop in affiliation by 1980 for manufacturing sectors over the figures of three years earlier of from 56 percent to 37 percent. In its 1983 congress, the UGT acknowledged that its affiliation had dropped to about 600,000 and Pérez Díaz argued that the Comisiones figure could not have been higher. Pérez Díaz, "Políticas económicas," 33 and 45. See also Víctor Pérez Díaz, "Los obreros españoles ante el sindicato y la acción colectiva en 1980," <u>Papeles de Economía</u>, 6 (1980); and Víctor Pérez Díaz, "Los obreros españoles ante la empresa en 1980," <u>Papeles de Economía</u>, 7 (1981). As Fishman suggests, the unions themselves were unaware of their active membership, and he agreed with the Pérez Díaz estimates. Spanish union affiliation may have been the lowest of any Western country.

11. At issue are the representation of collectivities by organizational units, in a manner similarly described by Olson, as well as the various types and levels of interactions between units, networks, levels of control over collectivities affected, passivity versus activity, the role of elites, and so forth. Amitai Etzioni, <u>The Active Society</u> (New York: The Free Press, 1968).

12. Minus a very unlikely PRI-ification of the Spanish party system (à la Partido Revolucionario Institutional, prior to the more recent evolution of the Mexican system), the longer the PSOE maintains its dominant position (which before the 1989 elections might have been described as "near-hegemonic"), the more likely the erosion of its ties to the UGT will play a greater public role. This clearly emerged in strains between the Socialist union and party which led to UGT leader Nicolás Redondo's resignation from parliament in 1987 and continued tension during 1988, culminating in the successful joint UGT-Comisiones general strike of 14 December 1988.

13. CEOE, "La conflictividad laboral en 1981," <u>Informes y estudios</u>, 12 (January 1982). Although there was a 53 percent increase in the number of official strikes in 1981 over 1980, with 36 percent more workers involved, there was a 31 percent reduction in man-hours lost. Removing from consideration those strikes by civil servants and in public services and those responding to "extra-laboral" demands (undefined), the CEOE calculated a 36 percent increase in the number of strikes, but a

33 percent decrease in the number of workers participating and a 32 percent drop in lost man-hours. Again considering solely official strikes with strictly "laboral" motivations, 1980 had registered a 26 percent decrease from 1979 in the number of strikes, with a 74 percent drop in the number of workers implicated, and a 67 percent drop in lost man-hours.

Level of Labor Conflicts	Absolute figures:			Percentage change over year-earlier:	
	1979	1980	1981	'80/'79	'81/'80
Number of strikes	1,789	1,315	1,792	-26.5	+36.3
No. establishments	10,068,712	3,140,485	1,748,766	-68.8	-44.3
Employees involved	5,752,304	1,506,324	1,016,221	-73.8	-32.5
Lost man-hours	171,067,049	57,235,591	34,800,106	-66.5	-32.2

14. Ashenfelter and Johnson, "Bargaining Theory," 39.

15. David Synder, "Institutional Setting and Industrial Conflict: Comparative Analyses of France, Italy and the United States," American Sociological Review, 40, 3 (June 1975): 260.
In their critique of Edwards, Tilly and Franzosi propose that an appreciation of institutional, political and economic variables simultaneously would prove beneficial in an analysis of strike activity.

> Reliance on one explanatory factor (such as the bargaining structure) to the exclusion of others (such as economic and political factors) may be quite misleading. Instead of contests to the death, we need integration among alternative explanations and models that have proved successful within particular domains.

Such an approach is key to the Spanish case. Charles Tilly and Roberto Franzosi, review of Strikes in the United States 1881-1974 (New York: St. Martin's Press, 1981), by P. K. Edwards, Industrial Relations Law Journal, 5 (1983): 437.

16. Synder, "Institutional Setting," 275.

17. Synder, "Institutional Setting," 264-265.

18. Much of the increase in strike activity in the mid-1980s was attributable to actions by workers already slated to loose their jobs.

19. Gunther, Sani, and Shabad, Spain after Franco, 35.

20. But the jump in labor unrest was impressive. Strikes increased from 931 in 1973, to 2,290 in 1974 and 17,731 in 1976. Lost man-hours rose from 14.5 million in 1975 to 150 million in 1976. José María Maravall, La política de la transición (Madrid: Taurus Ediciones, 1981), 27.

21. Such declarations of productivity growth may be somewhat exaggerated. However, overall enterprise output was maintained at most firms in the face of declines in manpower. Hence, an employer can validly calculate an increase in per capita worker productivity. Nearly two-thirds (64%) of our sample companies reduced their labor force over the five-year period to 1981. An additional 14 percent maintained the same number of workers. The workforce reductions in many firms were of a substantial magnitude. Thus, steady (or even some decreased) output with fewer workers, while indicating good productivity growth at the plant level, need not extend to aggregate indicators for the economy given the extremely high level of unemployment, disguised unemployment, and discouraged worker effects (i.e., very low labor force participation rates).

The "reabsorption" of the labor force into the agricultural sector and underemployment in agriculture has a substantial impact on aggregate productivity figures. Alcaide Inchausti estimated that a large 18.1 percent of the active labor force was in the agricultural sector in 1982. Yet the relative productivity of this sector was 37 percent compared to a construct for the economy as a whole set at 100. Industry stood at 103.9 percent, construction at 76.7 percent and services at 126 percent. Alcaide Inchausti, "El futuro de la sociedad," 15.

The Evolution in Labor Productivity
over 1973-1981 by the Change in Plant Size:

Evolution in productivity:	Number of workers - Change 1981/1976:			
	Decrease	No change	Increase	Total
Large increase	34.6	11.8	30.8	30.2
Small increase	35.8	55.9	32.1	37.3
No change	12.6	14.7	16.9	14.3
Small decrease	10.1	11.8	11.3	10.7
Large decrease	5.7	5.9	5.7	5.6
Other/don't know	1.3	0.0	3.8	2.0
	(159)	(34)	(53)	(252)

Changes in plant size have not substantially affected labor productivity. It was more likely to have

found a rise in productivity growth among those who decreased the size of their companies (70.4%) or who had
maintained the employment level steady (68%) than among
those who increased plant size (62%). If one notes the
relative proportion of each category of change in employment level, the aggregate employment effects for the
country are clear. Furthermore, maintained or increased
growth in the productivity of a unit of labor need not
extend to aggregate productivity growth, particularly
in light of the large majority having decreased the size
of their companies. Roughly a third of the chief
executives decreased company size by a fifth or more
over the five-year period in question. The unemployment
rate continued to deteriorate subsequently.

Inverting the relationship of the two variables,
changes in productivity produce no pattern in decisions
regarding plant size. Of those registering a large increase in productivity 72 percent reduced plant size;
21 percent increased it. Of those who suffered important
declines in productivity growth 64 percent reduced plant
size versus 21 percent who increased the size of their
companies.

22.   Only among the very small 6 percent having
suffered large decreases in productivity do we find
strong criticism of labor union activities as irresponsible. The level of criticism is extensive. Fully 80
percent considered union activities to have been fairly
or very irresponsible.

The 1983 DATA "Mentalities" survey found that 23
percent of Spaniards believed that both unions and employers associations acted responsibly, 19 percent believe that only the unions had been responsible players
and 5 percent only the associations. 35 percent believed
that neither the unions nor the associations behaved
responsibly and 19 percent had "no response."

23.   While the 49 percent unfavorable assessment
is high, an equivalent proportion (48%) viewed the
unions as having acted responsibly. Although not fully
a parallel question, Robert Fishman asked workplace
union leaders to assess the level of competence of the
management of their firms. It is interesting that the
workplace leaders split in equivalent, near-half proportions on the issue of management competence: 49 percent
regarded management as competent (9.3% very competent
and 39.2% fairly competent) and 49 percent viewed management as incompetent (36.4% not very competent and
13% as very incompetent). Fishman, "Working Class
Organization," 208.

24. Employers mentioning labor factors by province: Madrid, 57 percent; Barcelona, 69 percent; Vizcaya 60 percent; Valencia 46 percent; and Sevilla, 50 percent. In Madrid, large employers at 81 percent were very concerned with labor productivity issues, a level twice that registered among Madrid regular or intermediate firms.

25. The question did not ask employers to specify if the strike had been "official" or not, which may have led some respondents to avoid admitting to serious work disruptions.

26. The strike question asked the employer to describe the most recent strike experienced rather than whether his firm had experienced strike actions, implying an expectation that all companies had been struck. Thus, the employer would have had to reject the question as posed as irrelevant in the case of his own company. While probably leading to a higher admission of strikes, the question did not register how many strikes the company had suffered. Certainly, highly conflictual firms have had numerous job actions. A higher frequency of strikes in a single company may partially explain the relative weakness of the strike variable in accounting for changes in productivity. By implying the expectation that a strike had occurred, however, the phrasing of the question eased the hesitancy for an employer to admit that his company had experienced conflicts.

A number of employers of relatively well-off companies complained that the unions concentrated strike actions against their firms in the knowledge that their company might better weather labor actions. If there is any truth in this contention, it further contributes to a weakening of strike action as a variable (undifferentiated) in explaining changes in productivity. It is difficult to assess to what degree unions may "target" strike activity against better-endowed companies. Several factors may be at work. First, unions tend to be better organized in companies that are better organized (i.e., those stronger in economic terms). It also makes good economic sense not to strike companies which are in difficult straits. Hernes and Selvik state that "the closest cooperation between labor and capital is found in those firms that are in difficulties." Gudmund Hernes and Arne Selvik, "Local Corporatism," 111.

Large companies that are also well off will tend to sign company-specific agreements that will exceed more modest conditions achieved via industry-wide collective bargaining, which at times represent minimal settlements to which all companies can adhere. Thus, it is logical that unions strike in stronger companies, perhaps not as a test case for the industry, as a number of employers contend, but rather simply in the knowledge that they have the most to gain in such cases without jeopardizing the company.

But, we should not overemphasize any deterministic and complete logic on the part of unions. Union leaders involved will not generally possess the perfect information required to undertake such strike strategies consistently.

27.   For the total of firms having experienced strikes, 78 percent stated that the most recent strike had the support of the majority of employees and 21 percent only attained minority support.

28.   Some employers may have discounted losses due to strike action before calculating their productivity. For example, an employer may have thought simply, "in 1973 a worker in eight hours produced so much, whereas today he produces considerably more."

29.   In the 1980 union elections, Comisiones won 30.87 percent of the votes; the UGT 29.28 percent; and USO 8.68 percent.

30.   In comparison to the UGT in relation to its labor constituency, the risks for the CEOE relative to its business constituency were fewer, because it was favoring a second-ranking union perceived as more moderate, thereby denying Comisiones a protagonistic role as the primary spokespiece to business. Furthermore, any agreement restricting union demands, particularly in the wage area, would replace the perceived limitless options available to unions in the eventuality of no agreement.

In his treatment of the Central Working Community of German Employers and Employees (Zentralarbeitsgemein-schaft--ZAG), Feldman discusses the manner in which commitments to collaboration by employer and worker groups can "overstrain the organizational and ideological cohesion" of both organizations. Gerald D. Feldman, "German Interest Group Alliances in War and Inflation, 1914-1923," 225.

31.   In 1978, CCOO received 34.6 percent of the vote to UGT's 21.7 percent. In 1980, CCOO got 30.9 percent and the UGT 29.3 percent. UGT captured the top rank in the 1982 elections to workplace representatives when it received 37 percent of the workers' votes compared to 33 percent for Comisiones. In the 1986 workplace elections, UGT strengthened its vote share by capturing

40 percent to CCOO's 34 percent. However, <u>Comisiones</u> swept the vote in the majority of large companies and in many of the major (and strike-prone) public sector companies.

32. Fishman notes that analyses usually refer to "union elections," but the posts are really for representatives to works committees, which are non-union positions representing the totality of workers. Indeed, as our own data reflect, a number of independents (not affiliated to any union) did well at many companies.

33. See the chapter (no. 9) by Robert M. Fishman in the <u>FOESSA</u> study, 275-285.

34. The degree of change in the perception of the unions will always remain unclear given the lack of data for the period prior to the AMI. It could be the case that the UGT was already strongly favored by employers on grounds of experiences within their own companies or sectors or simply as representing an ideological position easier to swallow than a union composed of "untrustworthy" and unacceptable communists. While I stress the distaste by employers of <u>Comisiones</u> on ideological grounds, we should not forget that it works both ways. CCOO representatives, sensing their own more distant ideological positioning, would be less willing to face employers or employer groups.

Robert Fishman's 1981 survey work, conducted among the workplace union leadership of Barcelona and Madrid, provides an additional possibility. His data document the higher educational level and frequency of white collar to blue collar individuals active as UGT heads of works committees, as well as their older age. These personal characteristics might make it easier for many employers to deal with the union leaders involved, given the closer proximity in terms of deportment affected by class and generation. Fishman suggests that in purely personal terms from an employer's standpoint, many Comisiones workplace leaders had a rougher edge.

35. Employers acknowledging strike action, by the union controlling the works committees of their firms:

	Works committee union(s):						
Acknowledge strike:				CCOO	Others/	No	
	CCOO	UGT	Indep'ts	/UGT	combin.	Comité	Total
Yes	59.3	50.0	45.0	54.8	50.0	30.0	52.6
No	40.7	47.1	55.0	45.2	46.2	70.0	46.6
NR	0.0	2.9	0.0	0.0	3.8	0.0	.8
	(86)	(34)	(20)	(62)	(26)	(20)	(251)

36.   The difference may be greater in that Comi-siones-dominated companies might have suffered several strikes while UGT companies suffered but one, a critical distinction left undocumented in this data. Furthermore, important differences in the levels of tension might have been revealed had we detailed official versus unof-ficial or wildcat strike activity.

37.   The UGT tends to be more selective in sup-porting strikes whereas <u>Comisiones</u> tends to support most strikes, at both firm and industry level. As such, it would be reasonable to expect that a more cautious UGT would selectively support a higher proportion of strikes with the potential to succeed compared to a less dis-criminating CCOO.
Workers are more cautious than workplace leaders and more cautious, particularly, than <u>Comisiones</u> work-place leaders. The UGT may constitute a better "fit" for cautious workers than <u>Comisiones</u>. Additionally, the most cautious workers may be more inclined to vote UGT than CCOO.
Strike action undertaken by committees having both <u>Comisiones</u> and UGT membership, with neither in control, achieved majority worker adherence in two-thirds of the cases.

38.   In fact, 3.8 percent mentioned both the UGT and Comisiones. Another 3.3 percent mentioned UGT in combination with a third union.

39.   The only union that neared the UGT in main-taining a good image among the employers who had to deal with it in their own firms was USO. This observation is necessarily footnoted given that we had only four cases of committees with USO majorities and five more with it present as a competing minority (without any other union as a majority). Among the former (N=4), two employers considered USO the most responsible union and another mentioned it along with the UGT. The fourth employer mentioned UGT exclusively. Of the latter (N=5), one men-tioned USO; one mentioned USO and UGT both, and the re-mainder, UGT exclusively.

40.   This extends to the heads of firms whose committees have no majority and in which UGT is present along with Comisiones as minorities (with or without third or fourth unions). No such employer specified UGT. Of these 60 percent specified CCOO.

41. Overall, 54 percent of employers believe that the given candidate's personality and experience weighed more heavily than the union affiliation, while 36 percent believed the opposite. Logically, an over-whelming majority (90%) of those heading firms with in-dependents forming majorities on works committees chose the former over the latter consideration.

42. Some of these employers identified far-left unions or the anarchists. Had they been asked to compare only the UGT and _Comisiones_ or had they been questioned regarding how responsible they considered _Comisiones_ separately, a high proportion may have criticized the union. Others may have been satisfied.

43. However, of the employers heading _Comisiones_-dominated firms and well disposed towards the unions in general (11%), the majority (56%) identified the UGT exclusively as the most responsible union, and another 22.2 percent mentioned both socialist and communist unions.

44. The very weak position of _Comisiones_ on works committees in Vizcaya may account for a good deal of the 38% of Vizcaya associations without _Comisiones_ contacts. If the union is not present at a local sectoral level, there is obviously little impetus to forge channels. Madrid (17%) is a bit more difficult to interpret. The physical presence of the CEOE, with its more open antagonism toward the communist union, may have played a role.

45. The closed-ended question requested that em-ployers assess the more important of the two elements in influencing worker-employer negotiations.

Works committee union(s):

More important:	CCOO	UGT	Indep'ts	CCOO /UGT	Other groups	No Comité	Total
Position of the organizations	44.2	45.7	15.0	38.7	30.8	42.1	38.6
Attitudes of the individuals	48.8	48.6	80.0	56.5	61.5	57.9	55.8
Other responses	7.0	5.7	5.0	4.8	8.0	0.0	5.6
	(86)	(35)	(20)	(62)	(26)	(19)	(251)

46. Pérez Díaz, "La doble cara del neocorpora-tismo," 118.

47. Thirty-nine percent of those in Valencia and 36 percent of the Sevillanos argued that no such more responsible union existed. The wording of the statement was: "Some [unions], although they have little support, behave in a more responsible manner so as to gain [for themselves] the confidence of workers." The insertion of consideration of unions with only little support should have augmented the "yes" responses. Thus is the 28 percent no response particularly noteworthy.

48. Among those with independent works committees, 83 percent agreed with the statement and a minor 11 percent disagreed.

49. Furthermore, half of the 39 percent in question accepted that above 95 percent of strikes were normal, compared to 9 percent among regular and 7 percent among intermediate firm heads who had suffered strikes.

50. Of the thirty-two chief executives having completed some graduate work, twenty-seven actually held doctorates, 92 percent of whom were engineers. Two individuals were "lawyers of the State" (Abogados del Estado), a very prestigious official professional status, obtained through highly competitive exams (oposiciones), and one held an American MBA.

It is very interesting, but not really surprising, to note the high educational level attained by chief executives. Even the de Miguel and Linz data for 1960 uncovered a similar finding. Fully 46 percent of their chief executives held college degrees (licentiates or higher). Excluding semi-industrialized Spain, 49 percent held college degrees. Naturally, as in the 1981 survey, Linz and de Miguel admitted that over-representing the larger firms contributed to these findings. Nevertheless, the levels recorded remain impressive.

At firms of more than 1,000 employees in the 1960 data, 78 percent of chief executives held college degrees. Linz and de Miguel compared this to a 65 percent figure for American chief executives in 1952 in firms of the same size. For firms in the same size category, Linz and de Miguel found Spanish chief executives to be a more "elite and privileged" group than their U.S. counterparts. Surprisingly, for the 1981 data, the same 78 percent had completed college degrees among the heads   of large Spanish firms. However, we might note that the 78 percent in the 1981 data also included 26 percent of all large firm chief executives who, indeed, had completed graduate work as well.

For the 1960 data, Linz and de Miguel noted that: "Whatever the obstacles which large and giant Spanish firms have encountered in attempting to reach a world stature comparable to that of firms in other countries, without a doubt, the educational level of their directors is not among them." Amando de Miguel and Juan J. Linz, "Nivel de estudios del empresariado español," Arbor, 219 (March 1964): 33-42.

Linz and de Miguel found that educational level failed to explain much about numerous issues internal to the firm. Structural characteristics (including sector), social origins of the employer, and region all were, generally, of greater importance in explaining attitudes. Juan J. Linz and Amando de Miguel, "Los estudios de los empresarios españoles y su concepción del papel empresarial" (Paper delivered at the conference on "La formation des hommes et le développement économique," held under the auspices of the Centre de Sociologie Européenne, Madrid, October 26-31, 1964).

51.   Frank L. Wilson, "French Interest Groups," 897.

7

Business and European Integration

Spain achieved 5.5 percent real growth in its gross
domestic product (GDP) in 1987 and 5 percent in 1988,
double the European Community (EC) average, along with
surging corporate profits. Economic policy in the late
1980s and early 1990s was marked by extreme pragmatism
on the part of the Socialist government, engendering
severe antagonism from labor critics. Austerity marked
the PSOE's first government (1982-1986) under the stew-
ardship of "Super Minister" Miguel Boyer, who was both
minister of economy and of finance. The later 1980s saw
an emphasis on growth, at the expense, Socialist critics
declare, of progressive social policy. Although lacking
Boyer's prominence and flash, Boyer's successor, Carlos
Solchaga, did not move far from Boyer's basic liberalism
in economic policy. Further, the reappointment in 1988
of liberal-minded Mariano Rubio at the Banco de España,
Spain's central bank, augured for liberal consistency
in monetary as well as fiscal and social policy.

Spain signed its adherence to the Treaty of Rome
in June 1985 and officially entered the Common Market
effective 1 January 1986, eight and a half years after
having officially submitted its final, successful bid
for integration.[1] The years since have witnessed massive and rapid changes in the economy and an end to the
<u>crisis económica</u> that haunted Spain during its years of
democratic transition. While it is impossible to ascribe
Spain's recent "boom" to the EC, European integration
has had a substantial impact. In part that impact has
been directly economic, and in part it has been psychological, as business and society in general have attempted to adapt to perceptions of what is required to
succeed within Europe. 1987 and 1988 witnessed a rapid

expansion in output and rising consumer demand, which has led to important increases in import growth. Inflation was low by Spanish standards, 5.5 percent in 1987 and 5 percent in 1988, although it rose somewhat subsequently. Unemployment has been at above 20 percent for most of this period (the highest in the OECD, even exceeding Irish and Turkish levels), but it began a slow but significant decline in 1989. In contrast to declining employment throughout the early and mid-1980s (and a marked discouraged worker effect), employment has been steadily growing since the late 1980s. The labor force has improved, and labor-force participation has been growing. Employment grew roughly 3 percent each in 1987 and 1988, contrasting with declines of 1.8 percent in 1984 and 0.9 percent in 1985, and unemployment was substantially below 19 percent at the end of 1988, and expected to continue its steady decline.[2] The peseta has been strong. Continued and steady huge inflows of foreign, long-term capital have contributed to the growth of official reserves, which since 1987 have exceeded the level of external debt, which has been on a slow decline since 1983. The growth in long-term capital reflects the attractiveness of Spain to foreign investors and is consistent with liberal official policy encouraging such long-term operations.[3] Much of Spain's attractiveness to foreign investors is directly attributable to integration in the European Community.

Spain is exceedingly well placed for the changes Europe is undergoing as it pursues the goal of the single market and maximizing Spain's possibilities has been one of the government's primary economic objective. Spain assumed the "Presidency" of the EC from Greece on 1 January 1989. The government's desire to showcase Spain's effectiveness as EC leader during its six-month tenure in the presidency was tarnished by labor union unrest following the highly successful general strike called by the UGT and supported by Comisiones on 14 December 1988, the much-commented breakdown in the concertación social, and by pressures for early elections (which eventually were held 29 October 1989). Nevertheless, the heads of government at the EC's June 1989 Madrid summit closing Spain's presidency adopted the first phase of the Delors' report toward implementation of economic and monetary union ("EMU"; despite Margaret Thatcher's strong resistance, related to whether adherence to part one of the plan implied eventual concurrence on all three parts, including a European central bank).

To date, the full direct impact of European integration is difficult to confirm accurately, although undoubtedly the overall economic impact has been strongly positive. Nonetheless, as to trade flows, integration appears to have resulted more in trade diversion than in trade creation. Nevertheless, Spanish exports have been steadily growing, although imports from the EC have been growing even faster. Along with depressed wages, fast import growth has been a major factor in moderating inflation.

Prior to 1986, the Common Market issue had been an economic policy priority of Spanish governments, both authoritarian and democratic, for over twenty-five years. From the Spanish perspective, the topic always was phrased--and continues to be so--in staunchly political terms. Franquists hoped to mitigate Spain's isolation and achieve acknowledgement of the country's "European" character. Democratic governments hoped entry would assist in the consolidation of the democratic order and also linked the issue to other priority international policies, particularly NATO, but also Gibraltar. In fact, as it turned out, Spanish participation in NATO was upheld thanks to the manner in which the Socialists tied the issue to full participation in Europe (EC) in the March 1986 referendum. Democratic forces in opposition to Franco and during the early years of the transition argued that integration in the Common Market would be an important benefit achievable as a consequence of democratization and would serve to further democratic consolidation.

THE PREFERENTIAL TRADE AGREEMENT OF 1970

The commercial framework for EC-Spanish relations during the many years of negotiation of the final admission was the Preferential Trade Agreement signed between the EC and Franquist Spain in 1970.

The correct point of reference for viewing the Preferential Trade Agreement from the European perspective was within the context of the EC's so-called Mediterranean policy, a relatively haphazard collection of independently reached agreements that came to include practically all the non-EC Mediterranean states, and that, naturally, has been in disarray and reformation since the last two enlargements (Greece in 1981 and Spain and Portugal in 1986). Gerard Curzon called the EC's Mediterranean policy "an unplanned accident."[4] The EC maintained a wide range of disparate bilateral agreements, negotiated and signed at different points in time, without any over-reaching guiding logic, which were retroactively grouped under the rubric of a "Mediterranean policy." Alfred Tovias classified the agreements between the EC-9 (EC-6 at the time of the Spanish

agreement) and the various Mediterranean countries into
four types: (1) non-preferential trade agreements, for
example, Yugoslavia; (2) preferential trade agreements,
Spain and Israel; (3) cooperation agreements, the North
African countries; and (4) association agreements with
a view to membership, at that time, Greece and Turkey.[5]
To appear in compliance with GATT strictures, the Community packaged its Moroccan and Tunisian agreements as
free trade areas, despite the fact that neither agreement committed itself to such an objective. The Israeli
and Spanish agreements, both "preferential," were described, in the Israeli case, as an interim agreement
leading eventually to a free trade area, and, in the
Spanish, to a customs union, although the subsequent
intervening steps required were left undefined.[6]

At the time of the signing of the 1970 agreement,
Spain's effective rates of protection were lower than
those of the newly industrializing countries (NICs), but
considerably higher than the Six's Common External
Tariff (CET) or of the United States.[7] Furthermore, the
range of rates was considerably broader in Spain than
in the Common Market.[8] Effective rates of protection in
Spain ranged from 62 percent on durable goods, to 20
percent on nondurable consumer goods and negative 2 percent on transport equipment.[9] The preferences granted
by Spain under the agreement covered 61 percent of the
Common Market's 1968 exports to Spain,[10] and Spanish
concessions were divided into three lists, scheduling
tariff reductions annually until full objectives were
to be reached by 1 January 1977. List A items would be
reduced eventually to 60 percent from their starting
level, lists B and C would reduce to 25 percent each.[11]
Both parties were cautious in the preferences granted.
Almost half the tariff positions on list A, by far the
most "generous" schedule, corresponded to positions already at zero duty. Furthermore, items included on this
schedule of reductions fell into two very different, but
for this purpose, compatible categories: (1) those products in which Spain already had a comparative advantage,
and (2) those in which Spain had absolutely no hope of
ever being competitive.[12]

Likewise, on the EC side, effective rates of protection extended reduced the potential benefits for
Spain. Exports with a high raw materials content or
based on relatively labor-intensive manufactures, areas
in which Spain held or might have developed a comparative advantage, continued to face greater import obstacles. Fewer than half Spain's agricultural and fishery
commodities received any tariff reductions.[13] As is the
norm in trade agreements reached between a more advanced
industrial economy and an industrializing one, nominal

rates of EC protection were significantly lower than Spanish levels. Indeed, only in fewer than 10 percent of tariff positions were Spanish rates lower than their EC counterparts. Yet, significantly, more than half of those positions with higher nominal rates of protection by the EC were on agricultural commodities. CET concessions on most agricultural commodities were treated as "exceptions" and limited to a 30 percent to 50 percent range. However, despite the EC's hard line on agricultural commodities, the agreement from the Spanish perspective must also be viewed as having minimized then-increasing disadvantages relative to trading competitors among other Mediterranean producers already holding bilateral agreements with the EC. However, agricultural concessions granted other Mediterranean countries, generally, remained more generous. Yet despite these more generous agricultural preferences conceded other countries, Spain enjoyed unusually superior capacity and easier transport; its produce was often of better quality, and subject to somewhat differing seasons, all serving to mitigate negotiated paper disadvantages as compared with its Mediterranean competitors.

Labelling the items "sensitive," the EC restricted the preferences granted on a series of specific commodities in which Spain held a significant comparative advantage, including salt, woollens, synthetic fibers, stockings, undergarments, shoes, lead, and zinc. Additionally, the EC entirely excluded goods covered under the European Coal and Steel Community (ECSC), certain foodstuffs, a series of textile fibers, cork and cork products.[14] While nominal rates of protection by Spain to the EC remained relatively high, significantly they fell from an average of above 17 percent to 12.76 percent.[15] The CET average rate of slightly above 8 percent fell to 4.65 percent.[16] Gámir noted that the EC's preferences were greater than those conceded to Israel, but less favorable than those granted Greece, Turkey, Morocco, or Tunisia.[17]

Widely differing assessments of the agreement's results have been extended by different researchers. McQueen reported favorably on the agreements signed by Spain, Greece, Tunisia, and Morocco, stating that exports from these countries to the EC were "substantially higher than could be expected on the basis of the trend in the pre-agreement share of their exports in the imports of the EEC and the change in their competitive position in the markets of the rest of the world."[18] In fact, only in the case of Spain did McQueen find marked increased export diversification. Although less positive than McQueen, an early Círculo de Economía study attributed the consolidation of export expansion with the

EC to the 1970 agreement.[19] Gámir emphasized the relative decrease in production costs for exports versus domestic markets, that served to favor the flow of capital and labor toward goods to be sold abroad relative to the situation which would have prevailed had no agreement been signed. While stressing the very modest level of achieved preferences, Gámir concluded that there was some relative redistribution of resources toward export industries and the rise of more accurate cost criteria in the location of investment. Overall, Gámir saw a limited but positive impact.[20] The prominent marxist economist Tamames, on the other hand, emphasized the strong loss in theoretical customs collections resulting from tariff concessions and the severely limited or absent preferences granted agricultural commodities and industrial goods in which Spain was competitive. Tamames also argued that the limited agricultural preferences extended were entirely nullified by more favorable concessions granted other Mediterranean countries.[21] Overall, the comprehensive ESADE study comes out closer to Tamames than to Gámir. "It does not appear possible to infer that tariff reductions have visibly constituted a stimulative factor in favored sectors, nor a retardant in sectors apparently less favored by Community reductions."[22]

ESADE found no correlation between the actual commercial performance of goods favored by preferences and the consequences one would have expected given the extension of such concessions. "For the entirety of tariff positions, no uniformity has been detected between the magnitude of the reductions and the number of items which have augmented their degree of penetration."[23]

Given its much later publication, the ESADE study enjoyed an historical perspective not available to earlier studies and was able to appreciate the significant impact of exogenous factors that made isolated analysis of the agreement's effects difficult and inconclusive. Particularly important environmental changes impacting the agreement were the collapse of Bretton Woods, the first enlargement of the EC in 1973, the energy crisis, and the implementation of the generalized scheme of preferences under UNCTAD.

One characterization of the agreement on which both Tamames and Gámir agreed, and that is supported by a number of other observers, was the political dynamic involved. Both Tamames and Gámir denounced such a political dimension as inappropriate for inclusion in what should exclusively have been a commercial agreement. Gámir described the agreement as fundamentally an internal as well as external "political operation whose analysis rightfully pertains more to the sociological than the economic sciences."[24]

The context in which the agreement was sought and signed was certainly much more political from the domestic Spanish perspective than from that of the EC. But the EC was also sensitive to its potential political interpretations. The failure of the agreement to include any noteworthy political component was due to the conscious effort by the EC to diminish its political implications. The Franco regime wanted to assert Spain's "European" character by entering negotiations for integration, and the regime subsequently attempted to garner political mileage from the very limited agreement that resulted. That does not diminish the agreement's evident lack of a political framework, however. The heightened rhetoric domestically may have contributed to a greater awareness of political consequences by Spanish versus non-Spanish analysts of the agreement. Certainly a failure on the part of the Spanish negotiators to formulate a more adequate and effective commercial strategy, which has been observed by many non-Spanish investigators, may have been partially due to the overriding interest by the Franco regime in insuring that any agreement be forthcoming. Some more pro-Franquist observers even argued that the duration and difficulty in reaching agreement in and of itself reflected the EC's implicit recognition of Spain's European character.

In the conduct of the negotiations, the Spanish delegation increasingly realized that the agreement being reached would closely resemble those previously signed by the EC with Morocco and Tunisia, and particularly paralleled the one then under negotiation with Israel. They therefore attempted to gain recognition of Spain's historical European character.[25] While most of the agreements signed with various Mediterranean countries were written under the provisions of article 238 of the Treaty of Rome, however, those signed with Spain and Israel fell under the rubric of article 113. Article 238 refers to the establishment of "association" with other states and is phrased in terms of "reciprocal rights and obligations." Agreements reached under its provisions require unanimous action by all EC member states. Article 113, on the other hand, falls under commercial policy and can be acted upon by a qualified majority of the Council of Ministers.[26] A EC whose previously negotiated schedule of economic relations with Greece had been frozen in 1967 following the colonels' takeover could not have dealt otherwise with Franquist Spain.[27]

SPANISH BUSINESS AND THE 1970 PREFERENTIAL TRADE AGREEMENT

In looking at the business view of the 1970 agreement, an early survey among the heads of sixty-five Spanish companies in 1971 indicates that the largely favorable comments were based not on hard economic analysis but on "philosophy." The topic generated an "intense and somewhat mystifying political heat."[28] In his study of the Mediterranean enlargement, Tsoukalis emphasized the emotive Europeanist sentiment widely diffused in Spain, long outdated among the citizens of the original Six,[29] and which might be likened more to the fire of the neo-functionalist federalist heyday of the European Coal and Steel Community (ECSC).

Businessmen and women were asked about the exclusion of Spain from full integration into the Common Market at the time of the negotiation of the trade agreement. Was the exclusion of Spain from full integration on political grounds really the fundamental rationale or was it a pretext? Among individual chief executives, 29 percent considered the rationale given by Europe as the fundamental reason. Sixty-nine percent considered it a pretext.

Table 7.1 Employer Perceptions of the 1970 Exclusion of Spain from Full Integration in the EC

	Percentage Exports/Production:				Foreign capital participation:				Total
	0%	1-24	25-50	51-95	dom.	min.	maj.	MNC	
The political exclusion rationale was: The fundamental and real reason	23.5	31.0	31.7	33.3	24.7	20.0	33.3	61.9	28.9
A pretext	75.3	66.0	65.9	63.3	73.6	80.0	63.6	28.6	68.8
Other answers	1.2	3.0	2.4	3.3	1.7	0.0	3.0	9.5	2.3
	(85)	(100)	(41)	(30)	(174)	(25)	(33)	(21)	(256)

The degree of direct contact with foreign counterparts, either through participation in foreign markets (higher exports as a share of production) or by higher foreign capital equity ownership, appears to influence opinion on the 1970 exclusion of Spain from full participation in the expected direction. Those with more extensive foreign contacts tended more fully to accept Europe's positions about Spain's political inadequacies, fewer such individuals labelling the exclusion a pretext used to avoid feared economic competition. (Some die-hards, on the other hand, described the pretext as aris-ing not from fear of economic competition by Europe but from the leyenda negra.) The relationship by the level of foreign capital participation in the firm, in par-ticular, appears significant. While among fully domestic firms only 25 percent accepted Europe's premises, 62 percent of the heads of fully foreign-owned firms agreed with the EC.

Table 7.2 Employer Perceptions of the 1970 Exclusion by Assessment of Franco

| | Assessment of Franco: | | | | | |
	full approval	qualified approval	inter-mediate	qualified disap-proval	full disap-proval	Total
The political exclusion rationale was: The fundamental and real reason	8.3	26.9	15.6	40.4	37.5	28.9
A pretext	91.7	71.6	84.4	57.4	54.2	68.8
Other answers	0.0	1.5	0.0	2.1	8.3	2.3
	(12)	(134)	(32)	(47)	(24)	(256)

Not surprisingly, a chief executive's political views regarding the Franco regime also help explain opinions about the EC's arguments. The more favorably disposed toward the Franco regime, the more critical of the EC's policies toward Spain. This is not surprising given that the EC's actions excluding Spain throughout the 1960s and 1970s were targeted directly against its political regime. Among chief executives totally approv-ing of Franco, 92 percent labelled the exclusion a pre-text, compared to a substantially lower 54 percent among those who totally disapproved of Franco. That an impor-tant majority of those favorably disposed toward Franco should have been suspicious of the EC is not surprising. It is more intriguing, however, to note the persistence during the early 1980s of a strange anti-European legacy even among many Spaniards on the left.

Fifty-seven percent of chief executives believed that the EC had a political as well as an economic di-mension. One would expect that such individuals would also be somewhat more willing to accept the validity of Spanish exclusion on political grounds. Such proves not to be the case, however. There was no significant dif-

ference regarding the assessment of the 1970 agreement
between chief executives who viewed the EC as limited
to the economic realm and those acknowledging the existence of a political dimension.

THE VALIDITY OF THE EC'S EXCLUSION OF SPAIN

Regardless of a given chief executive's views
about whether the EC's denial of full integration was
the fundamental reason or merely a pretext, individuals
could independently consider whether the arguments extended by the EC were justifiable or not. Logically one
would expect that chief executives who labelled the exclusion a pretext would also consider it unjustified.
Likewise, the minority who viewed the EC's arguments as
the fundamental reason would largely also view those
arguments as valid or justifiable. Particularly in light
of the high correlation already established between
opinions on the EC's reasoning and political views about
Franco, one would expect a similar high correlation between opinions about the EC's reasoning and the validity
of such arguments.

Table 7.3 Justness of the EC's Grounds for Excluding Spain from
Full Integration

	Rationale: Fundamental Reason	Pretext	Other	Total
Exclusion was justifiable:				
Yes	75.7	38.9	50.0	49.8
No	21.6	57.1	33.3	46.3
Other answers	2.7 (74)	4.0 (175)	16.7 (6)	3.9 (255)

Not surprisingly, our findings are as expected.
Those closest to the EC view are the 76 percent (in the
first column) who both viewed the exclusionary arguments
as the fundamental reason and also considered them
justifiable. Although these represent 76 percent of
those who believed the EC's argument was the fundamental
reason, they represent only 22 percent of chief executives. These individuals accepted the parameters set by
the Treaty of Rome as valid and applicable against
Franquist Spain. The 22 percent in that column considering the EC arguments as the fundamental motives for

exclusion but considering them unjustifiable could include: (1) individuals somewhat more sympathetic to the Franco regime, that it sufficiently approximated a liberal state, at least in the economic realm, to warrant fuller participation in the EC; (2) business people believing that the political dimension of the EC, whether it existed or not, was essentially inappropriate for an organization whose objectives should be limited to the economic sphere; and (3) individuals who are fundamentally anti-EC or opposed to a federated Europe.

A substantial majority--57%--of those labelling the exclusionary arguments a pretext logically considered them unjustified (a significant 39% of chief executives). However, more interesting is the relatively high 39 percent (in the second column) who viewed the exclusionary premises as a pretext, probably motivated by economic factors, yet felt them to be justifiable. These individuals believed that the rejection of full Spanish participation was motivated more by economic considerations on the EC's side, but nevertheless conceded that the political status of Spain at the time was inappropriate for Europe given the strictures of the Treaty of Rome. This hypothesis is supported if the variables are controlled by the assessment of Franco.

Table 7.4 Justness of the EC's Grounds for Excluding Spain from Full Integration by Assessment of Franco

	Franco approvals: Rationale:			Franco disapprovals:		
	Fundamental reason	Pretext	Sub-total	Fundamental reason	Pretext	Sub-total
Exclusion justifiable:						
Yes	64.9	25.2	35.6	92.9	64.1	75.7
No	32.4	70.1	60.3	7.1	35.9	24.3
Other	2.7	4.7	4.1	0.0	0.0	0.0
	(37)	(107)	(146)	(28)	(39)	(70)

Among those who stated either full or qualified approval of Franco, 65 percent who believed that political criteria for exclusion extended by the EC were the fundamental reason also felt that it was justified. Among those disapproving of Franco's actions, fully 93 percent closely approximate the EC position: They believed that the exclusionary rational was the fundamental reason and also considered it justified in its application to Spain. While 70 percent of those indivi-

duals with pro-Franco sentiments considered the exclusion an unjustifiable pretext, only 36 percent, or
roughly half of that proportion, felt likewise among
those who were critical of Franco.

If we control the views about the justness of the
EC's grounds for exclusion of Spain by views regarding
the EC's areas of competence, we also derive expected
findings. A lower 66 percent of those who believe the
EC to be limited to the economic sphere believed the
exclusionary rational was a justifiable fundamental reason. Among those who believed the EC possessed a political dimension in addition to the economic, a significantly higher 84 percent approximated the EC posture.
Hence, some of those who considered the exclusion unjustified did so given that they opposed EC jurisdiction
in political arenas.

Thus, the 22 percent of chief executives who
considered the EC's exclusion as the fundamental reason
but considered it unjustifiable is largely explained by:
(1) those more favorable to Franco (32% in this category
versus 7% among anti-Franquists); and (2) those who considered the EC limited to economics (31% in this category versus 14% among those attributing a political
dimension to the EC).

JUSTIFICATION FOR THE EC'S EXCLUSION OF SPAIN

It is not surprising that a strong relationship
exists between one's views of the EC's criteria in excluding Spain and one's opinions about the Spanish political system. One would also expect other characteristics to provide further explanations as to opinions
about the EC's postures, but it proved difficult to
identify any such characteristics. Whereas companies
with greater foreign contacts, and those with high export levels or with high foreign capital participation,
tended to accept the EC arguments as the fundamental
motive, these indicators of more extensive foreign contacts fail to say anything interesting about attitudes
regarding the justness of the EC's exclusion.

The level of exports as a share of production
generally produces a pattern in the expected direction
(approximating the EC's view the higher the export
share), but with inconsistencies and at statistically
insignificant levels. Looking at the proportion of exports to the EC rather than overall export levels produces slightly more interesting figures, but still
includes inconsistencies and is not statistically significant. Among exporters with heavier EC market orientations, 58 percent of those with 20 percent to 50

percent of their exports destined to EC markets believed
that the exclusion was justifiable, as did 59 percent
of those with more than 50 percent of their exports going to the EC. Among non-exporters, 52 percent considered the exclusion justifiable. Also, size of firm is
not important in explaining EC attitudes.

Table 7.5 EC Exclusion as Justifiable by Province

Exclusion justifiable:	M	B	VZ	VA	S	Total
Yes	41.9	51.5	63.3	65.4	33.3	50.2
No	52.3	47.5	30.0	34.6	66.7	46.7
DK/NR	5.8	1.0	6.7	0.0	0.0	3.2
	(86)	(101)	(30)	(26)	(12)	(255)

Not surprisingly, a large majority in Vizcaya accepted the EC's criticism of the Franco regime as legitimate, and a higher percentage in Barcelona did so as
well relative to Madrid. However, Valencia is more interesting given its apparently incongruous position of
political conservatism in relation to Franco, but with
the highest proportion of any province labelling the
exclusionary rationale a pretext (89%), matched now with
the largest proportion accepting the exclusion as justifiable. The explanation probably lies in the very high
integration of Valencia into European markets.

Table 7.6 EC Exclusion as Justifiable by Assessment of Franco

	Assessment of Franco:					
	Full approval	Qualified approval	Inter- mediate	Qualified disapproval	Full disapproval	Total
Exclusion justifiable:						
Yes	33.3	35.8	55.9	69.6	87.5	49.8
No	58.3	60.4	38.2	30.4	12.5	46.3
DK/NR	8.3	3.7	5.9	0.0	0.0	3.9
	(12)	(134)	(34)	(46)	(24)	(257)

As stated at the outset, political characteristics
logically produce the strongest relationships. While
only a third of the most Franquist considered the exclusion justifiable, nearly nine-tenths of the most

critical of Franco considered the exclusion justifiable.
Clearly the vision of the EC at that time, given its
very clear statements regarding the incompatibility of
dictatorship with the principles embodied in the Treaty
of Rome, were very closely linked to one's own appreciation of the existing authoritarian political system.

Similar patterns appear by party vote. Fewer than
one-third of AP voters (1979 elections) considered the
exclusion justifiable, while half the UCD voters considered it so. Furthermore, greater proportions of supporters of the important regional parties, Convèrgencia
(56%) and the Basque Nationalists (83%), accepted the
EC's criteria.

Table 7.7 EC Exclusion as Justifiable by Preferred Role of the State in the
Economy

Exclusion justifiable:	Preferred State role in the economy:				
	Fully free enterprise	Some minimal indicative planning	Incentives & limited public sector	Large public sector	Total
Yes	42.3	49.1	50.8	67.7	49.8
No	55.1	45.6	46.0	32.3	46.3
DK/NR	2.6 (78)	5.3 (57)	3.2 (63)	0.0 (31)	3.9 (257)

It also appears that the more one supports greater
interventionism by the state in the economy, the more
likely one was to have supported the EC's 1970 criteria
as valid. But caution should be used in looking at economic preference by Spanish business at this time. The
Franquist state was highly interventionist and in no way
a free enterprise system. Yet, some in business perceived support for a large public sector as support for
Socialist policies. (Recall also that our survey was
long before the Socialists had proven themselves as genuine economic pragmatists.) Many in business supported
"free enterprise" as a political--and not economic--
posture.

A FRAMEWORK FOR ASSESSING THE EXPECTED IMPACT OF
INTEGRATION

In the 1980s, many Spaniards were worried about
the potential sectoral impact that integration would
bring. Before Spanish accession, few in business had a

clear idea of what EC integration portended for their own industries. Many important factors would have major sectoral impacts, including: (1) the adoption by Spain of the Common External Tariff (CET) and assumption of the major EC agreements with third countries, particularly those with the European Free Trade Association (EFTA), the Lomé Convention, and the global Mediterranean policies; (2) the common agricultural policy (CAP), whose eventual implementation in Spain in fact led to a major EC-U.S. trade dispute immediately following Spanish integration because of the considerable decline in imports of American cereals; (3) access to regional development funds; (4) the potential availability of full factor mobility; (5) adoption of the value added tax (VAT); (6) the application of a series of EC standards in areas of work and welfare; and (7) political ramifications.

That the EC was composed of a large number of strong diversified economies tended to diminish the losses that would be incurred as a consequence of trade diversion. The EC's standing agreement with EFTA countries, the EC's "hinterland," further diminishes losses from trade diversion.[30]

An early analysis by Balassa for the EC-Six, using 1958-1960 data for trade in manufactures, indicated that, with the exception of a relatively few commodities, the formation of the Common Market led to trade creation. Aggregating all third countries, losses from diversion in certain products was more than compensated for by gains from trade creation in others, although one has to look at the commodity composition of individual countries to calculate their net balances.[31]

Spanish integration clearly has led to significant trade diversion, but Spain also has boomed since integration. While technically it would be difficult to calculate the direct contribution of entry to the economic boom of the late 1980s, clearly investor confidence received a major boost. Expectations changed dramatically. It has been thanks to continued and steady huge inflows of foreign, long-term capital that official reserves stood at $38 billion in mid-year 1988, nearly three times the pre-integration level of 1985. In 1987, these reserves for the first time exceeded the level of external debt, which has slowly been declining since 1983. This growth in long-term capital inflows is a reflection of increased foreign investor confidence, a good deal of which was engendered by EC membership. We can also assume that in addition to any sense of greater economic policy stability--and dare I say political stability--many investors were attracted by the possibility of exploiting Spain's relatively lower factor costs and using the country as an export base for an ever more open EC. One should also recall that Spain's rapidly growing domestic market also remains somewhat less mature than those elsewhere in the EC, and as such might hold some attraction in of itself. Independent of the attractiveness of EC membership, however, the growth in foreign investment has also been consistent with official government policy encouraging liberal views towards such long-term operations.

A number of chief executives had, in fact, commented that clearer knowledge of what to expect given Spanish integration would prove more important that the actual tariff reductions and other negotiated settlements.

One threat posed by the southern enlargements (to twelve) mentioned by Tsoukalis was the possibility that the existing vertical division of labor between the more developed north and the three new entrants might be frozen. Of the three new EC states, however, the mix of Spanish exports and imports with the EC looked the most promising, and such appears now to be the case. Compared to Portugal or Greece, Spain's significantly more diversified export base and larger economy lent a pronounced intra-sectoral, rather than intersectoral, character to EC-Spanish trade, placing Spain in a more favorable position than either of the other two countries. The intra-industry specialization in Spanish trade with the EC already included broad groups of capital goods, product cycle goods in the Vernon-Hirsh sense, that sold well in Europe, including products in metal working, machinery, passenger car, and shipbuilding.[32]

While in the 1970s and early 1980s one might have generalized that Spain's comparative advantage rested on labor-intensive and resource-based products, one could also look at product cycle arguments, Spanish integration into the internationalization in the production of certain goods, and the institutional or targeted promotion of specific industries within Spain. Each could foretell some of the consequences of integration.

SECTORAL EXPECTATIONS OF INTEGRATION

Much of the economic literature available in Spain during the early 1980s on the EC's market impacts were not very encouraging. A major ESADE analysis of 935 industrial products was based on past trade performance. ESADE estimated the changes in trade that would be produced between Spain and the EC in the absence of tariff protection. Of the 935 items, only 19 percent (177) were classified as clearly well positioned. Furthermore, only

12 percent of these--that is to say, only 2 percent of all the 935 products analyzed--represented at least 10 percent of EC-Spanish trade in their given industry (for 1976). In contrast, 57 percent of the items demonstrated "very poor commercial performance" (the lowest possible of the four categories). These products with dismal outlooks included items from all nineteen of the major sectoral classifications used in the ESADE analysis.[33] Naturally, the ESADE study, as others of the pre-entry period, could not have foreseen the fundamental change in the investment climate, the availability of significant new sources of foreign capital, long-term political stability within Spain, and the advent of the internal market heralding major new potential for a reinvigorated Europe.

Spain's traditional weak trade balance was well-known. The country suffered a trade deficit of $11.7 billion in 1980, $10 billion in 1981, and $9.3 billion in 1982. Services, particularly tourism, and other net transfers play a crucial role in improving the overall current balance (which after a small surplus in 1979, was at a $5.2 billion deficit in 1980, $4.8 billion in 1981, and $4.2 billion in 1982). In 1980, the year before our interviews and the worst trade year throughout the 1970s-1980s period, exports represented not quite two-thirds of imports (64.6%). The trade balance with the EC was more favorable, however. Exports to the EC represented about 98 percent of imports.[34]

Given Spain's weak past trade performance and the low expectations in the economic analyses then available, both chief executives and association leaders were surprisingly optimistic about how their own industries would fare. Slightly more than one third expected that integration would have a positive impact in their own industry. Fewer than a third of chief executives and less than a fifth of association leaders held negative expectations.[35]

ESADE had found the highest number of products with favorable outlooks in consumer goods sectors, followed by intermediate goods products, particularly those at lower levels of sophistication.[36] Consumer products listed included food products, textiles, shoes, toys, furniture, and costume jewelry. Intermediate goods included tiles, mineral products, and tires. However, recall that ESADE also classified products from each of its nineteen major sectoral groupings in the very poor commercial performance category. Hence, it is not surprising to find dispersion of opinion among business people.

Table 7.8   Industry Expectations of the Impact of Integration

Chief Executives:

	Energy	Capital goods	Inter-mediate goods	Consumer goods	Con-struction	Total
Negative	12.5	37.0	23.5	32.1	6.3	29.2
Little/none	75.0	23.9	5.9	16.0	40.6	23.7
Compensatory	0.0	10.9	11.8	8.5	6.3	8.9
Positive	12.5	25.0	52.9	42.5	43.8	35.8
Other	0.0	3.3	5.9	.9	3.1	2.3
	(8)	(92)	(17)	(106)	(32)	(257)

Association Leaders:

	Capital goods	Consumer goods	Service sectors	Other*	Total
Negative	33.3	21.1	11.1	21.4	19.1
Little/none	11.1	18.4	31.1	7.1	20.9
Compensatory	33.3	15.8	20.0	35.7	22.6
Positive	16.7	42.1	35.6	28.6	33.9
Other	5.6	2.6	2.2	7.1	3.5
	(18)	(38)	(45)	(14)	(115)

* The few associations in energy products, intermediate goods and construction made separate treatment inappropriate. These are combined with intersectoral associations.

A 1979 sectoral study by Noelke and Taylor, done under contract for the EC, classified Spanish industry into thirteen sectors, which were disaggregated into eighty-one subsectors and categorized into four classes by their level of promise, from "clearly favorably positioned" to "clearly unfavorably positioned." Each commodity group was assessed for twenty-seven factors influencing competitive position, grouped into six major headings: demand factors; past performance; international competition and current levels of protection; sector-wide factors; factors at both sectoral and enterprise levels; and enterprise factors.[37] As in the ESADE study, all the major sectors (in this case thirteen)

included commodity groupings classed unfavorably, although in three of these sectors, such individual products only fared as poorly as the third class, "moder-
ately unfavorably positioned." All (eight) remaining
major groupings included products in the least favorably
positioned class. Noelke and Taylor assessed the aero-
nautic, electronic, chemical and automotive auxiliary
sectors as particularly poorly positioned overall. Product groupings clearly favored were fine yarns, nitrogen
and potassium fertilizers, and paper paste. Leather
footwear, tires, and ceramic tiles also fared well.[38]

It was interesting that roughly equivalent proportions of individual chief executives as of leaders, over
a third of each, held positive expectations. Similar
proportions, at above a fifth each, foresaw little or
no impact. More chief executives, at 29 percent, held
negative views than did leaders (19%). More leaders
(23%) held compensatory outlooks than did individual
chief executives (9%). To have more frequently expressed
expectations of both positive and negative results
(i.e., compensatory) was a more political response. Associations representing numerous companies, which often
had differing economic potentials, would tend to argue
that their companies would suffer different fates under
an integrated Spain. In part this response reflected
knowledge that association constituents differed in
their individual assessments.

**EXPORT LEVELS AND EXPECTATIONS OF THE SECTORAL IMPACT
OF INTEGRATION**

As one might have expected, the higher the proportion of production going to the EC, the more likely a
chief executive held strong views about the impact of
integration. Excluding non-exporting companies, we find
that the greater the orientation of exports toward the
EC-Ten, the less likely that chief executives were to
locate themselves on either of the two intermediate categories (little/none or compensatory impacts) and the
more likely either a positive or negative expectation.
Among those exporters without EC markets, 43 percent
believed integration would produce minimal or no sectoral impact or compensatory impacts. This figure declines consistently as the level of EC market orientation of exports increased. Thirty-eight percent fell
into intermediate impact categories among those with
minor EC market orientation (1%-19% of exports). Twenty-
four percent did so among those exporting 20 percent to
50 percent of the EC. Only 16 percent did so among those
sending over half of their exports toward EC markets.

Table 7.9   Expected Sectoral Impact among Exporting Companies

| | Percentage of firm's exports destined for EC markets: | | | | |
	zero	1-19%	20-50%	51-100%	Total
Negative	28.6	29.4	31.6	41.2	33.5
Little/none	34.3	23.5	13.2	7.8	18.0
Compensatory	8.6	14.7	10.5	7.8	10.2
Positive	22.9	29.4	44.7	43.1	36.5
Don't know	5.7	2.9	0.0	0.0	1.8
	(35)	(34)	(38)	(51)	(167)

High orientation of company production toward EC markets did not necessarily lead to positive expectations regarding the sectoral impact of integration. Relatively consistent increases emerge in the percentages of both negative and positive responses as the share of exports destined for the EC increase. Among those who were most committed to EC markets, there was a high 41 percent negative response and a high 43 percent positive response.

Table 7.9 does not control for the importance of exports as a share of production. Thus, included among "high EC oriented companies" are some for which exports are only of minor importance and others orienting most of their production for export markets. Among those companies (N=44) that can be identified both as oriented toward the EC market (with more than 20% of their exports going to the EC) and as export-focused (exports accounting for a quarter or more of production), 46 percent expected a negative impact, 12 percent little or none, 5 percent compensatory, and 39 percent a positive sectoral impact. A closer look reveals that an important distinction emerges between those exporting between 25 percent and 50 percent of production and those exporting over half. Looking only at these two high export groups, with each orienting a fifth or more of their exports to the EC-Ten, fully 65 percent of those exporting at between a quarter and a half of production expected negative consequences from integration compared to an insubstantial 11 percent among the most export-focused (exports above 50%). Fully two-thirds of the latter expected a positive impact, compared to a small 23 percent among the 25 percent to 50 percent export group. Hence, for companies with a high EC market orientation, the large percentages of chief executives fearing damaging impacts headed companies where the major portion of production continued to be targeted toward the domestic market and, as such, were fearful of increased competition within Spain. This holds independent of sector. In contrast, those already having a high EC orientation and with relatively less dependence on the Spanish market, logically expected only to benefit from reductions in barriers. Among these most export-focused, the higher the concentration in EC markets, the higher the positive expectations.

Among the most export-focused, there was a strong EC orientation for every firm size category. Size proved of minimal importance in determining the heavy European orientation of companies with high export levels, although we do find a much greater likelihood of more export focus as firm size increases. Among exporting firms, the Common Market was already very important. Thirty-one percent of all exporting companies destined over half of their exports to the EC. A further 23 percent sent between 20 percent and 50 percent of their exports to the EC. This group of exporters with a significant EC orientation represents a third of our firms. Among companies exporting at intermediate levels (exporting at between 25% and 50% of production) and high exporters (above 50%), over 60 percent of overall exports were bound for the EC. Among companies exporting less than a quarter of their production, 47 percent directed over 20 percent of these exports to EC markets. Thus, for firms that export at more modest levels, the EC, although of relatively lesser importance than among intermediate or high exporters, continues to weigh very heavily. Exporting firms that do not direct any of their trade to the EC are overwhelmingly found among the smallest export category. Eighty percent of companies that export, but not to the EC, are firms that export under a quarter of their production.

A third of our companies did not export at all, and an additional 16 percent exported but not at all to the EC. Firms exporting above a quarter of their production or more and with a strong EC orientation (above 20% of their exports going to the Common Market) represented 17 percent of the sample. Few regular firms were among the most export-focused and not as many intermediate as large firms were high exporters, although among high exporters, all appeared about equally and strongly oriented toward the EC regardless of size. Among regular firms that were high exporters, there existed a particularly strong EC focus.

Both Valencia and Barcelona firms were heavily committed to EC markets. Among "modest" exporters, however, Valencia firms were more EC-oriented than their

Barcelona counterparts. Adjusting the percentage of exports destined for the EC by the weight of exporting versus non-exporting firms in each province indicates that Valencia's level of "integration" in EC markets was roughly twice that of Barcelona, whose level of commitment to EC markets was comparable to that of Vizcaya companies. Fourteen percent of Madrid firms were high exporters with a strong EC orientation, as were 17 percent of Barcelona and Vizcaya firms, and 39 percent of Valencia firms. No firm in Sevilla was in that category.

There were fewer non-exporting firms among those fully or majority-controlled by foreign capital, but foreign controlled firms were also less likely to be high exporting firms than fully domestic or minority foreign firms. Fully foreign-owned or foreign-dominated firms fell into two groups--those established in Spain to service the domestic market, and those using the country as an export base.

Although a slightly smaller proportion of foreign companies figured among those exporting over a quarter of production, these firms tended to be much more heavily oriented toward Europe than their fully domestic or minority foreign counterparts. For the three exporting sectors in which both Spanish and foreign firms were present (capital goods, intermediate and consumer goods), only among intermediate goods producers was there a higher proportion of foreign-controlled firms that were high exporters compared to domestic firms (although all intermediate goods companies tended to have heavy export orientations).

Important foreign capital participation was present in the capital goods sector (32% either majority or fully foreign), intermediate goods sector (41%), and consumer goods sector (16%). In looking only at foreign controlled firms, 35 percent of consumer goods companies and 38 percent of capital goods companies had concentrations of 20 percent or more of their exports going toward the EC, as did 86 percent of foreign-controlled intermediate goods companies. Hence, whereas in the intermediate goods sector foreign capital invested in Spain with a view toward Europe, the Spanish domestic market loomed larger for foreign investors in the consumer and capital goods sectors. Nonetheless, it is significant that Europe was a more important destination for the exports of foreign-controlled companies than domestic.

For the group of 700 largest companies, Tsoukalis reported findings similar to our own. On average, substantial differences did not exist between foreign-owned and Spanish companies when looking at exports as a share of total sales. By industry, only in clothing, leather, and footwear (49.95%), paper (40.95%), iron and steel (29.5%), and non-electrical machinery (22.6%), did exports constitute a relatively large share of total production among foreign-controlled companies. Tsoukalis concluded that the domestic market provided the main incentive for most foreign direct investment. Perhaps ominously, Tsoukalis feared that the higher dependence by foreign companies on imported inputs could have unfavorable consequences for Spain following EC entry.[39] Some of this has been borne out in post-integration trade data.

SECTORAL EXPECTATIONS AND EUROPEANIST SENTIMENT

A priori, one would have expected economic factors and expectations to have an important impact on a business person's opinions with regard to a united Europe. Yet my data indicated otherwise. Spanish business generally favored a united Europe with Spain as a part of it. No differences emerged in expression of such Europeanist sentiment among Spanish companies exporting at different levels and higher export orientation specifically targeting EC markets also did not correlate with higher Europeanist sentiment--which I define as the desire for the ultimate unification of the continent. Among associations, economic expectations at the sectoral level affected the degree of European identification only to a minor extent. Indeed, among chief executives slightly higher proportions of those who were non-exporters or who headed companies less committed to European markets expressed Europeanist sentiments than those with a high EC export market presence.

Table 7.10 Preferred Degree of Ultimate European Integration by Expected Sectoral Impact among Chief Executives

Preferred degree of integration:	Expected sectoral impact:				
	Negative	Little /none	Compen- satory	Positive	Total
Solely economic	15.1	6.7	3.0	13.2	12.3
Certain common political policies	28.8	28.3	30.4	30.8	29.2
Unification	52.1	65.0	56.5	53.8	56.5
Other/DK/NR	4.1	0.0	0.0	2.2	2.0
	(73)	(60)	(23)	(91)	(253)

Over half of those expecting to suffer a deleterious impact in their own sectors from integration nevertheless favored ultimate European unification, equivalent to the 54 percent who were "pro-Europe" among
those expecting positive repercussions from integration.
In a parallel manner, only 15 percent of those fearing
integration also hoped Europe would unify solely in the
economic realm, as did 13 percent of those expecting to
profit from Spanish entry. Overall, the 12 percent who
hoped that European integration would achieve solely
economic ends is relatively inconsequential, particularly when compared to the 57 percent in favor of full unification.

In her 1975-1976 survey among Barcelona and Sevilla entrepreneurs, Bancroft found similar pro-European
sentiments. Twenty-two percent of her respondents
(N=154) believed Spain should make every effort possible
to gain entrance to the Common Market at a rapid pace;
61 percent favored negotiations to enter with precau-
tions but at an accelerated pace; 12 percent favored
negotiating only for more tariff preferences but without
efforts to gain membership; 3 percent wanted to maintain
existing preferences without further efforts; and 1 percent wanted to withdraw from all ties.[40] While the question posed was more commercial than political or emo-
tional, the high percentages in favor of bringing Spain
closer to Europe are very significant.

Official associational positions on Spanish entry
responded more to economic imperatives than did the
expression of pro-European sentiment among individual
chief executives. Not a single association whose leader
expected a negative impact had an official associational
position of unqualified support for Spanish integration.
Forty-six percent of those leaders expecting a positive
economic impact for their sectors also led associations
with positions of unqualified support for Spanish entry.
Only among those expecting a negative impact did we find
official associational opposition to Spanish entry,
albeit a minor 9 percent. Yet even among associations
whose leaders expected a negative economic impact, 50
percent had official positions of qualified support for
Spanish integration. Hence, as at individual companies,
one found more pro-European sentiment than was warranted
by straight economic imperatives. For associations, the
expected sectoral impact influences official policy but
very high percentages are favorably disposed toward entry among all associations and open opposition to entry
was almost non-existent. Associations in sectors more
fearful about economic impacts were much more likely not
to have an official position than to oppose Spanish
entry.

Table 7.11 Official Associational Position on Spanish Integration
by the Expected Sectoral Impact

| Association position: | Expected sectoral impact: | | | | |
	Negative	Little /none	Compen-satory	Positive	Total
Favorable	0.0	37.5	19.2	46.2	28.7
Qualified favorable	50.0	8.3	34.6	35.9	32.2
Intermediate	9.1	20.8	26.9	2.6	13.0
Qualified unfavorable	9.1	0.0	0.0	0.0	1.7
Unfavorable	0.0	0.0	0.0	0.0	0.0
Have no position	31.8	29.2	19.2	12.8	22.6
Other	0.0	4.2	0.0	2.6	1.7
	(22)	(24)	(26)	(39)	(115)

PROVINCE, SIZE, AND EUROPEANIST SENTIMENT

The larger a company, the more likely its chief executive was pro-European, although in individual provinces, greater proportions of Europeanists did not rise consistently by company size. Although Linz and de Miguel used a definition of Europeanist sentiment not directly comparable to our own, certain parallels emerge in the data. The Linz and de Miguel survey was undertaken during a period when very few Spaniards understood the early efforts at European integration. Correspondingly, "Europeanism" encompassed all those who supported Spanish entry into either the EEC or EFTA, or both, as the case might be![41] As with the 1981 data, overall, the larger the firm, the more likely to find a pro-European chief. At the provincial level, 62 percent of the chief executives in Madrid and Barcelona firms were classified as Europeanists by Linz and de Miguel, very close to the 61 percent we found among Madrid chief executives and 63 percent in Barcelona. As in 1981, Vizcaya had been considerably less Europeanist overall than Madrid or Barcelona with 45 percent in

1961. In 1981, the Vizcaya figure was 40 percent. In both surveys, significantly smaller proportions of regular and intermediate Vizcaya company chief executives were Europeanists, compared to much higher proportions among large companies.

Table 7.12 Europeanism and Chief Executives

Martínez data of 1981:

	M	B	VZ	VA	S	Total
Regular	59	47	25	33	50	46
Intermediate	46	63	22	57	33	51
Large	71	79	78	43	50	72
Total	61	63	40	42	42	57
	(86)	(101)	(30)	(26)	(12)	(255)

Linz and de Miguel data of 1960-1961:

	M	B	VZ	Total
Regular	63	67	35	59
Intermediate	61	63	42	60
Large	63	52	73	62
Total	62	62	45	60
	(77)	(156)	(71)	(460)

CONTACTS WITH THE EC AND EUROPEANIST SENTIMENT

Economic factors should have strongly influenced a businessman's opinions on a united Europe. Yet we have now seen that economic realities in relation to the EC did not necessarily determine attitudes on the ultimate European issue. Slightly higher proportions of non-exporters and those less committed to European markets expressed Europeanist sentiments than those with high EC export market concentration (those exporting at least a fifth of their exports to the EC). Among exporters with a high EC-market orientation, an impressive 51 percent favored unification, but this is nonetheless lower than the 57 percent overall average for all chief executives. Over a quarter of those chief executives who preferred that the EC limit itself to the economic sphere headed companies that oriented over half of their exports to the EC.

The failure for economic characteristics to explain attitudes about Spanish integration and the preferred ultimate objective of the EC is less surprising in light of the findings of the Linz and de Miguel work of twenty years earlier. They found the incongruous pattern wherein the worse the economic condition of the firm, the more likely its chief executive would be optimistic about the Common Market. They attributed this to poorer information available to such individuals. Those who were more concerned with the future well-being of their companies had generally exerted greater efforts in obtaining additional information and could better appreciative the potentially deleterious effects of integration, leading them to hold more reserved positions on Spanish entry. For the 1960 survey, personal and biographical factors, and not characteristics of the companies involved, proved the most telling in explaining attitudes held on the Common Market issue.[42]

Linz and de Miguel found the highest levels of Europeanist sentiment among younger chief executives, those whose fathers were from higher social levels (such as large employers, engineers, other professionals) and those who had travelled extensively. Looking at such sociological background characteristics among 1981 respondents, those from higher social or professional classes were not significantly more Europeanist than the average, but those chief executives whose fathers had been in the lowest two of our occupational categories, farmers and workers, expressed significantly lower levels of Europeanist sentiment (43%). Those favoring greater levels of state participation in the economy or who favored a large public sector, also had fewer Europeanists among them (45%), as did (1979) voters of AP/CD (37%), which is interesting because the most anti-Franquist also tended not to be pro-Europeanist (38%). Those declaring total approval of Franco registered 75 percent in favor of full European unification and those who voiced qualified support of Franco were also slightly more Europeanist than the average, while those voicing qualified disapproval of Franco were slightly less Europeanist.

THE ROLE OF ASSOCIATIONS ON THE EC ISSUE

Those chief executives whose companies were more integrated into European markets and who were, therefore, presumably better informed, tended to hold stronger views about the potential sectoral impact of entry and registered higher proportions in the negative and positive categories. This variable did not influence Europeanist sentiment, however. Among association leaders, economic expectations played a role in determining official policies, although high percentages of all associations favored Spanish entry and this is what should be stressed. The level of available information may also have played a role.

In looking at information available to associations, not surprisingly, a high correlation exists between associations with greater international contacts with foreign business associations and associations that had by 1982 already undertaken impact studies for their memberships. As one might have expected, direct CEOE affiliates, intermediate associations, and large associations with stronger budgets tended to be those that maintained more international contacts and that had undertaken studies.

Table 7.13 Information and Expected Sectoral Impact among Associations

| | Had conducted EC impact study for members: | | Level of contacts with counterpart associations in EC: | | | |
	No	Yes	None	Some	Member of International organization	Total
Negative	23.1	12.2	22.9	13.3	18.9	19.1
Little/none	26.2	14.3	27.1	16.7	16.2	20.9
Compensatory	12.3	36.7	16.7	23.3	29.7	22.6
Positive	33.8	34.7	31.3	40.0	32.4	33.9
Other	4.6	2.0	2.1	6.7	2.7	3.5
	(65)	(49)	(48)	(30)	(37)	(115)

In contrast to individual chief executives, associations with greater information--either by having conducted sectoral studies or through affiliation with international organizations--had leaders who tended in greater numbers to fall into one of the intermediate impact categories, namely the compensatory category (i.e., both positive and negative impacts). While chief executives of more "integrated" companies tended to fall more distinctly into either negative or positive categories, leaders with more access to information extended more nuanced responses. The overwhelming majority of associations in the early 1980s already had stated positions regarding Spanish entry into the Common Market, either generally strongly or generally supportive. Only slightly more than a fifth did not have any official position, with higher concentrations among indirect affiliates of the CEOE (28%) and among the smallest organizations (38% among those with budgets under 7 million pesetas). Not a single large association (over 30 million pesetas) failed to have a position. A relatively higher proportion of service sector associations (33%) than of either capital goods (28%) or consumer goods (16%) associations did not have an official position, a function particularly of the relative proportion (31%) of service sector associations whose leaders expected little or no sectoral impact (compared to 11% of capital goods association leaders and 18% of those heading consumer goods associations). The highest proportion of associations lacking an official posture were Vizcaya associations, where more than half (54%) did not have a position. This is particularly striking given that 70 percent of Vizcaya leaders expected either a positive or negative impact, and only 8 percent did not expect any impact. While Vizcaya leaders expected an impact, however, very few Vizcaya associations (8%) had actually undertaken sectoral impact studies, while about half of Madrid (47%) and Barcelona (50%) associations had done so. The greater ambivalence among Vizcaya associations may be related to the low level of Europeanist sentiment among Basque chief executives. The lowest level of Europeanist sentiment among chief executives was found in Vizcaya (40% compared to 61% Madrid chief executives and 63% in Barcelona). At the provincial level, Madrid associations were the most favorably disposed toward integration.

The availability of information appears to have played a role, although it was probably a two-way street; that is, those who were interested in integration would have tended to acquire more information. Among those lacking information and those without contacts with counterpart organizations in the EC, 29 percent did not have official positions, compared to 12 percent among those who had conducted impact studies and 18 percent among those who had contacts with business organizations of EC member states.

The EC process definitely represents a valuable area in which associations can develop the selective incentives that play a role in maintaining employer membership. Nevertheless, although the majority of associations had already adopted positions on the EC by early 1982, only 43 percent had undertaken studies, which would have been an ideal means by which to favor member firms over non-members. Chief executives were asked if their sectoral associations had offered any information or guidance on the EC. A surprisingly close 43.5 percent answered in the affirmative. An additional 2 percent responded that the associations had dealt with the topic, but in an unsatisfactory manner.

It remains as yet to be seen whether the integration of Spain into the EC and deepening of the internal market will contribute to a reversal of trends towards increased concentration of associational activities in the non-economic areas described at length in Chapters 3 and 4. Those associations approximating the role of trade associations in traditional molds may profit more from integration in consolidating employer support, given the reinforced need for such services.

Even in the early 1980s, an association like ASEFA, the association for synthetic fibers, was successful in its promotion of members' exports. ASEFA annually publishes extensive amounts of export and macroeconomic data, and placed a heavy emphasis on trade shows and trade missions abroad. ASEFA's 360 members were already heavily focused on EC markets and the presentation of their published data reflected a sensitivity to the emerging importance of the EC for Spain. By major product heading, 62 percent of ASEFA member company exports of finished textiles went to the EC, as did 37 percent of their yarns and threads and 32 percent of their fabric trimmings exports. This high and early EC export orientation contradicted the fact that none of these three product areas were favored in any of the major published sectoral analyses then available.[43] While other associations would not necessarily adopt similar trade activities to such an exclusive extent, more such activity could be expected.

The CEOE was very active and public on the EC issue. Most evident of the peak's interest was the office it already maintained in Brussels in the early 1980s and the early publication in February and December of 1981 of a brief, two-part analysis of Common Market integration. While not polemical, the CEOE document, La empresa española ante la adhesión al Mercado Común, approximated more a blueprint for government economic policy than a sectoral impact analysis. The introductory volume placed great stress on economic policies that the CEOE favored independently of EC integration, such as the granting of free dismissal, lower employer contributions to social security, and lower interest rates. The volume also stressed industrial restructuring (reconversión) and made a case in favor of lessening rigidities in within-firm wage and salary ratios (el abanico salarial), as opposed to the widespread use of either fixed-sum or proportional wage and salary in-

creases."[44] Volume two on the sectoral analyses of integration placed much less emphasis on comparative assessments and likely impacts, such as found in the more
analytical studies cited earlier, and instead emphasized
policy preferences and requirements for a number of important industries. Restructuring was a constant theme.
The CEOE's study was favorably disposed toward the EC
on balance, but called repeatedly for a ten-year transition. Nevertheless, Spain was described as a "new economic frontier,"[45] which was probably basically accurate.

As one might have expected, assessments by the
leaders of the CEOE's affiliated associations were
highly favorable regarding the peak's activities on the
EC. Member associations had been queried by the peak to
develop the 1981 policy piece. Seventy-eight percent of
the leaders assessed the peak's activities on the EC as
either positive or generally positive, and only 4 percent as negative. The directly affiliated were marginally more positive, as were intermediate organizations.
At 93 percent, Barcelona leaders were very positive,
while only 31 percent of Vizcaya leaders drew positive
assessments. Thirty-nine percent in Vizcaya were categorized with intermediate responses, and a high 31 percent were in the "don't know/no response" category.

High positive assessments of the CEOE's efforts on
the EC were found among associations regardless of their
official postures on EC entry. Two-thirds of those associations with intermediate official lines extended favorable assessments, as did 73 percent of associations
without any posture.

ADDITIONAL IMPACT CONSIDERATIONS

From a list of possible expected impacts from
integration, chief executives generally expected positive results in areas that were more directly economic
in nature. They overwhelmingly expected agriculture to
benefit (93%). Only on unemployment were they more
hesitant (57%).

In many countries that were already heavily re-
liant on foreign investment, more of the same might not
always be interpreted as entirely positive. However, to
expect more foreign investment, as did Spanish chief
executives (82%), indicated a belief that the investment
climate would be enhanced by entry into the Common Market. This high affirmative response by Spanish business
should be interpreted as a positive response, substantiated by other data indicating a widespread tolerance
of multinationals on grounds of relative equality with
domestic firms. Fifty-one percent of chief executives

felt that multinationals should not face any legal distinctions relative to domestic firms. Only 11 percent felt that multinationals should be restricted only to those activities that Spanish firms could not undertake and 10 percent believed that multinationals should face greater restrictions in obtaining credit.

On the more sensitive question of diminished regional conflicts, most did not expect that EC entry would have an impact. Vizcaya chief executives did not differ substantially from those elsewhere (Vizcaya had 40% "yes," Madrid 33%, Barcelona 37% and Valencia 39%). Chief executives did reflect the widely held public view that integration would ensure the consolidation of democracy.

Table 7.14 Expectations among Chief Executives of the Effects of EC Integration on Spain

Integration will:			Other/	
	Yes	No	DK/NR	(N)
1. Benefit agriculture	93.4	4.3	2.4	(258)
2. Lower unemployment	56.6	39.9	2.3	(258)
3. Facilitate industrial modernization given increased availability of new technologies	82.6	16.2	1.2	(259)
4. Increase foreign investment in Spain	81.7	14.4	3.9	(257)
5. Diminish regional economic conflicts within Spain	36.3	53.1	10.6	(256)
6. Guarantee the free market system	85.7	12.8	1.6	(258)
7. Guarantee consolidation of the democratic system	78.7	19.4	1.9	(258)
8. Reduce the importance of Spanish-U.S. relations	53.7	42.5	3.9	(259)
9. Damage Spanish-Latin American relations	12.4	85.3	2.3	(259)

In contrast to the general optimism regarding the repercussions of EC integration, and paralleling the more somber assessments of the sectoral impact of integration, both chief executives and associations leaders were considerably less sanguine about the expected impact of the application of the value added tax (VAT).[46] Although 36 percent of the chief executives expected a favorable impact from integration overall, only 20 percent expected a favorable impact from application of the VAT. Similarly, only 17 percent of association leaders viewed the VAT favorably, compared to the 34 percent who expected a favorable sectoral impact.

Fifty-eight percent of the chief executives opposing the VAT did so because of its expected inflationary impact. Another widespread concern was that the introduction of a new tax provided an opportunity for politicians to raise the overall tax level. Introduction of the VAT displaced the General Tax on Business Transactions (IGTE), a turnover or "cascade" tax that taxed gross receipts for goods and services at each production or distribution stage. Turnover taxes discriminate in favor of vertically integrated industries and production processes and against industries whose value added occurs early in the production process. They are also not transparent to consumers, as are value added taxes. The VAT also displaced the luxury tax, monopoly taxes, and export subsidies, as well as some special taxes, such as that on beverages.[47] Certainly, the VAT is simpler, less discriminatory, more transparent, and more rational than the IGTE. Nonetheless, introduction of the VAT in January 1986 was credited with contributing 2 percent to increased consumer prices that year (which rose 8.8% overall).[48]

CONCLUSIONS

The integration of Spain into the EC involved much more far-reaching adjustments for the EC than did the incorporation of Greece or Portugal. Correctly, large proportions of Spanish business (over a third of each survey) were confident integration would be achieved over the short term (1983-1985). Only 14 percent of leaders and 19 percent of chief executives did not expect Spain would be admitted before 1990 or later.

The PSOE, as the party in government after 1982, accelerated the European option for Spain and astutely linked it firmly to continuance in the Western Alliance. Thereby, a traditionally anti-West party ably convinced its electorate that adhesion to the most staunchly military symbol of the West made sense for broader foreign policy ends. Many also argued that continuance in NATO was politically expedient to calm the right and to "civilianize" the military through contacts with democratic military forces. Undoubtedly, Calvo Sotelo's precipitous entry into NATO made it easier for González, who would have faced a daunting task in taking Spain into the alliance had it not been done for him.

The PSOE further linked the EC-NATO matrix together with the preeminent national sovereignty issue, Gibraltar, and implied that resolution of Spain's international political status would help consolidate the democratic system. Specifically on the EC, no significant political force in Spain during the 1980s opposed entry and no force emerged to articulate the latent anti-European sentiments present among a sector of the population (primarily on the right).

In the EC's favor, the Spanish population as a whole was generally supportive. The 1983 "Mentalities" survey conducted by DATA found that 12 percent of the population was strongly supportive of integration, with an additional 44 percent fairly supportive. Twenty percent were somewhat unfavorable and 10 percent were strongly opposed. Among chief executives, we found a majority (57%) who believed Europe should eventually be unified.[49]

For the business sector, the level of involvement by firms abroad, via export share considerations, or by foreign capital participation within the company, influenced the views held regarding past EC decisions brought against Spain, such as those related to the Preferential Trade Agreement of 1970. Further, economic and political conservatism among chief executives was an important determining element in their attitudes toward the EC. Political conservatism was particularly important in explaining attitudes on the justification for the EC to limit Franquist Spain to a preferential agreement.

Access to adequate information influenced chief executives to expect stronger consequences from integration. For example, higher proportions of chief executives more deeply committed to European export markets expected both positive and negative repercussions. Generally, only companies with low export levels or with weak EC export orientation expected little or no impact from integration.

In contrast, the availability of more information by associations, either through investment in studies on integration or through membership in international organizations with large European business memberships, influenced leaders to expect compensatory impacts, that is, both positive and negative repercussions. Such varied impacts might have been conditioned on the health of member companies or the range of commodities produced by member companies. The adoption of such associational postures may have responded to heightened political sensitivity by the collective interest groups. Overall, particularly among individual chief executives, there was considerably more optimism about the sectoral outlook from integration than would have been warranted given the warnings from the analytical analyses then available.

Despite widespread business criticism of past EC posturing on Spain, there existed overwhelming support among both chief executives and their associational representatives in favor of Spanish integration and of full European unification. This was evident among both groups, regardless of the often negative sectoral expectations of entry. High levels of Europeanist sentiment or of official pro-integration postures existed even among those chief executives or associations expecting more immediate damage than profit accruing to their own industries. Outside their own industry, there existed generally favorable expectations from integration.

It was already crystal clear from our own 1981-1982 data that integration would contribute substantially to investor confidence, which, in fact, has proven to be the case. Not surprisingly, greater certainty and investor confidence can easily outweigh negotiated settlements in their beneficial economic impact.

NOTES

1. María Josefa Molina Requena, <u>España y la economía del Mercado Común</u> (Madrid: Ceura, 1987).

2. Organization for Economic Cooperation and Development, <u>Economic Surveys: Spain 1988/1989</u> (Paris: OECD, May 1989), 16.

3. Organization for Economic Cooperation and Development, <u>OECD Economic Surveys: Spain</u> (Paris: OECD, 1988), pp. 7, 21, 56.

4. Gerard Curzon, introduction to Alfred Tovias, <u>Tariff Preferences in Mediterranean Diplomacy</u> (London: World Policy Research Centre, 1977), xviii.

5. Tovias, <u>Tariff Preferences</u>, 12.

6. The GATT permits the lowering and elimination of tariffs among countries willing to surrender a degree of national sovereignty in so doing. Article XXIV of the General Agreement deals with "interim agreements" leading eventually to full elimination of tariffs on all trade. While the EC, for GATT purposes, may have treated the 1970 Spanish agreement as interim, it failed to clarify subsequent steps. Tovias, <u>Tariff Preferences</u>, 86.

7.   Eric N. Baklanoff, Economic Transformation, 34.

8.   ESADE (Escuela Superior de Administración de Empresa), Pere Puiz i Bastard, study coordinator, La industria española ante la CEE (Madrid: Instituto de Estudios Económicos, 1979), 249-252.

9.   Baklanoff, Economic Transformation, 34.

10.   Tovias, Tariff Preferences, 55.

11.   If the EC increased its concessions to 70 percent after 1974, list A preferences granted by Spain would be increased to 70 percent and list B items to 30 percent, list C remaining as originally planned. Such further mutual reductions were never undertaken given radical changes in EC-Spanish relations over the intervening period.

12.   Tovias, Tariff Preferences, 53-54.

13.   Jurgen B. Donges, "The Economic Integration of Spain with the EEC: Problems and Prospects," found in Avi Shlaim and G. N. Yannopoulos, eds., The EEC and the Mediterranean Countries (Cambridge: Cambridge University Press, 1976), 224-228.

14.   Tovias, Tariff Preferences, 53.

15.   Items on which Spain maintained its highest levels of protection included furniture and toys, followed by optical and other precision equipment, electrical material, and certain textile subsectors such as rugs and tapestries, piece items, and clothing. ESADE, La industria, 253-254.

16.   ESADE, La industria, 249 and 256.

17.   Luis Gámir, as cited in ESADE, La industria, 43.

18.   Matthew McQueen, "Some Measures of the Economic Effects of Common Market Trade Preferences for the Mediterranean Countries," in Shlaim and Yannopoulos, The EEC, 21.

19.   Círculo de Economía, La opción europea para la economía española (Madrid: Guadiana, 1974), 43-44.

20.   Gámir, ESADE, La industria, 192-197.

21.   Ramón Tamames, as cited in ESADE, La industria, 43-44. The two authors contrast ideologically. Gámir served as a UCD government minister and Tamames was a prominent PCE figure (although Tamames has changed specific labels frequently as the circumstances have warranted).

22.   ESADE, La industria, 44.

23.   ESADE, La industria, 273.

24.   Gámir, ESADE, La industria, 13.

25.   Antonio Sánchez-Gijón, El camino hacia Europa (Madrid: Ediciones del Centro, 1973), 331-332.

26.   J.A.S. Grenville, The Major International Treaties (New York: Stein and Day, 1974), 412-427.

27.   For Greece, which served as a precedent for the EC, see the article by Van Coufoudakis, "The EEC and the 'Freezing' of the Greek Association, 1967-1974," in Journal of Common Market Studies, 16, 2 (December 1977).

28.   Juan Viúdez, The Export Behaviour of Spanish Manufacturers--An Evaluation of Interviews (Kiel: Kiel Institute of World Economics, November 1972), 8.

29.   Loukas Tsoukalis, The European Community, 124.   The same comparative generalization was drawn by Eduardo Punset, former Spanish minister for the EC negotiations, interviewed by the author (Barcelona, 9 October 1981). Punset was followed in his post by Leopoldo Calvo Sotelo. Subsequent to Calvo Sotelo's departure to assume the position of prime minister in 1981, the post of head of negotiations was downgraded to the subministerial level.

30.   Tovias, Tariff Preferences, 13.

31.   Bela Balassa, "Trade Creation and Trade Diversion in the European Common Market," The Economic Journal (March 1967): 9-15.

32.   Donges, "Economic Integration," 221. The model of the product cycle holds that as products become increasingly standardized and established in markets, production input requirements change, such as, for example, less skilled labor being necessary. This leads to realignments among producer countries as a re-

flection of relative factor endowments. Raymond Vernon, "International Investment and International Trade in the Product Cycle," Quarterly Journal of Economics (May 1966): 190-207.

33. ESADE, La industria, 356-377.

34. With a 32 percent increase in exports, Spain registered a first-ever favorable trade balance with the EC in 1983 of some 21.7 billion pesetas, which compared to a 50.7 billion peseta deficit in 1982. Exports to the EC represented 48.3 percent of total exports, and imports, 32.3 percent. The trade balance was most favorable with the Netherlands, which imported twice what it exported to Spain, as well as very favorable with France, Spain's single primary export market. ABC, Madrid, 7 March 1984, international edition.

35. DATA's 1983 "Mentalities" survey found that 9 percent of all Spaniards expected integration to prove "strongly beneficial," 48 percent "beneficial," 15 percent expected it would have little impact, 11 percent a damaging impact, and 4 percent a very damaging impact. Thirteen percent did not respond.

36. ESADE, La industria, 377.

37. Sector-wide factors included inputs, foreign technological dependence, labor costs, state participation, and so forth. Sector and enterprise factors were technological-level employed, availability of qualified labor inputs, and infrastructural realities. Enterprise level factors included credit facilities, firm size, level of specialization, management factors, and age of physical plant.

38. Michael Noelke and Robert Taylor, "L'Industrie espagnole face à la Communauté Economique Européenne: l'impact de l'adhésion" (European Research Associates, Brussels, October 1979): 1-47. The automotive outlook was more positive than that for the "automotive auxiliary" sector.

39. Tsoukalis, European Community, 94.

40. Bancroft, Industrial Entrepreneurship, 225-226.

41. Juan J. Linz and Amando de Miguel, "El Mercado Común, el capital extranjero y el empresario español," Productividad, 26 (January-March 1963): 18-41.

42.   Ibid., 29-41.

43.   Yarns and threads figured favorably, the others less so. Total sales in 1980 of ASEFA member firms for all three commodities exceeded $124 million. ASEFA, "Memoria 1980," (Madrid). ASEFA stands for "Agrupación Sindical Económica de las Fibras Artificiales y Sintéticas Cortadas." It is interesting that an association like ASEFA, which played a more traditional <u>trade</u> association role, also maintained its Franco-era name, inherited from Sindicato times--an infrequent, but not unique phenomenon among the previously Sindicato-integrated associations. ASEFA was founded in 1953.

44.   CEOE, <u>La empresa española ante la adhesión al Mercado Común</u>, vol. I (Madrid: February 1981), 15-27.

45.   Ibid., 15.

46.   On the trajectory of the adoption of the VAT by Spain see Thomas D. Lancaster, "A Price for Entry: The European Community, Spain and the Value-Added Tax" (Paper delivered at the conference of the American Political Science Association, Chicago, August 1983).

47.   It was not surprising that the association with the most fully developed position on the VAT was the one representing companies in the non-alcoholic beverages subsector. Indeed, its leader became quite animated when the topic was introduced.

48.   OECD, <u>OECD Economic Surveys: Spain 1987/1988</u> (Paris: OECD, 1988), 17-18.

49.   Interestingly, the Spanish population as a whole remained quite pro-European after four years of EC membership. A population survey conducted in late 1989 found that 55 percent of Spaniards felt EC membership on the whole had brought more favorable than unfavorable changes to their country, compared to 52 percent in France, 51 percent in the Federal Republic and 28 percent in the United Kingdom. "Los españoles, los más europeístas de la CE," <u>El País</u> edición internacional (Madrid: 20 November 1989), 1.

8

Conclusions

Looking back more than fifteen years from the perspective of the booming Spain of the early 1990s, it already
is difficult to appreciate the achievement represented
by the transition. Things did not have to turn out as
they did. Moderation did not have to win out over radicalism or retrenchment--but it did, due primarily to
capable leadership and the willingness by the vast majority of Spaniards to defer less demanding and more
parochial interests, and to accept a politics of consensus that eventually resulted in the achievement of a
more immediate collective objective--a consolidated
democracy.

Moderation characterized the major political parties that cooperated with Suárez, who, with the support
of the monarch, and through negotiations with party
elites, first won agreement for sweeping political reform and then approval of a pluralistic constitutional
order. At frequent intervals--the December 1976 referendum on the political reform, the June 1977 parliamentary elections, and the December 1978 referendum on
the constitution--the Spanish population as a whole
overwhelmingly endorsed the direction being taken by
political elites and supported the emerging system.
Noteworthy in this regard was the electorate's support
for political parties legitimating the system through
their platforms and activities. Perhaps among the most
emotionally laden manifestations of public support for
the system were the massively attended demonstrations
held nation-wide in major cities and small towns alike
on 27 February 1981, days after the abortive military
coup.

Some of the legitimacy accorded to the emerging

system by the broad public was due in part to the moderating influence of elites heading components of the
civil society, such as labor. The empirical work by
Fishman among workplace union leaders in Barcelona and
Madrid documents that the moderation expressed by national union leaders was, perhaps, even better articulated through the actions and posturing of local-level
leaders in individual firms who directly expressed and
implemented workers' demands for the consolidation of
the new democracy even above the full immediate ful-
fillment of their economic and social aims. Business,
for its part, also played a critical role. A loss of
confidence by the business community in the new system
could have been irreparable for democratic consolidation. Business, both collectively and through the aggregate of individual business decisions, cast its lot
with change. Some business sectors enthusiastically supported change. Others supported it more hesitantly but
were nonetheless cognizant that Spain required greater
coherence between its political system and achieved economic well-being. A more open political system would
better channel articulation of competing demands extended by a more affluent society.

Dahl's early work on polyarchies stated that there
appeared to be a high correlation between polyarchies
and more highly developed economies. I contend that
democracy is exceedingly likely in developed countries
when market control is relatively diffused. With hindsight, it was not really surprising to have found overwhelming support for a democratic system within the
Spanish business sector. A highly educated business
elite, directing a developed economy, and with individual market power at their personal disposal, could
only have supported a strengthened "free market" in
political power to better pursue both political-social
and economic ends on their own. Business wanted a political voice unencumbered by outdated bureaucratic restrictions and that reflected its achieved economic and
market self-confidence. And business, as did much of
Spain, wanted to be a part of Europe.

Much otherwise worthwhile academic work on democracy in other regions, particularly in the Latin America of the 1960s and 1970s, confused "state capitalism"
or other oligopolistic, pseudo-market systems in not
fully modernized societies with free markets in capitalist societies—to the detriment of our understanding
of the function of truly free markets on increasing
demands for democratization. Diffused economic control
can result in competition for the instruments of control
available to a regime attempting artificially to maintain a closed system. Furthermore, the more diffused the

market power, the less likely an authoritarian regime will be able to maintain its hegemony. The more diffused the benefits of free markets in the population overall, the more likely change will be moderate, the less likely it will be radical. While many commentators in the Western media were amazed by the success of the Spanish transition, the Spain of 1975 was not the Hemingwayesque Spain of the 1930s many still depicted in the press. Indeed, the "two Spains" or "la otra España" still existed in 1975, but the fervor of the divisions that made sense in 1936 were no longer present. Spain had enjoyed years of rapid growth, and although the distribution of growth's benefits were far from equitable, many individuals of modest means had enough material and social assets worth protecting from unnecessary and risky upheaval.

Business supported the <u>reforma</u> even on strictly political grounds. But many in business also perceived that the economic bases for a resumption of growth with the means afforded by the existing authoritarian system were bankrupt. The Franquist system was already facing major structural bottlenecks that were stymieing growth and that were aggravated by the generalized global economic downturn of the 1970s. While attitudinal vestiges of the paternalistic, statist policy preferences of many business people emerged in our research, it is also true that many recognized that the system was increasingly too far removed from market imperatives. With regard to labor, the existence of levels of strike activity comparable to European experiences even prior to the death of Franco made it exceedingly clear to many that fundamental modifications were necessary in existing mechanisms for collective bargaining.

Business was not monolithic or homogeneous. Although much of the business sector constituted one of the major, passive sources of the Franco regime's support, very important segments of the business community were significantly more distant from the authoritarian regime. Most notable in this regard were the Catalan and Basque business communities. These segments of Spanish business are not equatable to economic interests in peripheral nationality regions elsewhere in Europe. Catalonia and the Basque Country were the first regions of Spain to develop and still constitute a huge share of the total Spanish economy. The Catalan business community, in particular, played a critical role in the moderation that typified business discourse over the late 1970s and early 1980s. Catalan business, we should recall, was well established and less tainted by Franquist economic policy and flourished in a region with a rich civil society and in which business had long enjoyed a public legitimacy not accorded elsewhere in Spain.

An attempt by political leaders to address all the seemingly clamorous issues put forward by competing groups during a political transition can lead to an overloaded agenda and increase the potential for a failed consolidation. Not all the relevant groups may realize the need to moderate their postures. It may be left to leadership accurately to steer away from "pressing" needs and toward the building of the exigent consensus. Not enough emphasis has been placed in the literature on democracy on the fortuitous incidence political leadership has had at critical junctures. While overwhelmingly embracing democracy, business nevertheless failed to credit its primary architect, Adolfo Suárez. Indeed, business dissatisfaction eventually contributed substantially to the erosion and eventual demise of the UCD, thereby opening the way for the assumption of power by the theoretically antithetical Socialists (who, as we found, were not as despised by business as public perceptions of business would have had us think). However, it would be a serious mistake to misinterpret the decline in business support for the Centrist government with any questioning of the democratic system itself. The UCD was coming apart from the inside as well as being criticized externally. While business retreated from its support of Suárez over 1980 and eventually withheld its initially halting support of Calvo Sotelo in 1982, business was not siding with the opponents of democracy but was seeking a more assertive government in economic and "efficiency" terms. The unraveling of the UCD was attributable to numerous factors, prominent among which was the internally driven "feuding barons" syndrome described in the work of Share and that of Huneeus. Further, a politics of consensus in the public domain could not have endured indefinitely. The need for such consensus under an established constitutional rubric, within the framework of a competing party system, would necessarily erode as time progressed. As such, criticism of policy could become increasingly public and detailed, with less trepidation about potential unsavory consequences. In analyzing the crisis of the UCD and how business grew increasingly critical, Huneeus stated that: "It has not been the intention of our analysis to ascribe causality to the CEOE in the collapse of the UCD, the origins of which [collapse] are found within [the UCD] itself."[1]

The politics of consensus necessary to build the system even among political elites had largely ended by the early 1980s, although, naturally, the 1981 coup attempt led to some retreat from public divisiveness.

Share, for example, argues that after the 1979 elections the PSOE "abandoned the code of political conduct that had prevailed during the first years of the transition" and began to perform more as a "true opposition party."[2] Share argues that the Socialists--as did many political and economic opponents--stepped up their pressure on Suárez during 1980 partly as a result of the disintegration of the UCD.[3] The shift by the CEOE and many in business in part responded to changes taking place within the UCD and also reflected shifting perceptions among the electorate as a whole. In some ways, the period up to about 1980 reflected an almost excessive fear of open conflict by the many parties to democratization, a fear that any open disagreement would strengthen the hand of those willing to strike down the emerging democracy. In certain respects, such fear-- not entirely unfounded--was the product of a system in which institutionalized conflict was still not consolidated. In fact, a more conciliatory PSOE line following the abortive coup should be read as a reawakening of the latent fears about the system's soundness; fears that otherwise had been declining since the 1979 elections. PSOE-UCD cooperation in 1981 and 1982 on the LOAPA, the law whose intent it was to "harmonize" the process of regional devolution, can be interpreted within the framework of concern over open dispute, particularly in an area credited with having contributed substantially to uneasiness for many on the semi-loyal right.[4] Hence, we should similarly be cautious in our interpretation of a more independent business line as time progressed.

As noted before, all this is not to criticize Suárez. His tenure would have been exceedingly brief and the change in regime less peaceful had he attempted to meet the many demands emanating from numerous sectors, notable among them the conflicting demands of business and labor.

Important structural elements characterizing the business sector had an impact on business posturing during the transition. Indubitably among the more prominent of such features are regional dissimilarities and the related issue of the differing degrees of continuity with the earlier authoritarian system.

While much of the Spanish population did not appreciate the need to address regional demands at the time of the transition, it is to the credit of the political elites that they recognized its importance. Consideration of the strength of regionalist sentiment and of Spain's multicultural heritage is key to understanding the dynamics of business and business organization in the country. The location of two of the country's three primary industrial foci in the regions with the strongest regionalist or, alternatively, regional-nationalist aspirations, reinforces the exigency of considering regional factors. That Catalonia and the Basque Country were also the first regions of Spain to industrialize and the areas with the longest trajectories of wide-scale collective business activity emerges as a prime consideration in a business study emphasizing the organizational dimensions of employer activity. Throughout we noted the salience of regional differences in explaining much of the variance among business attitudes. Indeed, the study could validly have concentrated on the regional dimension in business attitudes and organization as its primary focus and still have said a great deal about business and the democratic system.

Continuity figures as a paramount characteristic explaining both organizational realities and much of the apparent inconsistency in the attitudes of individual chief executives. A good deal of the distinctiveness of the Catalan organizational configuration is accounted for by continuity. Elsewhere in Spain, continuity within the Sindicato Nacional or with policies of the economic growth years of the 1960s were still discernable in treating many political issues and topics related to associability. On the issue of associability and on the Common Market, the data document the endurance of diacritical elements among business and women with attitudes and practices uncovered twenty-one years earlier by Linz and de Miguel. This is particularly striking given the fundamental changes experienced by the economy and the political system over the intervening period.

An important part of the strength of the CEOE hierarchy in its early years of existence must be attributed precisely to the historical continuity of many of its affiliate organizations at both base and intermediate levels. While in general this was a positive element in affording a quickly consolidated collective business input during the transition, there also persisted foci of resistance to change. Some segments among the formerly Sindicato-integrated organizations defended outdated traditional prerogatives of collective action. These attitudes were apparent on political issues and manifested themselves in an outmoded exposition of reactive justifications for associability and in a desire that the state take up the standard against encroaching economic liberalism (although it would never be enunciated as such). Some of these trends were evident among individual chief executives as well.

A static view of business associability would underscore the widespread apathy and disinterest that characterized much of employer opinion on topics related

to collective action. Even among many of those who openly supported their associations, the issue was not much
of a priority. Entrepreneurs are pragmatic and indi-
vidualistic by nature. They often perceive their professional activity as a vocation. They do not define their
status in relation to a greater collectivity. Often, the
only "collectivity" to which they feel an attachment is
their own company. Organized collective action correspondingly suffers. Many of those employers actively
supporting collective action do so only insofar as it
has an immediate impact on their subsector or in their
province. Hence, breaches open between many base associations and the CEOE hierarchy, weaknesses often further aggravated rather than ameliorated by lower level
association leaders.

   Nonetheless, the CEOE quickly achieved a sufficient level of consolidation and legitimacy to speak on
behalf of business and be heard. Perhaps the single most
striking element uncovered by our research was the impressive degree of similarity and apparent broad agreement between employers and the leaders of their collective interest organizations. With minor differences in
the expected directions, individual chief executives and
association leaders stood on common ground on issues of
associational competencies. Significantly, both groups
opposed inappropriate associational activities in political forums and both had clear ideas as to which associational functions were appropriate and which were not.

   Spain has continued to evolve since the time of
our field work. In the October 1982 elections, the
governing party, the UCD, virtually disappeared
overnight--a phenomenon probably unprecedented in any
Western democracy--and the PSOE came to power.[5]   From
1982-1983 until about 1987, the Socialists could be described as having enjoyed a near-hegemonic position at
local, regional, and state levels. In addition to having
achieved the first absolute parliamentary majority in
Spain, they held a majority position in the governments
of thirteen of the seventeen regional autonomous communities and controlled about two-thirds of the country's municipal halls.[6]   What has this meant for business? Although this takes us beyond the ken of the data,
we can guess that a good number of business people are
embarrassed to admit just how pro-business PSOE policies
have been.

   In many areas, pragmatic Socialist government policies from the very beginning appealed to many in business. The two main thrusts of early PSOE government,
economic austerity and industrial restructuring, found
substantial support among sectors of business. Many
business people saw economic austerity as necessary to

prepare the economy for sustained growth and applauded the government's limitation of wage growth. While industrial restructuring focused on public sector firms (starting with iron and steel, home appliances and textiles, and, later, shipbuilding), business supported restructuring on a philosophical level, and its concomitant easing of dismissal policies to implement the downsizing without which other restructuring policies would have been fruitless. Many employers also hoped that the layoffs that materialized relatively early in restructuring the public sector indicated that an easing of dismissal policy would eventually be realized in the private sector as well. On both wage restraint and restructuring, the PSOE, given its constituency and near-hegemonic electoral position, was able to implement policies with relatively harsh social costs that the timid and electorally unsteady UCD would never have been able to put into practice. The disappearance of the UCD following the 1982 elections left the political center effectively occupied by the PSOE, which had already been moving away from the left for several years. The PCE split on the PSOE's left flank, not effectively corrected until the rise of the Izquierda Unida coalition before the 1989 elections, meant that the Socialists were better able to chart a course of relatively moderate foreign policy and liberal technocratic economic and social policy without great fear of losing support on the left. On the right, AP's publicly perceived far-right positioning and internal divisiveness further lowered concerns over policy issues for the PSOE leadership.

The acuerdo interconfederal (AI) signed by the government, CEOE, CEPYME, UGT and Comisiones in February 1983 reflected a de facto broad acceptance of austerity by economic actors. The two-year acuerdo económico y social (AES) signed in October 1984 by the CEOE, CEPYME, the UGT and the government (Comisiones refused), moved further in business' direction by limiting wage increases to below the expected rate of inflation and introducing modest flexibility into labor markets, specifically, allowing for part-time and temporary hiring and easing some restrictions on layoffs and firings. The AES lapsed at the end of 1986 and, although employers appeared willing to explore the possibilities for a new social pact, the UGT was not.[7] In some ways, the end of the negotiations of pacts reflected rising government difficulties with its increasingly less pliant union partner, the UGT, which culminated in the successful December 1988 general strike. Wages and prices dropped consistently year over year during the 1980s.[8]

Miguel Boyer's early implementation of austerity

and clamping down on wage growth succeeded in breaking
a natural and long-standing policy inclination in Spain
toward inflation. While wage cum inflation and employment policy areas were of most importance, some other
early PSOE policies would have been favored by business.
For example, immediately upon assuming office, the Socialists ended the "horas intensivas" (intensive hours)
work schedule at all ministries and public offices.
Public administration employees would no longer enjoy
an 8 A.M. to 3 P.M. schedule. During one 1981 interview at
a large Barcelona company, located in the interior of
the province, one chief executive related a joke that
undoubtedly reflected widely shared business perceptions
of the public administration:

> One time, a small businessman from a rural province needed some paperwork
> taken care of at the Ministry of Industry in Madrid. He arrived at 4 P.M.
> and was surprised not to find anyone at the Ministry. He commented to the
> custodian, "I didn't know they didn't work in the afternoons." The
> custodian corrected him: "No sir, they don't come in the afternoons. It's
> in the mornings when they don't work!"

Promulgation of legislation on incompatibilidades
by the PSOE government, which was in development prior
to their 1982 victory, meant that bureaucrats would no
longer be allowed to hold outside employment and would
have to dedicate themselves exclusively to their primary job. While many business people have grumbled about
"packing" of the administrative system with Socialist
party loyalists, many of them were pleased with the
initial shake-up of the bureaucracy which, was perceived as bloated and inefficient.

Generally, business favored PSOE efforts for fiscal restraint in the health and legal areas and in social security. In 1985, the Socialists tightened eligi-
bility rules for some social security spending, such as
raising from ten to fifteen the number of years required for pension vesting. Additionally, pension benefits would hence-forth be calculated on the basis of
the average of the eight best consecutive years, rather
than two. Annual cost of living increases would be peg-
ged to the government's inflation target, rather than
to the actual inflation rate subsequently experienced.

Although the number of work days lost to strikes
increased in 1984 as a result of the so-called hot summer that year, lost time to strikes even in 1984 only
matched the 1980 level, and 1983, 1985, and 1986 were
all years of relatively lower strike activity. Furthermore, some of the strike action during this period was
related to workers in subsectors already slated for
reconversión lay-offs.

Finally, business activity appears to be rising in respectability among important segments of public opinion. Rapid economic growth has led to the creation of an emerging, truly entrepreneurial class and revitalized numerous business enterprises (while dooming others). In sociological terms, the phenomenon of widespread disinterest or lack of prestige accorded to business as a profession appears to be waning, especially among young professionals, particularly in areas where the perception of business already was better, such as Catalonia. Young Spaniards are increasingly attracted to the study of business, and greater numbers are entering MBA programs. IESE (Instituto de Estudios Superiores de la Empresa), a Barcelona school that offers a two-year American style graduate business program, has an cosmopolitan student body and is internationally recognized as among Europe's top business schools.[9] The backside of this, naturally, is rising criticism of a crass and superficial consumer culture. A few on the ideological left have attacked the emergence of a "casino" mentality. Antonio García Santesmases, of the small, censorious "Socialist Left" current within the PSOE said that: "The Socialists who govern us are primarily interested in maximizing the accumulation of capital, the rapid earning of money, enjoying easy business deals and exquisite consumption, while social policy is crippled."[10]

In contrast to the favorable policies and trends from the business perspective, many in business would object to the substantial jump in general government expenditures and the increasing role of public spending as a share of the economy. Government spending has risen rapidly and consistently from under 25 percent of GDP at the time of Franco's death, to over 40 percent in the late 1980s.[11] Nonetheless, this remains below the OECD average. A widely held perception in the business community, not entirely groundless, is that a good proportion of the increase in government has been attributable to the development of the <u>autonomías</u>. Naturally, many, particularly outside the historic minority nationalities regions, complain about the creation of unnecessary and duplicative autonomous bureaucracies.[12] The composition of government borrowing has changed substantially. Whereas central government debt, including the financing of social security, has stabilized, regional budgets, which had basically been balanced in the early 1980s, are now accumulating significant amounts of debt.[13]

While corporate tax rates have remained relatively stable and tax credits were made available for job creation and investment, corporate taxes have increased significantly as a share of GDP since the early 1980s (after years of relative stability). Government plans to reduce subsidies for investment and job creation, including recent subsidies for employer contributions to social security for new hires, are likely to increase tax pressures on business.

Average marginal tax rates on individuals have climbed substantially in the early years of PSOE government, climbing from 19.9 percent in 1983 to 33.1 percent in 1986.[14] The highest marginal tax rate is comparatively high, as are the number of tax brackets.[15] Despite all of this, however, Spain is not a highly taxed country by European standards, although business people are more likely to compare their tax burden to their own earlier experiences than to the situation elsewhere.

> The overall tax burden has risen much faster in Spain over the past two decades than on average in other OECD countries. Yet, excluding Turkey, the tax share is still the smallest among OECD countries. This primarily reflects low revenues from personal income taxation. In terms of GDP they averaged just 6 per cent in the mid-1980s, the lowest figure for the OECD area along with France, Greece and Turkey. By contrast, the relative weight of social security contributions has been well above the OECD average. In particular, employers' contributions are among the heaviest in the OECD area, following France and Sweden. Taxes on goods and services represented a relatively low share of GDP until the introduction of VAT but have since picked up sharply, both in relation to GDP and as a share of total government revenues.[16]

Employer contributions to social security were a significant bone of contention even before the PSOE came to office. Skyrocketing social security costs stabilized somewhat in the late 1980s, in part due to the pension changes undertaken in 1985. However, the financial impact of government plans to increase minimum retirement benefits remains to be seen. Our data indicated that business was already wary of the VAT in 1981. Undoubtedly, most business opinion considers the VAT a tax on business.

The Socialists' industrial restructuring and the opening of Spain to investment would threaten some traditional sectors of Spanish industry, but, in general, would be more favored than opposed by business. Foreign direct investment, which averaged 1 percent of GDP from 1970 to 1985, doubled to 2 percent after 1985. As time goes on, such liberalization will result in a more progressive business sector in economic terms as less competitive industries fall by the wayside. In 1987, the Socialists also relaxed restrictions on capital exports.[17] Official reserves grew steadily after the mid-

1980s and in 1987, for the first time, exceeded the
level of external debt, which slowly ebbed after 1983-
1984. The growth in long-term capital inflows is a reflection of the attractiveness of Spain to foreign investors, many of them increasingly using the country as
an export base, and is consistent with official policy
favoring inflows of foreign long-term capital.[18]

Many business people will criticize PSOE policies,
but overall they would have to admit that the business
climate has been very good. It is a monumental achievement for Spain that the prime focus of economic debate
is on issues that are admittedly less interesting and
not fundamental for the system, like the double tax-
ation of corporate income or reorganization of pension
benefits, and not on the monarchy, the constitution, or
the legality of various political organizations.

More recently, analysts have attempted to understand what might be learned from the south European experience of democratization in Spain, Greece, and Portugal that has applicability to Eastern Europe. There
are, in fact, very important parallels, but the differences are probably more significant.

As was the case in southern Europe, in the east,
one is dealing with newly democratizing countries. All
three south European countries became democratic during
the same historical period, and with many of the same
factors at work. The communist order collapsed throughout the east. The dictatorships of the right were delegitimized and deteriorated in the south. Neither a
Hungary under Communism, nor a Spain under dictatorship
could ever have become an active participant in the
development of a new Europe. Only the rise of democracy
in both regions afforded these countries the political
credentials necessary eventually to participate within
the European Community, or at least, to cooperate much
more closely with it. The trajectory of Spanish efforts
to join the EC and the final dénouement attest to this.

Even on the political side, however, there are
important differences between southern Europe and
eastern. In the East, for the most part, there has been
a total collapse of the previous political order,
whereas change in some parts of the Mediterranean, particularly in Spain, was much less precipitated. This is
perhaps less true for Greece, and certainly much less
true for Portugal, which went through revolutionary
turmoil in its transition to democracy.

In the case of Spain, conservative political
sectors--including the vast majority in business--
supported democratic change when it came in the mid-
1970s. While seeking a more open political order,
however, the previous regime was not entirely

discredited in their eyes. Franco's forty years in power meant that by his death in November 1975 the period of widespread and harsh repression of his regime, which occurred mostly in the 1940s, had long passed. In the 1960s and early 1970s, Spain had prospered. By 1975, there was already a certain degree of opening in the regime. As such, the climate for moderate change was enhanced. The wounds of the past had for the most part healed, and the democratic opposition was willing to attempt moderate rather than radical change. In many ways, this contrasts with more recent democratic change in parts of Latin America, such as in Argentina, Chile, or Uruguay, where the memory of repression has been much more recent, potentially serving as an obstacle to full democratic consolidation. The Romanian situation may be another such case.

Also importantly, the Franco regime, as those of Salazar in Portugal, and the colonels in Greece, was an authoritarian regime, <u>not</u> a totalitarian regime like the Communist regimes in Eastern Europe. Although many in the West might speak fashionably of "Fascist Spain," to do so is a misnomer. The Spanish fascists, the Falangists, were, in fact, one the of earliest and most vociferous of Franco's supporters. But Franco was not, himself, a fascist. Franco was, above all, a "Franquist." As he did with many other groups, such as business, the Church, and above all the military, Franco used the Fascists as one of the sources of support for his regime. But that base of support was not static and the role of the fascists within the system declined as the regime endured over time.

To label a system "authoritarian" is not to say that it was any less repressive than a totalitarian regime. But it does say important things about ideology and, more significantly, about institutionalization, that had important consequences for management-labor issues during the transition. By nature, authoritarian regimes rely much more heavily on the personality of the leader in charge than do institutionalized totalitarian regimes, that also have the crutch of ideology on which to hang their legitimacy. Thus, authoritarian regimes are often faced by crises of continuity whenever the leader dies. They are much less institutionalized, and the possibility for change historically has been greater at such junctures than in totalitarian systems.

Totalitarian regimes, unlike authoritarian ones, are mobilization societies in which the state intervenes much more directly into the <u>daily</u> lives of individual citizens. The level of control is greater and reaches into private life as well as the public realm.

Those who piloted the Spanish political transition through its turbulent waters used the political instruments available under the previous system--the existing Franquist legal order--to effectuate change. Hence, it was the last Franquist parliament that in 1976 agreed to approve the Law of Political Reform, through its own legislative procedures, and amazingly, thereupon also agreed to legislate itself out of existence. Similarly, the referendum laws used by the primary architect of democratic change, Adolfo Suárez, to validate democratic change popularly were the same referendum laws available under the Franquist regime. That change was effected in such a manner is important. By using Franquist legal instruments to democratize the country, the architects of change legitimated change even in the eyes of many Franquists, who could not argue that the change was illegal.

There are some parallels in Eastern Europe. The Hungarians in particular studied the Spanish transition closely and have conducted much of their change in a consciously similar manner. To a certain extent, change in Poland has also been done within the legal framework of the previous regime. However, change in East Germany, and even more so in Czechoslovakia, has not followed this pattern. Change in Romania, of course, has broken completely with the past. Nonetheless, in all of Eastern Europe, it is clear that the previous regimes were significantly more delegitimized among much wider sectors of the population than was the case in Spain.

Economics also had a role to play in why things were different in Spain. Contrary to the assessment of many, even academic, analysts of the period, by the time of Franco's death, it was erroneous to depict Spain as a more successful, lesser-developed, or newly industrializing country. Spain's level of industrial output, its character of inter- versus intra-sectoral trade, product specialization, and labor force sectoral distribution, its available institutional mechanisms in the industrial realm, and its historical evolution, placed the _problématique_ of the country's industrial realities firmly among those of developed West European states, constituting the correct standards against which to compare Spain. These were also the standards against which Spanish policy makers and industrialists compared themselves. From 1959 until 1973, Spain's GNP rose at an average annual rate of over 7, percent the highest in the West during that period, except for Greece and Japan. Real per capita income more than doubled. The Franquist economic policies of the 1960s allowed Spain to participate in the world-wide boom and led to a profound transformation of Spanish society.

From the EC's perspective, the size and strength of the Spanish economy placed its candidacy for membership in a fundamentally different position from those of Greece and Portugal--which were more easily digestible.

Hence, another contrast with Eastern Europe. In the fall of 1989, <u>BusinessWeek</u> ran a cover story on Eastern Europe that drew references to the Spanish economy for comparison. The physical size of Spain and its population is comparable to that of Poland. Spain's level of industrial production and some measures of individual economic well-being were considered as somewhat similar to those of East Germany. But care should be taken in comparisons. Easy economic comparisons are very difficult when one is dealing with economies with non-convertible currencies was the case in Eastern Europe.

Significantly, the Spanish transition was essentially limited to the political system. Spain was already a modern industrial state with an operative market economy, and very much a participant in international economic exchanges (albeit recognizing the paternalism, the restrictions and interventionism of the vestiges of corporatist elements). The transitions in the east face greater obstacles. Importantly, the transitions taking place are not limited to the political realm. The East European countries are attempting simultaneously to transform both their economic as well as their political orders. As such, the potential for political breakdown and failure is much greater.

When the Mediterranean countries were democratizing, the international political climate strongly endorsed their change. Fortunately, a similar situation exists today, which may be the saving grace for what is going on in Eastern Europe. Western Europe recognizes its own critical role in helping the East. How that will play out, and the role, specifically, of the EC, remains fully to be seen. But in the end, the political decision by Europeans to support change may prove the determining factor.

At the time of the transition, business recognized that a country at Spain's level of economic and social development required a more open and competitive political system. Business people individually and collectively contributed to the peaceful change steered by elites and overwhelmingly endorsed by the Spanish citizenry. Business has thrived under democracy and has become a driving force behind Spain's efforts fully to become an integral part of the new Europe that continues to emerge and evolve.

NOTES

1.   Huneeus, <u>La Unión de Centro Democrático y la transición a la democracia en España</u> (Madrid: Centro de Investigaciones Sociológicas, 1985), 373.

2.   Donald Share, <u>Dilemmas of Social Democracy</u> (Westport, Conn.: Greenwood Press, 1989), 58.

3.   Share believes that the pressures of writing the Constitution, achieving the economic pacts, and the process of regional devolution, wore down the UCD's cohesiveness. Recall also that the UCD was really a coalition of widely varying political stripes. Ibid., 59.

4.   Significantly, the LOAPA (Ley de Armonización del Proceso Autonómico) was perceived as braking excessive devolution to the regions and was forcefully criticized by regionalist-nationalist opinion. Many read the LOAPA as placating some of the disquietudes on the right about the weakening of central control and the slow dismemberment of the country.

5.   The UCD went from 168 parliamentary seats to 12 and dropped from 35 percent of the vote in 1979 to 6.7 percent. Early in 1983, the party was dissolved.

6.   In the June 1986 general elections, the PSOE held on to its parliamentary majority but dropped significantly from 202 of the 350 lower house seats to 184 seats. The Socialist vote share fell by over 4 percent to 43.4 percent. Over the course of 1987, their electoral position declined from "near-hegemony" of the political system to "mere" dominance. In the "triple" elections of June 1987 (votes in thirteen of the seventeen autonomous regions, municipal and European parliamentary elections), the PSOE's vote share dropped below 40 percent for the first time since its 1982 sweep. In the October 1989 general elections, the PSOE's maneuverability was further eroded when it won only half the parliamentary seats (175 seats with 39.6% of the vote). The PSOE would now depend on independents to put its policies into place. Probably more importantly, the loss of the absolute majority meant that the PSOE could no longer reserve to itself the exclusive right to set the daily legislative calendar and would face difficulties in blocking opposition initiatives. Izquierda Unida (IU), a communist coalition, was the primary beneficiary of the PSOE's electoral decline. Nonetheless, the Socialists' staying power, and that of Felipe González specifically, have proven remarkable.

7. Labor market conditions for many were so severe by 1986 that the UGT needed to distance itself from PSOE government policies. Already in 1985, UGT Secretary General Nicolás Redondo and other UGT members did not vote with the government on its pension reform legislation. In October 1987, Redondo resigned his parliamentary seat over government wage targets. Over 1987 and 1988, Redondo effectively ousted all those in UGT leadership positions who towed the government line on economic and social policy and replaced them with persons in his confidence. At a special union congress of the metal sector held in Barcelona in March 1988, Redondo forced the secretary general of the metal sector union, Antonio Puerta, and his leadership to resign. All of them had been identified as close to the government. This was the first such ouster ever effectuated without a full congress being called. Luis Peiro, "El PSOE reacciona ante el 'Nicolazo'," Cambio 16 (Madrid: 11 April 1988), 18-22.

8. Consumer prices, which rose 14.4 percent in 1982 and 12.2 percent in 1983, were down to a 4.8 percent increase in 1988. The average increase in contractual wages went from a 12 percent rise in 1982 and 11.4 percent in 1983 to 5.3 percent in 1988. OECD, Spain 1988/1989, 106.

9. Shawn Tully, "Europe's Best Business Schools," Fortune (New York: 23 May 1988), 106-110.

10. Gonzalo San Segundo, "El dinero, la nueva furia de los españoles," Cambio 16 (Madrid: 15 August 1988), 17.

11. OECD, Spain 1988/1989, 47.

12. See the Círculo de Empresarios, "Empresa y autonomías," Boletín 29 Extraordinario (Madrid: May 1985).

13. OECD, Spain 1988/1989, 74-75.

14. The rates described are on personal income for an "average production worker." Part of the rapid rise in personal income taxes was achieved by not indexing tax brackets for inflation in given years, such as 1986. OECD, Spain 1988/1989, 69-73.

15. At 56 percent, the top rate is exceeded in the OECD only in the Netherlands (60%), Ireland (58%) and France (57%). Only Luxembourg, with twenty-four, has

more tax brackets than Spain's sixteen. Círculo de Empresarios, "Taxes and Public Expenditure in a Context
of Internationalization," policy statement (Madrid: 20
July 1989), 10.

   16.   OECD, Spain 1988/1989, 66-67.

   17.   Ibid., 83.

   18.   Robert E. Martínez, "Spain: Pragmatism and
Continuity," Current History 87, no. 532 (Philadelphia:
November 1988), 375-376.

Appendix

1981 SURVEY OF CHIEF EXECUTIVES

The survey of chief executives was realized between February and November of 1981 and the interviews directed exclusively to the director-general, managing director, or president of each company. The objective was to locate the individual actually managing the operations of the company on a daily basis. The original sample of 300 industrial and construction companies with corporate headquarters in Madrid, Barcelona, Vizcaya, Valencia, and Sevilla provinces was divided by their relative provincial industrial weights, measured by industrial value added (including construction), based on Banco de Bilbao data. Each provincial sample was divided into thirds: (1) regular firms, employing from 50 to 199 employees; (2) intermediate firms, with 200 to 999; and (3) large firms at 1,000 or more employees. Province was determined by the location of corporate headquarters. Size was the total number of employees within Spain.

The most current issue of <u>Las 1500 mayores empresas españolas</u>, published annually by Fomento de la Produccion (Barcelona), was used to compile lists of firms with a thousand or more employees. Given that Fomento de la Produccion lists companies by sector rather than province, the list was grouped by province and numbered alphabetically so as to draw a random sample. Regular- and intermediate-size companies were numbered as listed in the Industrial Registry of the Ministry of Industry.

It was unnecessary to contact most large companies to determine the identity of their chief executive prior to requesting the interview in writing. The information provided in the Fomento de la Produccion publication is very reliable. An important minority of intermediate company chief executives was also listed in the Fomento volume. Although other, larger directories of business people are available, such as the well-known DICODI (Directorio de consejeros y directores), they proved sorely inaccurate. Hence, almost all regular and intermediate firms were called by phone to identify their chief executives.

Table A.1 Chief Executives by Province and Company Size

	Madrid		Barcelona		Vizcaya	
	(N)	%	(N)	%	(N)	%
Regular	27	10.4	30	11.6	12	4.6
Intermediate	25	9.7	38	14.7	9	3.5
Large	36	13.9	35	13.5	9	3.5
Totals	88	34.0	103	39.8	30	11.6

	Valencia		Sevilla		Total	
	(N)	%	(N)	%	(N)	%
Regular	12	4.6	4	1.5	85	32.8
Intermediate	7	2.7	6	2.3	85	32.8
Large	7	2.7	2	.8	89	34.4
Totals	26	10.0	12	4.6	259	100.0

A letter signed by Prof. Linz advised the chief executive that I would formally request an interview. My letter followed, describing the study. Both letters assured that the data would be maintained in the strictest confidence. A handful of chief executives in mining and metallurgical companies received a third letter from Prof. Manuel Lopez-Linares, professor at the Madrid Escuela de Minas. About twelve Barcelona chief executives received letters from Fomento del Trabajo Nacional. About twenty, primarily Catalan, chief executives received letters from Jose Antonio Gefaell, a director at the Banco Industrial de Vizcaya in Barcelona. About a dozen Madrid chief executives received letters from Fernando Fernandez Rodriguez, an executive with the Banco de Bilbao in Madrid. One Barcelona interview was scheduled through a friend of mine, a nephew of the chief executive. Chief executives do not readily sacrifice one or two hours of time for an academic study, which explains the letters sent before the phone call. A refusal over the phone to grant an interview could almost never be reversed.

After the original random sample of 300 was drawn, substitutions were realized for interview rejections, and a survey termination date set for November 1981. Almost all the interviews at large companies were conducted by the author. Professional interviewers from the Centro de Investigaciones Sociologicas conducted the majority of interviews at regular- and intermediate-size companies. Overall, the author realized 36 percent of the chief executive interviews. The average duration of each was an hour and a half.

Table A.2 Industry Disaggregation by Province and Company Size

	Madrid:				Barcelona:				Vizcaya:			
	R	I	L	T	R	I	L	T	R	I	L	T
Energy products	0.0	4.0	5.6	3.4	0.0	.0	8.6	2.9	8.3	0.0	0.0	3.3
Intermediate goods	40.7	24.0	41.7	36.4	33.3	26.3	51.4	36.9	25.0	77.8	44.4	46.7
Capital goods	3.7	4.0	11.1	6.8	6.7	7.9	2.9	5.8	16.7	11.1	0.0	10.0
Consumer goods	29.6	40.0	25.0	30.7	53.3	55.3	34.3	47.6	33.3	11.1	22.2	23.3
Construction	22.2	24.0	16.7	20.5	6.7	10.5	2.9	6.8	16.7	0.0	33.3	16.7
Other	3.7	4.0	0.0	2.3	0.0	0.0	0.0	0.0	0.0	0.0	0.0	0.0
	(27)	(25)	(36)	(88)	(30)	(38)	(35)	(103)	(12)	(9)	(9)	(30)

	Valencia:				Sevilla:				Total Sample
	R	I	L	T	R	I	L	T	
Energy products	0.0	0.0	0.0	0.0	0.0	16.7	0.0	8.3	3.1
Intermediate goods	8.3	14.3	42.9	19.2	50.0	33.3	0.0	33.3	35.9
Capital goods	16.7	0.0	0.0	7.7	0.0	0.0	0.0	0.0	6.6
Consumer goods	66.7	85.7	57.1	69.2	50.0	33.3	100.0	50.0	41.3
Construction	8.3	0.0	0.0	3.8	0.0	16.7	0.0	8.3	12.4
Other	0.0	0.0	0.0	0.0	0.0	0.0	0.0	0.0	.8
	(12)	(7)	(7)	(26)	(4)	(6)	(2)	(12)	(259)

The most recent INE (Instituto Nacional de Estadística) census, that for 30 April 1978, registered 177 companies with a thousand or more employees; 1,795 with 200 to 999; and 6,788 with 50 to 199. These figures are understated. The Labor Ministry (Oficina de Información Pública) listings of workplaces that submitted records of elections to workplace provincial delegates (July 1978) indicated 260 companies at more than 1,000 employees. The Fomento de la Producción publication yielded 317 companies in this size category. Many of these were service sector companies and, therefore, outside our universe. Nevertheless, available sources were deficient and contradictory.

The rejection rate overall was about 20 percent. Additionally, many companies had gone bankrupt since the compilation of the Industrial Registry and much time and effort was expended in attempting to contact companies that were casualties, for the most part, of the economic crisis.

Table A.3 Foreign Capital Participation by Company Size and Province

Degree of foreign ownership:	Size:			Province:					
	R	I	L	M	B	VZ	VA	S	Total
None	85.5	64.3	57.3	58.0	68.0	86.7	88.5	66.7	68.8
Minority	8.4	7.1	13.5	13.6	8.0	6.7	7.7	8.3	9.8
Majority	4.8	15.5	19.1	18.2	14.0	6.7	3.8	8.3	13.3
Complete	1.2	13.1	10.1	10.2	10.0	0.0	0.0	16.7	8.2
	(83)	(84)	(89)	(88)	(100)	(30)	(26)	(12)	(256)

All the questionnaires were coded by the author.

1982 SURVEY OF LEADERS OF ASSOCIATIONS

Except for the first interview, conducted in December 1981, the association interviews were done between January and July of 1982. The survey was directed to the chief functionary at each association, handling the operations of the organization on an ongoing basis. In the majority of cases (72.2%) the individual in question was the secretary general. In 9.6 percent of the associations, the interviewee held the title of director-general or managing director, and 16.5 percent were presidents. Given the research interest in organi-

zational internal dynamics, it was decided to contact
the top managerial position conducting daily affairs.
Those presidents interviewed were in smaller associations without full-time managers, where the top managerial and elected representation roles coincided in the
same person. A couple of secretary-generals also faced
membership election (versus than the usual selection by
a board of directors). Two interviewees (1.7% of the
sample) were executive vice-presidents.

Table A.4 Associations by Affiliation and Province

CEOE affiliation:	Madrid (N)	%	Barcelona (N)	%	Vizcaya (N)	%	Total (N)	%
Direct	52	45.2	6	5.2	0	0.0	58	50.4
Indirect	21	18.3	23	20.0	13	11.3	57	49.6
Totals	73	63.5	29	25.2	13	11.3	115	100.0

The sample universe consisted of all the sectoral
associations directly affiliated to the state-wide peak
employers association, the CEOE (Confederación Española
de Organizaciones Empresariales), which fell within the
geographic scope of the survey (Madrid, Barcelona, and
Vizcaya), and a random sample of sectoral and intersectoral, territorial associations affiliated indirectly
to the peak association.

All sixty-six valid sectoral affiliates of the
CEOE in the survey area (as per the CEOE annual report
for 1981) were contacted and fifty-eight interviews
(88%) were conducted. Five additional sectoral direct
affiliates were not contacted as they were located outside the three provinces included in the survey. A random selection of twenty-five associations each was drawn
from among the affiliates of CEIM (Confederacion Empresarial Independiente de Madrid) and the Barcelona affiliates of FTN (Fomento del Trabajo Nacional). CEIM
and FTN are the Madrid province and Catalan region
territorial peak associations, respectively. While a
territorial association exists for Barcelona province,
Fomento actually directly conducts all activities in the
province (not the case in the other three Catalan provinces). By the end of the survey period, and with a random substitution system for rejections, twenty-one
interviews were realized among the forty-nine affiliates
of CEIM (43%) and twenty-three among the fifty affiliates of Fomento located in Barcelona province (46%).
Both lists of associations were prepared from the annual

reports of their respective territorial confederations. With roughly a 10 percent rejection rate, the proportions of active associations that were interviewed are actually understated in that a number of the affiliates proved inoperative (and were subsequently scratched from the list of "valid" indirect affiliates). These were uncovered randomly in the course of contacting associations for interviews. Hence, operating affiliates were fewer than the forty-nine in Madrid and fifty in Barcelona quote above.

Table A.5 Associations by Membership-Order Level and Affiliation

CEOE affiliation:						
	Indirect:		Direct:		Total:	
	(N)	%	(N)	%	(N)	%
Membership-Order:						
Base	49	42.6	38	33.0	87	75.7
Intermediate	8	7.0	20	17.4	28	24.3
Total	57	49.6	58	50.4	115	100.0

As with the survey of chief executives, interviews averaged an hour an half in duration. I conducted 70 percent of the interviews and a colleague from the Facultad de Ciencias Politicas y Sociologicas of the Universidad Complutense, Rafael Pardo Avellaneda, conducted the remainder. The author coded all of the questionnaires.

Table A.6 Associations by Sector and Province

	Madrid	Barcelona	Vizcaya	Total
Energy products	4.1	0.0	0.0	2.6
Intermediate goods	17.8	6.9	23.1	15.7
Capital goods	2.7	0.0	0.0	1.7
Consumer goods	27.4	51.7	23.1	33.0
Construction	2.7	3.4	0.0	2.6
Service sector	41.1	27.6	53.8	39.1
Intersectoral	4.1	10.3	0.0	5.2
	(73)	(29)	(13)	(115)

While the CEOE itself was of great help, in no instance did they assist in gaining entry as this certainly would have affected interview responses. A letter from Professor Linz and myself was adequate. Leaders playing public roles, such as these individuals, were more willing to be interviewed than the chief executives.

Bibliography

Aguila, Rafael del, and Ricardo Montoro. El discurso
    político de la transición española. Madrid: Centro
    de Investigaciones Sociológicas, 1984.
Aguilar Solé, Salvador. "L'empresariat i les seves
    organitzacions." Unpublished paper delivered at
    the   conference of the Associació Catalana de
    Sociología, Barcelona, June 1983.
Alcaide Inchausti, Julio. "El futuro de la sociedad es-
    pañola: la distribución de la renta nacional."
    Unpublished paper, Banco de Bilbao, Madrid, 1983.
Almendros Morcillo, Fernando; Enrique Jiménez-Asenjo;
    Francisco Pérez Amorós; and Eduardo Rojo Torre-
    cillo. El sindicalismo de clase en España (1939-
    1977). Barcelona: Ediciones Península, 1978.
Amsden, Jon. Collective Bargaining and Class Conflict
    in Spain. London: London School of Economics and
    Political Science, 1972.
Anderson, Charles. The Political Economy of Modern
    Spain.   Madison: University of Wisconsin Press,
    1970.
Andrés Orizo, Francisco. La sociedad española en el
    umbral de los 80. Madrid: Mapfre, 1984.
Apter, David. The Politics of Modernization. Englewood
    Cliffs, N.J.: Prentice-Hall, 1968.
Ashenfelter, Orley, and George E. Johnson. "Bargaining
    Theory, Trade Unions, and Industrial Strike Ac-
    tivity." The American Economic Review 59-1 (March,
    1969).
Asociación para el Progreso de la Dirección. Estudio
    socio-laboral de la empresa española. Madrid:
    Asociación para el Progreso de la Dirección, 1981.

Baklanoff, Eric N. The Economic Transformation of Spain
    and Portugal. New York: Praeger Publishers, 1978.
Balassa, Bela. "Trade Creation and Trade Diversion in
    the European Common Market." The Economic Journal
    77 (March, 1967).
Banco de Bilbao. Renta nacional de España. Madrid: 1977
    and 1980 editions.
Bancroft, Janet E. Industrial Entrepreneurship in Spain:
    Barcelona and Sevilla. Ph.D. dissertation, The
    Johns Hopkins University, 1978.
Barnes, Samuel; Max Kaase; et al. Political Action: Mass
    Participation in Five Western Democracies. Beverly
    Hills: Sage Publications, 1979.
Bauer, Raymond A., and Ithiel de Sola Pool. American
    Businessmen and International Trade. Glencoe,
    N.Y.: The Free Press, 1960.
Berle, Jr., Adolf A., and Gardiner C. Means. The Modern
    Corporation and Private Property. New York: Com-
    merce Clearing House, 1932.
Blank, Stephen. Industry and Government in Britain.
    Westmead, England: D. C. Heath Ltd., 1973.
Braunthal, Gerhard. The Federation of German Industry
    in Politics. Ithaca, N.Y.: Cornell University
    Press, 1965.
Cabrera, Mercedes. La patronal ante la II República.
    Madrid: Siglo Veintiuno de España Editores, 1983.
Caciagli, Mario. Elecciones y partidos en la transición
    española. Madrid: Centro de Investigaciones
    Sociológicas, 1986.
Cámara de Comercio, Industria y Navegación de Barcelona.
    España y las Comunidades Europeas. Barcelona:
    Cámara de Comercio, Industria y Navegación de
    Barcelona, 1973.
Campo, Salustiano del; José Félix Tezanos; and Walter
    Santin. "The Spanish Political Elite: Permanency
    and Change." In Moshe M. Czudnowski (ed.). Does
    Who Governs Matter? Elite Circulation in Contem-
    porary Societies. DeKalb: Northern Illinois
    University Press, 1982.
Carr, Raymond, and Juan Pablo Fusi Aizpurua. Spain:
    Dictatorship to Democracy. London: George Allen &
    Unwin, 1979.
Chilcote, Ronald H. Spain's Iron and Steel Industry.
    Austin, Tex.: Bureau of Business Research, 1968.
Círculo de Economía. Círculo de Economía 1958-1983.
    Barcelona: Círculo de Economía, 1983.
___. La opción europea para la economía española.
    Madrid: Guadiana, 1974.
Círculo de Empresarios. Actitud y comportamiento de las
    grandes empresas españolas ante la innovación.
    Madrid: Círculo de Empresarios, 1988.

___. "Empresa y autonomías." <u>Boletín</u>, May 1985.
___. "Taxes and Public Expenditures in the Context of Internationalization." Policy Statment. Madrid: October 1989.
Confederación de Empresarios de Andalucía. "Andalucía es empresa de todos." Pamphlet, May 1982.
___. "Entérate bien y entérate a tiempo." Pamphlet, May 1982.
Confederación Española de Organizaciones Empresariales. "La conflictividad laboral en 1981." <u>Informes y estudios</u>, January 1982.
___. <u>La empresa española ante la adhesión al Mercado Común</u>. Madrid: Confederación Española de Organizaciones Empresariales, February 1981.
___. "Estatutos y normativa sobre régimen interior de la CEOE." Madrid: Confederación Española de Organizaciones Empresariales, 1978.
___. <u>Memoria</u>. Madrid: Confederación Española de Organizaciones Empresariales, 1980, 1981, 1982, 1986 and 1987 editions.
Confederación Española de Pequeñas y Medianas Empresas. "¿Qué es CEPYME?" Madrid: 1980.
Coufoudakis, Van. "The EEC and the 'Freezing' of the Greek Association." <u>Journal of Common Market Studies</u> 16-2 (December, 1977).
Curzon, Gerard. Introduction to Alfred Tovias. <u>Tariff Preferences in Mediterranean Diplomacy</u>. London: World Policy Research Centre, 1977.
Dahl, Robert A. <u>Democracy and Its Critics</u>. New Haven: Yale University Press, 1989.
___. <u>Polyarchy</u>. New Haven: Yale University Press, 1971.
___. "Business and Politics: A Critical Appraisal of Political Science." <u>American Political Science Review</u> 53-1 (March, 1959).
DiPalma, Guiseppi. "Founding Coalitions in Southern Europe: Legitimacy and Hegemony." <u>Government and Opposition</u> 15-2 (1980).
Donges, Jurgen B. "The Economic Integration of Spain with the EEC: Problems and Prospects." In Avi Shlaim and G. N. Yannopoulos (eds.). <u>The EEC and the Mediterranean Countries</u>. Cambridge: Cambridge University Press, 1976.
Dülfer, Eberhard. <u>Problemática de colaboración y promoción industrial en Andalucía</u>. Sevilla: Ediciones del Instituto de Desarrollo Regional, 1975.
Edinger, Lewis J., and Donald D. Searing. "Social Background in Elite Analysis: A Methodological Inquiry." <u>American Political Science Review</u> 61 (June 1967).
Ehrmann, Henry W. <u>Organized Business in France</u>. Princeton: Princeton University Press, 1957.

___. Interest Groups on Four Continents. Pittsburgh:
    University of Pittsburgh Press, 1958.
Eibert, Mark E. "The Spanish Constitutional Tribunal in
    Theory and Practice." Stanford Journal of Inter-
    national Law, Vol. 18, Summer 1982.
Escuela Superior de Administración de Empresa, Pere Puiz
    i Bastard, study coordinator. La industria es-
    pañola ante la CEE. Madrid: Instituto de Estudios
    Económicos, 1979.
Estatuto de los trabajadores. Boletín Oficial del Esta-
    do. Madrid: Spanish Government Printing Office,
    March 1980.
Etzioni, Amitai. The Active Society. New York: The Free
    Press, 1968.
Farnetti, Paolo. Imprenditore e societá. Turin: Li/Ed
    L'impresa, 1970.
Feldman, Gerald D. "German Interest Group Alliances in
    War and Inflation." In Suzanne Berger (ed.).
    Organizing Interests in Western Europe. Cambridge:
    Cambridge University Press, 1981.
Fernández Romero, Andrés. El autodiagnóstico de la pe-
    queña y mediana empresa. Madrid: Asociación para
    el Progreso de la Dirección, 1981.
Finer, S. E. "The Federation of British Industries."
    Political Studies 4-1 (February, 1956).
Fishman, Robert M. "Working Class Organization and Po-
    litical Change: The Labor Movement and the Tran-
    sition to Democracy in Spain." Ph.D. dissertation,
    Yale University, 1985, published as Working Class
    Organization and the Return to Democracy. Ithaca,
    N.Y.: Cornell University Press, 1990.
Fomento de la Producción. Las 1500 mayores empresas
    españolas. Barcelona: Fomento de la Producción,
    September 1980.
Fomento del Trabajo Nacional. "¿Qué es Fomento del Tra-
    bajo Nacional?" Barcelona: Fomento del Trabajo
    Nacional, 1980.
Friedrich, Carl J. Constitutional Government and Demo-
    cracy. Boston: Ginn and Company, 1950.
___. "Some Observations on Weber's Analysis of Bureau-
    cracy." In Robert A. Merton, Ailsa P. Gray, Barba-
    ra Hockey, and Hanan O. Selvin (eds.). Reader in
    Bureaucracy. Glencoe, N.Y.: The Free Press, 1952.
Fundación Friedrich Ebert. Documentos y legislación de
    la transición. Madrid: Fundación Friedrich Ebert,
    1982.
Gámir, Luis. Las preferencias efectivas del Mercado
    Común a España. Madrid: Ediciones Moneda y Cré-
    dito, 1972.
García San Miguel, Luis. "Las ideologías políticas en
    la España actual." Sistema 48 (January, 1981).

García-Delgado, José L., and Julio Segura. Reformismo
    y crisis económica. Madrid: Editorial Saltés,
    1977.
Geneen, Harold S. "Why Directors Can't Protect the
    Shareholders." Fortune. Vol. 110-6 (September,
    1984).
Giles, Michael W., and Thomas D. Lancaster. "Political
    Transition, Social Development and Legal Mobi-
    lization in Spain." American Political Science
    Review 83-3 (September, 1989).
González, Bernardo, and Miguel Angel Noceda. "Campaña
    electoral sucia: Andalucía pierde." Mercado, 21-
    27 May 1982.
Gonzáles González, Manuel-Jesús. La economía política
    del franquismo (1940-1970). Madrid: Editorial
    Tecnos, 1979.
Gordon, Robert A. "The Executive and the Owner-Entre-
    preneur." In Robert Merton, Ailsa P. Gray, Barbara
    Hockey, and Hanan O. Selvin (eds.). Reader in
    Bureaucracy. Glencoe, N.Y.: The Free Press, 1952.
Graell, Guillermo. Historia del Fomento del Trabajo Na-
    cional. Barcelona: Imprenta en Viuda de Luis
    Tasso, 1911.
Granick, David. Managerial Comparisons of Four Developed
    Countries: France, Britain, United States and
    Russia. Cambridge, Mass.: The MIT Press, 1972.
Grant, Wyn. "British Employers' Associations and the
    Enlarged Community." Journal of Common Market
    Studies 11-4 (June, 1973).
Grant, Wyn and David Marsh. The Confederation of British
    Industry. London: Hodder and Soughton, 1977.
Grenville, J.A.S. The Major International Treaties. New
    York: Stein and Day, 1974.
Gunther, Richard. Public Policy in a No-Party State.
    Berkeley: University of California Press, 1980.
Gunther, Richard, Giacomo Sani, and Goldie Shabad, Spain
    After Franco: The Making of a Competitive Party
    System. Berkeley: University of California Press,
    1986.
___. "Party Strategies and Mass Cleavages in the 1979
    Spanish Elections." Paper delivered at the con-
    ference of the American Political Science Associa-
    tion, Washington, D.C., August 1980.
Hartman, Heinz. "Cohesion and Commitment in Employers'
    Organizations." World Politics 11-3 (April, 1959).
Hernes, Gudmund, and Arne Selvik. "Local Corporatism."
    In Suzanne D. Berger (ed.). Organizing Interests
    in Western Europe. Cambridge: Cambridge University
    Press, 1981.
Herz, John H. (ed.). From Dictatorship to Democracy:
    Coping with the Legacies of Authoritarianism and

<u>Totalitarianism</u>. Westport, Conn.: Greenwood Press, 1982.

Horowitz, Morris. A. <u>Manpower and Education in Franco Spain</u>. Hamden, Conn.: Archon Books, 1974.

Huneeus, Carlos. <u>La Unión de Centro Democrático y la transición a la democracia en España</u>. Madrid: Centro de Investigaciones Sociológicas, 1985.

Iglesias Selgas, Carlos. <u>El sindicalismo español</u>. Madrid: Doncel, 1974.

___. <u>Los sindicatos en España</u>. Madrid: Ediciones del Movimiento, 1965.

Instituto de Estudios Económicos. <u>Programas económicos frente a la crisis</u>. Madrid: Instituto de Estudios Económicos, 1980.

___. <u>La terminación del contrato de trabajo en Europa occidental</u>. Madrid: Instituto de Estudios Económicos, 1979.

Instituto Nacional de Estadística. <u>Censo industrial de España-1978</u>. Madrid: Instituto Nacional de Estadística, 1978.

Instituto Nacional de Industria. <u>Memoria INI</u>. Madrid: 1980.

Izquierdo Escribano, Antonio. "Sobre la evolución electoral de los partidos políticos parlamentarios en las elecciones catalanas." <u>Mientras tanto</u>, 1980.

Johansen, Lars Norby. "Organization of Business Interests in the Danish Metal-Working and Construction Industries." Paper delivered at the conference of the International Sociological Association, Mexico City, August 1982.

Johansen, Lars Norby, and Ole P. Kristensen. "Corporatist Traits in Denmark, 1946-1976." In Gerhard Lehmbruch and Philippe Schmitter (eds.). <u>Patterns of Corporatist Policy-Making</u>. Beverly Hills: Sage Publications, 1982.

Keller, Suzanne. <u>Beyond the Ruling Class: Strategic Elites in Modern Society</u>. New York: Random House, 1963.

Keohane, Robert O. "Economics, Inflation and the Role of the State." <u>World Politics</u>, Vol. 31 (October, 1978).

Korpi, Walter, and Michael Shalev. "Strikes, Industrial Relations and Class Conflict in Capitalist Societies." <u>British Journal of Sociology</u> 30 (June 1979).

Kurth, James R. "Industrial Change and Political Change: A European Perspective." In David Collier (ed.). <u>The New Authoritarianism in Latin America</u>. Princeton: Princeton University Press, 1979.

Lancaster, Thomas D. <u>Policy Stability and Democratic Change: Energy in Spain's Transition</u>. University

Park: The Pennsylvania State University Press, 1989.

___. "A Price for Entry: The European Community, Spain and the Value-Added Tax." Paper delivered at the conference of the American Political Science Association, Chicago, August 1983.

LaPalombara, Joseph. Interest Groups in Italian Politics. Princeton: Princeton University Press, 1964.

Lehmbruch, Gerhard. "Liberal Corporatism and Party Government." Comparative Political Studies 10-1 (April, 1977).

___. "Introduction: Neo-Corporatism in Comparative Perspective." In Gerhard Lehmbruch and Philippe Schmitter (eds.). Patterns of Corporatist Policy-Making. Beverly Hills: Sage Publications, 1982.

Linz, Juan J. Conflicto en Euskadi. Madrid: Espasa Calpe, 1986.

___. Crisis, Breakdown, and Reequilibrium. Vol. I of Juan J. Linz and Alfred Stepan (eds.). The Breakdown of Democratic Regimes. Baltimore: The Johns Hopkins University Press, 1978.

___. "The Basques in Spain: Nationalism and Political Conflict in a New Democracy." In W. Phillips Davison and Leon Gordenker (eds.). Resolving Nationality Conflicts. New York: Praeger, 1980.

___. "La crisis de un estado unitario, nacionalismos periféricos y regionalismo." In La España de las autonomías. Madrid: Espasa Calpe, 1981.

___. "From Falange to Movimiento-Organización: The Spanish Single Party and the Franco Regime 1939-1968." In S. Huntington and C. Moore (eds.). Authoritarian Politics in Modern Societies: The Dynamics of Established One Party Systems. New York: Basic Books, 1970.

___. "La frontera sur de Europa: tendencias evolutivas." Revista Española de Investigaciones Sociológicas. Vol. 9 (January-March 1980).

___. "Legitimidad y eficacia en la evolución de los regímenes políticos." In Cajas de Ahorros y Monte de Piedad de Granada. Problemas del subdesarrollo. Granada: 1978.

___. "Opposition In and Under an Authoritarian Regime: The Case of Spain." In Robert Dahl (ed.). Regimes and Oppositions. New Haven: Yale University Press, 1973.

___. "Peripheries within the Periphery." In Per Torsvik (ed.). Mobilization in Center-Periphery Structures and Nation-Building. Bergen, Norway: Universitetsforlaget, 1981.

___. "Totalitarian and Authoritarian Regimes." In Fred I. Greenstein and Nelson W. Polsby (eds.). Hand-

book of Political Science. Reading, Mass.:
Addison-Wesley, 1975.

Linz, Juan J. and Amando de Miguel, Los empresarios ante
el poder público. Madrid: Centro de Estudios
Políticos, 1966.

____. El prestigio de profesiones en el mundo empre-
sarial. Madrid: Instituto de Estudios Políticos,
1963.

____. "Asociaciones voluntarias. La realidad asociativa
de los españoles." In Confederación Española de
Cajas de Ahorros. Sociología española de los años
setenta. Madrid: Confederación Española de Cajas
de Ahorros, 1971.

____. "Bureaucratisation et pourvoir discrétionnaire dans
les enterprises industrielles espagnoles." Sociologie du Travail. 6-3 (July-September 1964).

____. "Características estructurales de las empresas es-
pañolas: tecnificación y burocracia." Racionaliza-
ción. Vol. 17 (1964).

____. "The Eight Spains." In Richard L. Merritt and
Stein Rokkan (eds.). Comparing Nations. New Haven:
Yale University Press, 1966.

____. "El empresario ante los problemas laborales." Re-
vista de Política Social 60 (October-December
1963).

____. "Los empresarios españoles y la banca." New York:
Bureau of Applied Social Research, reprint no. A-
371, 1961.

____. "Los estudios de los empresarios españoles y su
concepción del papel empresarial." Paper delivered
at the conference on "La formation des hommes et
le développement économique," held in Madrid by
the Centre de Sociologie Européenne, October 1964.

____. "Fundadores, herederos y directores en las empresas
españolas." Revista Internacional de Sociología,
January-March 1963. English version is "Founders,
Heirs, and Managers of Spanish Firms." New York:
International Arts and Sciences Press, Spring-
Summer 1974.

____. "El Mercado Común, el capital extranjero y el
empresario español." Productividad 26 (January-
March 1963).

____. "Los problemas de la retribución y el rendimiento,
vistos por los empresarios." Revista de Trabajo 1
(March, 1963).

____. "La representación sindical vista por nuestro em-
presariado." Revista de Fomento Social XX-78
(April-June 1965).

Linz, Juan J.; Manuel Gómez-Reino y Carnota; Francisco
Andrés Orizo; and Darío Vila. Informe sociológico
sobre el cambio político en España 1975-1981.

Madrid: Fundación FOESSA, 1981.

___. _Atlas electoral del País Vasco_. Madrid: Centro de Investigaciones Sociológicas, 1981.

López Pintor, Rafael. _Sociología industrial_. Madrid: Alianza Editorial, 1986.

Ludevid, Manuel. _Cuarenta años de sindicato vertical_. Barcelona: Editorial Laia, 1976.

___. _Los protagonistas en las relaciones laborales en la España contemporánea: las organizaciones empresariales_. Barcelona: ESADE, n.d.

Makler, Harry Mark. _A Elite Industrial Portuguesa_. Lisbon: Centro de Economia y Finanças, 1969.

Malo de Molina, José Luis. "Rigidez del mercado de trabajo y comportamiento de los salarios en España." _El trimestre económico_, April–June 1984.

Maravall, José María. _Dictatorship and Political Dissent: Workers and Students in Franco's Spain_. London: St. Martin's Press, 1978.

___. _La política de la transición_. Madrid: Taurus Ediciones, 1981.

Martinelli, Alberto. "The Italian Experience." In Raymond Vernon and Yair Aharoni (ed.). _State-Owned Enterprise in the Western Economies_. New York: St. Martin's Press, 1981.

Martínez, Robert E. "Spain: Pragmatism and Continuity." _Current History_ 87-532 (November, 1988).

Maxwell, Kenneth (ed.). _The Press and the Rebirth of Iberian Democracy_. Westport, Conn.: Greenwood Press, 1983.

McCarthy, W. E. "A Survey of Employers' Association Officials." London: Royal Commission on Trade Unions and Employers' Associations, Research Paper 7, 1967.

McDonough, Peter, and Antonio López Pina. "Disenchantment and Dealignment in Spanish Politics." Paper delivered at the conferences of the American Political Science Association, Washington D.C., August 1980.

McLure, Jr., Charles E. _The Value-Added Tax_. Washington, D.C.: American Enterprise Institute, 1987.

McQueen, Matthew. "Some Measures of the Economic Effects of Common Market Trade Preferences for the Mediterranean Countries." In Avid Shlaim and G. N. Yannopoulos (eds.). _The EEC and the Mediterranean Countries_. Cambridge: Cambridge Univesity Press, 1976.

Medhurst, Kenneth N. _Government in Spain: The Executive at Work_. Oxford: Pergamon Press, 1973.

Menéndez Roces, César. _La marginación de la pequeña y mediana empresa_. Madrid: Editorial Mañana, 1978.

Michels, Robert. Political Parties: A Sociological Study
    of the Oligarchical Tendencies of Modern Democ-
    racy. New York: Dover, 1959.
Miguel, Amando de. Recursos humanos, clases y regiones
    en España. Madrid: Cuadernos para el Diálogo,
    1977.
___. Sociología del franquismo. Barcelona: Editorial
    Euros, 1975.
Miguel, Amando de, and Juan J. Linz. "Movilidad social
    del empresario español." Revista de Fomento Social
    75-76 (July-September and October-December 1964).
___. "Nivel de estudios del empresariado español." Arbor
    219 (March, 1964).
Ministerio de Industria y Energía. La industria y la
    CEE. Two volumes. Madrid: Ministerio de Industria
    y Energía, 1979 and 1980.
Ministerio de Trabajo. Comentarios al acuerdo marco
    interconfederal sobre negociación colectiva.
    Madrid: 1980.
Molas, Isidre. Lliga catalana. Barcelona: Ediciones 62,
    1972.
Molina Requena, María Josefa. España y la economía del
    Mercado Común. Madrid: Ceura, 1987.
Morisi, Massimo. "Aspectos esenciales de la relación
    entre estado y economía en una Constitución de la
    crisis." In Alberto Predieri and Eduardo García
    de Enterría (eds.). La Constitución española de
    1978. Madrid: Editorial Civitas, 1981.
Moya Valganon, Carlos. El poder económico en España
    (1939-1970). Madrid: Tucar Ediciones, 1975.
Munns, V. G. "The Functions and Organisation of Em-
    ployers' Associations in Selected Industries."
    London: Royal Commission on Trade Unions and
    Employers' Associations, Research Paper 7, 1967.
Nadal, Jordi. El fracaso de la revolución industrial en
    España 1814-1913. Barcelona: Editorial Ariel,
    1978.
Navalón, Antonio, and Francisco Guerrero. Objetivo
    Adolfo Suárez. Madrid: Espasa Calpe, 1987.
Noelke, Michael, and Robert Taylor. "L'Industrie espag-
    nole face à la Communauté Economique Européenne:
    l'impact de l'adhésion." Brussels: European
    Research Associates, October 1979.
O'Donnell, Guillermo A. Modernization and Bureaucratic
    Authoritarianism. Berkeley: Institute of Inter-
    national Studies, University of California, 1973.
O'Donnell, Guillermo; Philippe C. Schmitter; and
    Laurence Whitehead (eds.). Transitions from
    Authoritarian Rule: Prospects for Democracy.
    Baltimore: The Johns Hopkins University Press,
    1986.

Offe, Claus, and Helmut Wiesenthal. "Two Logics of Collective Action: Theoretical Notes on Social Class and Organizational Form." In _Political Power and Social Theory_. Greenwich, Conn.: JAI Press, 1979.

Olarra Ugartemendía, Luis. _Postfranquismo: proyecto de futuro_. Bilbao: Ediciones Deusto, 1977.

Olson, Mancur. _The Logic of Collective Action_. Cambridge, Mass.: Harvard University Press, 1971.

___. _The Rise and Decline of Nations_. New Haven: Yale University Press, 1982.

Organization for Economic Cooperation and Development. _OECD Economic Surveys: Spain 1987/1988_. Paris: OECD, May 1988.

___. _OECD Economic Surveys: Spain 1988/1989_. Paris: OECD, May 1989.

Pascual, Julio. "El empresario español de la transición." Paper delivered at the Club Siglo XXI, Madrid, June 1979.

Peiro, Luis. "El PSOE reacciona ante el 'Nicolazo'." _Cambio 16_, April 11, 1988.

Pempel, T. J., and Keiichi Tsunekawa. "Corporatism Without Labor? The Japanese Anomaly." In Philippe Schmitter and Gerhard Lehmbruch (eds.). _Trends Towards Corporatist Intermediation_. Beverly Hills: Sage Publications, 1979.

Pérez Díaz, Víctor. "Políticas económicas y pautas sociales en la España de la transición: la doble cara del neocorporatismo." In Juan J. Linz (ed.). _España: un presente para el futuro_. Madrid: Instituto de Estudios Económicos, 1984. Published subsequently in Víctor Pérez Díaz, _El retorno de la sociedad civil_. Madrid: Instituto de Estudios Económicos, 1987.

___. "Los obreros españoles ante la empresa en 1980." _Papeles de Economía_, 1981.

___. "Los obreros españoles ante el sindicato y la acción colectiva en 1980." _Papeles de Economía_, 1980.

Poulantzas, Nicos. _Classes in Contemporary Capitalism_. London: Humanities Press, 1976.

___. _The Crisis of the Dictatorships_. London: Humanities Press, 1976.

Punset, Eduardo. _La salida de la crisis_. Barcelona: Editorial Argos Vergara, 1980.

Reder, Melvin W. "The Theory of Union Wage Policy." _Review of Economics and Statistics_ 34 (February 1952).

Reder, Melvin W., and George R. Neuman. "Conflict and Contract: The Case of Strikes." _Journal of Political Economy_ 88-5 (October, 1980).

Rodríguez Ibañez, José Enrique. Después de una dicta-
    dura: cultura autoritaria y transición política en
    España. Madrid: Centro de Estudios Constituciona-
    les, 1987.
Rodríguez Sahagún, Tomás. Alternativas del poder en la
    empresa. Madrid: Ibérico Europea de Ediciones,
    1977.
Rojos Alejos, Manuel; Prosper Lamothe Fernández; and
    Enrique Moreau Moya. Financiación de la pequeña y
    mediana empresa. Madrid: Asociación para el
    Progreso de la Dirección, 1981.
Román, Manuel. The Limits of Economic Growth in Spain.
    New York: Praeger Publishers, 1971.
Rosen, Sherwin. "Trade Union Power, Threat Effects and
    the Extent of Organization." Review of Economic
    Studies 36-106 (April 1969).
Rubio, Rafael, and Norberto Gallego. "¿Quién le teme?"
    Mercado, March 5, 1982.
____. "En 1983, Felipe González en la Moncloa." Mercado,
    March 5, 1982.
Sabel, Charles. "The Internal Politics of Trade Unions."
    In Suzanne Berger (ed.). Organizing Interests in
    Western Europe. Cambridge: Cambridge University
    Press, 1981.
San Segundo, Gonzalo. "El dinero, la nueva furia de los
    españoles." Cambio 16, August 15, 1988.
Sánchez-Gijón, Antonio. El camino hacia Europa. Madrid:
    Ediciones del Centro, 1973.
Savage, Dean. Founders, Heirs and Managers: French
    Industrial Leadership in Transition. Beverly
    Hills: Sage Publications, 1979.
Schmitter, Philippe. "Still the Century of Corporatism?"
    In Frederick B. Pike and Thomas Stritch (eds.).
    The New Corporatism. South Bend, Ind.: University
    of Notre Dame Press, 1974.
Schwartz, Pedro. "La empresa como soporte de la visión
    empresarial." Paper delivered at the conference on
    El Balance social de la empresa y las institucio-
    nes financieras, Madrid, February 1981.
Schwartz, Pedro, and Manuel-Jesús González González. Una
    historia del Instituto Nacional de Industria.
    Madrid: Editorial Tecnos, 1978.
Share, Donald. The Making of Spanish Democracy. New
    York: Praeger, 1986.
____. Dilemmas of Social Democracy. Westport, Conn.:
    Greenwood Press, 1989.
Sierra, Fermín de la, Juan José Caballero, and Juan
    Pedro Pérez Escanilla. Los directores de grandes
    empresas españolas ante el cambio social. Madrid:
    Centro de Investigaciones Sociológicas, 1981.

Stoetzel, Jean. Les valeurs du temps présent: une enquete européenne. Paris: Presses universitaires de France, 1983.

Synder, David. "Institutional Setting and Industrial Conflict: Comparative Analyses of France, Italy and the United States." American Sociological Review 40-3 (June, 1975).

Tamames, Ramón. La oligarquía financiera en España. Barcelona: Editorial Planeta, 1977.

Tilly, Charles, and Roberto Franzosi. A book review of P. K. Edwards. Strikes in the United States 1881-1974. New York: St. Martin's Press, 1981. Industrial Relations Law Journal 5 (1983).

Tovias, Alfred. EEC Enlargement - The Southern Neighbors. Sussex, U.K.: Sussex European Research Centre, 1979.

____. Tariff Preferences in Mediterranean Diplomacy. London: World Policy Research Centre, 1977.

Tsoukalis, Loukas. The European Community and its Mediterranean Enlargement. London: George Allen & Unwin, 1981.

Tully, Shawn. "Europe's Best Business Schools." Fortune, May 23, 1988.

Vernon, Raymond. Big Business and the State. Cambridge, Mass.: Harvard University Press, 1974.

____. "International Investment and International Trade in the Produce Cycle." Quarterly Journal of Economics, May 1966.

Viúdez, Juan. The Export Behaviour of Spanish Manufacturers - An Evaluation of Interviews. Kiel, Germany: Kiel Institute of World Economics, November 1972.

Vogel, David. "How Business Responds to Opposition: Corporate Political Strategies During the 1970s." Paper delivered at the conference of the American Political Science Association, Washington, D.C., August-September 1979.

Weber, Max. Max Weber on the Methodology of the Social Sciences. Edited by Edward A. Shils and Henry A. Finch. Glencoe, Ill.: The Free Press, 1949.

____. "The Presuppositions and Causes of Bureaucracy." In Robert Merton, Ailsa P. Gray, Barbara Hockey, and Hanan O. Selvin (eds.). Reader in Bureaucracy. New York: The Free Press, 1952.

Wilson, Frank L. "French Interest Group Politics: Pluralist or Neocorporatist?" American Political Science Review, December 1983.

Wilson, James Q. Political Organizations. New York: Basic Books, 1973.

Witney, Fred. Labor Policy and Practices in Spain. New York: Praeger, 1965.

Wright, Alison. The Spanish Economy, 1959-1976. London: Macmillan Press, 1977.

Zafra Valverde, José. Régimen político en España. Pamplona: Ediciones Universidad de Navarra, 1973.

Index

About the Author

ROBERT E. MARTÍNEZ is with Strategic Planning at Norfolk Southern Corporation. Previously, he served as the Associate Deputy Secretary of Transportation at the U.S. Department of Transportation where he managed the portfolio for intermodal transportation. Prior to that, he was the Deputy Maritime Administrator at the department from early 1990 to 1992. In this role, Martínez helped manage the sealift for Operation Desert Shield/Desert Storm. He has worked as a consultant on Spain and Latin America, and he has published articles on business and politics in Spain and on maritime, sealift, and intermodal transportation.